DATE DUE

NOV 2 7 2003	

BRODART   Cat. No. 23-221

Anxiety Disorders in Children and Adolescents

BIOBEHAVIOURAL PERSPECTIVES ON HEALTH AND DISEASE PREVENTION

From the perspective of behavioural science, the series examines current research, including clinical and policy implications, on health, illness prevention, and biomedical issues. The series is international in scope, and aims to address the culturally specific, as well as the universally applicable.

Series Editor: Lydia R. Temoshok, PhD, Institute of Human Virology, Division of Clinical Research, University of Maryland Biotechnology Center, 725 West Lombard Street, Room N548, Baltimore, Maryland 21201, USA

Anxiety Disorders in Children and Adolescents: Epidemiology, Risk Factors and Treatment

Edited by

Cecilia A. Essau
*Westfälische Wilhelms-Universität,
Münster, Germany*

Franz Petermann
Universität Bremen, Germany

First published 2001 by Brunner-Routledge
27 Church Road, Hove, East Sussex, BN3 2FA

Simultaneously published in the USA and Canada
by Taylor & Francis Inc,
29 West 35th Street, New York NY 10001

Brunner-Routledge is an imprint of the Taylor & Francis Group

© 2001 Brunner-Routledge

Printed and bound in Great Britain by Biddles Ltd, Guildford and King's
Lynn

British Library Cataloguing in Publication Data
A catalogue record for this book is available from the British Library

Library of Congress Cataloging-in-Publication Data
A catalogue record for this book is available from the Library of Congress

ISBN 1-58391-232-0

Contents

List of Figures

List of Tables

List Of Contributors

Fumiyo Aihara
Department of Clinical Psychology
University of Bremen
Grazerstr. 6, 28359 Bremen
Germany

Kemie L. Alexander
Department of Psychology
Virginia Polytechnic Institute and State University
Blacksburg, VA
USA

Susanne Al Wiswasi
Department of Clinical Psychology
University of Bremen
Grazerstr. 6, 28359 Bremen
Germany

Paula Barrett
Griffith University, Gold Coast Campus
PMB 50 Gold Coast mail centre
Queensland 9726
Australia

James Bowers
Fairleigh Dickinson University
Child Anxiety Disorders Clinic
Teaneck-Hackensack Campus
Teaneck, New Jersey 07666
USA

Lisa K. Brien
Fairleigh Dickinson University
Child Anxiety Disorders Clinic
Teaneck-Hackensack Campus
Teaneck, New Jersey 07666
USA

Bruce F. Chorpita
Department of Psychology
University of Hawaii
2430 Campus Road
Honolulu, HI 96822
USA

Andrew R. Eisen
Fairleigh Dickinson University
Child Anxiety Disorders Clinic
Teaneck-Hackensack Campus
Teaneck, New Jersey 07666
USA

Cecilia A. Essau
Psychologisches Institut I
Westfälische Wilhelms-Universität Münster
Fliednerstr. 21
48149 Münster
Germany

Amie E. Grills
Department of Psychology
Virginia Polytechnic Institute and State University
Blacksburg, VA
USA

Chris Hayward
Stanford University
Department of Psychiatry and Behavioural Sciences
401 Quarry Road, Room 1316
Stanford, CA 94305-5722
USA

Catherine Moffitt
Department of Psychology
University of Hawaii
2430 Campus Road
Honolulu, HI 96822
USA

Thomas H. Ollendick
Virginia Polytechnic Institute and State University
Child Study Center
Blacksburg, VA
USA

Franz Petermann
Department of Clinical Psychology
University of Bremen
Grazerstr. 6, 28359 Bremen
Germany

Ronald M. Rapee
Department of Psychology
Macquarie University, Sydney, 2109
Australia

Berit Reiss
Department of Clinical Psychology
University of Bremen
Grazerstr. 6, 28359 Bremen
Germany

Daniel S. Schechter
College of Physicians & Surgeons of Columbia University
New York, NY 10032
USA

Michael A. Southam-Gerow
Department of Psychology
University of California at Los Angeles
Franz Hall, Los Angeles, CA 90095-1563
USA

Melanie Steinmeyer
Department of Clinical Psychology
University of Bremen
Grazerstr. 6, 28359 Bremen
Germany

Arielle Strudler
248 Independence Drive
Chestnut Hill
MA 02467
USA

Lynne Sweeney
Neutral Bay Medical Centre
2/24 Young Street, Neutral Bay
2089 Sydney, N.S.W
Australia

Per Hove Thomsen
Psychiatric Hospital for Children and Adolescents
University Hospital of Aarhus
Harald Selmersvej 66
DK-8240 Risskov
Denmark

M. Cevdet Tosyali
Departments of Child and Adolescent Psychiatry, and
Developmental Psychobiology and Pediatrics
Columbia College of Physicians & Surgeons
Columbia University and the New York State Psychiatric Institute
New York, NY
USA

Preface

The presence of anxiety disorders in childhood and adolescence has traditionally been viewed as a normal part of development. Yet, children and adolescents with anxiety disorders comprise a large portion of patients treated at child mental health settings. Further evidence for the common prevalence of anxiety disorders in children and adolescents come from recent epidemiological studies which reported these disorders as one of the most common disorders in this age group. As shown in our Bremen Adolescent Study, anxiety disorders were the most frequent disorders, with a frequency of 18.6%. When considering the subtype of anxiety disorders, phobia (agoraphobia, specific and social phobia) were the most common. Posttraumatic stress disorder and obsessive-compulsive disorder occurred less frequently with rates below 2%. The least common of all anxiety disorders were panic disorder and generalized anxiety disorder, both have rates well below 1%.

Some major changes have taken place in the latest version of the DSM (DSM-IV). First, among the three types of anxiety disorders (separation anxiety disorder, avoidant disorder, and overanxious disorder) that are specific to children and adolescents in DSM-III-R, only separation anxiety disorder remains. Avoidant disorder has now been subsumed under social phobia, and overanxious disorder under generalized anxiety disorder. In addition to the "childhood-specific" anxiety disorders, DSM-IV also includes anxiety disorders that may be applied to adults as well as to children and adolescents: specific phobia, social phobia, panic disorder, obsessive compulsive disorder, generalized anxiety disorder, posttraumatic stress disorder, acute stress disorder, anxiety disorder due to a general medical condition, and substance-induced anxiety disorder. Second, the text and criteria for a panic attack have been provided in a separate section. Third, the term "simple phobia" has now been changed to "specific phobia". This change was considered necessary in order to avoid the misleading sense of mildness that "simple" implies. Fourth, numerous changes have also been undertaken in the criteria of some subtypes of anxiety disorders. The extend to which these changes may influence the kind of information we will have about anxiety disorders (e.g., in the prevalence and incidence rates of anxiety disorders) in future studies is still unknown.

The aim of this volume is to present a comprehensive summary of the state-of-the-art information on anxiety disorders in children and adolescents. The book is divided into three sections. Part I covers general issues related to anxiety disorders in children and adolescents including an introduction to the topic, research methods, and assessment strategies. Part II contains 7 chapters addressing each subtype of anxiety disorders: separation anxiety disorder, panic disorder, social phobia, specific phobia, generalized anxiety disorder, obsessive-compulsive disorder, and posttraumatic stress disorder. The topics cover in each chapter include: definition and classification, epidemiology, risk factors, comorbidity, course and outcome, prevention/intervention, and concluding remarks. Part III contains a chapter on progress and unresolved issues in the study of anxiety disorders in children and adolescents and provides some recommendations for future studies.

This volume is conceptualized as a tool for advanced students, researchers and other professionals working in the fields of psychiatry, psychology, pediatrics, social work, and other mental health professions. Researchers and professionals working in clinical practice will find this book useful because of its wide coverage, ranging from epidemiology and risk factors through intervention of the subtypes of anxiety disorders. Advanced students will benefit from a broad review of anxiety disorders.

We wish to acknowledge the efforts of the contributors, whose expertise and dedication to the project have been outstanding. Without them, a comprehensive coverage of the various topics would not have been easily achieved. Additionally, we wish to acknowledge the support and cooperation of the staff at Harwood Academic Publishers.

Cecilia A. Essau
Franz Petermann

PART I
GENERAL ISSUES

1 FEARS, WORRIES, AND ANXIETY IN CHILDREN AND ADOLESCENTS

Thomas H. Ollendick
Amie E. Grills
Kemie L. Alexander

Although terms such as fear, worry, and anxiety are often used inter-changeably, a clear distinction among them can be seen in the empirical literature. At the most basic level, this distinction lies in the definitions and descriptions of these phenomena. For instance, fear has been described as a reaction to accurately perceived dangers that are associated with unpleasant feelings (Erol and Sahin, 1995; Marks, 1987a). More broadly, fear can be defined as a painful feeling of impending danger when confronted by life-threatening dangers. In contrast, worry has been characterized as anxiety-related thought processes (Borkovec *et al.*, 1983). Worry is generally considered to be a cognitive component of anxiety, involving uncontrollable negative thoughts about future events. Thus, the primary difference between these two anxiety-related phenomena is that fear occurs in the presence of an actual threatening stimulus, whereas worry pertains to future-oriented thoughts about the threatening stimulus, but in the absence of that stimulus (Muris *et al.*, 2000). Finally, anxiety has been conceptualized as a more global term that encompasses physiological tension and arousal, cognitions of threat, and behavioural avoidance (Hagopian and Ollendick, 1997). Clearly the anxiety response has adaptive value when an individual is actually confronted by dangerous stimuli. However, when this reaction occurs in response to an unreasonably perceived danger or with excessive intensity, thus causing impairment to the individual, an anxiety *disorder* is said to exist.

Despite definitional distinctions among fear, worry, and anxiety, questions regarding what differentiates normal and pathological variants of these emotional states remain. For instance, worry has been described as a component of a number of classifiable anxiety disorders. For example, excessive worry is the essential feature of generalized anxiety disorder and worry about separation from a primary caregiver is the core feature of separation anxiety disorder. Moreover, fear of particular stimuli is clearly the major symptom of specific phobias. Still, both worry and fear characterize social phobia. Further complicating this issue is the fact that researchers continually use these terms interchangeably in both research studies and scale development without clearly distinguishing their intended meaning.

Despite the controversy over the use of anxiety related terms, researchers in the past several years have become increasingly interested in the specific aspects of each of these three overlapping, yet relatively discrete, areas of study. Research within the first two of these areas (i.e., fear and worry) has been primarily focused on their prevalence and expression in normal children. In contrast, the majority of empirical studies regarding anxiety disorders has been conducted using clinic referred samples. Nevertheless, there exists a growing body of literature that has also examined anxiety at the symptom, as opposed to the syndromal, level.

For example, anxiety is commonly depicted as either reflecting state or trait characteristics. State anxiety has been defined by Spielberger (1975) as a reaction, "consisting of unpleasant consciously-perceived feelings of tension and apprehension, with associated activation of the autonomic nervous system" (pp. 115–143). On the other hand, trait anxiety has been described as a general anxiety-proneness that is a characteristic of an individual's general disposition or personality. Regardless of the individual's age, most studies have examined relationships solely between psychopathology and anxiety-proneness or trait anxiety (Comunian, 1989; Maddux and Stanley, 1986; Messer and Beidel, 1993). Nevertheless, research with adults (Hodges and Felling, 1970) as well as children (Gaudry and Poole, 1972) has demonstrated that those with high trait anxiety levels react to evaluative situations with higher degrees of state anxiety than those with low trait anxiety. This suggests that these two aspects of anxiety are related and that state anxiety might be more easily activated in those individuals high in trait anxiety and predisposed to react in an anxious manner.

Thus, researchers who are interested in anxiety at the symptom level have generally embraced more of a dimensional scheme, where a continuum from normal to clinically impairing anxiety is described. Thus, similar to fear and worry, there also exists research on the prevalence and appearance of anxiety symptomology in normal children.

Fears in Normal Children

Most children experience some degree of fear throughout the course of their development. In fact, one recent study of 190 normal children between 4 and 12 years of age from the Netherlands found that 75.8% reported being fearful of at least one stimulus (Muris *et al.*, 2000) and a majority of these children were fearful of multiple stimuli. Nevertheless, — childhood fears generally tend to be mild, age-related, and transitory despite variance in their frequency, intensity, and duration (Hagopian and Ollendick, 1993; Marks, 1987b; Ollendick *et al.*, 1994a). This notion can be illustrated through delineation of the typical developmental pattern of fears in children. For most children the initial experience of a fearful reaction occurs during infancy when a loud noise or loss of support produces a startle-response. Following this, an increased panic-like fear tends to result in older infants when they are exposed to new situations, unfamiliar people, or separation from major attachment figures. Later, children between the ages of two and four begin to develop fears of imaginary creatures (i.e., ghosts, monsters) as well as animals and the dark. School-related fears tend to appear shortly after this when the child first enters formal schooling. These fears may also reappear if changes in schools or grades (i.e., a move into middle school) occur. Finally, during — adolescence, the primary fear is commonly related to social and evaluative concerns (i.e., embarrassment in front of peers; Ollendick and Vasey, 1999).

This fairly specific developmental pattern has been demonstrated in several studies of childhood fears. For example, Bauer (1976) divided children into three age groups (e.g., 4–6, 6–8, 10–12) and found that 74% of the youngest group of children reported fears of ghosts and monsters, as compared to 53% of the 6–8 year olds and only 5% of the 10–12 year olds. Conversely, only 11% of the youngest group of children reported fears of bodily injury or physical danger as compared with 53% and 55% of the two older groups of children. More recently, Muris *et al.* (2000) found similar findings in their study of normal children. These researchers reported findings regarding the top three fears indicated by children in age groups of 4–6, 7–9, and 10–12 years of age. For children in all three of these age groups the most frequently reported feared stimuli were animals. However, the next most frequently reported fear among the 4–6 and 7–9 year olds was imaginary creatures, whereas for the 10–12 year olds it was social threats. Finally, the third most frequently reported fears were environmental threats (4–6 year olds), frightening dreams/movies (7–9 year olds), and being kidnapped (10–12 year olds). Thus, similar to the results of Bauer, the fears reported by children in this study also appear to follow a developmental pattern. Regardless of developmental age, it appears that children's fears are consistently related to harm coming to themselves. It appears that as children grow to recognize the "imaginary" nature of their earlier fears of harm, these fears do not completely dissipate but instead transfer to other more age appropriate stimuli.

The prevalence of fears also appears to change with age and gender. For instance, whereas the overall prevalence of fears in the Muris *et al.* (2000) study was 75.8%, significant age differences also emerged. These findings revealed that fears were most commonly reported by seven to nine year olds (87%), followed by 4–6 year olds (71%), and finally 10–12 year olds (67.8%). Furthermore, girls in this study reported a significantly greater percentage of fears regarding being kidnapped whereas boys tended to report more fears about imaginary creatures. This finding is consistent with other researchers who have found that girls tend to report significantly more fears than boys. For instance, Ollendick and colleagues have repeatedly found that girls report a greater level and number of fears as compared to boys (King *et al.*, 1989; Ollendick *et al.*, 1989, 1996; Ollendick and Yule, 1990).

One of the major advances for the study of childhood fears occurred with Ollendick's (1983) revision of the Fear Survey Schedule for Children (Scherer and Nakamura, 1968). The Revised Fear Survey Schedule for Children (FSSC-R) has proved to be one of the most commonly used measures in the study of anxiety related phenomena. The numerous studies utilizing this measure have provided a rich body of literature from samples within the United States as well as a number of other countries. For example, studies conducted in Australia, Belgium, China, Great Britain, Holland, Kenya, Nigeria, and Turkey have provided information on cultural norms as well as cross-cultural differences. Although distinct cultural and environmental experiences can be expected to influence children's fears, studies utilizing this measure in different countries have consistently revealed similar findings regarding the types of fears reported. In line with the previous description of the developmental pattern of fears, the most frequently endorsed fears in all countries tend to be related to physical harm and dangerous situations (Dong *et al.*, 1994; Erol and Sahin, 1995; Ingman *et al.*, 1999; Muris *et al.*, 1997a, 1997b, 2000; Ollendick *et al.*, 1985, 1989, 1991, 1996). For example, Ollendick *et al.* (1985) found the 10 most commonly rated fears in an American sample of children aged 7–18 to be being hit by a car or truck (42%), not being able to breathe (38%), fire or getting burned (38%), death or dead people (36%), bombing attacks or being invaded (34%), getting poor grades (34%), a burglar breaking into your house (33%), having my parents argue (33%), looking foolish (31%), falling from high places (30%), and being sent to the principal (30%). In addition to these, other commonly reported fears have included illness, earthquakes, spiders, and snakes (Muris et al., 1997a). Although these percentages clearly reflect fears of harmful acts occurring to oneself, there are also school related and familial fears interspersed.

Furthermore, another group of researchers has examined the utility of the FSSC-R with regard to diagnostic differentiation, particularly among subtypes of specific phobia (Weems et al., 1999). These researchers investigated the utility of the FSSC-R subscales in a sample of 120 clinically phobic children and their parents. The primary purpose of the study was to determine whether children's or parent's reports on this measure could be used to differentiate among children diagnosed with social phobia, specific phobia of the dark/sleeping alone, specific phobia of animals, or specific phobia of shots/doctors. The results of this study revealed that both children's and parents' reports could discriminate among the specific phobias. In addition, parent reports were found to distinguish among the specific and social phobias. These findings suggest that specific phobias in clinically referred children are similar to those reported by normal children. However, in phobic children the severity of these fears/phobias is significantly greater.

Worries in Normal Children

In contrast to the vast amount of research that has examined childhood fears, few empirical studies of worry in children have been conducted. Nevertheless, from these studies a number of similarities regarding worries and fears in normal children have become evident. In particular, these studies have revealed similar prevalence rates, content of worries, developmental patterns, and gender differences.

To begin, consistently high prevalence rates have been reported for childhood worries. Regarding the overall number of worries reported by children, Orton (1982) reported that more than 70% of primary school children reported 10 or more things about which they worried. Similarly, Silverman et al. (1995) found children aged 7–12 reported an average of 7.64 different worries. Furthermore, Muris et al. (2000)

noted that 67.4% of their overall sample of children reported at least one worry. Finally, Bell-Dolan et al. (1990) reported that up to 30% of normal children in their sample (aged 5–19) exhibited subclinical levels of excessive worry. Thus, as has been reported with fears, worries are also common in normal children.

Another similarity with the findings regarding fearfulness involves the content of worries that are frequently reported by normal children. That is, the majority of studies have revealed self-referent (e.g., threats to oneself rather than to other people) childhood worries (Muris et al., 1998a, 2000; Silverman et al., 1995). Moreover, the content of these worries has been found to change in accord with the child's age. For instance, Vasey et al. (1994) divided children into three age groups (5–6, 8–9, 11–12) and found that self-referent worries were rated the highest among the 5–6 year olds. However, these types of worries decreased significantly as the children's age increased. In the two older groups of children, worries related to behavioural competence, social evaluations, and psychological well being were reported with increased frequency. Furthermore, the older groups of children evidenced a greater array of areas about which they reported worrying.

The findings of Vasey et al. (1994) were essentially replicated in a recent study by Muris et al. (2000) that examined specific worries across children of different ages. This investigation revealed that although separation from parents was rated as the most intense worry for four to six year olds (24.1%), it dramatically decreased with the children's increase in age (5.6%, 0% for 7–9 and 10–12 year olds, respectively). Interestingly, the opposite pattern emerged for test performance which was not reported by any of the youngest children but was indicated as the third highest worry among 7–9 year olds and as the topmost (reported by 46.7%) worry by 10–12 year olds. Thus, childhood worries also appear to be transient and reflective of the child's age and particular life circumstances.

A number of additional findings regarding worry in normal children were revealed in an extensive investigation of 273 second through sixth grade children (Silverman et al., 1995). Children in this study completed self-report measures as well as an interview that sought to determine the nature and features of worry from each of 14 previously identified areas. Health, school, and physical harm were the three most commonly reported worries in this study. In fact, the most frequently reported worry pertained to physical harm or attacks from others and was listed by a striking 56.6% of the children. In addition, the intensity of the worries paralleled this finding, as worries about security and personal safety were rated as the most intense. However, this was also one of the lowest rated situations in terms of the frequency that it actually occurred. That is, although the children worried excessively about security and personal safety, rarely did such threats to the self actually occur.

As has been found in fear research, gender differences have also emerged in the study of worries in normal children. For example, in the studies by Silverman *et al.* (1995) and Muris *et al.* (2000), girls indicated a significantly greater number of worries than boys. However, these two studies revealed differences in the content of the worries reported. In particular, whereas Silverman *et al.* (1995) found that girls reported more worries about school, classmates, future events, and appearance, Muris *et al.* (2000) found that girls reported significantly more worries about being kidnapped as compared to boys who reported significantly more worries about being punished. Such differences might be related to the different countries in which these studies were conducted (the United States and The Netherlands, respectively).

Interestingly, Muris *et al.* (2000) also found an interaction between gender and the prevalence rates of worry. Although prevalence rates were comparable between genders for 4–6 year olds (girls—48.3%, boys—45.5%), this dramatically changed in the prevalence of worries reported by seven to nine year olds. More specifically, girls (88.9%) between the ages of 7–9 reported significantly more worries than boys (66.7%). Of interest, these percentages returned to comparable ranges for girls and boys aged 10–12 (girls—78.8%, boys—73.1%). Thus, results of this study suggest that gender differences may be specific to the age of the children being investigated.

Another recent examination by Muris and colleagues ties all of this information together and thus more completely illustrates what has been discovered regarding worry in normal children. In this study, 193 children from The Netherlands and Belgium who ranged in age from 8–13 were asked to provide information about their main intense worry. Consistent with the previously cited findings, 68.9% of these children reported that they worry "every now and then". The frequency with which children reported having their main intense worry was two to three days per week (Muris *et al.*, 1998a).

Furthermore, in line with Silverman *et al.* (1995), the most commonly indicated worries were related to school performance, dying/health concerns, and social contacts. However, the majority of children (70.7%) were unable to recall an event that had led to the onset of their worry.

Nevertheless, 12.8% reported that their worry became worse after experiencing an aversive or threatening event and 16.5% indicated that their main worry was caused by such an event. In addition, although on average children reported that they attempted to resist thinking about their worries, they also indicated that they found these thoughts difficult to stop. Despite these difficulties, the children reported relatively mild interference and anxious feelings resulting from their worries. Another similarity that emerged between the worries reported in the study by Silverman *et al.* (1995) and those by Muris *et al.* (1998a) was in regard to gender differences. Overall, gender differences were discovered such that, girls reported greater worry and anxiety than boys on self-report questionnaires. In particular, girls reported significantly more specific concerns regarding sports and appearance. Thus, consistent with Silverman *et al.*'s findings, girls appeared to report more social and performance related concerns.

Finally, these children were questioned as to the coping strategies they used to deal with their worrisome thoughts. The majority of children (55.6%) reported that they distracted themselves by engaging in some activity or thought about more pleasant things (37.6%), whereas a smaller percentage of children reported that they discussed worries with some other person (8.3%). In addition, 27.8% of the children indicated that their particular worry had helped them to cope with difficult future events in a more effective manner.

Anxiety Symptoms in Normal Children

As previously noted, researchers have also examined the degree to which normal, nonreferred children experience anxiety symptoms associated with various anxiety disorders. For instance, a factor analytic study of anxiety symptoms by Spence (1997) revealed that normal children fell into categories that closely matched those specified in the DSM-IV. Furthermore, in Bell-Dolan *et al.*'s (1990) study, anxiety symptoms, specifically those associated with generalized anxiety disorder and specific phobias, were found to be rather common in nondiagnosed children, occurring in as many as 20–30% of those sampled from the general population. In addition to the subclinical anxiety observed in these children, Bell-Dolan *et al.* (1990) discovered that the children neither came from anxious families nor had dissimilar adjustment and outcomes of children who were asymptomatic. That is, presence of these symptoms did not signal poor adjustment or negative outcomes. However, the general findings were similar to those of studies of fears and worry such that girls reported more symptoms than boys and younger children endorsed more symptoms of separation anxiety compared to older children, who reported more generalized anxiety symptoms (Bell-Dolan *et al.*, 1990).

In response to findings such as these, a continuum of anxiety symptoms ranging from normal to clinically significant has been proposed (Gruner *et al.*, 1999). Subsequently, Muris and colleagues have conducted several studies that have sought to examine these symptoms in normal samples of children. These studies have revealed that anxiety disorder symptoms are indeed common in normal children (Muris *et al.*, 1998b). Furthermore, anxiety symptoms in normal children tend to evidence the same patterns as those found for fears and worries in normal children. For instance, consistent with previous findings (Birmaher *et al.*, 1997), a general decline of anxiety disorder symptomology has been revealed with increased age (Muris *et al.*, 1998b, 1998c).

In addition, Muris and colleagues have found consistent gender differences related to anxiety symptomology using the Screen for Child Anxiety Related Emotional Disorders, a self-report questionnaire designed to measure symptoms of DSM-IV anxiety disorders (SCARED; Muris *et al.*, 1998b, 1998c). For instance, overall girls have been found to evidence a greater degree of anxiety disorder symptoms than boys. In particular, girls have been found to score significantly higher regarding symptoms of environmental-situation phobia, animal phobia, blood-injection-injury phobia, separation anxiety disorder, panic disorder, and total anxiety score as measured by the FSSC-R and the SCARED (Muris *et al.*, 1998b, 1998c).

One final area of research that has been conducted regarding anxiety disorder symptoms in normal children concerns self-statements (Muris *et al.*, 1998d). Self-statements can be defined as subjective thoughts or comments that an individual makes based on his/her self-perceptions. In general, it has been accepted that a greater number of negative self-statements are associated with higher levels of anxiety (Fox *et al.*, 1983; Zatz and Chassin, 1985). Thus, Muris *et al.* (1998d) examined the relationship between negative self-statements and anxiety disorder symptomology in normal children. Two primary findings were revealed. First, a positive relationship was discovered between anxiety symptoms and negative self-statements (i.e., the more symptoms, the more negative self-statements). Second, findings varied according to the particular nature of these self-statements. For example, anxious self-statements (e.g., "I thought I would fail") were more often present in children who had relatively high levels of anxiety symptoms. However, depressive (e.g., "Life is terrible") as well as anxious *and* depressive self- statements were found to be positively associated with the presence of more severely debilitating symptoms of anxiety disorders in normal children, such as generalized anxiety disorder, obsessive-compulsive disorder, and separation anxiety disorder. Interestingly, in contrast to findings regarding the prevalence and content of fears and worries, this study did not reveal gender differences. Thus, it seems that girls and boys may report self-statements in a similar manner, although such a conclusion is in need of additional empirical support.

In all, the findings of Muris and colleagues are consistent with those of studies that have looked at fear and worry in normal children. In all of these areas of research, prevalence, developmental trends, and gender differences have been found to follow the same patterns. In addition, as evidenced by the prevalence and type of symptoms found in normal children, it appears that each of these areas has provided evidence for the suggested continuum of anxiety symptomology. The implications of these findings for the distinctiveness of fear, worry, and anxiety await additional inquiry.

Worries and Anxiety Symptoms Across Cultures

In general, research has indicated that child and adolescent psychopathology may be heavily influenced by cultural factors. However, cross-cultural research on children's fears, worries, and anxiety symptoms has been relatively neglected (although see above comments for exceptions) and, as a result, our ability to determine whether certain behaviour patterns can be generalized across cultures has been compromised. To date, cross-cultural studies have tended to examine and validate Western theories that were developed to explain the origin and maintenance of these negative emotional states in normal children (Ollendick *et al.*, 1994a). Although the importance of biological factors has not been ignored in these theories, social/environmental factors have been emphasized. In particular, culturally mediated values, traditions, and beliefs associated with socialization practices have been hypothesized to play a critical role in the types of problems children display. Thus, a comparison of fears, worries, and anxiety displayed by children across cultures may allow us to determine the scope and extent of such cultural differences.

Such possibilities are nicely illustrated in a study of fear and anxiety in African children conducted by Opolot (1976). Consistent with American scores on the Children's Manifest Anxiety Scale, Opolot found Ugandan girls to report higher scores than Ugandan boys. However, results also indicated that Ugandan children scored higher than American children. Opolot hypothesized that these scores were indicative of cultural differences between American and Ugandan socialization practices. Ugandans tend to be conservative and restrictive in their socialization practices, which are believed to lead to heighten anxiety levels in children. Recently, Dong *et al.* (1994) and Ingman *et al.* (1999) reported similar differences on the Fear Survey Schedule for Children-Revised with Chinese and African children. However, it must be noted that conflicting results were found in an early study by Pela and Reynolds (1982) using the Revised Children's Manifest Anxiety Scale with Nigerian primary school children. Unexpectedly, results of this study indicated that there were no significant differences between Nigerian girls and boys on level of anxiety. Nor were there significant differences between Nigerian and American children on levels of anxiety. Perhaps subtle cultural differences between Ugandan and Nigerian children account for these discrepant findings.

Furthermore, our postulated conclusions about relations between age and gender and fear can be examined more precisely through cross-cultural research. A vast amount of literature indicates that older children report fewer fears than younger children. For example, Erol and Sahin (1995) studied children's fears in terms of characteristics such as gender and age in a Turkish population of 9–13-year-olds. Their findings indicated that girls had more intense and frequent fears than boys, and that younger children reported more fears than older ones. In fact, there was no single item on which the girls did not score lower than the boys, and, on most of the items, younger children scored higher than older ones. In this study, fears related to death and separation were highly endorsed by children as well as religious fears (i.e., going to hell). Thus, although similarities in age and gender findings might be consistent across cultures, important content differences might prevail. Dong *et al.* (1994) and Ollendick *et al.* (1996) reported important content differences in fear between Chinese and American children.

Furthermore, cultural differences have been found between European-American children and African-American children in the United States. The majority of studies on American children's fears have been conducted with a middle-class white population. In fact, few studies have examined fears in nonwhite children. African-Americans comprise 8%–12% of the population in the United States, yet little information is available on anxiety symptoms or disorders in this group. According to Neal and Turner (1991), several reasons exist for the lack of research on anxiety disorders in African-Americans. First, African-Americans may make a judgment about whether proposed research is being conducted solely for its stated purpose or for ulterior purposes that might harm them. Second, instead of seeking help from mental health professionals, African-Americans are more likely to seek help from a medical doctor and/or a minister. Third, most researchers have simply not included African-Americans in their empirical studies. Still, some important studies have been undertaken.

The extant research on African-American children's fears, scant as it is, suggests that fears of black children may differ significantly from fears displayed by white children. African-American children not only report more fears but their fears appear to be more reality based than those of white children (LaPouse and Monk, 1959; Nalven, 1970). For example, Nalven (1970) found that African-American children were more likely to report specific fears (rats, poisons), whereas white children are more likely to use generic terms in reporting fears of animals and events. Neal and Turner (1991) suggest that prevalence differences reported between Blacks and Whites are rooted in semantics and may not represent true differences.

In addition, previous research on the FSSC-R with European-American children has consistently found that the scale contained five factors: fear of failure and criticism, fear of the unknown, fear of injury and small animals, fear of danger and death, and medical fears (Ollendick, 1983; Ollendick et al., 1985, 1989). In addition, results from Australian (King et al., 1990, 1989) and British (Ollendick et al. 1989, 1991) studies are consistent with those found in white American studies. Neal et al. (1993) used the FSSC-R to examine the factor structure and stability of FSSC-R in 109 African-American and 124 white children aged 6–12. Indeed, results confirmed a five-factor solution for white children; however, a three-factor solution was obtained for the African-American children. The most notable difference was the absence of a school-fears factor for African-American children and the presence of a factor related to fear of embarrassment. In addition, the 11 most common fears for African-American and white children were compared and eight of the 11 fears were the same for both groups of children. These eight common fears were not being able to breathe, being hit by a car, falling, from high places, germs or getting a serious illness, getting lost in a strange place, bombing attacks-being invaded, a burglar breaking into our house, and fire- getting burned. The three other highest rated items reported by African-American children were getting a shock from electricity, bears or wolves, and strange or mean looking dogs; whereas, Caucasian children reported death or dead people, being sent to the principal, and getting poor grades. Again, differences in concrete versus more ambiguous fears were evident. In addition, Silverman *et al.*'s (1995) study of children's worries in elementary school aged children and its relation to anxiety found that girls reported more worries than boys, as noted earlier. Furthermore, African-Americans reported more worries than Caucasians or Hispanics. For African-Americans, however, no sex differences were apparent. Moreover, African-Americans reported more worries pertaining to family, war, and personal harm than either Caucasians or Hispanics.

It is apparent that there is conflicting evidence on the importance of cultural variables as mediating factors in the kinds of anxiety-related problems children and adolescents display. Needless to say, there is urgent need for cross-cultural research to examine existing theories on the development and expression of fears, worries, and anxiety in children of varying cultures.

Anxiety Disorders in Clinic-Reffered Children

PHENOMENOLOGY OF CHILDHOOD ANXIETY DISORDERS

Phenomenology refers to the descriptions of distinctive symptoms used to classify disorders and their associated features. The Diagnostic and Statistical Manual of Mental Disorders (DSM) is the most commonly used classification system in the world. Since its initial publication in 1952, the DSM has undergone a number of alterations with greater focus on developmental issues in each subsequent revision. In regard to anxiety disorders, the latest version of the DSM (DSM- IV; APA, 1994) exhibits many differences from the two previous versions (DSM-III [APA, 1980], DSM-III-R [APA], 1987). Whereas previous editions of the DSM provided for three distinct diagnostic categories of anxiety disorders in children (i.e., overanxious disorder, OAD; avoidant disorder, AD; and separation anxiety disorder, SAD), the current version has subsumed OAD and AD under adult anxiety disorder categories (generalized anxiety disorder and social phobia, respectively). Thus, while it is clear that a variety of anxiety disorders occurs in children and adolescents as well as adults, separation anxiety disorder is the only anxiety disorder that is included within the section "disorders usually first diagnosed in infancy, childhood, or adolescence". However, as with previous versions of the DSM, the remaining adult categories of anxiety disorders included in the current edition may be applied to children and adolescents as well. Furthermore, with the exception of panic disorder (with or without agoraphobia) and agoraphobia without a history of panic disorder, all of the anxiety disorders described in DSM-IV include diagnostic specifications for children (Ollendick *et al.*, 1994b).

Whereas all of the anxiety disorders are characterized by excessive or inappropriate anxiety that causes the individual significant impairment in functioning, the distinction among these disorders is primarily in regard to the nature of the feared stimulus and the anxiety response produced by it. Furthermore, in order to receive a diagnosis of an anxiety disorder in the DSM-IV, the symptoms cannot be better accounted for by another of the mental disorders, a general medical condition, or as a result of substance use (APA, 1994).

Separation anxiety disorder (SAD) is characterized by excessive and recurrent anxiety regarding separation from the home or individuals to whom the child is attached. In addition, associated features with SAD include: persistent reluctance to attend school, remain alone, and go to sleep without a major attachment figure present, as well as nightmares involving the theme of separation and the expression of a number of physical complaints when separation occurs or is anticipated (APA, 1994).

Specific phobia is defined as excessive and persistent fear that results in response to or anticipation of an explicitly feared object or situation. The primary difference between this disorder and the fears described previously is that specific phobias tend to be involuntary, inappropriate, and limiting to the child's life (Anderson, 1994). The DSM-IV indicates that children may not be cognizant of the unreasonable or excessive nature of their fears and that these fears may be expressed through crying, tantrum, freezing, or clinging behaviours. In addition, the feared stimulus is usually avoided or endured with intense anxiety or distress. Finally, in order to separate the typical developmental fears experienced by most children (which tend to dissipate over time), a duration parameter of 6 months has been included for the diagnosis of specific phobia in children under the age of 18.

The criteria for a diagnosis of social phobia are identical to those of specific phobia with the exception that the fear and avoidance occur in social situations or other situations in which the person may be scrutinized in a manner that could lead to embarrassment. In addition, a number of other specifications are made for diagnosis of social phobia in children. For instance, the child must exhibit: age-appropriate social relationships with familiar people, anxiety within interactions involving peers as well as adults, and fear which can be expressed through crying, tantrums, freezing, or shrinking from social situations with unfamiliar people. However, the child need not recognize the unreasonable or excessiveness of his/her social anxiety.

Panic disorder (PD) is characterized by recurrent panic attacks that occur unexpectedly and are followed by at least 1 month of either persistent concern about having another attack, worry about the consequences of the attack, or a change in behaviour related to the attack. Agoraphobia is characterized by anxiety resulting from situations in which escape or avoidance may be inhibited or in which help may not be available if panic symptoms were to occur. These two disorders can either co-occur or occur independent of one another. Although there is ample evidence that these disorders occur among adolescent and adult populations, it remains unclear whether the presence and nature of them is similar in children (Ollendick et al., 1994b).

Obsessive-compulsive disorder (OCD) is characterized by obsessions and/or compulsions that cause distress, are time consuming, and interfere with the child's daily life. Obsessions are defined as recurrent and intrusive thoughts, impulses, or images that the child attempts to neutralize or suppress with other thoughts or actions. Compulsions are repetitive behaviours or mental acts that are performed in response to an obsession or used to reduce or prevent distress of a dreaded event. Often the child feels driven to perform the compulsive acts and if interrupted or prevented from doing so may feel intense anxiety or panic (Reed et al., 1995).

Posttraumatic stress disorder (PTSD) results from the experiencing or witnessing of an event that is perceived as threatening or dangerous and that involves a response of intense fear, helplessness, disorganized, or agitated behaviour. The child suffering from PTSD continues to reexperience the event through distressing memories and intense psychological distress or physiological arousal resulting from internal or external cues that are associated with the event in some way. Persistent avoidance of stimuli associated with the event, numbing of general responsiveness, and persistent symptoms of arousal that were not present prior to the event also characterize PTSD.

The essential feature of generalized anxiety disorder (GAD) is excessive anxiety and worry about a variety of events that the child finds difficult to control. These behaviours must be exhibited for more days than not over the course of at least 6 months. In addition, the anxiety and worry are associated with at least one of a number of difficulties such as restlessness, fatigue, difficulty concentrating, irritability, muscle tension, and sleep disturbance.

PREVALENCE OF ANXIETY DISORDERS IN CHILDREN

Epidemiological estimates of childhood anxiety disorders within community settings have been found to range from 2.4% to 17.7% (Kearney *et al.*, 1995; Muris and Merckelbach, 1998; Ollendick *et al.*, 1997). The broadness of this estimated figure appears to be related to the degree of clinical impairment reported. For example, Hagopian and Ollendick (1997) reported prevalence rates between 2.4% to 8.7% for children meeting criteria for an anxiety disorder with clinical impairment and 6.8% to 17.3% for children who meet criteria without impairment. Similarly, Kashani and Orvaschel (1988) reported the prevalence of any anxiety disorder in a sample of 150 adolescents without clinical impairment at 17.3%. However, when clinical impairment was considered, these percentage rates dropped to half (8.7%). Furthermore, it has been suggested that these percentages would nearly double if anxiety-related disorders such as school refusal behaviours, selective mutism, and sleep problems were included in the estimates (Kearney *et al.*, 1995). Regardless, anxiety disorders are consistently cited as the most prevalent disorders in children (Anderson, 1994; Anderson *et al.*, 1987; Beidel, 1991; Kashani and Orvaschel, 1988; Messer and Beidel, 1993).

DIFFERENTIAL DIAGNOSIS

As previously noted, differentiation among the various anxiety disorders reflects the nature of the feared stimulus and the response that it produces. Thus, a child who is phobic of closed spaces may be distinguished from a child with social phobia or agoraphobia on the basis of their fear. The phobic child's fear may be related to concerns of closed spaces in general (e.g., claustrophobia, specific phobia), concerns that being in closed spaces leads to increased social evaluation (social phobia), or concerns that being in a closed space will lead one to have a panic attack during which escape will be difficult (agoraphobia). Furthermore, although prevalence rates generally tend to be higher among girls and older children (Ollendick and Hagopian, 1997), a differentiation among the anxiety disorders has been observed with regard to gender and age. For instance, in clinical samples it appears that gender differences do not begin to emerge until adolescence (Last *et al.*, 1992). In addition, for some of the anxiety disorders, prevalence rates have been found to differ with regard to age (Anderson, 1994; Bernstein and Borchardt, 1991). For example, separation anxiety disorder is the most common diagnosis found in younger children while generalized anxiety disorder is the most common in older children and adolescents. Similarly, whereas specific phobias are more common in younger children, social phobia does not usually develop until adolescence.

A study by Last *et al.* (1992) further illustrates the differentiations that have been found among the DSM anxiety disorders. This study examined the clinical and sociodemographic characteristics among DSM-III-R anxiety disorders in a sample of 188 children and adolescents from an outpatient clinic. Although all DSM-III-R disorders were assessed, only those disorders that remain in the current DSM-IV will be reviewed here (cf. Last *et al.*, 1992 for information on overanxious and avoidant disorders). Overall, SAD was found to be the most prevalent disorder at intake (27.1%), followed by specific phobia (19.7%) and social phobia (14.9%). In contrast, PD, OCD, and PTSD were less commonly diagnosed disorders in this sample (9.6%, 6.9%, 3.2%, respectively). A similar pattern was also observed for a lifetime history of these disorders with SAD as the most common (44.7%) and PTSD (3.7%) as the least common.

In addition, a number of other findings from the Last *et al.* (1992) study deserve mention. For example, it was discovered that SAD (7.5 years) and specific phobia (8.4 years) tended to occur at a younger age, whereas PD (14.1 years) and social phobia (11.3 years) tended to have a later age of onset. These findings are consistent with previous research regarding these disorders (Last *et al.*, 1987a; Last and Strauss, 1989), and in accord with our review of fears, worries, and anxiety in normal children. In contrast to the research previously described regarding anxiety-related behaviours in normal children, however, a relatively equal distribution of gender was found across the anxiety disorders. Finally, two remarkable findings were reported for children with SAD. First, although the majority of children in this clinic sample came from intact families (52.5–64.3% intact), this was not the case for children with SAD who tended to come from single parent families (36.9% intact). This finding suggests that children from single-parent families may be more likely to develop fears of separation, perhaps in response to the separation that has already occurred with one parent. A second interesting finding regarding children with SAD was that they were more likely to be from low socioeconomic (52.4%) status households as compared with children with other diagnoses (35.7–45.9%). Although this study revealed a number of interesting results, future research that replicates these findings as well as examines the specific DSM-IV anxiety disorders is clearly necessary.

Comorbidity

Anxiety disorders have consistently been reported as having high rates of comorbidity with both internalizing and externalizing psychiatric disorders. For example, comorbidity rates among anxiety disorders in general population samples have been reported as 39% for children (Anderson *et al.*, 1987; Kashani and Orvaschel, 1990) and 14% for adolescents (Anderson, 1994; Kashani and Orvaschel, 1988; McGee *et al.*, 1990). Furthermore, Last *et al.* (1992) found that overanxious disorder (96%) and panic disorder (63%) evidenced the greatest degree of comorbidity with other anxiety disorders.

Comorbid depression in children and adolescents with anxiety disorders also appears to be extremely high, ranging from 17% to 69% in general population and clinical samples (Berstein and Garfinkel, 1986; Kashani *et al.*, 1987; King *et al.*, 1990, 1991; Last *et al.*, 1987b; Ollendick and Yule, 1990; Seligman and Ollendick, 1998; Strauss *et al.*, 1988). Identifying comorbid anxiety disorders or depression seems particularly important considering the combination of these disorders has been associated with increased psychopathology and severity of symptoms (Bernstein, 1991). For instance, Strauss *et al.* (1988) examined differences between 140 children and adolescents (age 5–17) who presented with either comorbid anxiety and depression or anxiety alone. As compared with the children with anxiety alone, the comorbid group of children reported significantly more state, trait, and physiological anxiety as well as a greater number of fears, worry, and oversensitivity. Furthermore, in a companion study, Strauss *et al.* (1988) found that children with comorbid anxiety and depression also evidenced less positive social outcomes as compared with children with anxiety alone.

Externalizing disorders are also frequently found to be comorbid with anxiety disorders (23–69%; Anderson *et al.*, 1987, Kashani *et al.*,

1987). Although the impact of comorbid externalizing disorders is less clear than that with internalizing disorders, it has been found that children with an anxiety disorder more commonly present with comorbid attention-deficit hyperactivity symptoms, whereas adolescents with anxiety disorders typically show increased signs of oppositional or conduct disorders (Anderson, 1994; Ollendick *et al.*, 1997). In addition, children with comorbid anxiety and ADHD have been found to differ in terms of age (Pliszka, 1992), impulsivity (Livingston *et al.*, 1990; Pliszka, 1992), and family patterns of these two disorders (Biederman *et al.*, 1991a). Comorbid conduct disorder with an anxiety disorder was estimated at approximately 40% in a clinical sample of 177 boys (Walker *et al.*, 1991).

These researchers also found that the anxious symptoms in the conduct/anxiety disorder boys seemed to abate the conduct disorder behaviours to some extent as evidenced by a decrease in problems exhibited as compared to those without comorbid anxiety symptoms. However, Ollendick *et al.* (1999) did not find evidence of anxiety as a protective factor with incarcerated delinquent adolescents. The chronic nature of the conduct disturbance in the incarcerated youth may have affected the potential mitigating role of anxiety.

In addition to comorbid psychiatric disorders, anxious children have also been found to evidence school refusal behaviours (Bernstein and Garfinkel, 1986), social incompetence (La Greca *et al.*, 1988), and feelings of loneliness (Crick and Ladd, 1993) with greater frequency. In fact, significant correlations between anxiety, loneliness, and peer relationship problems have been consistently cited in empirical literature with North American samples (Crick and Ladd, 1993; La Greca *et al.*, 1988; Strauss *et al.*, 1986) as well as across other cultures (e.g., South Pacific, Israeli; Ginter *et al.*, 1996).

The Etiology of Fears, Worries, and Anxiety in Children

The etiology of fears, worries, and anxiety in children is not fully understood at this time. As a part of normal development, these emotional states wax and wane—sometimes being more evident and, at other times, being relatively absent. In addition, as described earlier, the content of these anxiety-related phenomena tend to change over time. Furthermore, many fears function as protective factors and constitute adaptive responses to dangerous stimuli. However, many fears and worries that would normally dissipate over time may be reinforced and continue long after their survival value has declined.

A considerable amount of research suggests that the expression of anxiety symptomatology and disorders is related to the interaction between the environment and developmental processes that occur throughout life. Developmentally, for example, children universally experience normative fears (Marks, 1987a, b). Undoubtedly, the risk for the emergence of certain fears changes in accordance with important developmental process. Maintenance or persistence of age-appropriate fears may result in pathology, specifically anxiety disorder in later life. These developmental periods of increased vulnerability, in combination with certain life events, may lead to the expression of any one specific anxiety disorder (Ollendick and King, 1994). This developmental process is mutually influenced by, and influences, life events and experiences and can result in learning experiences that shape or occasion subsequent anxious behaviour. Children can learn to associate aversive outcomes through classical, operant, and vicarious learning. In addition, they learn that avoidant and fearful behaviour result in consequences that may be reinforcing. For example, there is a higher probability that children of anxious parents observe overly anxious behaviour in their parents, and they are more likely to be reinforced for their fearful behaviour than are children whose parents are less anxious. Unfortunately, the child's fearful behaviour is being reinforced and shaped by their parents, whereas the parents' behaviour may be negatively reinforced by the anxious child becoming calm (Hagopian and Slifer, 1993), resulting in an ongoing transactional process.

Genetic influences and temperament tendencies may predispose the child to general fearfulness, behavioural inhibition, and anxiety disorder; however, specific forms of parental psychopathology and specific conditioning histories are seemingly necessary to set the stage for the development of specific anxiety disorders. Thus, several risks and prognostic factors for the development and long-term course of anxiety disorder include heredity, temperament, attachment, learning history, and parenting practices, each of which will be reviewed next.

HEREDITY

There appears to be a genetic predisposition for the development and maintenance of anxiety-related phenomena and anxiety disorder in children. Information supporting this view is obtained from familial concordance studies and twin studies. A number of familial concordance studies have illustrated high concordance rates of anxiety disorders among first degree relatives of anxiety disordered patients (Turner *et al.*, 1987; Weissman *et al.*, 1984). Specifically, there is a growing body of literature that suggests there is an increased risk for anxiety disorder in children whose parents have anxiety or affective disorders. For example, Weissman *et al.* (1984) found significantly higher rates of these disorders in children of parents with major depression than in children of normal controls. Although major depression was the most prevalent (13.1%) diagnosis, attention deficit disorder and anxiety disorder were found to have the second highest prevalence rates with (10.3%) of the children experiencing each of these disorders (Seligman and Ollendick, 1998). Similarly, Turner *et al.* (1987) investigated psychopathology in children of parents with an anxiety disorder (i.e., obsessive-compulsive disorder, agoraphobia), parents with dysthymic disorder, and parents without a disorder. Results indicated that children of anxious parents were seven times more likely to be diagnosed with an anxiety disorder than were children of parents without a disorder. In addition, the study showed that risk for an anxiety disorder was not significantly different for children of anxiety-disordered parents and children of dysthymic parents. Importantly, the authors indicated that the disorders manifested in children of dysthymic disordered parents were all anxiety disorders (i.e., SAD, OAD, SP).

In another study, children of clinically depressed and anxious parents were assessed to determine the probability of their subsequent risk for an anxiety disorder in later life (Biederman *et al.*, 1991b). The study examined offspring of parents with panic disorder and agoraphobia only; children of parents with panic disorder with agoraphobia and with major depression; and children of parents with major depression alone. Biederman *et al.* (1991b) found that children of parents with panic disorder and agoraphobia, both with and without comorbid depression, were at increased risk for anxiety disorder. Furthermore, results indicated that children of depressed parents were not at an increased rate for an anxiety disorder per se. Although this latter finding is discordant with the findings reported by Weissman *et al.* (1984) and Turner *et al.* (1987), the majority of findings support the notion that offspring of both anxiety and affective disorder parents are at increased risk for the development of anxiety disorders.

In addition, concordance rates of anxiety symptoms and disorders in MZ twins have been shown to be higher than that in DZ twins (Kendler *et al.*, 1992; Thepar and Mc Guffin, 1995). Even though these studies support a genetic predisposition to the development of anxiety symptoms and disorders, the difference in concordance rates among MZ twins to DZ twins is low in comparison to other psychiatric disorders. Therefore, as noted earlier, the expression of anxiety disorders is more likely related to an interaction between genetic predisposition, developmental processes and life circumstances.

TEMPERAMENT

Temperamental characteristics appear to act as risk factors for the development, progression, and outcome of anxiety disorders in children. According to Kagan and his colleagues, one aspect of temperament that has been identified as a risk factor for the development of anxiety in children is behavioural inhibition to the unfamiliar (Kagan *et al.*, 1984, 1988). These researchers assert that a behaviourally inhibited child who is shy and cautious will experience physiological arousal, and will withdraw when exposed to unfamiliar situations. In addition, this tendency toward behavioural inhibition has been shown to be a stable characteristic that has been identified in infants (Garcia-Coll *et al.*, 1984; Kagan *et al.*, 1998). Several studies have linked behaviour inhibition to anxiety disorder. For instance, in a study involving children of parents with panic disorder with agoraphobia, Rosenbaum *et al.* (1988) reasoned that these children may be considered at high risk for anxiety disorder based on family history. Furthermore, they argued that these children would evidence higher rates of behavioural inhibition. Their findings supported their hypotheses: 76% of children of parents with panic disorder with agoraphobia showed characteristics of behavioural inhibition. In addition, these children were found to have higher rates of anxiety disorder than children who were uninhibited. An examination by Biederman *et al.* (1990) also investigated the association between the development of an actual anxiety disorder and behavioural inhibition. Results showed that children classified as behaviourally inhibited at 21 months showed higher rates of anxiety disorder between the ages of 7 and 8 years opposed to those children who were assessed as uninhibited. These results were significant only for comparisons involving 7- and 8-year-olds with a phobic disorder; however, there was an inclination for behaviourally inhibited children to demonstrate a significantly higher rate of multiple (2 or more) anxiety disorders as well.

Another aspect of temperament is what is frequently referred to as the three basic dimensions of personality: emotionality-activity-sociability. Rende (1993) measured temperament in children at ages 1, 2, 3, and 4 years of age and at age 7 assessed behavioural and emotional problems and found that emotionality and sociability in infancy and early childhood were positively related to emotional problems in girls. For boys, emotionality but not activity or sociability was positively correlated to anxiety and depression. More research along this line is obviously needed.

ATTACHMENT

Early experiences of stress lead to styles of coping, which may predispose children to or protect them from anxiety in later life (Mattis and Ollendick, 1997; Warren et al., 1997). For instance, a secure attachment relationship is one in which the child is confident that his or her parent will be available and return to them after brief periods of separation. Bowlby (1973) noted that once an infant becomes attached to the caregiver, there is a period in which they are made anxious by even brief separations. A child who has a secure attachment relationship is less likely to feel anxious by brief separations, however. In contrast, a child who has an insecure attachment relationship may become anxious more frequently.

Ainsworth et al. (1978) described two primary types of insecure attachment relationships: anxious-avoidant and anxious resistant. Briefly, anxious-avoidant infants whose mothers frequently rejected them when the infant sought comfort, demonstrated avoidance behaviours (i.e., looking away, moving away) after being separated from and reunited with their mothers. In contrast, mothers of anxious-resistant infants showed inconsistent care giving. These infants displayed resistant, angry, and ambivalent feelings upon reunion. According to Mattis and Ollendick (1997), this group of insecurely attached infants is thought to be at risk for development of anxiety disorders later in life.

To illustrate, Warren et al. (1997) conducted a longitudinal study of 172 children (81 females, 91 males) and their mothers. At the time of delivery, mother's age ranged from 12 to 37 years, 62% were not married, they were of low socioeconomic status, and their lives were marked by high levels of stress (84% were Caucasians, 11% were African-American, and 5% were Native American or Hispanic). Ainsworth's Strange Situation Test was administered when the infants were 12 months of age to test the quality of the attachment relationship. Results were derived from eight episodes, including two brief separations from and subsequent reunions with the mother. When the 172 children were 17.5 years old, a structured diagnostic interview was administered to assess past and present anxiety disorders. Results indicated that 26 (15%) of the late adolescents had at least one past or current anxiety disorder. In particular, 20 had one anxiety disorder, 5 had two anxiety disorders, and 1 had five anxiety disorders. In addition, results indicated that these young adults were classified as anxious/resistant infants more frequently than youth without anxiety disorders. In fact, 13% of the adolescents who were not anxiously/resistant attached developed anxiety disorders; whereas, 28% of youth who were anxiously/resistant attached developed anxiety disorder.

In a related study, Manassis and Bradley (1994) investigated behavioural inhibition, attachment style, and anxiety in 20 children (14 boys, 6 girls) of mothers with anxiety disorders. Fourteen mothers were diagnosed with panic disorder, three with generalized anxiety disorder, and one with obsessive-compulsive disorder. All mothers were married Caucasian women of varying socioeconomic backgrounds. Anxiety in the children was assessed with diagnostic criteria and a parent completed checklist. Three of the children met criteria for an anxiety disorder. Behavioural inhibition and attachment security were measured in standard laboratory ways. Results revealed that 65% of these children were classified as inhibited (13 inhibited, 7 uninhibited) and 80% were classified as insecurely attached. It is important to note that the demarcation between insecure-avoidant and insecure-resistant was not differentiated. In addition, and unexpectedly, no significant relationship was found between behavioural inhibition and security of attachment.

LEARNING HISTORY

Children do not exist in a vacuum. They are constantly changing and evolving. Moreover, they interpret environmental cues differently, dependent upon their specific learning histories. Therefore, Rachman's (1991) three pathways to fear acquisition model may provide a useful framework for studying the origins of fears, anxieties, and worries in children. According to this theory, there are three types of discrete, but overlapping learning experiences that play a fundamental role in the acquisition of these anxiety-related phenomena: aversive classical conditioning; modeling (vicarious learning); and negative information transmission. Unfortunately, there have been only a few studies, which have attempted to test Rachman's theory.

Ollendick and King (1991) found considerable support for Rachman's theory in their investigation of Australian and American school-aged children from a community sample. In their study, a short questionnaire was administered to children who indicated "a lot" of fear to FSSC-R items such as not being able to breathe and snakes. The questionnaire asked these children whether they had experienced conditioning, modeling, and/or informational events related to the stimuli or situations that had been endorsed as causing "a lot" of fear. The authors found that a majority (88%) of children endorsed negative information transmission as the source of their fear. Modeling and conditioning events were less frequently attributed to fear acquisition in children (56.2% and 35.7%, respectively).

In a similar study, Muris *et al.* (1999) tested the frequency of children who reported conditioning, modeling, and negative information experiences as etiologic factors in the origin of nighttime fears. The vast majority of children (77.5%) attributed their fear to negative information processes (largely from watching television). Children who reported conditioning and modeling experiences were considerably lower (25.6% and 13.2%, respectively). It is important to note, however, that 24% of the children did not know where their nighttime fears came from and did not endorse any of the pathways as links to their fear acquisition. The study also investigated parental views of fear acquisition in their children. Of interest, parents reported similar percentages as to the pathways of their children's nighttime fears: 61.9% of the parents indicated that exposure to negative information led to the acquisition of fear in their children. Negative information transmission was followed by conditioning (23.6%), and modeling (9.0%) influences. About a third of the parents (34.5%) mentioned none of the pathways. Furthermore, the authors reported that the main difference between children and parents' reports on the origins of nighttime fears was that negative information by television was more frequently mentioned by the children than the parents.

Yet another study that assessed the extent to which modeling, negative information, and conditioning contribute to the development of common childhood fears and worries in children is that recently reported by Muris *et al.* (2000). In this study, the fears, worries and scary dreams in 4- to 12-year old children were assessed. Results indicated the origin of scary dreams for children could be attributed primarily to the information pathway. Most children (55.2%) reported that these dreams were about something that they had recently seen on television. However, only a small portion mentioned conditioning or modeling experiences in relation to their scary dreams (33.1% and 25%, respectively). In contrast, modeling was the most frequently mentioned pathway for fears, and direct conditioning was the most frequent mode for worries. Collectively, these findings suggest that different pathways may be associated with fears, worries, and anxiety. The import of this conclusion for the origin and onset of these anxiety-related phenomena remains unexplored at this time.

PARENTING PRACTICES

As noted throughout this chapter, fear, worry, and anxiety are common among children and may occur as part of normal development. Parental rearing practices are believed to play a role in the development of these anxiety-related phenomena and the anxiety disorders themselves (see review by Rapee, 1997).

Measures of childrearing have focused on a wide array of behaviours and attitudes including such notions as neglect, hostile detachment, and expression of affection. To make sense of the large variety of childrearing concepts, several researchers have conducted factor analytic studies of childrearing questionnaires (Gerlsma et al., 1991; Schwartz et al., 1985; Schwartz and Mearns, 1989). Typically these studies have indicated two main factors. The largest factor describes behaviours and attitudes related to acceptance, or on the reverse side, warmth. This factor is often conceptualized in terms of negative or hostile feelings by the parent towards the child. The second factor refers to the parents' granting of autonomy to the child or, on the reverse side, the amount of control the parents impose or have over their children. These factors are termed parental rejection and control, respectively (Rapee, 1997). According to Muris and Mercklebach (1998), empirical support for the role of parenting variables comes from two primary sources, first by obtaining retrospective measures of anxiety and child rearing from non-clinical adult samples, and second by obtaining retrospective surveys from adult anxiety disordered patients. For example, Arrindell et al. (1983) asked anxiety disordered patients and normal controls to retrospectively judge the rearing practices of their parents. This study demonstrated that anxiety disordered patients reported their parents to be more rejecting and controlling than did the normal control adults. In addition, the patients reported that their parents were less emotionally warm when they were growing up. Thus, retrospective research suggests parental rejection and control may be risk factors for developing anxiety disorders.

In more recent work, Muris and Merckleback (1998) have directly examined the relationship between perceptions of parental rearing behaviours and anxiety disorders symptomatology in normal school children. Results indicated a positive relationship between anxious rearing and control. This was especially true for symptoms of generalized anxiety disorder, separation anxiety disorder, and environmental-situational phobia. Thus, significant and positive relationships were found between anxious rearing behaviours and parental control. Evidence for differences in parenting styles characterized by rejection were less evident, however.

In addition, in an even more recent study, Gruner *et al.* (1999) further examined the relationship between parental rearing practices (anxious behaviours) and anxiety disorders symptomatology in normal children. In their study, 117 school children between 9 and 12 years completed a questionnaire that measures perceptions of parental rearing behaviours and the Children's Anxiety Scale (CAS). Results showed that there were significant and positive associations between parental rejection, anxious rearing, and parental control with anxiety symptoms in children. It is important to note however that emotional warmth was not related to anxiety symptoms in this study. Parental control and anxious rearing were also related positively to the CAS anxiety scales; however, the strongest relationship emerged between parental rejection and CAS scores. Furthermore, parental rejection appeared to be the most important predictor of anxiety symptoms in children. Therefore, it is believed that perceived parental rearing behaviours contribute to levels of anxiety in children in complex ways.

Summary

Children experience many fears, worries, and anxieties over the course of normal development. These fears are usually short-lived. Moreover, they are frequently adaptive responses to a world that is not fully comprehended nor understood by them—a world replete with situations, objects, and events that seem uncontrollable and unpredictable to them. However, these phenomena are not unusually problematic for children because they desist over time and with increased experiences of control and predictability in the world. However, for some children, these reactions persist over time and do cause considerable distress and interference in their lives. They develop phobic and anxiety disorders. The etiology and maintenance of these disorders remain perplexing issues for us because they involve the complex interplay of familial, biological, developmental, and environmental contextual variables. The specific expression of any one anxiety disorder is likely related to the interaction between life circumstances, learning histories, developmental, and biological processes. We conclude that we know much about childhood fears, worries, and anxieties but that we have much more to learn before we can assert that we fully understand their onset, course, and long-term sequels. The challenge is before us.

References

Ainsworth, M.D.S., Blehar, M.C., Waters, E., & Wall, S. (1978). *Patterns of Attachment: A Psychological Study of the Strange Situation*. Hillsdale, NJ: Earlbaum.

American Psychiatric Association (1980). *Diagnostic and Statistical Manual of Mental Disorders* (3rd Ed.) (DSM-III). Washington, DC: American Psychiatric Association.

American Psychiatric Association (1987). *Diagnostic and Statistical Manual of Mental Disorders* (3rd Ed., Rev.) (DSM-III-R). Washington, DC: American Psychiatric Association.

American Psychiatric Association (1994). *Diagnostic and Statistical Manual of Mental Disorders* (4th Ed.; DSM-IV). Washington, DC: American Psychiatric Association.

Anderson, J.C. (1994). Epidemiological issues. In T.H. Ollendick, N.J. King, & W. Yule (Eds.), *International Handbook of Phobic and Anxiety Disorders in Children and Adolescents*. New York: Plenum Press.

Anderson, J.C., Williams, S., McGee, R., & Silva, P.A. (1987). DSM-III disorders in preadolescent children: Prevalence in a large sample from the general population. *Archives of General Psychiatry, 44,* 69–76.

Arrindell, W.A., Emmelkamp, P.M.G., Monsma, A., & Brilman, E. (1983). The role of perceived parental rearing practices in the aetiology of phobic disorders: A controlled study. *British Journal of Psychiatry, 143,* 183–187.

Bauer, D.H. (1976). An exploratory study of developmental changes in children's fears. *Journal of Child Psychology and Psychiatry, 17,* 69–74.

Beidel, D.C. (1991). Social phobia and overanxious disorder in school-age children. *Journal of the American Academy of Child and Adolescent Psychiatry, 30,* 545–552.

Bell-Dolan, D., Last, C.G., & Strauss, C.C. (1990). Symptoms of anxiety disorders in normal children. *Journal of the American Academy of Child and Adolescent Psychiatry, 29,* 759–765.

Bernstein, G.A. (1991). Comorbidity and severity of anxiety and depressive disorders in a clinic sample. *Journal of the American Academy of Child and Adolescent Psychiatry, 30,* 43–50.

Bernstein, G.A., & Borchardt, C.M. (1991). Anxiety disorders of childhood and adolescence: A critical review. *Journal of the American Academy of Child and Adolescent Psychiatry, 30,* 519–532.

Bernstein, G.A., & Garfinkel, B.D. (1986). School phobia: The overlap of affective and anxiety disorders. *Journal of the American Academy of Child Psychiatry, 25,* 235–241.

Biederman, J., Faraone, S.V., Keenan, K., Steingard, R., & Tsuang, M.T. (1991a). Familial association between attention deficit disorder and anxiety disorders. *American Journal of Psychiatry, 148,* 251–256.

Biederman, J., Rosenbaum, J.F., Bolduc, E.A., Faraone, S.V., & Hirshfeld, D.R. (1991b). A high risk study of young children of parents with panic disorder and agoraphobia with and without comorbid major depression. *Psychiatry Research, 37,* 333–348.

Biederman, J., Rosenbaum, J.F., Hirshfield, D.R., Faraone, S.V., Bolduc, E.A., Gersten, M., Meminger, S.R., Kagan, J., Snidman, N., & Reznick, S. (1990). Psychiatric correlates of behavioral inhibition in young children without psychiatric disorders. *Archives of General Psychiatry, 47,* 21–26.

Birmaher, B., Khetarpal, S., Brent, D., Cully, M., Balach, L., Kaufman, J., & McKenzie Neer, S. (1997). The screen for child anxiety related emotional disorders (SCARED): Scale construction and psychometric characteristics. *Journal of the American Academy of Child and Adolescent Psychiatry, 36,* 545–553.

Borkovec, T.D., Robinson, E., Pruzinsky, T., & De Pree, J.A. (1983). Preliminary exploration of worry: Some characteristics and processes. *Behaviour Research and Therapy, 21,* 9–16.

Bowlby, J. (1973). *Attachment and Loss: Separation, Anxiety, and Anger.* New York: Basic Books.

Comunian, A.L. (1989). Some characteristics of relations among depression, anxiety, and self-efficacy. *Perceptual and Motor Skills, 69,* 755–764.

Crick, N.R., & Ladd, G.W. (1993). Children's perceptions of their peer experiences: Attributions, loneliness, social anxiety, and social avoidance. *Developmental Psychology, 29,* 244–254.

Dong, Q., Yang, B., & Ollendick, T.H. (1994). Fears in Chinese children and adolescents and their relations to anxiety and depression. *Journal of Child Psychology and Psychiatry, 35,* 351–363.

Erol, N., & Sahin, N. (1995). Fears of children and the cultural context: The Turkish norms. *European Child and Adolescent Psychiatry, 4,* 85–93.

Fox, J.E., Houston, B.K., & Pittner, M.S. (1983). Trait anxiety and children's cognitive behaviors in an evaluative situation. *Cognitive Therapy and Research, 7,* 149–154.

Garcia-Coll, C.G., Kagan, J., & Reznick, J.S. (1984). Behavioral inhibition in young children. *Child Development, 55,* 1005–1019.

Gaudry, E., & Poole, C. (1972). The effects of an experience of success or failure on state anxiety level. *Journal of Experimental Education, 41,* 18–21.

Gerlsma, C., Arrindell, W.A., Van der Veen, N., & Emmelkamp, P.M.G. (1991). A parental rearing style questionnaire for use with adolescence: Psycometric evaluation of the EMBU-A. *Personality and Individual Differences, 12*, 1245–1253.

Ginter, E.J., Lufi, D., & Dwinell, P.L. (1996). Loneliness, perceived social support, and anxiety among Israeli adolescents. *Psychological Reports, 79*, 335–341.

Gruner, K., Muris, P., & Merckelbach, H. (1999). The relationship between anxious rearing behaviours and anxiety disorders symptomatology in normal children. *Journal of Behavior Therapy and Experimental Psychiatry, 30*, 27–35.

Hagopian, L.P., & Ollendick, T.H. (1993). Simple phobia in children. In R.T. Ammerman & M. Hersen (Eds.), Handbook of behavior therapy with children and adults: A developmental and longitudinal perspective. *General psychology series, Vol. 171.* Boston, MA, USA: Allyn & Bacon, Inc.

Hagopian, L.P., & Ollendick, T.H. (1997). Anxiety Disorders. In R.T. Ammerman and M. Hersen (Eds.), *Handbook of prevention and treatment with children and adolescents.* New York: John Wiley & Sons.

Hagopian, L.P., & Slifer, K.J. (1993). Treatment of Separation Anxiety Disorder with graduated exposure and reinforcement targeting school attendance: A controlled case study. *Journal of Anxiety Disorders, 7*, 271–280.

Hodges, W.F., & Felling, J.P. (1970). Types of stressful situations and their relation to trait anxiety and sex. *Journal of Consulting and Clinical Psychology, 34*, 333–337.

Ingman, K.A., Ollendick, T.H., & Akande, A. (1999). Cross-cultural aspects of fears in African children and adolescents. *Behaviour Research and Therapy, 37*, 337–345.

Kagan, J., Reznick, J.S., Clarke, C., & Snidman, N. (1984). Behavioral inhibition to the unfamiliar. *Child Development, 55*, 2212–2225.

Kagan, J., Reznick, J.S., & Snidman, N. (1988). The physiology and psychology of behavioral inhibition in children. *Child Development, 58*, 1459–1473.

Kashani, J.H., Beck, N.C., Hoeper, E.W., Fallahi, C., Corcoran, C.M., McAllister, J.A., Rosenberg, T.K., & Reid, J.C. (1987). Psychiatric disorders in a community sample of adolescents. *American Journal of Psychiatry, 144*, 584–589.

Kashani, J.H., & Orvaschel, H. (1988). Anxiety disorders in mid-adolescence: A community sample. *American Journal of Psychiatry, 145*, 960–964.

Kearney, C.A., Eisen, A.R., & Schaefer, C.E. (1995). General issues underlying the diagnosis and treatment of child and adolescent anxiety disorders. In A.R. Eisen, C.A. Kearney & C.E. Schaefer (Eds.), *Clinical handbook of anxiety disorders in children and adolescents.* New Jersey: Jason Aronson Inc.

Kendler, K.S., Neale, M.C., Kessler, R.C., Heath, A.C., & Eaves, D.K. (1992) Generalized Anxiety Disorder in women: A population-based twin study. *Archives of General Psychiatry, 49*, 267–272.

King, N.J., Gullone, E., & Ollendick, T.H. (1990). Childhood anxiety disorders and depression: Phenomenology, comorbidity, and intervention issues. *Scandinavian Journal of Behaviour Therapy, 19*, 59–70.

King, N., Ollendick, T.H., & Gullone, E. (1991). Negative affectivity in children and adolescents: Relations between anxiety and depression. *Clinical Psychology Review, 11*, 441–459.

King, N.J., Ollier, K., Iacuone, R., Schuster, S., Bays, K., Gullone, E., & Ollendick, T.H. (1989). Child and adolescent fears: An Australian cross-sectional study using the Fear Survey Schedule for Children. *Journal of Child Psychology and Psychiatry, 30*, 775–784.

La Greca, A.M., Dandes, S.K., Wick, P., Shaw, K., & Stone, W.L. (1988). Development of the social anxiety scale for children: Reliability and concurrent validity. *Journal of Clinical Child Psychology, 17*, 84–91.

LaPouse, R., & Monk, M.A. (1959). Fears and worries in a representative sample of children. *American Journal of Orthopsychiatry, 29*, 803–818.

Last, C.G., Hersen, M., Kazdin, A.E., Finkelstein, R., & Strauss, C.C. (1987a). Comparison of DSM-III separation anxiety and overanxious disorders: Demographic characteristics and patterns of comorbidity. *Journal of the American Academy of Child and Adolescent Psychiatry, 26*, 527–531.

Last, C.G., Perrin, S., Hersen, M., & Kazdin, A.E. (1992). DSM-III-R anxiety disorders in children: Sociodemographic and clinical characteristics. *Journal of the American Academy of Child and Adolescent Psychiatry, 31*, 1070–1076.

Last, C. G., & Strauss, C. C. (1989). Panic disorder in children and adolescents. *Journal of Anxiety Disorders, 3*, 87–95.

Last, C.G., Strauss, C.C., & Francis, G. (1987b). Comorbidity among childhood anxiety disorders. *Journal of Nervous Mental Disorders, 175*, 726–730.

Livingston, R.L., Dykman, R.A., & Ackerman, P.T. (1990). The frequency and significance of additional self reported psychiatric diagnoses in children with attention deficit disorder. *Journal of Abnormal Child Psychology, 18*, 465–478.

Maddux, J.E., & Stanley, M.A. (1986). Self-efficacy theory in contemporary psychology: An overview. *Journal of Social and Clinical Psychology, 4*, 249–255.

Manassis, K., & Bradley, S.J. (1994). The development of childhood anxiety disorders: Toward an integrated model. *Journal of Applied Developmental Psychology, 15*, 345–366.

Marks, I. (1987a). The development of normal fear: A review. *Journal of Child Psychology and Psychiatry, 28*, 667–697.

Marks, I. (1987b). Fears, phobias, and rituals. New York: Oxford University Press.

Mattis, S.G., & Ollendick, T.H. (1997). Children's cognitive responses to the somatic symptoms of panic. *Journal of Abnormal Child Pyschology*, *25*, 47–57.

McGee, R., Feehan, M., Williams, S., Partridge, F., Silva, P., & Kelly, J. (1990). DSM-III disorders in a large sample of adolescents. *Journal of the American Academy of Child and Adolescent Psychiatry*, *29*, 611–619.

Messer, S.C., & Beidel, D.C. (1993). Psychosocial correlates of childhood anxiety disorders. *Journal of the American Academy of Child and Adolescent Psychiatry*, *33*, 975–984.

Muris, P., Meesters, C., Merckelbach, H., Sermon, A., & Zwakhalen, S. (1998a). Worry in normal children. *Journal of the American Academy of Child and Adolescent Psychiatry*, *37*, 703–710.

Muris, P., & Merckelbach, H. (1998). Perceived parental rearing behaviour and anxiety disorders symptoms in normal children. *Personality and Individual Differences*, *25*, 1199–1206.

Muris, P., Merckelbach, H., & Collaris, R. (1997a). Common childhood fears and their origins. *Behaviour Research and Therapy*, *35*, 929–937.

Muris, P., Merckelbach, H., Gadet, B., & Moulaert, V. (2000). Fears, worries, and scary dreams in 4- to 12-year old children: Their content, developmental pattern, and origins. *Journal of Clinical Child Psychology*, *29*, 43–52.

Muris, P., Merckelbach, H., Mayer, B., & Meesters, C. (1998b). Common fears and their relationship to anxiety disorders symptomatology in normal children. *Personality and Individual Differences*, *24*, 575–578.

Muris, P., Merckelbach, H., Mayer, B., & Sneider, N. (1998d). The relationship between anxiety disorder symptoms and negative self-statements in normal children. *Social Behavior and Personality*, *26*, 307–316.

Muris, P., Merckelbach, H., Meesters, C., & Van Lier, P. (1997b). What do children fear most often? *Journal of Behavior Therapy and Experimental Psychiatry*, *28*, 263–267.

Muris, P., Merckelbach, H., Ollendick, T.H., King, N.J., & Bogie, N. (1999). Children's nighttime fears: Parent-child ratings of frequency, content, origins, coping behavior, and severity. *Journal of Child Psychology and Psychiatry*.

Muris, P., Merckelbach, H., van Brakel, A., Mayer, B., & van Dongen, L. (1998c). The screen for child anxiety related emotional disorders (SCARED): Relationship with anxiety and depression in normal children. *Personality and Individual Differences*, *24*, 451–456.

Nalven, F.B. (1970). Manifest fears and worries of ghetto vs middle-class suburban children. *Psychological Reports*, *27*, 285–286.

Neal, A.M., Lilly, R.S., & Zakis, S. (1993). What are African-American children afraid of? A preliminary study. *Journal of Anxiety Disorders*, *7*, 129–140.

Neal, A.M., & Turner, S.M. (1991). Anxiety disorders research with African Americans: Current status. *Psychological Bulletin*, *109*, 400–410.

Ollendick, T.H. (1983). Reliability and validity of the revised Fear Survey Schedule for Children (FSSC- R). *Behaviour Research and Therapy, 21*, 685–692.

Ollendick, T.H., Hagopian, L.P., & King, N.J. (1997). Specific phobias in children. In G.C.L. Davey (Ed.), *Phobias: A handbook of theory, research, and treatment*. Chichester: Wiley.

Ollendick, T.H & King, N.J. (1991). Origins of childhood fears: An evaluation of Rachman's theory of fear acquistion. *Behaviour Research and Therapy, 29*, 117–123.

Ollendick, T.H., & King, N.J. (1994). Diagnosis, assessment, and treatment of internalizing problems in children: The role of longitudinal data. *Journal of Consulting and Clinical Psychology, 62*, 918–927.

Ollendick, T.H., King, N.J., & Frary, R.B. (1989). Fears in children and adolescents: Reliability and generalizability across gender, age, and nationality. *Behaviour Research and Therapy, 27*, 19–26.

Ollendick, T.H., King, N.J., & Yule, W. (Eds.) (1994a). *International handbook of phobic and anxiety disorders in children and adolescents*. Boston: Allyn and Bacon.

Ollendick, T.H., Matson, J.L., & Helsel, W.J. (1985). Fears in children and adolescents: Normative data. *Behaviour Research and Therapy, 23*, 465–467.

Ollendick, T.H., Mattis, S.G., & King, N.J. (1994b). Panic in children and adolescents: A review. *Journal of Child Psychology and Psychiatry, 35*, 113–134.

Ollendick, T.H., Seligman, L.D., & Batcher, A.T. (1999). Does anxiety mitigate the behavioral expression of severe conduct disorders in delinquent youth? *Journal of Disorders, 13*, 565–574.

Ollendick, T.H., & Vasey, M.W. (1999). Developmental theory and the practice of clinical child psychology. *Journal of Clinical Child Psychology, 28*, 457–466.

Ollendick, T.H., Yang, B., King, N.J., Dong, Q., & Akande, A. (1996). Fears in American, Australian, Chinese, and Nigerian children and adolescents: A cross-cultural study. *Journal of Child Psychology and Psychiatry, 37*, 213–220.

Ollendick, T.H., & Yule, W. (1990). Depression in British and American children and its relation to anxiety and fear. *Journal of Consulting and Clinical Psychology, 58*, 126–129.

Ollendick, T.H., Yule, W., & Ollier, K. (1991). Fears in British children and their relationship to manifest anxiety and depression. *Journal of Child Psychology and Psychiatry, 32*, 321–331.

Opolot, J.A. (1976). Normative data on the Children's Manifest Anxiety Scale in a developing country. *Psychological Reports, 39*, 587–590.

Orton, G.L. (1982). Comparative study of children's worries. *Journal of Psychology, 110*, 153–162.

Pela, O.A., & Reynolds, C.R. (1982). Cross-cultural applications of the Revised Children's Manifest Anxiety Scale: normative and reliability data for Nigerian primary school children. *Psychological Reports, 51,* 1135–1138.

Pliszka, S.R. (1992). Comorbidity of attention-deficit hyperactivity disorder and overanxious disorder. *Journal of the American Academy of Child and Adolescent Psychiatry, 31,* 197–203.

Rachman, S.J. (1991). Neoconditioning and the classical theory of fear acquisition. *Clinical Psychology Review, 11,* 155–173.

Rapee, R.M. (1997). Potential role of childbearing practices in the development of anxiety and depression. *Clinical Psychology Review, 17(1),* 47–67.

Reed, L.J., Carter, B.D., & Miller, L.C. (1995). Fear and anxiety in children. In C.E. Walker & M.C. Roberts (Eds.), *Handbook of clinical child psychology.* New York: Wiley.

Rende, R.D. (1993). Longitudinal relations between temperament traits and behavioral syndromes in middle childhood. *Journal of the American Academy of Child and Adolescent sychiatry, 32,* 287–290.

Rosenbaum, A.F., Biderman, J., Gersten, M., Hirshfield, D.R., Meminger, S.R., Herman, J.B., Kagan, J., Reznick, S., & Snidman, N. (1988). Behavioral inhibition in children of parents with Panic Disorder and agoraphobia. *Archives of General Psychiatry, 45,* 463–470.

Scherer, M.W., & Nakamura, C.Y. (1968). A Fear Survey Schedule for Children (FSS-FC): A factor analytic comparison with manifest anxiety (CMAS). *Behaviour Research and Therapy, 6,* 173–182.

Schwartz, J.C., Barton-Henry, M.L., & Pruzinsky, T. (1985). Assessing child-rearing behaviors: A comparison of ratings made by mother, father, child, and sibling on the CRPBI. *Child Development, 56,* 462–479.

Schwartz, J.C., & Mearns, J. (1989). Assessing parental childrearing behaviors: A comparison of parent, child, and aggregate ratings from two instruments. *Journal of Research in Personality, 23,* 450–468.

Seligman, L.D., & Ollendick, T.H. (1998). Comorbidity of anxiety and depression in children and adolescents: An integrative review. *Clinical Child and Family Psychology Review, 1,* 125–144.

Silverman, W.K., La Greca, A.M., & Wasserstein, S. (1995). What do children worry about? Worries and their relation to anxiety. *Child Development, 66,* 671–686.

Spence, S.H. (1997). Structure of anxiety symptoms among children: A confirmatory factor-analytic study. *Journal of Abnormal Psychology, 106,* 280–297.

Spielberger, C.D. (1975). Anxiety: State-trait process. In C.D. Spielberger & I.G. Sarason (Eds.), *Stress and anxiety,* Vol. 1. Washington, D.C.: Hemisphere/Wiley.

Strauss, C.C., Last, C.G., Hersen, M., & Kazdin, A.E. (1988). Association between anxiety and depression in children and adolescents with anxiety disorders. *Journal of Abnormal Child Psychology, 16,* 57–68.

Thepar, A., & McGuffin, P. (1995). Are anxiety symptoms in childhood heritable? *Journal of Child Psychology and Psychiatry, 36,* 439–447.

Turner, S.M., Beidel, D.C., & Costello, A. (1987). Psychopathology in the offspring of anxiety disorder patients. *Journal of Consulting and Clinical Psychology, 55,* 229–235.

Vasey, M.W., Crnic, K.A., & Carter, W.G. (1994). Worry in childhood: A developmental perspective. *Cognitive Therapy and Research, 18,* 529–549.

Walker, J.L., Lahey, B.B., Russo, M.F., Frick, P.J., Christ, M.A., McBurnett, K., Loeber, R., Stouthamer-Loeber, M., & Green, S. (1991). Anxiety, inhibition, and conduct disorder in children: I. Relations to social impairment. *Journal of the American Academy of Child and Adolescent Psychiatry, 30,* 187–191.

Warren, S.L., Huston, L., Egeland, B., & Sroufe, L.A. (1997). Child and adolescent anxiety disorders and early attachment. *Journal of the American Academy of Child and Adolescent Psychiatry, 36,* 637–644.

Weems, C.F., Silverman, W.K., Saavedra, L.M., Pina, A.A., & Lumpkin, P.W. (2000). The discrimination of children's phobias using the Revised Fear Survey Schedule for Children. *Journal of Child Psychology and Psychiatry, 40,* 941–952.

Weissman, M.M., Leckman, J.F., Merikangas, K.R., Gammon, G.D., & Prusoff, B.A. (1984). Depression and anxiety disorders in parents and children. *Archives of General Psychiatry, 41,* 845–852.

Zatz, S.L., & Chassin, L. (1985). Cognitions of test anxious children under naturalistic test-taking conditions. *Journal of Consulting and Clinical Psychology, 53,* 393–401.

2 RESEARCH METHODS IN CHILDHOOD ANXIETY

Bruce F. Chorpita
Catherine Moffitt

The study of childhood anxiety has become an area of increased focus over the past 20 years, fueled by both an increased understanding of the scope of anxiety conditions and their sequelae (Kashani and Orvashel, 1990; Lewinsohn *et al.*, 1993) and an accumulation of sophisticated theories of anxiety in adults (e.g., Barlow *et al.*, 1996; Clark, 1986; Clark and Watson, 1991, Fowles, 1995). This development of the childhood anxiety literature has distinguished itself with some considerable achievements, including major advances in treatment (e.g., Barrett *et al.*, 1996; Kendall, 1994; Kendall *et al.*, 1990), diagnostic assessment (Silverman and Albano, 1996) and theory (Chorpita and Barlow, 1998; Lonigan and Philips, in press; Thompson, in press; Vasey and Dadds, in press). From a research and methodology perspective, the process has involved a dialectic or bootstrapping process (Cronbach and Meehl, 1955), with each successive achievement inspiring revisions in the basic understanding of the domain, revisions which in turn foster new developments in a feed-forward cycle.

The childhood anxiety literature is no longer in its infancy, and accordingly, continued study in this area deserves increased attention to sophisticated methodological strategies that may catalyze continued development of ideas. With this aim in mind, the present chapter reviews research and methodology issues that are germane to the study of childhood anxiety and its broader conceptual domain. Obstacles, strategies, and recommendations are divided into the following four areas: (1) *construct network issues*, which involve the traditional notions of validity and reliability in articulating and measuring constructs relevant to the area of study; (2) *process and theory issues*, which further involve the notion of validity by testing and developing theories or models of the relations among these articulated constructs; (3) *clinical assessment issues*, which involve definition and evaluation of classification models and methods; and (4) *treatment issues*, which typically involve the application and extension of knowledge from the first three areas to their most applied ends.

These four areas can be organized within a larger framework or matrix, as pictured in Figure 2.1. The columns of this matrix divide areas into dimensions of *measurement* and *relational structure*. *Measurement* issues are those aimed at defining the network of constructs relevant to the domain of interest (i.e., asking, "what are the variables?"). *Relational structure* issues involve investigation of the operations of those constructs on each other (i.e., asking, "how does one variable influence the others?"). The rows of the matrix further divide the areas into dimensions of *basic* and *applied* research, with the former involving concept and theory development and the latter involving clinical assessment and treatment procedures. Clearly, these divisions are not definitive, as the four cells of the matrix overlap and impact each other considerably. Figure 2.1 notes how information moves from the construct development area to the treatment outcome area, informing new ideas along the way (inside arrows), while at the same time evidence from the treatment outcome area feeds all the way back to construct development (outside arrows). As is implied by the figure, one should consider the upper left cell of the matrix as the foundation for all substantive developments in the matrix. It is the theme of this chapter that methodological practice in the area of childhood anxiety will benefit most from continued attempts to (a) foster specific developments within each of the four cells of the matrix and (b) facilitate the feed-forward and feed-back channels relating the areas represented by these four cells. Within this proposed frame of reference, specific attention is paid to examples of methodological obstacles facing the childhood anxiety literature as well as to their potential solutions.

Basic Research: Elaboration of the Network of Constructs

As mentioned above, the very basis of the study of any domain rests on the clear articulation of the network of relevant constructs. As suggested in Figure 2.1, before the relations within the domain can be examined, constructs themselves must be identified or outlined in some way. In other words, investigation of measurement is typically prerequisite to investigation of relational structure. Similarly, basic research often sets the stage for any substantive applied work. Thus, developments in the child anxiety literature fully depend upon the issues represented in the upper left cell of the matrix in Figure 2.1. The importance

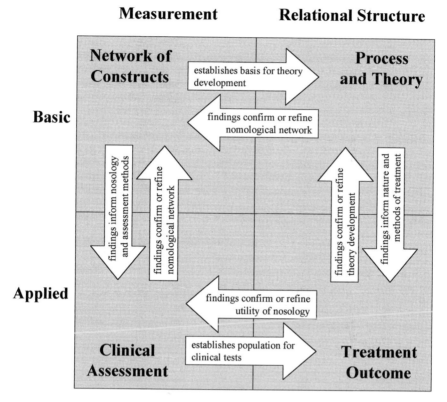

Figure 2.1   Matrix of research areas and their interrelations

of this issue cannot be overstated, as the child anxiety literature faces some particular challenges in this area. These challenges are best addressed through an examination of basic methodological principles regarding construct development and validity.

Articulating a Nomological Network

In their classic monograph on construct validation, Cronbach and Meehl (1955) offered the term *nomological network* to describe "the interlocking system of laws which constitute a theory" (p. 290). The network presumes testable relations among various constructs, which are defined as "some postulated attribute[s] of people, assumed to be reflected in test performance" (Cronbach and Meehl, 1955, p. 283). In this sense, Cronbach and Meehl argued that in order to understand the meaning of any chosen construct, we must have certain ideas about how it will relate to other constructs. It follows that "learning more about a theoretical construct is a matter of elaborating the nomological network in which it occurs, or of increasing the definiteness of its components" (p. 290).

To bring this discussion back to the context of childhood anxiety, what is the network in that literature? What, indeed, are the constructs thought to be a part of that network? Presumably, "anxiety" is a central construct, but to what degree does the network reflect that "anxiety" is related to such constructs as "sadness," "inhibition," "processing speed," or "avoidance," for example? This obscurity raises considerable problems, in that we now know that the nomological network is a prerequisite to theory construction, and in the childhood anxiety literature, much of the network remains poorly articulated. One of the first issues that needs to be examined, then, is why the nomological network is indefinite.

To begin with, the essence of the childhood anxiety nomological network is comprised of unobservable psychological constructs. The APA Committee on Psychological Tests (1954) stated, "the problem of construct validation becomes especially acute in the clinical field since for many of the constructs dealt with it is not a question of finding an imperfect criterion but of finding any criterion at all" (pp. 14–15). Although Cronbach and Meehl (1955) recommended that a minimum of constructs within the nomological network represent observable behaviors, only a small minority of studies in the childhood anxiety literature examine observable constructs. In this sense, the childhood anxiety literature is not entirely unique; however, it does face some comparatively formidable challenges, given the often discreet nature of its subject matter. It is therefore not surprising that (a) measurement of presumed behavioral outputs of anxiety is often time consuming, expensive, or unreliable (Beidel, 1991; Dadds and Sanders, 1992; Foster and Cone, 1986), and (b) there is no consensus regarding definitive validity criteria for anxiety (e.g., Chorpita et al., 1998; Lonigan et al., 1994).

CONTENT VERSUS PROCESS DIMENSIONS

Some considerations that may help in the task of refining measurement strategies involve the distinction between the content and the process of anxiety phenomena in children. For example, in research on worry, procedures have been used to analyze the content of children's worries (e.g., worries about illness, interpersonal situations, natural phenomena; Silverman *et al.*, 1995). Content measures are important for, among other things, analyses of the manner in which children's worries change according to cognitive and social development (Vasey and Daleiden, 1994). Within the same area, other questionnaires examine a specific process of the anxiety experience—its frequency, intensity, disruption, and uncontrollability (Borkovec *et al.*, 1991). For example, the Penn State Worry Questionnaire for Children (Tracey *et al.*, 1997) focuses on the degree of uncontrollably of the worry. Such a distinction between content and process is potentially important, in that content factors appear to discriminate across age groups (Barrios and O'Dell, 1998), whereas process dimensions appear to be better at separating normal from pathological worry (Borkovec *et al.*, 1991; Chorpita *et al.*, 1997). These issues have obvious implications for related research on such topics as fears and phobias.

SELF-REPORT IN CHILDHOOD ANXIETY

Many studies in the childhood anxiety literature involve some self-report measure of anxiety as their means of defining groups or evaluating outcomes. However, some of the most widely used measures in the childhood anxiety literature (e.g., Revised Children's Manifest Anxiety Scale, RCMAS, Reynolds and Richmond, 1978; Fear Survey Schedule for Children—Revised, FSSC-R, Ollendick, 1983; State Trait Anxiety Inventory for Children, STAIC-T, Spielberger, 1973) were developed prior to many of the recent theoretical advances in the understanding of emotional disorders (e.g., Barlow, 1988; Clark and Watson, 1991; Gray and McNaughton, 1996). Thus, these measures represent constructs in a network that has been refined or in some instances even invalidated by an accumulation of new evidence.

For example, Joiner and colleagues (1996) and Chorpita *et al.* (1998) both demonstrated problems with the factorial validity of the RCMAS and a measure of childhood depression, the Children's Depression Inventory (CDI; Kovacs, 1981), by showing that items from the two measures better factored not into two dimensions of "anxiety" and "depression," as the names of the measures would suggest, but rather into three dimensions as articulated in Clark and Watson's (1991) tripartite model of emotion. Similarly, Lonigan and colleagues (1994) demonstrated that anxious and depressed children were best discriminated not by RCMAS or CDI scores, but by totaling only a specific subset of items from the CDI. These findings suggest that anxiety and depression may not themselves represent unitary constructs, but rather are possible combinations of elements in a more detailed network of constructs. A tentative example of such a network was articulated by Chorpita (in press) and can be seen in Figure 2.2. Notice the absence of the general traits of anxiety and depression.

In general, accumulating evidence suggests that the broad term "anxiety" may be multifactorial and many of its measures therefore over-inclusive. Not surprisingly, some measures of childhood anxiety have demonstrated problems with discriminant validity. For example, Perrin and Last (1992) found that the RCMAS, FSSC-R, and a modified version of the STAIC-T (Fox and Houston, 1983) failed to discriminate boys with anxiety disorders from those with ADHD and that the FSSC-R failed to discriminate boys with anxiety disorders from boys with no history of psychiatric illness. The laws of the nomological network, however preliminary, would suggest that children with anxiety disorders should score higher on anxiety measures than children with other disorders or with no disorders. Similar results have been found with the related construct of Anxiety Sensitivity, a measure

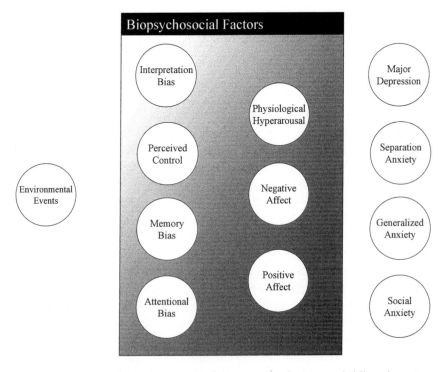

Figure 2.2   Hypothetical network of constructs relevant to childhood anxiety and its disorders

of which failed to discriminate children with ADHD from children with anxiety disorders (Rabian *et al.*, 1993).

At this point, the researcher is left to ponder whether such problems are due to the measures or to the constructs themselves. In other words, (a) can we make better measures of "anxiety," or (b) is there perhaps no definitive dimension that we can label "anxiety," and can we then articulate and evaluate a new network of related dimensions? Unfortunately, in the childhood anxiety literature, it is often difficult to separate what are method issues and what are construct issues, because constructs are so frequently defined with a single measure (i.e., mono-operation bias; Cook and Campbell, 1979).

MULTI-TRAIT MULTI-METHOD APPROACHES

Addressing this very issue, Campbell and Fiske (1959) argued that variance can be partitioned into effects of method and effects of the traits or constructs using the multi-trait multi-method matrix (MTMM). This operation specifies that at least two traits be evaluated using at least two different assessment methods. By evaluating the magnitude of correlation among all elements in the MTMM, one can draw inferences about the differential contributions of methods and traits to the variance of individual measures. This process ultimately helps us understand in the face of negative findings whether problems lie with our constructs or with our measures.

In this pursuit, researchers of childhood anxiety face two considerable challenges: (1) the difficulty of finding multiple adequate measures for even the most basic constructs in the network, and (2) the even greater difficulty of finding multiple methods to assess those constructs. It is a ubiquitous observation within the child anxiety literature that parents and teachers are rather poor informants regarding their children's or students' negative emotions (Handwerk *et al.*, in press; Klein, 1991), leaving the researcher few choices with which to abide by the principles of Campbell and Fiske (1959). For example, Achenbach and colleagues (1987) showed that correlations of parent measures with child measures average about .30, and that these are typically lower when measuring internalizing constructs (e.g., anxiety and depression).

Complications go one step further when considering the more technical elements of measurement theory. For example, it has recently been shown that MTMM investigation alone may yield incorrect identification of latent variables under many conditions (Bollen and Lennox, 1991; Kenny and Kashy, 1992). This concept will be illustrated with an example, presented earlier by Chorpita *et al.* (1998, see Figure 2.3). In this example, two latent constructs, *anxiety* and *depression*, are highly correlated at $r = .80$ and each construct is being measured by two scales. One or more of the measures of anxiety and depression has only moderate reliability, such as a reliability coefficient of .55 (as can be true for childhood self-report, e.g., Saylor *et al.*, 1984). Under these conditions, it is possible for one of the depression measures to be more highly correlated with one of the anxiety measures than with the second depression measure, thus leading one to the incorrect identification of factors. That is, in Figure 2.3, the depression measure *d1* would demonstrate a higher observed correlation with the anxiety measure *a2* ($r_{d1a2} = .51$) than with the other depression measure *d2* ($r_{d1d2} = .41$), simply because of measurement error artifacts (see Bollen and Lennox, 1991, for a detailed discussion). Further, this example already assumes the construct validity of the anxiety and depression factors, an assumption which may not be defensible, as noted above. Thus, even commendable attempts to abide by the basic principles of construct validation outlined by Cronbach and Meehl

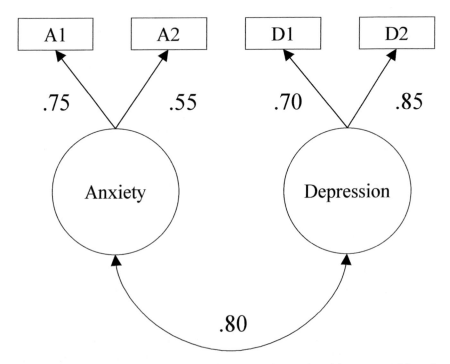

Figure 2.3   Example of the relation between observed and latent variables of anxiety and depression

(1955) and Campbell and Fiske (1959) can easily be derailed by serious methodological obstacles.

OBSERVATIONAL METHODS

Because of some of these issues, it is often advisable to use assessment procedures other than self-report, despite the highly subjective nature of anxiety (Barrios and Hartmann, 1997). One such procedure is the behavioral avoidance test (BAT), in which a child encounters a feared stimulus. The child may be asked to gradually move closer to and interact with the stimulus or the stimulus may be moved closer to the child. What is assessed in this situation is the child's length of time to respond, distance traveled toward stimulus, and time in contact with object or time spent in feared situation (Strauss, 1993). Behavioral avoidance tests can be done in laboratory or naturalistic settings. They have been used to assess fears of heights (Van Hasselt et al., 1979), social interaction (Eisen and Silverman, 1991), blood (Van Hasselt et al., 1979), animals (Evans and Harmon, 1981) and darkness (Kelly, 1976). Behavioral avoidance tests are useful for evaluating children's anxiety, but, as noted by Barrios and Hartmann, (1997), they do have a number of limitations as well as specific benefits. The absence of a standardized BAT makes cross-study comparisons difficult, and at least one study (Kelly, 1976) has indicated that differences in the instructions that are given can influence the outcome of a BAT. Also, because of the high level of control the subject has in a BAT (e.g., a feared animal may be caged, a subject is often told they can stop whenever they wish), results may not generalize (Lick and Unger, 1977). Use of the BAT in more naturalistic circumstances may provide a more externally valid result.

The benefits of the BAT (Barrios and Hartmann, 1997) include that the procedure is straightforward and easy to standardize, that it allows for assessment of multiple motor responses, and that it allows for concurrent monitoring of different types of responses (e.g., physiological responses and approach behavior). Furthermore, the BAT is one of the best methods for determining frequency and severity of symptoms, behaviors, antecedents and consequences (Silverman and Serafini, 1998).

Observational rating scales are another method that has been used to assess anxious mannerisms and behaviors in response to the feared stimulus, they are often used in natural environments, making them more generalizeable than laboratory BATs. More psychometric data exist on observational rating scales than on any other observational instrument (Barrios and Hartmann, 1997). Checklists, on the other hand, are instruments that retrospectively record behavior in occurring in the natural environment. They can cover a wide range of behaviors and time periods, and the observers can include researchers, parents and teachers.

In addition to specific issues encountered by particular observational methods, there are some measurement issues that all observational methods share in common (Barrios and Hartmann, 1997). One such issue is accuracy, which is the ability to obtain data that reflect the domain under investigation without distortion (Foster *et al.*, 1988). In order to ensure accuracy, observational methods must be compared with an objective criterion; however, oftentimes such a criterion does not exist, so the accuracy of observational methods cannot be assured (Foster and Cone, 1980). Another issue is reactivity, meaning that the mere presence of observers can influence the behavior being observed (Tyron, 1998), leading the subjects to act differently than they would otherwise. There is some evidence, however, that children are not as prone to reactivity as adults are (Foster and Cone, 1980). Some methods for minimizing reactivity include using participant observers, using video cameras or tape recorders, minimizing subject-observer interaction and allowing enough time for reactivity to lessen (Haynes and Horn, 1982). Yet another issue is factors that can bias the reports of observers, such as expectancies and observer drift. For example, if observers know the experimenter's expectations, that might influence their observations. Observer drift describes tendency of trained observes to rate the same events differently over time (Tyron, 1998). Regular agreement checks and effective observer training are important to minimize observer bias (Harris and Lahey, 1982). A final problem with direct observation methods is that they are not able to assess the cognitive and affective components of anxiety (Jacobson, 1985).

In summary, although behavioral observation methods clearly have a place in anxiety research, they will likely work best when supplemented with other methods, such as structured interviews, self-report measures, psychophysiological measurement, and self-monitoring to obtain a full picture of the phenomenon of anxiety.

RECOMMENDATIONS

In general, the challenges of establishing and articulating a definitive nomological network represent possibly the greatest impediment currently facing the childhood anxiety literature. As will be discussed in more detail below, many of the most promising ideas in the childhood anxiety literature seek to relate constructs that have not been subject to multiple empirical challenges or that are operationalized by a single assessment measure or protocol. Childhood anxiety researchers continue to need to know both (a) the boundaries of the constructs (what are "anxiety," "fear," "anxiety sensitivity," "panic," "inhibition," etc.), and (b) the degree to which measures of these constructs contain method variance. The use of multiple assessment strategies is therefore essential.

This caveat is not intended to minimize any of the accomplishments in the extant childhood anxiety literature. Indeed, as mentioned above, tremendous gains have been made (e.g., Kendall, 1994; Vasey and Dadds, in press). However, while we may all find ourselves in agreement, for example, that "exposure works," a suitable reply is "exposure works on what?" Does it affect symptom expression, memory processing, attributions, temperamental negative affectivity, behavioral inhibition, serotonin levels? All of these? Will it impact comorbid syndromes? For how long? In this example, only a well-articulated nomological network underlying investigations of exposure will help childhood anxiety researchers refine existing treatments. The same principles are true with respect to other cells in the matrix in Figure 2.1. Research on theory or clinical assessment is similarly impeded by a poorly defined network of constructs.

Of course, there are some methods for confronting these obstacles. Such efforts would likely begin at the level of factor analysis. Recent developments in models of anxiety (Barlow et al., 1996; Clark and Watson, 1991; Fowles, 1995; Gray and McNaughton, 1996; Kagan et al., 1987), have suggested the relevance of depression, temperamental variables, and information processing dimensions within the nomological network of "anxiety." Currently, there is a better understanding of specific conceptual factors that may constitute the theoretical domain. Again, a few of these factors are outlined in Figure 2.2, which features dimensions of the tripartite model of emotion as well as specific cognitive or information processing dimensions. With some improved understanding of the childhood anxiety domain, the following three avenues appear to hold promise.

- The development of new self-report measures or adaptation of existing measures should continue, with increased attention to item content and discriminant validity (e.g., Haynes et al., 1995). Initial item pools for developing instruments should be over-inclusive, to allow discriminant validity to be build into the test construction process (Loevinger, 1957). For example, if developing a measure of *autonomic arousal*, a preliminary measure should initially also contain items related to *central nervous system arousal* or some other discriminant construct, so that the boundary of autonomic arousal can be established empirically through factor analysis. Following such analysis, central nervous system arousal items could be discarded, provided that they did not factor with the autonomic items. In general, the choice of items for the initial pool will be particularly important for the development of new measures, and will need to be guided by the most current and well-supported theories of childhood anxiety. It is not sufficient to develop a scale without strong hypotheses about factor structure and discriminant validity (Haynes *et al.*, 1995). Finally, the supplemental use of confirmatory factor analyses in these efforts will protect against misspecified factors, and will heighten the role of theory in test construction.

- Specific parent and teacher assessment measures should continue to be evaluated and developed in parallel with child measures. Although parent or teacher agreement with child self-report for internalizing disorders is notoriously low, such research efforts may increase the understanding of which dimensions—or even which items—are reliably reported by other informants. Such research has the potential to suggest optimal rules for combining information from various sources, which may ultimately inform clinical strategies (see Figure 2.1), while providing important MTMM avenues for investigating construct validity.

- Additional methods of assessment need to continue to be developed and evaluated against parent and child measures. For example, interview strategies that require children to describe or interpret certain events (e.g., ambiguous situations paradigm, Butler and Mathews, 1983), elaboration of observational strategies that produce some behavioral index (e.g., interoceptive challenges, BATs), or cognitive production strategies (e.g., "think aloud" technique) will all be critical elements of the nomological network. Although such methods are more time intensive, their application is the only way to establish the meaning of the ubiquitous self-report measures that are a fundamental part of most research procedures. As before, these procedures should be heavily influenced by theory, and should themselves attempt to investigate method variance within their operation. For example, a researcher employing a procedure designed to have children interpret symptoms of arousal should consider the use of both a checklist format and a free-response format to measure children's inter-pretation. In this way, there is some safeguard against particular findings being mere procedural artifacts. These more detailed assess-ment procedures have relevance not only to test construction, but also to theory development, and some of these ideas will be discussed in more detail below.

Applied Research: Classification and Clinical Assessment

At some point, the constructs evaluated within the nomological network represent dimensions with special relevance to clinical intervention. In Figure 2.2, these dimensions are seen in the rightmost column and repre-sent the most widely used classification system for psychological disor-ders, the Diagnostic and Statistical Manual of Mental Disorders (DSM-IV; American Psychiatric Association, 1994). These dimensions are not the only ones that may have utility for treatment, as will be discussed below; however, the DSM-IV nosology has clearly been subject to the most research and application in classification.

STRUCTURED INTERVIEWS

The current state of the art for clinical diagnosis involves the structured diagnostic interview (Edelbrock and Costello, 1990; Matarazzo, 1983). As compared with unstructured interviews, structured diagnostic inter-views offer superior reliability through clear specification of the domains to be assessed and employment of a standard format to reduce variability among interviewers. As compared with unstructured clinical interviews, structured diagnostic interviews (a) yield more objective and quantifiable data, (b) facilitate a comprehensive assessment of a range of disorders, and (c) increase the specificity of the information gathered (DiNardo et al., 1983; Edelbrock and Costello, 1990). All of these properties are important given the advent of a particularly differentiated taxonomy within the anxiety disorders that employs more explicit diagnostic criteria (Edelbrock and Costello, 1990).

One of the most commonly used structured interviews for childhood anxiety disorders is the Anxiety Disorders Interview Schedule for DSM-IV, Child and Parent Versions (ADIS-IV-C/P; Silverman and Albano, 1996). The ADIS-IV-C/P is a structured clinical interview for parents and children that is specifically designed for *DSM-IV* diagnosis of childhood anxiety disorders and related mood disorders and that allows the clinician to rule out alternative diagnoses such as behavior disorders. A particular strength of the ADIS-IV-C/P is its detail with respect to multiple parameters of anxiety disorders. For example, it often asks about such important parameters as severity, intensity, interference, avoidance, uncontrollability, both at the symptom and syndrome levels. Ironically, although the ADIS-IV-C/P appears particularly well suited for research with childhood anxiety, no data regarding its psychometric properties have been reported in the literature (Silverman, 1999, personal communication). Nevertheless, the ADIS-IV-C/P is a revision of the Anxiety Disorders Interview Schedule for Children (Silverman and Nelles, 1988), which has been shown to possess satisfactory reliability across a range of parameters and ages (Rapee *et al.*, 1994; Silverman and Eisen, 1992). Given the high utility of the ADIS-IV-C/P for research of childhood anxiety, it would be important to establish reliability and validity estimates for this instrument in future research.

ALTERNATIVE CLASSIFICATION MODELS: A FUNCTIONAL APPROACH

Some sophisticated approaches to classification focus not on the topography of the behavior but rather on functional dimensions relevant to treatment (Kearney, 1993, 1995). Drawing from the tradition of behavior therapy and assessment, Kearney's model of school refusal behavior rates children's actions along four functional dimensions: (1) avoidance of negative affectivity (e.g., anxiety and depression), (2) escape from aversive social and/or evaluative situations (e.g., peer interactions, tests), (3) attention seeking (e.g., tantrums), and (4) positive tangible reinforcement (e.g., watching television and sleeping late rather than attending class). Conditions 1 and 2 describe children who refuse school for negative reinforcement, while conditions 3 and 4 describe children who refuse school for positive reinforcement (Kearney, 1995). This functional approach is highly useful in that it bridges the gap between assessment and treatment planning. The development of treatment goals and focus of treatment interventions can be derived from knowledge about the function of the school refusal behavior. Specifically, treatment is administered by adapting specific therapeutic procedures to match the functional dimensions of the child's problem (e.g., Kearney and Silverman, 1990). In addition to its high utility,

Kearney's approach is a good example of how there can be dimensions other than topography that are able to be evaluated within a particular domain.

ALTERNATIVE CLASSIFICATION MODELS: DIMENSIONAL APPROACHES

Another alternative to diagnostic classification is a dimensional system. One of the most well known approaches involves the empirically derived factors of Internalizing and Externalizing behaviors (Achenbach, 1991; 1993; Achenbach and Edelbrock, 1983). Based upon extensive studies using the Child Behavior Checklist (CBCL; Achenbach, 1993), the structure of child psychopathology has been outlined specifying two broad, higher-order factors, Internalizing and Externalizing, and multiple lower order factors. The three lower-order within the Internalizing domain are Anxious/Depressed, Withdrawn, and Somatic Complaints. A great advantage of this system is that developmental variables are accounted for, and clinical profiles for specific populations are based on separate age and gender groupings.

A potential disadvantage of such a system for the study of childhood anxiety disorders is that it has relatively low correspondence with specific pathological syndromes. Thus, although the CBCL may be helpful in identifying children with anxiety or depression, it has difficulty in identifying specific diagnostic membership within that domain (Jensen et al., 1993). Nevertheless, given its extensive empirical support, the CBCL remains an extremely helpful tool in terms of outlining the nomological network discussed above, and the possibility remains that inconsistency between its structure and that of the DSM are due to problems with the DSM nosology rather than with the CBCL. Very few empirical investigations of the structure of DSM anxiety disorders have been conducted as of yet (Chorpita et al., 1999; Spence, 1997).

One recently evaluated dimensional approach that may be a suitable complement to the DSM classification strategy involves the use of Clinical Severity Ratings (CSRs). These are ratings that represent clinician judgement on a Likert scale regarding the degree to which features of a disorder are present within the child. Ratings are usually made following the administration of a structured interview and possible behavioral observation. Such ratings can be combined for an overall index of anxious psychopathology (Chorpita et al., 1998) or used to represent the presence of specific syndromes. Recently, Chorpita and colleagues (1999) evaluated the reliability and validity of these ratings for several anxiety disorders and depression in children and found excellent inter-rater agreement as well as significant concurrent validity for DSM-IV diagnosis.

One of the only self report measures designed to provide dimensional indices of a number of the childhood anxiety disorders was recently developed by Spence (Spence Children's Anxiety Scale, SCAS, 1997; 1998). Using confirmatory factor analysis, Spence (1997) found support for a six-factor model of anxiety symptoms, encompassing the factors of panic-agoraphobia, social phobia, separation anxiety, obsessive-compulsive problems, generalized anxiety, and fear of physical injury. Preliminary reliability and validity data are supportive. This measure has recently been revised using both exploratory and confirmatory factor analysis in nearly 2,000 children and adolescents (Revised Child Anxiety and Depression Scale; RCADS, Chorpita et al., 1999). The SCAS was further modified by incorporating a Depression scale and by removing the Fear of Physical Injury Scale, which had both limited psychometric properties and lower correspondence to a specific DSM syndrome. Data from two large studies have shown preliminary support for the reliability and validity of the RCADS in non-referred children (Chorpita et al., 1999). Few other self-report measures exist that are relatively specific to DSM-IV syndromes at this time, perhaps with the exception of measures of social anxiety (e.g., Beidel et al., 1996).

RECOMMENDATIONS

A number of important goals exist for research in this area. First, the continued improvement of structured interviews through evaluation of both reliability and validity will be important. Arguably, few validity criteria exist, yet supplemental measures of specific syndromes (e.g., Beidel et al., 1996; Berg et al.,1986; Chorpita et al., 1997) may help in the dialectic or bootstrapping process of refining the boundaries of the nosology. It is imperative that multiple validity criteria continue to be developed and evaluated. In addition, evaluations of classification systems should seek to evaluate the reliability and validity of not only diagnosis or dimensional diagnostic ratings, but also symptom level variables, such as panic attacks, uncontrollability of worry, or poor concentration. Finally, the evaluation of the relations between the diagnostic syndromes and their constituent symptoms should be evaluated more closely. That is, how many or which symptoms are most or least predictive of which syndromes? Ultimately, such tools as ROC analysis may suggest which algorithms are optimal for defining particular syndromes (e.g., Tracey *et al.*, 1997).

Further, continued investigation of alternatives to topographical classification is essential. To the extent that Kearney's (1995) functional model has shown promise for clinical utility, such systems as these should be expanded and more fully evaluated. The prescriptive approach—like many other areas of the literature—is driven largely by a single questionnaire. Investigation of complementary procedures for the system as well as evaluations of its reliability and validity will likely be fruitful for clinical applications (Daleiden *et al.*, in press). This particular system is likely to have important implications not only for school refusal but for anxiety disorders in general.

Finally, the continued refinement of any nosology rests upon the nomological network of constructs discussed above. Future research endeavors would benefit from linking diagnostic categories to the broader system of constructs (see Figure 2.1). For example, questions regarding whether and how generalized anxiety disorder is distinct from negative affectivity or autonomic arousal will likely help refine our understanding of the disorder. This pursuit will most likely be aided by the use of measures that allow correlational or factor analytic procedures, such as the use of dimensional ratings of syndromes or symptoms or the use of self- or parent-report measures that target specific diagnostic syndromes (Beidel *et al.*, 1996; Berg *et al.*, 1986; Chorpita *et al.*, 1997; Spence, 1998).

BASIC RESEARCH: RELATIONAL ISSUES AND THEORY CONSTRUCTION

Along with the task of outlining the relevant constructs in the domain of childhood anxiety, an equally critical part of research in this area involves investigations of the relations among these constructs. Before proceeding with a review of specific examples of such tests within the childhood anxiety literature, it is first necessary to address basic issues of the types of relations that may exist. Addressing such issues in the context of childhood depression, Cole and Turner (1993) described the lack of specific attention in the literature to the differentiation of moderational and mediational processes implicitly hypothesized to be involved with emotional disorders. Specifically, they highlighted that a mediational model is operative when one variable (the mediator) is influenced by another variable and simultaneously influences the outcome variable. A moderational relationship, on the other hand, indicates the statistical interaction of the mediator with other variables to jointly influence the outcome variable.

A moderational model best characterizes the implicit diathesis-stress conceptualizations of most cognitive and cognitive-affective theories (e.g., Alloy et al., 1990; Barlow et al., 1996; Beck and Emery, 1985), whereas a mediational model is thought to characterize early development of anxiety and depression (Chorpita et al., 1998; Turner and Cole, 1994). It is important to note, as well, that moderational and mediational models are not mutually exclusive and may be combined to represent more complex models and sophisticated theory building (Baron and Kenny, 1986).

Considering the hypothesized constructs in Figure 2.1, a large number of specific relations could be hypothesized and tested. For example, cognitive dimensions could mediate between experience and the expression of disorders, or they could moderate the effects of experiences on the expression of disorders. In light of these issues, the following section reviews selected paradigms and procedures involved with the investigation of relational structure in child anxiety. Often the investigation of such relations is only implicit in the design, but an increased focus on these issues in future study is likely to help move these investigations towards a more unified and organized framework. In some respects, this work has already begun, however, much still remains to be done.

COGNITION

One of the best examples of the investigation of relations among constructs involves the area of cognition and anxiety. There are a number of studies investigating the relationship between anxiety and such constructs as attention and attribution (see Figure 2.2). Many studies have investigated how attention to threatening stimuli may interfere with information processing in those with anxiety. Initial studies used the Stroop color-naming task, where subjects must name the color of a word while ignoring the content (e.g., Matthews, 1990), to show that anxiety interfered with processing of information. More recent research has begun to elaborate on the nature of this interference, examining such factors as whether an attentional shift is toward or away from threatening stimuli (e.g., Vasey *et al.*, 1995). Although these studies have begun to demonstrate that children with anxiety, like their adult counterparts, seem to have a bias toward attending to threatening stimuli, many questions remained to be answered. Research with adults (Fox, 1993) has questioned whether those with anxiety have a general inability to focus attention rather than a bias toward threatening stimuli. Also, more studies are needed on how the biases differ among specific disorders. Research with adults shows that spider-phobic individuals show a bias toward spider-related stimuli, while for those with generalized anxiety disorder, interference varied according to whether the stimuli were congruent with the content of their worries (Matthews, 1990). Furthermore, research is needed to explicate the relationship between attention and emotional constructs such as negative and positive affectivity.

More studies have examined the quantity of negative thoughts and negative self-evaluation in children and adolescents than have examined the role of attributions (i.e., causal inferences) per se, but studies that have looked at attributions have tended to find that anxious children's attributions differ from those of children who are not anxious. One study, (Epkins, 1996), investigated the relationship between events, attributions, avoidance and inhibition using ambiguous scenarios and found that internal attributions for social failure were related to high ratings of avoidance and inhibition. Another study that looked at the relationship between events and attribution (Chorpita *et al.*, 1996) found that high-anxiety children were more likely to interpret ambiguous scenarios as threatening and to plan more avoidant responses.

As with attention, further studies investigating attributions in anxious children could examine whether specific disorders are associated with specific types of attributions. Also, given that attributional biases play a key role in depression (Alloy *et al.*, 1990; Beck *et al.*, 1979), it is possible that attributional biases are related not just to anxiety, but to underlying factors thought to be related to both disorders, such as negative affectivity. Another area in need of investigation is how are attention and attribution differ. Some (e.g., Craske and Barlow, 1991) have suggested that they both may reflect some underlying process, such as an overactive danger schema.

Research has demonstrated that cognitive biases of attribution and attention play an integral role in the anxiety disorders, but there are further areas to investigate. For example, cognitive biases appear to exist in other areas such as memory and perception of control, areas which have received less research attention in children (cf. Chorpita *et al.*, 1998; Daleiden, 1998). If these additional cognitive biases are confirmed in multiple tests, the relationship among multiple cognitive constructs (e.g., see Figure 2.2) would need to be explicated. For example, if biases in memory exist in children, how are they related to interpretational biases? In addition, future research should look for mediators and moderators of the relationship between anxiety and cognitive biases (Chorpita *et al.*, 1998), for example, state anxiety, memory, stress, influence from parents, perceived control.

FAMILY STUDIES

The area of family studies encompasses a diverse group of methodologies and techniques. Among the groupings of studies in this area are studies that investigate prevalence of anxiety in relatives of children with anxiety disorders, studies that examine the role of family environment in the etiology and maintenance of anxiety symptomatology, and twin studies that attempt to identify what portion of the risk for anxiety disorders comes from hereditary versus shared or individual environmental factors. What this diverse group of studies has in common is the investigation of how anxiety disorders are transmitted in families. As we will discuss below, most family studies seem to support the existence of an inherited general risk factor for negative emotions, but there is some evidence to support a role for environmental factors as well.

Prevalence in relatives. Most of the studies that have been done in this area have explored differences between the offspring of those with anxiety disorders, using either questionnaires or structured interview, and most have found that prevalence of anxiety disorders is higher in relatives of those with anxiety disorders. Mancini and colleagues (1996) using structured interviews, found that 49% of children of socially phobic parents had an anxiety disorder. Beidel and Turner (1997), using similar methodology, found that children of parents with an anxiety disorder were nearly five times more likely to have a psychiatric disorder and 5.4 times more likely to have an anxiety disorder than children without any psychiatric disorder. Studies that have looked at parents of children with anxiety disorders have found similar results (e.g., Last *et al.*, 1987).

Twin studies. Twin studies investigate the concordance rates for anxiety disorders between monozygotic and dizygotic twins in an attempt to elucidate the genetic, shared environmental and individual environmental causes and maintaining factors in anxiety. Shared environment refers to those factors that produce similar outcomes for all of the offspring of one family, while nonshared environment refers to those factors which produce different outcomes for each offspring in a family (Reiss *et al.*, 1995). Twin studies have demonstrated that the majority of the environmental influence on depression is from nonshared environmental factors (Wierzbicki, 1987). Few studies have examined genetic and environmental influences in child anxiety. Thapar and McGuffin (1995), found that symptoms of anxiety as rated by parents were best explained by genetic transmission, but self-rated anxiety symptoms were best explained by shared environmental factors. Conversely, Topolski *et al.* (1997) found that shared environmental factors played a small role in overanxious disorder, which appeared to be explained mostly by genetic and nonshared environmental factors; however, separation anxiety disorder was best explained by shared and nonshared environmental effects. Further twin studies could benefit from the methods used by Reiss *et al.* (1995), in which multiple sources of information were used (parent and child) and structural equation modeling was implemented to adjust for method variance, thereby yielding more accurate estimates of the effects of genetics and environment.

Family environment. A further step in examining environmental influences on anxiety disorders is to look at what unique or shared experiences are associated with the development of anxiety. Several authors (e.g., Parker, 1981) have suggested that certain types of parenting style may lead children to experience anxiety or depression later in life. Some studies that have examined the role of parenting style in childhood anxiety have had an improved design over older studies that used retrospective reports from adult participants. Instead of retrospective reports, these studies have used clinical and community samples of children and adolescents and have used multiple methods to gather information about parenting style, including self-report measures and observers' ratings (Reiss *et al.*, 1995; Siqueland *et al.*, 1996).

More research is needed to explicate connections between family environment and the larger nomological network. For example, is the observed connection between family environment and anxiety disorders mediated or moderated by cognitive variables (Chorpita *et al.*, 1998). While some evidence has been provided for the role of perceived control; attention, memory and attribution have not been studied much as mediators or moderators of this process. Furthermore, the role of such emotional factors as negative and positive affect could be examined further, perhaps by looking at the research on risk factors such as behavioral inhibition that tend to occur in families.

CULTURE AND ETHNICITY

Another area that has received comparatively little research attention involves the study of cultural and ethnic variables and their relation to childhood anxiety. Although often conflated with culture, ethnicity refers to the individual's ancestry, e.g., whether a child's family is from Ireland, Samoa, or South Africa. Culture, on the other hand, refers to a broad constellation of cognitive, behavioral, and environmental variables relevant to an individual. In general, many studies which have looked at culture have defined it only in terms of ancestry, but to truly measure cultural identity one must look at the extent to which an individual identifies with and practices the traditions of a specific group (e.g., Marsella and Yamada, in press). To do this requires the assessment of ethnocultural identity, which includes such things as one's cultural beliefs, style of dress, patterns of socialization, and use of language. From a research perspective, the examination of culture rather than ethnicity is likely to be more fruitful endeavor, simply because culture is presumably more proximally related to the constructs of interest. That is, we are typically interested in variables like parenting style, religiosity, or shame, which are cultural variables. Although such cultural variables are roughly indexed by ethnicity, in this increasingly diverse world, it is quite possible for example to have a Caucasian family that participates in Latin American culture. In such an instance, the researcher may wish to know the extent to which that family participates in Latin American cultural practices.

In the childhood anxiety literature, studies of culture and ethnicity issues appear to involve two different kinds of studies: studies across two different nationalities (e.g., China vs. US), which tend to be referred to as "cross-cultural" and studies of different ethnic and racial groups within a single country (e.g., Hispanic vs. Caucasian), which are intended to look at the influence of culture (although more accurately are studies of ethnicity).

Many studies have found differences in children's anxiety and fears across both cultures and ethnic groups. In particular, there have been a wealth of studies on how children's fears differ according to culture (e.g., Last and Perrin, 1993; Ollendick and King, 1991) or by ethnic group (Kashani and Orvaschel, 1988; Last and Perrin, 1993; Shore and Rapport, 1998; Tikalsky and Wallace, 1988). Fewer studies have looked at dimensions other than fears or anxiety disorders across cultures and ethnic groups.

Although many differences have been found between various cultural and ethnic groups, the question remains, what do these differences mean? What is it about culture and ethnicity that sometimes results in differences in anxiety and fear? Culture is mediated by many other variables, and it may be a somewhat distal variable in terms of its relation to the development of anxiety disorders. Culture is a marker for beliefs, actions, and other factors that influence the development of anxiety. Attitudes toward mental health and psychological treatment may differ, e.g., African Americans may be less likely to seek help from settings where clinical research is conducted (Neal and Turner, 1991). Clinic samples may be biased because of biases in who gets referred or differences in ability to afford treatment. Child rearing practices and social customs may account for some differences. Culture may influence the content and focus of anxiety disorders (Kirmayer et al., 1995). Culture influences not only what symptoms occur, but which are considered salient by patients, clinicians (Kirmayer et al., 1995) and parents. For example, studies by Weisz and colleagues (Weisz et al., 1988, 1991) found that Thai parents, teachers, and psychologists rated over-and undercontrolled behavior as significantly less serious and worrisome and less likely to reflect personality traits than did their American counterparts.

RECOMMENDATIONS

A key to theory construction is forming connections. The following recommendations are some guidelines for how and where connections might be formed to construct helpful theories in child and adolescent anxiety.

- Future research in the developmental psychopathology of anxiety in children and adolescents is needed to elucidate complex issues such as longitudinal comorbidity or heterotypic continuity (whereby the symptomatic expression of an underlying pathology differs over the course of development; e.g., Caspi et al., 1988). For example, many researchers have suggested that negative affect may be responsible for the high correlation between anxiety and depression in children (e.g., Cole et al., 1997). Also, it is important to investigate the factors that mediate or moderate developmental pathways, such as genetic risk factors, choices that shape one's environment, cognitive and social skills, cognitive sets, and links between experiences (Rutter, 1989). Longitudinal research will be necessary to investigate these topics and to answer questions that exist about the direction of effects between various constructs. Also, reliable and valid measures of dimensions such as negative affect will be needed. Further MTMM investigations using techniques such as confirmatory factor analysis to reduce method variance will be helpful in explicating the true relationships among these constructs.

- Further research is needed into the nature and structure of risk factors for the development of negative emotions, with an eye toward their place in the nomological network. For example, several studies have suggested that behavioral inhibition may be a risk factor for the later development of anxiety disorders (e.g., Biederman et al., 1990; Hirshfeld et al., 1992). Another proposed risk factor is anxiety sensitivity (Silverman et al., 1991). How might these risk factors interact with events, information processing dimensions, and emotional constructs in the development of anxiety disorders? For example, does the inherited component of anxiety disorders consist of risk factors for specific disorders, or a general risk factor? As Kendler and colleagues (1992) have suggested, it may be that different disorders are the result of a common, genetically influenced neurobiologic vulnerability. Could such a vulnerability constitute an underlying risk factor that is responsible for longitudinal comorbidity? Do risk factors function as moderating or mediating variables? How is behavioral inhibition distinct from negative affect? Elucidation of these relationships will depend on having reliable and valid measures of these constructs, as mentioned in the first section, as well as reliable and valid tools for assessing anxiety disorders, as mentioned in the second section.

- Finally, the ideas discussed herein have been divided into separate theoretical areas, and only a few researchers have started to form connections among these areas. In general, connections need to be formed among constructs in a larger nomological network, whether it is the network illustrated in Figure 2.2, or another network of constructs that appears to describe the factors involved in the occurrence of anxiety in children and adolescents. As we have stated previously in this section, some work has begun in relating cognitive, family and cultural concepts to our broader network of information processing dimensions and emotional constructs, but much remains to be done.

Here, too, reliability and validity of constructs and measures will be of key importance in assuring an accurate picture of the relationships and in minimizing measurement error.

Applied Research: Treatment Outcome

The final cell in the matrix involves research on treatment. This involves understanding the effects of various clinical protocols or manipulations on some aspect of anxiety pathology. The study of treatments of childhood anxiety has a considerable history, involving many exposure-based approaches in single subject or small n designs (Barrios and O'Dell, 1989). Only recently have treatments for childhood anxiety been subject to randomized clinical trials (Barrett *et al.*, 1996; Kendall, 1994). Such designs involve the random assignment of children to an active treatment group and a control group (e.g., waitlist, or alternative treatment). This strategy is quite powerful and provides some of the strongest support for the notion that treatment works relative to a control condition.

Some difficult issues arise in employing such methodology. For example, given the accumulation of support for exposure based treatments, it is becoming increasingly difficult to justify the use of a waitlist condition. One solution to this problem is to compare two alternative treatments. However, some degree of experimental control is lost in such an approach, particularly when both conditions produce changes in the dependent variable (Kazdin *et al.*, 1993). Although a waitlist was also included in their study, Barrett *et al.* (1996) compared the efficacy a cognitive behavioral treatment for childhood anxiety with and without a family component and found that the family component enhanced treatment effects. Similar studies could still be fruitful without requiring a waitlist condition. Even comparison of alternative treatments can be problematic, however, if the alternative treatment is not empirically supported, in that assignment to an alternative condition is essentially withholding treatment that is known to help.

Although it is one of the most powerful tools available for evaluating treatments, the RCT has received a number of other criticisms. In particular, the RCT appears to work best with the testing of manualized and highly standardized treatments. Addressing this point, Persons (1991) noted that treatment outcome literature in general suffers in that it does not represent the more ideographic and flexible nature of interventions administered in clinical settings. Recently, Wilson (1996) outlined frequently noted problems with manualized treatments, among those, conceptual inconsistency with treatment approach (cf. Wolpe, 1989), and the preclusion of a proper case formulation. However, this problem may be an artifact of the recentness of treatment manualization. That is, evidence is accumulating that manuals or protocols that are designed to be flexible can be reliably evaluated and may represent an improvement over non-flexible protocols (e.g., Jacobson et al., 1989; Wilson, 1996), and as manuals continue to be refined, they may incorporate algorithms for branching to, omitting, or combining multiple strategies. Such manuals have yet to be developed within the area of childhood anxiety.

Another important consideration involves the distinction between efficacy and effectiveness of treatments. The APA Task Force on Psychological Intervention Guidelines (1995) outlined a template for the development of guidelines for interventions with psychological disorders. The first major dimension of the template involves the evaluation of treatment efficacy, that is, how well a treatment is known to bring about change in the target problem. The second major dimension of the template involves the effectiveness of the interventions, which involves their feasibility, generalizability, and cost/benefit ratio. Ideally, treatment research should seek to strike a balance of demonstrating both high efficacy and high effectiveness for interventions. However, this balance is almost impossible to achieve.

Another important concern involves the generalizability of effects. Although the issue is not unique to childhood anxiety, there are important considerations regarding the acceptability of treatments across different ethnic, socio-economic, and cultural groups. Kendall's (1994) RCT for childhood anxiety employed a sample of 78% Caucasian and 22% African American, whereas Barrett et al. (1996) did not report the ethnic composition of their sample. No RCTs of childhood anxiety have reported socio-economic or cultural variables, although the efficacy demonstrated across two different countries is clearly supportive of the treatment approach. Inclusion of non-Western cultural groups (e.g., African, Asian, Latin American) will be important in future studies, as will inclusion of participants from low-income urban or rural settings.

Recently, some researchers have described an interesting strategy to circumvent many of these issues noted above (Strosahl et al., 1998). The manipulated training design differs from the RCT in that therapists—not the individuals seeking treatment—are randomized to conditions. Some therapists are trained in the experimental protocol, and therapists in the control group are either given no training or training in an alternative approach. The outcomes of cases are then tracked for a specified number of months or cases. This rather elegant approach allows the investigator a tremendous degree of latitude regarding treatment flexibility and conceptual orientation. For example, it is likely that not all individuals would receive the same elements of treatment or the same length of treatment, and the diagnostic composition in the study could be completely heterogeneous, which is a particularly salient issue in childhood anxiety, with its wide range of disorders and high comorbidity. One final advantage of the manipulated training design is its high relevance to clinical settings. Treatments evaluated in this manner would seem to be more likely to survive the transition into clinical service settings, as the design allows for the treatments to be tested in these settings.

RECOMMENDATIONS

The following recommendations are offered in the area of evaluating treatments for childhood anxiety.

- The field has benefited greatly from the establishment of a manual based treatment for childhood anxiety disorders. Future research would be best aimed at evaluating the degree to which treatments can be adapted for different populations and or situations. For example, one important movement is toward school based intervention, and the evaluation of such a protocol adapted for school based therapy would be important. In addition, it will be important to examine the degree to which current cognitive behavioral techniques can be mixed and matched to provide the most appropriate treatment plan for a given child. This is particularly important given the probability of multiple diagnoses in children with internalizing disorders, and such investigations would be consistent with the recommendations of Persons (1991) regarding case formulation and Kearney (1995) regarding treatment structure.
- Additional emphasis should be placed on external validity in future studies. For example, it will be important to use such new designs as the manipulated training design to test the effects of a particular approach on a broadly defined clinical population. Such studies will also likely provide answers to questions regarding training and dissemination issues, identifying how much training is important to see effects and which types of therapists perform better than others.

• Finally, research on treatment should always seek to test or inform basic theoretical issues (e.g., Forsyth, 1997). Perhaps the best example of this in the childhood anxiety literature is the work of Australian researchers Mark Dadds, Paula Barrett, Ron Rapee, and colleagues, who have investigated family processes in research on cognition and have used these findings to develop and test family-based treatments in RCTs. Such highly programmatic research endeavors operate in multiple cells of the matrix outlined in Figure 2.1 and facilitate the feed-back and feed-forward cycles detailed therein. Such programs are likely to make great contributions to the literature in the long run.

SUMMARY

The field of childhood anxiety has advanced considerably over the last 20 years. New models and treatment approaches have emerged and have provided considerable gains in the understanding of basic phenomena underlying childhood anxiety. Future research in this area will likely benefit from careful consideration of research strategies that address the particular obstacles created by the subject matter (e.g., assessment issues). Increased use of multiple assessment methods will help continue to refine the constructs that comprise the theoretical domain. In addition, researchers in this area will clearly benefit from directing future efforts towards integration of paradigms and models. Such attempts will help provide a larger organized framework for the continued advancement of theory on childhood anxiety and will perhaps accelerate the dialectical process of advancing and discarding competing ideas.

References

Achenbach, T.M. (1991). *Manual for the Child Behavior Checklist/4–18 and 1991 Profile*. Burlington, VT: University of Vermont Department of Psychiatry.
Achenbach, T.M. (1993). Implications of multiaxial empirically based assessment for behavior therapy with children. *Behavior Therapy, 24*, 91–116.
Achenbach, T.M. & Edelbrock, C.S. (1983). *Manual for the Child Behavior Checklist and Revised Child Behavior Profile*. Burlington, VT: University of Vermont, Department of Psychiatry.

Achenbach, T.M., McConaughy, S.H., & Howell, C.T. (1987). Child/ adolescent behavioral and emotional problems: Implications of cross-informant correlations for situational specificity. *Psychological Bulletin, 101*, 213–232.

Alloy, L.B., Kelly, K.A., Mineka, S., & Clements, C.M. (1990). Comorbidity of anxiety and depressive disorders: A helplessness-hopelessness perspective. In J.D. Maser & C.R. Cloninger (Eds.), *Comorbidity of mood and anxiety disorders* (pp. 499–543). Washington, DC: American Psychiatric Press.

American Psychiatric Association. (1994). *Diagnostic and statistical manual of mental disorders*, (4th ed.). Washington, DC: Author.

American Psychological Association Committee on Psychological Tests (1954). Technical recommendations for psychological tests and diagnostic techniques. *Psychological Bulletin Supplement, 51*, 1–38.

Barlow, D.H. (1988). *Anxiety and its disorders: The nature and treatment of anxiety and panic.* New York: Guilford.

Barlow, D.H., Chorpita, B.F., & Turovsky, J. (1996). Fear, panic, anxiety, and the disorders of emotion. In D.A. Hope (Ed.), *Perspectives on anxiety, panic, and fear* (Vol. 43, pp. 251–328). Lincoln, NE: University of Nebraska Press.

Baron, R.M. & Kenny, D.A. (1986). The moderator-mediator variable distinction in social psychological research: Conceptual, strategic, and statistical considerations. *Journal of Personality and Social Psychology, 51*, 1173–1182.

Barrett, P.M., Dadds, M.R., & Rapee, R.M. (1996). Family treatment of childhood anxiety: A controlled trial. *Journal of Consulting and Clinical Psychology, 64*, 333–342.

Barrios, B.A. & O'Dell, S.L. (1998). Fears and anxieties. In E.J. Mash & R.A. Barkley (Eds.), *Treatment of childhood disorders* (2nd ed., pp. 249–337). New York: Guilford Press.

Barrios, B.A. & O'Dell, S.L. (1989). Fears and anxieties. In E.J. Mash & R.A. Barkley (Eds.), *Treatment of childhood disorders* (1st ed., pp. 167–221). New York: Guilford Press.

Barrios, B.A. & Hartmann, D.P. (1997). Fears and anxieties. In E.J. Mash & L. G. Terdal (Eds.) *Assessment of childhood disorders* (pp. 230–327). New York: Guilford Press.

Beck, A.T., Rush, A.J., Shaw, B.F., & Emery, G. (1979). *Cognitive therapy of depression.* New York: Guilford Press.

Beck, A.T. & Emery, G. (1985). *Anxiety disorders and phobias: A cognitive perspective.* New York: Basic.

Beidel, D.C. (1991). Determining the reliability of psychophysiological assessment in childhood anxiety. *Journal of Anxiety Disorders, 5*, 139–150.

Beidel, D.C. & Turner, S.M. (1997). At risk for anxiety: I. Psychopathology in the offspring of anxious parents. *Journal of the American Academy of Child and Adolescent Psychiatry, 36*, 918–924.

Beidel, D.C., Turner, S.M., & Fink, C.M. (1996). Assessment of childhood social phobia: construct, convergent, and discriminative validity of the social phobia and anxiety inventory for children (SPAI-C). *Psychological Assessment, 8,* 235–240.

Biederman, J., Rosenbaum, J.F., Hirshfeld, D.R., Faraone, S.V., Bolduc, E.A., Gersten, M., Meminger, S.R., Kagan, J., Snidman, N., & Reznick, J.S. (1990). Psychiatric correlates of behavioral inhibition in young children of parents with and without psychiatric disorders. *Archives of General Psychiatry, 47,* 21–26.

Berg, C.J., Rapoport, J.L., & Flament, M. (1986). The Leyton Obsessional Inventory—Child Version. *Journal of the American Academy of Child and Adolescent Psychiatry, 25,* 84–91.

Bollen, K.A. & Lennox, R. (1991). Conventional wisdom on measurement: A structural equation perspective. *Psychological Bulletin, 110,* 305–314.

Borkovec, T.S., Shadick, R., & Hopkins, M. (1991). The nature of normal and pathological worry. In R.M. Rapee & D.H. Barlow (Eds.), *Chronic anxiety, generalized anxiety disorder, and mixed anxiety depression.* New York: Guilford Press.

Butler, G. & Mathews, A. (1983). Cognitive processes in anxiety. *Advances in Behavior Research and Therapy, 5,* 51–62.

Campbell, D.P. & Fiske, D.W. (1959). Convergent and discriminant validity by the multi-trait multi-method matrix. *Psychological Bulletin, 56,* 81–105.

Caspi, A., Elder, G.H., & Bem, D.J. (1988). Moving away rom the world: Life-course patterns of shy children. *Developmental Psychology, 24,* 824–831.

Chorpita, B.F. (in press). Vulnerability for anxiety and depression: Structure and development. In K.D. Craig, R.J. McMahon, & K.S. Dobson (Eds.), *Proceedings of the 29th Banff International Conference on Behavioral Science.* New York: Sage.

Chorpita, B.F., Albano, A.M., & Barlow, D. (1998). The structure of negative emotions in a clinical sample of children and adolescents. *Journal of Abnormal Psychology, 107,* 74–85.

Chorpita, B.F., & Barlow, D.H. (1998). The development of anxiety: The role of control in the early environment. *Psychological Bulletin, 117,* 3–19.

Chorpita, B.F., Brown, T.A., & Barlow, D.H. (1998). Perceived control as a mediator of family environment in etiological models of childhood anxiety. *Behavior Therapy, 29,* 457–476.

Chorpita, B.F., Plummer, C.P., & Moffitt, C. (1999). *Dimensions of the childhood anxiety and mood disorders and their relation to dimensions of negative emotion.* Manuscript submitted for publication.

Chorpita, B.F., Tracey, S., Brown, T.A., Collica, T.J., & Barlow, D.H. (1997). Assessment of worry in children and adolescents: An adaptation of the Penn State Worry Questionnaire. *Behaviour Research and Therapy, 35,* 569–581.

Chorpita, B.F., Yim, L., Moffitt, C., Umemoto, L.A., & Francis, S.E. (1999). *Assessment of symptoms of DSM-IV anxiety and depression in children and adolescents: A Revised Child Anxiety and Depression Scale.* Manuscript submitted for publication.

Cronbach, L.J. & Meehl, P.E. (1955). Construct validity in psychological tests. *Psychological Bulletin, 52,* 281–302.

Clark, D.M. (1986). A cognitive approach to panic. *Behaviour Research and Therapy, 24,* 461–470.

Clark, L.A., & Watson, D. (1991). Tripartite model of anxiety and depression: Psychometric evidence and taxonomic implications. *Journal of Abnormal Psychology, 100,* 316–336.

Cole, D.A., Truglio, R., & Peeke, L. (1997). Relation between symptoms of anxiety and depression in children: A multitrait—mutimethod—multi-group assessment. *Journal of Consulting and Clinical Psychology, 62,* 110–119.

Cole, D.A. & Turner, J.E. (1993). Models of cognitive mediation and moderation in child depression. *Journal of Abnormal Psychology, 102,* 271–281.

Cook, T.D. & Campbell, D.T. (1979). *Quasi-experimentation: Design and analysis issues for field settings.* Chicago: Rand McNally.

Craske, M.G. & Barlow, D.H. (1991). Contributions of cognitive psychology to assessment and treatment of anxiety. In P.R. Martin (Ed.), *Handbook of behavior therapy and psychological science: An integrative approach* (pp. 151–168). New York: Pergamon.

Cronbach, L.J. & Meehl, P.E. (1955). Construct validity in psychological tests. *Psychological Bulletin, 52,* 281–302.

Dadds, M.R. & Sanders, M.R. (1992). Family interactions and child psychopathology: A comparison of two observation strategies. *Journal of Child and Family Studies, 1,* 371–391.

Daleiden, E. (1998). Childhood anxiety and memory functioning: A comparison of systemic and processing accounts. *Journal of Experimental Child Psychology, 68,* 216–235.

Daleiden, E.K., Chorpita, B.F., Kollins, S.H., & Drabman, R.S. (1999). Factors affecting clinical judgements about the function of children's school refusal behavior. *Journal of Clinical Child Psychology, 28,* 396–406.

DiNardo, O'Brien, G.T., Barlow, D.H., Waddell, M.T., & Blanchard, E.B. (1983). Reliability of DSM-III anxiety disorder categories using a new structured interview. *Archives of General Psychiatry, 40,* 1070–1074.

Edelbrock, C. & Costello, A.J. (1990). Structured interviews for children and adolescents. In G. Goldstein & M. Hersen (Eds.), *Handbook of psychological assessment* (2nd ed., pp. 308–323). Elmsford, NY: Pergamon Press.

Eisen, A.R. & Silverman, W.K. (1991). Treatment of an adolescent with bowel movement phobia using self-control therapy. *Journal of Behavior Therapy and Experimental Psychiatry, 22,* 45–51.

Epkins, C.C. (1996). Cognitive specificity and affective confounding in social anxiety and dysphoria in children. *Journal of Psychopathology and Behavioral Assessment, 18*, 83–101.

Evans, P.D. & Harmon, G. (1981). Children's self-initiated approach to spiders. *Behavior Research and Therapy, 19*, 543–546.

Forsyth, J. P. (1997). It was the age of wisdom, it is the age of hope. *Behavior Therapy, 28*, 397–401.

Foster, S., Bell-Dolan, D.J., & Burge, D.A. (1988). Behavioral Observation. In A. S. Bellack & M. Hersen (Eds.), *Behavioral assessment: A practical handbook* (3 ed., pp. 119–160). New York: Pergamon Press.

Foster, S.L. & Cone, J.D. (1980). Current issues in direct observation. *Behavioral Assessment, 2*, 313–338.

Foster, S.L. & Cone, J.D. (1986). Design and use of direct observation procedures. In A.R. Ciminero, K.S. Calhoun, & H.E. Adams (Eds.), *Handbook of behavioral assessment* (2nd ed., pp. 253–324). New York: Wiley.

Fowles, D.C. (1995). A motivational theory of psychopathology. In W.D. Spaulding (Ed.), *Integrated views of motivation, cognition, and emotion: Nebraska Symposium on Motivation* (Vol. 41, pp. 181–238). Lincoln, NE: University of Nebraska Press.

Fox, E. (1993). Attentional bias in anxiety: Selective or not? *Behaviour Research and Therapy, 31*, 487–493.

Fox, J.E. & Houston, B.K. (1983). Distinguishing between cognitive and somatic trait and somatic state anxiety in children. *Journal of Personality and Social Psychology, 45*, 862–870.

Gray, J.A. & McNaughton, N. (1996). The neuropsychology of anxiety: Reprise. In D.A. Hope (Ed.), *Perspectives on anxiety, panic, and fear: Nebraska Symposium on Motivation* (Vol. 43, pp. 61–134). Lincoln, NE: University of Nebraska Press.

Handwerk, M.L., Larzelere, R.E., Soper, S.H., & Friman, P.C. (1999). Parent and child discrepancies in reporting severity of problem behaviors in three out of home settings. *Psychological Assessment, 11*, 14–23.

Harris, F.C. & Lahey, B.B. (1982). Recording system bias in direct observational methodology: A review and critical analysis of factors causing inaccurate coding behavior. *Clinical Psychology Review, 2*, 539–556.

Haynes, S.N. & Horn, W.F. (1982). Reactivity in behavioral observation: A review. *Behavioral Assessment, 4*, 369–385.

Haynes, S.N., Richard, D.C.S., & Kubany, E.S. (1995). Content validity in psychological assessment: A functional approach to concept and methods. *Psychological Assessment, 7*, 238–247.

Hirshfeld, D.R., Rosenbaum, J.F., Biederman, J., Bolduc, E.A., Faraone, S.V., Snidman, N., Reznick, J.S., & Kagan, J. (1992). Stable behavioral inhibition and its association with anxiety disorder. *Journal of the American Academy of Child and Adolescent Psychiatry, 31*, 103–111.

Jacobson, N.S. (1985). Uses versus abuses of observational methods. *Behavioral Assessment, 7,* 323–330.

Jacobson, N.S., Schmaling, K.B., Holtzworth-Munroe, A., Katt, J.L., Wood, L.F., & Follette, V.M. (1989). Research-structured vs. clinically flexible versions of social learning-based marital therapy. *Behaviour Research and Therapy, 27,* 173–180.

Jensen, P.S., Salzberg, A.D., Richters, J.E., & Watanabe, H.K. (1993). Scales, diagnoses, and child psychopathology: I. CBCL and DISC relationships. *Journal of the American Academy of Child and Adolescent Psychiatry, 32,* 397–406.

Joiner, T.E., Catanzaro, S.J., & Laurent, J. (1996). Tripartite structure of positive and negative affect, depression, and anxiety in child and adolescent psychiatric inpatients. *Journal of Abnormal Psychology, 105,* 401–409.

Kagan, J., Reznick, J.S., & Snidman, N. (1987). The physiology and psychology of behavioral inhibition. *Child Development, 58,* 1459–1473.

Kashani, J.H. & Orvaschel, H. (1988). Anxiety disorders in mid-adolescence: A community sample. *American Journal of Psychiatry, 145,* 960–964.

Kashani, J.H. & Orvashel, H. (1990). A community study of anxiety in children and adolescents. *American Journal of Psychiatry, 147,* 313–318.

Kazdin, A.E., Mazurick, J.L., & Bass, D. (1993). Risk for attrition in treatment of antisocial children and families. *Journal of Clinical Child Psychology, 22,* 2–16.

Kearney, C.A. (1993). Measuring the function of school refusal behavior: The School Refusal Assessment Scale. *Journal of Clinical Child Psychology, 22,* 85–96.

Kearney, C.A. (1995). School refusal behavior. In A. R. Eisen, C.A. Kearney, and C.E. Shaefer (Eds.), *Clinical handbook of anxiety disorders in children and adolescents.* Northvale, NJ: Jason Aronson, Inc.

Kelly, C.R. (1976). Play desensitization of fear of darkness in preschool children. *Behavior Research and Therapy, 14,* 79–81.

Kearney, C.A. & Silverman, W.K. (1990) A preliminary analysis of a functional model of assessment of school refusal behavior. *Behavior Modification, 14,* 340–366.

Kendall, P.C. (1994). Treating anxiety disorders in children: Results of a randomized clinical trial. *Journal of Consulting and Clinical Psychology, 62,* 100–110.

Kendall, P.C., Kane, M., Howard, B., & Siqueland, L. (1990). *Cognitive behavioral therapy for anxious children: Treatment manual.* (Available from Philip C. Kendall, Department of Psychology, Temple University, Philadelphia, PA, 19122.)

Kendler, K.S., Neale, M.C., Kessler, R.C., Heath, A.C., & Eaves, L.J. (1992). Major Depression and Generalized Anxiety Disorder: Same genes, (partly) different environments? *Archives of General Psychiatry, 49,* 716–722.

Kenny, D.A., & Kashy, D.A. (1992). Analysis of the multitrait-multimethod matrix by confirmatory factor analysis. *Psychological Bulletin, 112,* 165–172.

Kirmayer, L.J., Young, A., & Hayton, B.C. (1995). The cultural context of anxiety disorders. *Cultural Psychiatry, 18,* 503–521.

Klein, R.G. (1991). Parent child agreement in clinical assessment of anxiety and other psychopathology: A review. *Journal of Anxiety Disorders, 5,* 187–198.

Last, C.G., Hersen, M., Kazdin, A.E., Francis, G., & Grubb, H.J. (1987). Psychiatric illness in the mothers of anxious children. *American Journal of Psychiatry, 144,* 1580–1583.

Last, C.G. & Perrin, S. (1993). Anxiety disorders in African-American and white children. *Journal of Abnormal Child Psychology, 21,* 153–164.

Last, C.G., Phillips, J.E., & Statfeld, A. (1987). Childhood anxiety disorders in mothers and their children. *Child Psychiatry and Human Development, 18,* 103–112.

Lewinsohn, P.M., Hops, H., Roberts, R.E., Seeley, J.R., & Andrews, J.A. (1993). Adolescent psychopathology: I. Prevalence and incidence of depression and other DSM-III-R disorders in high school students. *Journal of Abnormal Psychology, 102,* 133–144.

Loevinger, J. (1957). Objective tests as instruments of psychological theory. *Psychological Reports, 3,* 635–694.

Lonigan, C., Carey, M., & Finch, A.J. (1994). Anxiety and depression in children: Negative affectivity and the utility of self-reports. *Journal of Consulting and Clinical Psychology, 62,* 1000–1008.

Lonigan, C.J. & Philips, B. (2000). Temperamental factors. In Vasey M.W., & Dadds, M. R. (Eds.), *The developmental psychopathology of anxiety* (pp. 60–91). New York: Oxford.

Mancini, C., Van Amerigen, M., Szatmari, P., Fugere, C., & Boyle, M. (1996). A High-risk pilot study of the children of adults with social phobia. *Journal of the American Academy of Child and Adolescent Psychiatry, 35,* 1511–1517.

Marsella, A.J. & Yamada, A.M. (2000). Culture and mental health: An introduction and overview of foundations, concepts and issues. In I. Cuellar & F. Paniagua (Eds.). *The handbook of multicultural mental health: Assessment and treatment of diverse populations.* New York: Academic Press.

Matarazzo, J.D. (1983). The reliability of psychiatric and psychologic diagnosis. *Clinical Psychology Review, 3,* 103–145.

Matthews, A. (1990). Why worry? The cognitive function of anxiety. *Behaviour Research and Therapy, 28,* 455–486.

Neal, A.M. & Turner, S.M. (1991). Anxiety disorders research with African Americans: Current Status. *Psychological Bulletin, 109,* 400–410.

Ollendick, T.H. (1983). Reliability and validity of the Revised Fear Survey Schedule for Children (FSSC-R). *Behaviour Research and Therapy, 21,* 685–692.

Ollendick, T.H. & King, N.J. (1991). Origins of childhood fears: An evaluation of Rachman's theory of fear acquisition. *Behaviour Research and Therapy, 29*, 117–123.

Perrin, S. & Last, C.G. (1992). Do childhood anxiety measures measure anxiety? *Journal of Abnormal Child Psychology, 20*, 567–578.

Persons, J.B. (1991). Psychotherapy outcome studies do not accurately represent current models of psychotherapy: A proposed remedy. *American Psychologist, 46*, 99–106.

Rabian, B., Peterson, R.A., Richters, J., & Jensen, P.S. (1993). Anxiety sensitivity among anxious children. *Journal of Clinical Child Psychology, 22*, 441–446.

Rapee, R. M., Barrett, P. M., Dadds, M. R. & Evans, L. (1994). Reliability of the DSM-III-R childhood anxiety disorders using structured interview: Interrater and parent-child agreement. *Journal of the American Academy of Child and Adolescent Psychiatry, 33*, 984–992.

Reiss, D., Hetherington, M., Plomin, R., Howe, G.W., Simmens, S.J., Henderson, S.H., O'Connor, T.J., Bussell, D.A., Anderson, E.R., & Law, T. (1995). Genetic questions for environmental studies. *Archives of General Psychiatry, 52*, 925–936.

Reynolds, C.R. & Richmond, B.O. (1978). What I Think and Feel: A revised measure of children's manifest anxiety. *Journal of Abnormal Child Psychology, 6*, 271–280.

Rutter, M. (1989). Pathways from childhood to adult life. *Journal of Child Psychology and Psychiatry and Allied Disciplines, 30*, 23–51.

Saylor, C.F., Finch, A.J., Spirito, A., & Bennett, B. (1984). The children's depression inventory: A systematic evaluation of psychometric properties. *Journal of Consulting and Clinical Psychology, 52*, 955–967.

Shore, G.N. & Rapport, M.D. (1998). The Fear Survey Schedule for Children-Revised (FSSC-HI): Ethnocultural variations in children's fearfulness. *Journal of Anxiety Disorders, 12*, 437–461.

Silverman, W.K. & Albano, A.M. (1996). *Anxiety Disorders Interview Schedule for Children-IV, Child and Parent Versions*. San Antonio, TX: The Psychological Corporation.

Silverman, W.K. & Eisen, A.R. (1992). Age differences in the reliability of parent and child reports of child anxious symptomatology using a structured interview. *Journal of the American Academy of Child and Adolescent Psychiatry, 32*, 117–124.

Silverman, W.K., Fleisig, W., Rabian, B., & Peterson, R.A. (1991). Childhood Anxiety Sensitivity Index. *Journal of Clinical Child Psychology, 20*, 162–168.

Silverman, W.K., LaGreca, A. M., & Wasserstein, S. (1995). What do children worry about? Worries and their relation to anxiety. *Child Development, 66*, 671–686.

Silverman, W.K. & Nelles, W.B. (1988). The Anxiety Disorders Interview Schedule for Children. *Journal of the American Academy of Child and Adolescent Psychiatry, 27*, 772–778.

Silverman, W.K. & Serafini, L.T. (1998). Assessment of child behavior problems: Internalizing disorders. In A. Bellack & M. Hersen (Eds.), *Behavioral asssessment: A practical handbook* (4 ed., pp. 342–360). Boston.

Spence, S.H. (1997). Structure of anxiety symptoms among children : A confirmatory factor-analytic study. *Journal of Abnormal Psychology, 106*, 280–297.

Spence, S.H. (1998). A measure of anxiety symptoms among children. *Behaviour Research and Therapy, 36*, 545–566.

Spielberger, C.D. (1973). *Preliminary test manual for the state-trait anxiety inventory for children.* Palo Alto: CA: Consulting Psychological Press, Inc.

Strosahl, K.D., Hayes, S.C., Bergan, J., & Romano, P. (1998). Assessing the field effectiveness of acceptance and commitment therapy: An example of the manipulated training research method. *Behavior Therapy, 29*, 35–64.

Thapar, A. & McGuffin, P. (1995). Are anxiety symptoms in childhood heritable? *Journal of Child Psychology and Psychiatry and Allied Disciplines, 36*, 439–447.

Thompson, R. (2000). Attachment and emotion regulation processes. In Vasey M.W., & Dadds, M.R. (Eds.), *The developmental psychopathology of anxiety* (pp. 160–182). New York: Oxford.

Tikalsky, F.D. & Wallace, S.D. (1988). Culture and the structure of children's fears. *Journal of Cross-Cultural Psychology, 19*, 481–492.

Topolski, T.D., Hewitt, J.K., Eaves, L.J., Silberg, J.L., Meyer, J.M., Rutter, M., Pickles, A., & Simonoff, E. (1997). Genetic and environmental influences on childr reports of manifest anxiety and symptoms of separation anxiety and overanxious disorders: A community-based twin study. *Behavior Genetics, 27*, 15–28.

Tracey, S.A., Chorpita, B.F., Douban, J., & Barlow, D.H. (1997). Empirical evaluation of DSM-IV generalized anxiety disorder and adolescents. *Journal of Clinical Child Psychology, 26*, 404–414.

Turner, J.E. & Cole D.A. (1994). Developmental differences in cognitive diatheses for child depression. *Journal of Abnormal Child Psychology, 22*, 15–32.

Tyron, W.W. (1998). Behavioral Observation. In A. Bellack & M. Hersen (Eds.), *Behavioral assessment: A practical handbook* (4 ed., pp. 79–103). Boston: Allyn & Bacon.

Van Hasselt, V.B., Hersen, M., Bellack, A.S., Rosenblum, N.D., & Lamparski, D. (1979). Tripartite assessment of the effects of systematic desensitization in a multi-phobic child: an experimental analysis. *Journal of Behavior Therapy and Experimental Psychiatry, 10*, 51–55.

Vasey M.W. & Dadds, M.R. (Eds.) (2000). *The developmental psychopathology of anxiety.* New York: Oxford.

Vasey, M.W. & Daleiden, E.L. (1994). Worry in children. In G. Davey & F. Tallis (Eds.), *Worrying: Perspectives on theory, assessment and treatment* (pp. 185–207). New York: Wiley.

Vasey, M.W., Daleiden, E.L., Williams, L.L., & Brown, L.. (1995). Biased attention in childhood anxiety disorders: A preliminary study. *Journal of Abnormal Child Psychology, 23*, 267–279.

Weisz, J.R., Suwanlert, S., Chaiyasit, W., Weiss, B., Walter, B.R., & Anderson, W.W. (1988). Thai and American perspectives on over- and undercontrolled child behavior problems: Exploring the threshold model among parents, teachers, and psychologists. Journal of Consulting and Clinical Psychology, 56, 601–609.

Weisz, J. R., Suwanlert, S., Chaiyasit, W., Weiss, B., & Jackson, E.W. (1991). Adult attitudes toward over- and undercontrolled child problems: Urban and rual parents and teachers from Thailand and the United States. *Journal of Child Psychology and Psychiatry and Allied Disciplines, 32*, 645–654.

Wierzbicki, M. (1987). Similarity of monozygotic and dizygotic child twins in level and lability of subclinically depressed mood. *American Journal of Orthopsychiatry, 57*, 33–40.

Wilson, G.T. (1996). Manual-based treatments: The clinical application of research findings. *Behaviour Research and Therapy, 34*, 295–314.

Wolpe, J. (1989). The derailment of behavior therapy: A tale of conceptual misdirection. *Journal of Behaviour Therapy and Experimental Psychiatry, 20*, 3–15.

3 DEVELOPMENTAL ISSUES IN THE ASSESSMENT OF ANXIETY

Cecilia A. Essau
Paula Barrett

Psychological assessment represents a fundamental step in understanding anxiety problems in children and adolescents. The development and implementation of a successful intervention generally depends on a comprehensive assessment of the presenting complaints (Essau *et al.*, 1997). More recently the focus of assessment has been on objectively quantifying thoughts, feelings, and behaviour. Since the release of DSM-III, one goal of childhood assessment has been to reliably and validly differentiate anxiety from other syndromes and further, to discriminate between the different categories of anxiety disorders. To achieve this goal, several methods of assessment have been developed including self-report instruments, behaviour rating scales, diagnostic interviews, and behavioural observation. While methods of assessing childhood anxiety have experienced a significant increase and refinement over the past decade, several developmental issues have limited their reliability and validity. In this chapter, we discuss the often overlooked issue of developmental context in the assessment of anxiety in children and adolescents. These issues include: (i) a developmentally bereft diagnostic system, (ii) the matter of validity across different age groups, and (iii) the lack of procedural guidelines for combining information from multiple informants. Before discussing these developmental issues, we describe and critique the different methods for assessing anxiety in young people.

Types of Assessment

The common goals of assessment are to classify, select, evaluate, and investigate (Kendall *et al.*, 1998). Assessment always precedes treatment and the success of the intervention is often dependent on the information initially provided about the problem. In the assessment of childhood anxiety problems, this task is more difficult by the necessity of obtaining reliable and valid information from multiple informants. Parent and teacher reports are notoriously problematic in the assessment of anxiety because of the lack of overt signs and symptoms displayed by the child. Furthermore, child reports, particularly from younger children, also have questionable validity because the ability to respond to questions about ones internal state is dependent upon cognitive and social maturity. To compensate for these difficulties, a multimethod approach is commonly utilised in clinical practice as well as in research methodologies. The main characteristics of the multimethod approach is the use of various assessments that use different informants and in several settings (Table 3.1). Such method could reduce the amount of error variance in the assessment and presents a comprehensive picture of the child's behavioural, social, and emotional functioning. Each approach to assessment is now reviewed.

SELF-REPORT QUESTIONNAIRES

While some behavioural manifestations of anxiety, namely avoidance of feared objects or situations, are evident in children, the internal cues such

Table 3.1 Multimethod approach of assessment

Approach	Method/Measure

Assessment Methods	<ul><li>Diagnostic Interviews
	  – Highly structured interview (e.g., DISC)
	  – Semi-structured interview (e.g., ADIS-C; K-SADS, CAPA)</li><li>Direct observation (e.g., BAT, POSA)</li><li>Rating scales (e.g., CBCL)</li><li>Self-report questionnaires (e.g., RCMAS, FSSC-R, STAIC, MASC, SCAS, SCARED)</li></ul>

Informants	<ul><li>Child/Adolescent</li><li>Parent</li><li>Teacher</li><li>Clinician</li></ul>
Setting	<ul><li>Home</li><li>School</li><li>Other naturalistic environment (e.g., playground)</li><li>Laboratory setting</li><li>Clinic/Hospital</li></ul>

as thoughts, feelings, and physiological arousal, that accompany the behaviours are measurable only by child self-report (March and Albano, 1998). The aim of self-report questionnaires is to identify specific anxious symptoms and behaviours, and quantify their occurrence (Silverman and Serafini, 1998). The standard format of these scales are Likert-style responses to items in terms of frequency, impairment, or both. Self-report instruments are insufficient for determining a child's specific diagnosis, but are necessary to assess the anxiety experience from the perspective of the child (March and Albano, 1998). In research, questionnaires are frequently used to quantify symptoms before and after treatment, to compare responses across different diagnoses, and as a means of screening children in the community (Silverman and Serafini, 1998). In clinical practice, self-report instruments are typically administered as part of a comprehensive assessment. The responses can be used to assist a clinician in the initial evaluation by providing a guide as to the probability of a particular problem and as a tool for quantifying the child's presenting symptoms.

On a general level, these self-report instruments have been criticised for being contaminated by faking and bias (Nietzel et al.,1988), having questionable validity across other domains of assessment (Silverman and Serafini, 1998), failing to target child-specific symptoms, and for confounding the scores by including items from other clinical syndromes (March and Albano, 1998). Although self-reporting will always be intrinsically biased due to its reliance on the truthfulness and insight of the respondent, this means of assessment is recognised as an important method of data collection. To this end, researchers have attempted to overcome limitations of existing measures by designing developmentally appropriate, anxiety-specific self-report instruments. Further work is needed to design self-report measures that can be used to adequately identify children and adolescents who require treatment, and appropriate for use in the assessment of treatment outcome.

Numerous self-report instruments have been developed and examined in the literature. The most commonly used of these are the Fear Survey Schedule for Children—Revised (FSSC-R; Ollendick, 1983), the Revised Children's Manifest Anxiety Scale (RCMAS; Reynolds and Richmond, 1978; 1985), and the State-Trait Anxiety Inventory for Children (STAIC; Spielberger et al., 1976). Other instruments have been tailored for specific diagnostic categories, including social anxiety, social phobia, test anxiety, and obsessive-compulsive disorder.

Revised Children's manifest Anxiety Scale (RCMAS; Reynolds and Richmond, 1978) is a widely used instrument for assessing physiological anxiety, worry and oversensitivity, and social concerns/ concentration. The 37 items on this scale are to be rated on a yes–no basis. The unique feature of this instrument is its ability to calculate a lie score, or a measure of social desirability, a characteristic which is common in anxious children (Kendall and Flannery-Shroeder, 1998). All the positive (yes) responses, except "lie-scale items", are used to compute total anxiey scores. The RCMAS has been shown to have good psychometric properties. Reported internal consistency coefficients for the three factors have ranged from 0.56 to 0.80, and for the total anxiety score above 0.80. The test-retest reliability coefficients for the three factors for the 3-week interval was 0.9, and a 9-month interval 0.68 (Reynolds and Paget, 1983). However, the scale failed to reliably discriminate between children with different subtypes of anxiety disorders, or between those with anxiety disorders and other psychiatric disorders (Perrin and Last, 1992).

State-Trait Anxiety Inventory for Children (STAIC) comprises two measures of anxiousness, including both a measure of trait anxiety (A-Trait) and state anxiety (A-State) (Spielberger *et al.*, 1973). Trait anxiety reflects chronic, stable anxiety across time and situations. The 20 items on the A-Trait scale can be answered "hardly ever", "sometimes", or "often". State anxiety is situation-specific, transitory anxiety at the time of completing the instrument. The 20 items on the A-state scale are answered "very calm", "calm", or "not calm". All of these measures have demonstrated adequate internal consistency and test-retest reliability. The test-retest reliability coefficients have been reported to ranged from 0.65 to 0.72 for the A-state, and between 0.44 to 0.94 for the A-Trait (Kendall and Ronan, 1990). An early study by Spielberger (1973) has shown the internal consistency estimates to range from 0.78 to 0.87.

The Multidimensional Anxiety Scale for Children (MASC) is a 39-item instrument designed specifically to assess childhood anxiety according to DSM-IV diagnostic categories (March *et al.*, 1997). The items in the MASC cover a wide range of anxiety symptoms commonly reported by children aged 8 to 17 years. A 4-point Likert-scale is used to rate each item in terms of frequency from "never" to "otfen". Empirical investigations of the instrument demonstrated four robust factors: physical symptoms; social anxiety; harm avoidance; and separation anxiety (March *et al.*, 1997). These factors were consistent across age and gender in a sample of 374 young people. The MASC showed good to excellent reliability with Cronbach alphas ranging from 0.75 on the separation anxiety factor to 0.85 on the physical symptoms factor for the total sample. Test-retest reliability was also satisfactory. The MASC was highly correlated with the RCMAS ($r = 0.63$) but not with a measure of depression ($r = 0.19$) thus demonstrating good convergent and divergent validity. However, the validity of the MASC was established on a small clinical sample of only 24 children, hence further research is necessary to demonstrate the utility of the instrument across different ages, cultures, and diagnostic categories.

The Spence Children's Anxiety Scale (SCAS) is a 44-item measure of anxiety in children aged 8 to 12 years (Spence, 1997, 1998). Like the MASC, the SCAS items reflect the DSM-IV anxiety disorder categories including separation anxiety, social phobia, obsessive-compulsive disorder, panic/agoraphobia; specific phobia (specifically physical injury fears), and generalised anxiety disorder. The SCAS also includes 6 positively-framed filler items (e.g. "I am good at sports") to decrease negative bias in the reporting of anxiety symptoms. Each item is rated on a 4-point scale in terms of its frequency from "never" (0) to "always" (3). To obtain a total score, the 0 to 3 ratings of the 38 anxiety items are summed, with higher scores, indicates greater anxiety symptoms. To assess the psychometric properties of the scale, the SCAS was administered in a counterbalanced order with the RCMAS to a large cohort of 2052 nonclinic children. A smaller sample of 218 children completed both scales, as well as the Children's Depression Inventory (CDI). A clinical sample of 40 children presenting with social phobia or social phobia with separation anxiety, were also recruited. An age- and gender-matched sample of 20 nonclinic children was obtained. Analyses indicated a six, correlated factor model reflecting the diagnostic categories outlined above showed the best fit for the data, although intercorrelations between the factors was notably high (range: $r = 0.55$ to $r = 0.91$) (Spence, 1998). Overall, the psychometric data for the SCAS were found to be adequate, but not as superior as the MASC. Firstly, internal and test-retest reliability were satisfactory, with correlation coefficient being 0.60. Secondly, the SCAS demonstrated acceptable convergent validity as demonstrated by a significant correlation with the RCMAS ($r = 0.71$). Divergent validity was not strongly supported as shown by moderate correlations with the CDI ($r = 0.48$), although this relationship was significantly lower than correlations with the RCMAS. Finally, comparisons between clinical and nonclinical groups of children supported the social phobia factor, but differentiation of separation anxiety was not clear cut. Both clinical groups did, however, score significantly higher than the nonclinic group but not each other. Overall, the SCAS has acceptable psychometric properties and the size of the normative sample is excellent.

Fear Survey Schedule for Children-Revised (FSSC-R) is an instrument designed to assess the intensity of fear associated with 80 items in children aged 9 to 12 years (Ollendick, 1983). The kind of fears included in the FSSC-R are those related to school, home, social, physical, animal, travel, classic phobia, and miscellenous. In order to "accomodate the developmental and cognitive limitations of young children" (Ollendick, 1983, p. 685), the response format was changed from a 5-point to a 3-point Likert scale (1="not scared" to 3="very scared"). A total fear scale is obtained by summing scores for all items. Factor analysis produced the following factors: "fear of failure and criticism", "fear of the unknown", "fear of injury and small animals", "fear of danger and death", and "medical fears". The FSSC-R has been used in children and adolescents in different countries, including Australia (Ollendick *et al.*, 1989), England (Ollendick and Yule, 1990), and China (Dong *et al.*, 1994). It has been reported to show high internal consistency, with coefficient alphas over 0.90; it is highly reliable and stable over a 1-week interval ($r = 0.82$), but is only moderately stable over a 3-month interval ($r = 0.55$). The validity of this scale was supported through its significant correlation with the RCMAS and the A-Trait Scale of the STAIC (Gullone and King, 1992).

Social Anxiety Scale for Children-Revised (SASC-R) consists of 22 items designed for measuring social anxiety and fear of negative evaluation (La Greca and Stone, 1993). Children indicate on a 3-point or 5-point scale as to how much they felt the item was true for them. Factor analysis yielded three factors: (i) "Fear Negative Evaluation (FNE)", which reflects children fear, concern, or worry about negative evaluations from peers; (ii) "Social Avoidance and Distress-Specific to New Peers or Situations (SAD-New)", represents social avoidance, inhibition or distress commonly reflect in new situations or with unfamiliar peers; and "Social Avoidance and Distress-General (SAD-G)", which reflects a generalized social avoidance, behavioural inhibition, and social discomfort with peers. All these factors have acceptable internal consistency; the standardized reliability coefficients for FNE was 0.86, SAD-New 0.78, and SAD-G 0.69. Their result also support the concurrent validity of the SASC-R in that children who scored highly on the FNE and the SAD-New and SAD-G also perceived themselves as having lower social acceptance, lower self-worth and poorer behavioural conduct than children who were less socially anxious. Neglected and rejected children also had higher scores on the FNE subscale compared to the popular children. Neglected children had significantly higher scores on SAD-New and on SAD-G compared to children in the popular, rejected and average groups.

The Screen for Child Anxiety Related Emotional Disorders (SCARED) is a 38-item self-report questionnaire to assess DSM-IV childhood anxiety disorders (Birmaher *et al.*, 1997). Factor analysis yielded five factors: somatic/panic, generalized anxiety, separation anxiety, social phobia and school phobia. Each factor was found to have good internal consistency, with coefficient alpha values ranging from 0.74 to 0.89. Test-retest reliability based on two occasions (ranging from 4 days to 15 weeks) has been found to be relatively good, with intraclass correlation coefficients for the total score being 0.86, and for the individual factors ranging from 0.70 to 0.90. The SCARED also has good discriminant validity, both between children with anxiety compared to other disorders, as well as among the subtypes of anxiety disorders. Children with anxiety disorders can be significantly differentiated from those with disruptive disorders on the total anxiety and on each of the five factors of the SCARED. The SCARED can furthermore be used to discriminate children with anxiety and depression on the child's total score, somatic/panic, separation anxiety, and school phobia factors.

In addition to these specific self-report questionnaires designed to assess anxiety symptoms, numerous self-report measures are available that contain items or scales for assessing anxiety symptoms. The most commonly used measure is that of *Symptom Checklist-90-Revised* (SCL-90-R; Derogatis, 1977). The SCL-90-R is a 90-item scale for the assessment of psychological distress. Each item is rated on a 5-point scale (ranging from "not at all" to "extremely") to indicate the severity of the symptom over the past 7 days. Although this scale was developed for adults, it can and has been used in adolescents aged 13 and older with a reading level of at least 6th grade. The inventory assesses 9 primary symptom dimensions, 4 of which are related to anxiety: obsessive-compulsive behaviour, anxiety, interpersonal sensitivity, and phobic anxiety. The other clusters are somatization, depression, hostility, paranoid ideation, and psychoticism. In addition to numerous research studies establishing the reliability and validity of this scale, it has age-appropriate non-patient norms available for adolescents between 13 and 17 years of age.

BEHAVIOUR RATING SCALES

Another means of assessing anxious symptoms is via parent or teacher observations or judgement on behaviour rating scales. These judgements are made by using a standardized rating format. This approach to assessment elicits information through asking informants to indicate the frequency of specific behaviours. The most widely used behaviour rating instrument is the Child Behavior Checklist (CBCL; Achenbach and Edelbrock, 1983), although its place is predominantly in the field of research rather than in clinical settings (Silverman and Serafini, 1998). The parent, teacher and youth rating scales of the CBCL are designed to assess social competence and behaviour problems in children and adolescents between the ages of 4 and 18 years. The items are rated according to frequency from "not true" to "very true or often true" and represent a broad range of problem behaviours. Several composite dimensions are obtained from scores on these instruments, including "Internalizing Problems" (anxiety/depression, somatic complaints). The CBCL has good test-retest reliability ranging from 0.72 on the Youth Self Report Form to 0.92 for the Teacher Report Form. The instrument demonstrates significant correlations ranging from 0.52 to 0.88 with the Connors Parent Rating Scale and the Revised Problem Behaviour Checklist (Kearney and Socha, 1997). The parent scale has a downward extension for very young children aged 2 to 3 years, has a total of 99 items, of which 44 were designed specifically for this age group. The psychometric properties of this instrument are also satisfactory. Additionally, a teacher form is available for children aged 2 to 5 years. The main limitation of the CBCL and other behaviour rating scales is the general inadequacy of the internalizing subscale to differentiate between clinical and nonclinical groups, as well as among clinical groups. One reason for this may be the high rates of comorbidity in children with internalising disorders; another possible explanation is the lack of focus on specifically identifying anxiety as opposed to the presence of general childhood psychopathology (Silverman and Serafini, 1998).

The main advantage of behaviour rating scales is that the child is characterised across a variety of internalising and externalising dimensions based on the frequency of that child's reported behaviours in comparison with their same-aged peers. The most important consideration in the utilisation of behaviour rating scales for assessing childhood anxiety, however, is the accuracy of the informants. Cross-informant correspondence is often quite low for internalising problems (Achenbach et al., 1987). Research indicates that children are the best reporters of anxiety (Klein, 1991), although the more severe the problem, the more likely parents and teachers will be more accurate informants (Laurent and Potter, 1998). Rating scales are less expensive compared to direct behavioural observation in terms of professional time and training required. Unfortunately, the behaviour rating scales do not provide guidelines for integrating the information from different sources (Essau *et al.*, 1997), nor has a clearly defined link between the scores on these instruments and specific diagnoses been identified (Silverman and Serafini, 1998). Another problem is related to the so-called bias of response, which is the way in which the informants complete rating scales may create additional error in the resulting scores. At this point in time, behaviour rating scales are limited to identification.

DIAGNOSTIC INTERVIEWS

In clinical practice and research, the clinical interview remains the primary source of information about a child's presenting symptomatology. Interviews are typically classified as either structured or unstructured. Unstructured interviews make no attempt to standardise the gathering of information across respondents (Richardson *et al.*, 1965) and are commonly used in clinical settings. When the goal of the interview is to establish a reliable diagnosis by accurately identifying key DSM-IV symptoms, such as in research, the structured interview is the method of choice (March and Albano, 1998). Interview schedules have been developed for use with children and all of these have parallel parent versions.

Structured interview can further be divided into: highly structured and semi-structured. Highly structured interviews contain exact wording and sequence of questions, well-defined rules for recording, and rating of the respondents' answers. Highly structured interviews attempt to reduce variability in obtaining information by specifying the items to be investigated and providing instructions for rating the presence and severity of the items. Due to their highly structured forms, no clinical judgement is needed and that they can be administered by lay interviewers with training in using the instruments. Such interviews have mostly been developed for used in large epidemiologic studies. Semi-structured interviews contain flexible guidelines for conducting the interview to ensure consistent coverage of topics and recording of information. As such they are primarily designed for use by trained clinicians, usually in clinical setting. However, since the interview maybe conducted in a slightly different way by each clinician, close attention needs to be paid to reliability.

While the use of structured and semi-structured interviews has increased the reliability of DSM diagnoses, the problems of clinician error and disagreement (Silverman and Serafini, 1998), and cross-informant inconsistencies remain. Methodological differences across studies examining the diagnostic interviews also presents a major obstacle in drawing conclusions about their comparative reliability. For example, one study investigating the ADIS-C settled clinician disagreements by consensus (Silverman and Nelles, 1988); another utilising the K-SADS arrived at a diagnosis based on the live interviewer's decision (Last *et al.*, 1992). Cross informant inconsistency is also a problem. Interviews rely on the accurate reporting of the child's presenting symptoms which may be affected by the parents motivation to have their child accepted into treatment ("faking bad") and by the child's social desirability ("faking good") (Kendall and Flannery-Shroeder, 1998). A further criticism of the diagnostic interview is its focus on arbitrarily defined criteria which fail to assess individual thoughts and behaviours (Kendall and Flannery-Shroeder, 1998). Finally, interviews have also been hampered by changing DSM criteria for the anxiety disorders. The removal of overanxious disorder and avoidant disorder from DSM-IV, makes comparisons with DSM-III-R studies very difficult. Diagnostic stability is a fundamental requirement in evaluating the reliability and validity of the structured interview. A problem with most structured interviews is that items are often "gated" which lead to loss of information. That is, if the essential "symptoms" are answered negatively, none of the subsequent symptoms will be asked and that the interview will skip to the next diagnostic category. The most commonly used interviews for assessing anxiety in young people are the modified Schedule for Affective Disorders and Schizophrenia in School-Age Children (K-SADS) and the Anxiety Disorders Interview Schedule for Children (ADIS-C).

The Diagnostic Interview Schedule for Children (DISC) is a highly structured diagnostic interview developed for use by trained lay interviewers (Piacentini *et al.*, 1993; Schwab-Stone *et al.*, 1993). It was designed for children aged 9–17 to assess the presence of different subtypes of anxiety disorders (separation anxiety, avoidant disorder, agoraphobia, social phobia, simple phobia, panic disorder, obsessive-compulsive disorder) and other psychiatric disorders, including: attention-deficit disorder, conduct disorder, anorexia nervosa, bulimia, functional enuresis and encopresis, alcohol abuse/dependence, cannabis abuse/dependence, tobacco dependence, schizophrenia, cyclothymic disorder, and substance abuse, and affective disorder. The DISC requires the interviewer to read each question exactly as written. Most response options are limited to "yes", "no", and "sometimes" or "somewhat". DISC questions can be grouped into two categories: (a) "stem" questions which ask about the presence of behaviours. A "no" response to the "stem question" means that the interview has to move forward past more specific prompts of that general question; (b) "contingent" questions inquire only if a stem question is answered positively to determine whether the elicited behaviour meets a diagnostic criterion; these questions may reduce the false positive responses, and help to determine whether the symptom meets the specifications for a diagnostic criteria; and (c) another types of questions has been added in the later versions of the DISC, which are asked at the end of each diagnostic section when certain number of symptoms have been positively answered. These questions assess age at which the first "episode" appeared, impairment associated with the current episode, the context in which the current symptoms may have arisen or been exacerbated, and the need for or receipt of any treatment intervention for the specific conditions.

The Diagnostic Interview for Children and Adolescents—Revised (DICA-R) is a structured interview designed to assess the major psychiatric disorders of childhood and adolescence according to DSM-III-R criteria, together with onset, duration, severity, and associated impairments of the symptoms (Herjanic and Reich, 1982). This interview schedule is available in three versions, one for children (ages 6–12), one for adolescents (ages 13–17), and another for parents. The diagnostic categories covered included anxiety disorders (separation anxiety disorder, overanxious disorder, simple phobia, obsessive-compulsive disorder), attention-deficit disorder, oppositional disorder, conduct disorder, alcohol use, cigarette smoking, drug use, anorexia nervosa, bulimia, mood disorders, somatization disorder, enuresis, encopresis, menstruation, gender identity disorder, sexual experience, psychotic symptoms, and psychosocial stressors. Questions are also available for the interviewer to evaluate the child's general appearance, affect, motor behaviour, speech, attention, flow of thought, general responses to the interview, and subjective clinical impressions of the interview.

The Kiddie-Schedule for Affective Disorders and Schizophrenia (K-SADS) is a semi-structured diagnostic interview designed to measure the presence or absence of disorders (Puig-Antich and Chambers, 1978), according to DSM-III and Research Diagnostic Criteria. The interview begins with an unstructured interview to establish rapport, to gain information about the child's social environment and social functioning (e.g., family relations, peer relations), and to obtain a history of the present illness, as well as to determine current symptoms, their severity, and chronicity. The structured section of the K-SADS focusses on specific symptoms. The six point severity ratings are scaled from: "no information" to "extreme". The "essential symptoms" (i.e., screening or gating question) of a disorder are first asked to evaluate the presence of an episode of illness before evaluating additional "qualifying symptoms". If the response to the screening question is negative, the clinician then skips to the next diagnostic category.

The Child and Adolescent Psychiatric Assessment (CAPA) is a semi-structured, symptom-oriented, diagnostic interview for children and adolescents aged 8–18 years (Angold *et al.*, 1995). It contains diagnostic algorithms that provide diagnoses according to DSM-III-R, DSM-IV, and ICD–10 for anxiety disorders, depressive disorders, somatization disorders, food-related disorders, sleep problems, elimination disorders. The interview comprises of three phrases: (i) the introduction, which is usually used to establish a rapport with the child; (ii) the symptom review; and (iii) the inacapacity rating for measuring the effects of symptoms on various life areas. When questioning about the symptom, the interviewers ask the context in which it has occurred and its consequences. The information obtained is then matched with the operational definitions and levels of severity given in the glossary.

The Anxiety Disorder Interview Schedule for Children (ADIS-C) is a semi-structured interview that provides a detailed coverage of the DSM-IV anxiety disorders and most other categories relevant to children and adolescents (Silverman and Albano, 1996). It is available in two forms: the child version (ADIS-C) and the parent version (ADIS-P). Each interview requires 60 to 90 minutes for administration. Some questions can be answered yes/no, but most required elaboration. Items address situationally and cognitive cues for anxiety, intensity of anxiety, extent of avoidance and precipitaing events. The parent interview addresses history and effects on the child, while the child interview addresses symptomatology in greater detail. Although the ADIS appears less able to reliably discriminate among specific anxiety disorders, interrater agreement for most categories is moderate to high. Silverman and Eisen (1992) reported moderate Kappa coefficients of 0.46 for the ADIS-C and 0.54 for the ADIS-P.

Diagnostic interview schedules designed for adults have also been used with adolescents, including the Diagnostic Interview Schedule (Robins *et al.*, 1981), the Composite International Diagnostic Interview (Essau and Wittchen, 1993; Wittchen *et al.*,1991), and the Structured Clinical Interview for DSM-III-R (Spitzer *et al.*, 1988).

The Diagnostic Interview Schedule (DIS) is a fully structured diagnostic interview that permits, the derivation of current and lifetime diagnoses according to the Feighner Criteria, the Research Diagnostic

Criteria (RDC), and the DSM-III-R. In addition to assessing anxiety disorders, the DIS can also be used to assess other psychiatric disorders such as somatization, affective, eating, drug and alcohol disorders, organic brain syndrome, and the subtypes of these disorders (Robins *et al.*, 1981). The latest version (Robins *et al.*, 1996) of the DIS includes the following additions: disorders arising in childhood (attention-deficit/hyperactivity disorder, separation anxiety disorder, oppositional defiant disorder, and conduct disorder), chronic and acute pain disorder, specific phobia, and depressive episode due to medical condition, substance induced disorders, and those with post-partum onset. The DIS contains both the age of onset and recency questions related to the symptom of each disorder, and determines whether these symptoms have been continous between those ages. It also contains questions as to time periods of being symptom-free for at least a year. "Standard impairment questions" ask the extend to which respondent report that the symptoms caused impairment in various life domains and indicate their duration and severity. Respondents are also asked whether they ever talked to a doctor or other health professional about the symptoms of the disorder.

The Composite International Diagnostic Interview (CIDI) is a fully standardized interview designed for used by well-trained lay interviewers (Wittchen *et al.*, 1991). It provides adult diagnoses according to both the ICD-10 and the DSM-IV (Essau and Wittchen, 1993; Wittchen *et al.*, 1991). The CIDI incorporates "symptom" and "time-related" questions. "Symptom questions" ask about problems or experiences that the respondents have had. Positive answers to these questions are explored further with fully specified probes to determine the clinical significance of the symptom and whether it could have been entirely explained by physical causes or ingesting substances. "Time-related questions" allows making diagnoses on a lifetime and a cross-sectional basis. The first CIDI question concerning a symptom asks whether it has ever occurred in the respondent's lifetime. If the symptoms have ever occurred, the respondents are asked as to how recently they occurred, and when the first of the symptoms of the disorder occurred. If the last occurrence was more than a year ago, the respondent is asked the age at which the symptom first appeared.

The Structured Clinical Interview for DSM-III-R (SCID) is a semi-structured interview for the assessment of DSM-III-R diagnoses of anxiety disorders, bipolar disorder, cyclothymia, major depression, dysthymia, and mood disorders not otherwise specified (Spitzer *et al.*, 1988). The SCID assesses for problems that occur within the past month (current) and over the lifetime, with responses being coded as: ?=inadequate information, 1=absent or false, 2=subthreshold, and 3=threshold. It also documents information about the onset, course of illness, partial or full remission, impairment or Global Assessment of Functioning, and the differentiation of symptoms from organic causes. Since the SCID is modularized, the interviewer, usually a clinician, can tailor their interview with their prefered diagnostic coverage.

BEHAVIOURAL OBSERVATION

Observational procedures are widely accepted as the best method for developing a formal functional analysis of a child's presenting problem (March and Albano, 1998; Silverman and Serafino, 1998). The typical types of symptoms and behaviours that might be observed include verbal behaviour, such as positive/negative self-references, and nonverbal behaviour, including body posture and avoidance. These variables can be measured in terms of frequency or response duration. Most behavioural observation assessment techniques used naturalistic methods in that they are usually conducted in the child's normal environment (e.g., the classroom, playground). Another method of observation is that of analog, which is conducted in a contrived situation (e.g., laboratory, clinic) developed to stimulate the natural environment.

The Preschool Observation Scale of Anxiety (POSA) is an observation system for anxiety in preschool children (Glennon and Weisz, 1978). It contain 30 behaviour that contain direct signs of fear (e.g., trembling), indirect signs of fear (e.g., cry, nail biting) and other behaviour which reflect fears (e.g., silence, rigid body posture). It has been used to study children's verbal (e.g., screaming) and physical (e.g., trembling lip) behaviours in children aged under 5 years during forced separation from their mothers at preschool. In that study, a sample of 36 children attending a University-based preschool and their mothers were observed. The 30 items of the POSA demonstrated adequate interrater reliability ($r = 0.78$) and correlated significantly with teachers' and parents' ratings of the childrens' anxiety ($r = 0.47$ and $r = 0.37$, respectively). The children's own ratings of their anxiety showed no significant relationship, suggesting that behavioural observation may be a reliable and valid means of assessing anxiety in young children who are unable to accurately report their own internal state.

The Behavioural Avoidance Task (BAT) is the most widely used method of behavioural observation with anxious children. This assessment device exposes the child to an anxiety-provoking object or situation, usually for between 5 and 10 minutes. The BAT is designed to be voluntary and is usually conducted without parents present. The distance between the child and the object/situation or the duration of the exposure are often used to assess the degree of fear and avoidance. Subjective ratings of distress and cognitive self-talk (via thought listing) can be taken before, during, and after the BAT. A typical example of this task would involve observing a child with social phobia giving a verbal presentation in front of a small group of people who are unfamiliar to that child. This mimics as closely as possible the naturally-occurring triggers in a social performance situation and allows the clinician to assess the child's tolerance for anxiety and degree of impairment/distress (March and Albano, 1998). A BAT has the additional advantage of providing the clinician with an ongoing measure of change across treatment (March and Albano, 1998). Behavioural exposure tasks have been developed for assessing children with simple or social phobia, separation anxiety disorder, and generalised anxiety disorder.

Another less widely used, yet equally valuable, type of behavioural observation task is family interaction. Barrett and colleagues (1996) devised an interaction task to assess the influence of family processes on children's processing of threat. The study involved 152 children aged between 7 and 14 years with a primary diagnosis of either separation anxiety, overanxious, or social phobia. Children and their parents were presented with ambiguous hypothetical situations, representing physical (e.g., "On the way to school, you [your child] feel(s) funny in the tummy") and social threats (e.g., "You [your child] see a group of students from another class playing a great game. You (your child) walk over and want to join in and hear them laughing"). After each situation, the child and parent were separately asked to provide an interpretation and plan of action. Following this, each family discussed the situations with the aim of generating a mutually agreeable solution. After the discussion, the child was again asked to interpret and provide a plan of action for each situation. This design assessed the degree to which parents model and reinforce anxious responses in their children. The respondent's interpretation of the situations were classified as threatening or non-threatening, and their plans of action as either avoidant, aggressive, or proactive. Compared with nonclinic control children, anxious children reported more threatening interpretations of the ambiguous situations. Furthermore, these children selected more avoidant plans of action in comparison with nonclinic and oppositional children. The children's responses following the family discussion demonstrated an interesting phenomenon. Compared to before the interaction, the anxious children chose even more threatening interpretations and more avoidant solutions. This result was termed the FEAR effect ("Family Enhancement of Anxious Responding") because it appeared that parents contribute to the enhancement of the cognitive interpretative style of their children. Similarly, these results have been replicated by Chorpita and colleagues (1996).

Like other assessment methods, direct behaviour observation has its problems. A major problem with this method is the phenomenon of observer drift, which is the tendency of observers to gradually depart from originally agreed-on behaviour definition. Future research should focus on developing a checklist which may help to reduce this problem. Such checklist needs to contain the three basic components of anxiety disorders: (1) the behavioural component (e.g., nervous, nail biting, avoid eye contact, crying, screaming, whining, excessive clining to parents, stuttering, avoidance behaviour), (2) the physiological component (e.g., increase heart rate, palpitation, sweating, increased in pulse volume, headache, stomachaches, dizziness), and the (3) cognitive component (e.g., self-critical thoughts, self-deprecatory thoughts, and feeling incompetence). The responses in each of these components, although different, have similar function. Responses in the behavioural component reflect impairment, responses in physiological component somatovisceral arousal, and in the cognitive component they reflect psychological distress

SELF-MONITORING

Self-monitoring allows individual to systematically record ongoing subjective states or behaviours, either at regular intervals or whenever they occur (Haynes, 1978). The most commonly used self-monitoring procedure in children and adolescents is that of daily diaries, either in pictorial and printed versions. Daily diaries can be used to elicit situational variables, time of the day, location, behavioural consequences, and anxiety rating. According to an early study by Beidel and colleagues (1991), daily dairies is useful in providing information related to the intensity, precipitators, consequences of anxious reactions, and the associated cognition. These authors also showed daily dairies as a reliable and valid method in the assessment of anxiety.

One of the major problems with self-monitoring is related to compliance. Children and adolescents may fail to complete their self-monitoring homework, especially if they are to do the recording at a frequent basis. In studies among adults, non-compliance behaviour can be reduced by giving patients the rationale of self-monitoring and by a regular discussion of the assignment with the patients (O'Brien and Barlow, 1984). Among anxious children, family participation led to over 90% compliance in utilizing daily diary (Israel *et al.*, 1987).

FAMILY ASSESSMENT

Familial factors have been suggested as crucial in the development and maintenance of anxiety factors. The use of family assessment scales to augment the clinician's observation of in-session family interactions, and enable the clinicians to evaluate the family member's viewpoint. The inclusion of parent assessment may be useful in planning family interventions. Having family members involved in the treatment of anxiety could facilitate psychological interventions since parents usually act as providers of reinforcement and punishment, and the models of adaptive behavior.

The two commonly used family assessment scales are the Family Environment Scale (FES; Moos and Moos, 1986) and the Family Adaptability and Cohesion Evaluation Scale—III (FACES-III; Olson *et al.*, 1985). The FES comprises of 90 items that can be used to measure perceptions of social and family environmental characteristics. The 10 subscales of the FES include independence, achievement orientation, cohesion, control, organization, intellectual-cultural orientation, moral-religious emphasis, active-recreactional orientation, conflict, and expressiveness. The FACES-III consists of 20 items which can be used to assess family cohesion and adaptability. The cohesion subscale measures the extend to which families are disengaged, separated, connected, or enmeshed. The adaptability dimension measures the degree to which family members are rigid, structured, flexible, or choatic.

TEMPERAMENT ASSESSMENT

One of the potential risk factors for anxiety disorders is temperament. The most well-known laboratory-based temperamental construct has been the "behavioral inhibition to the unfamiliar" (Kagan, 1989). It refers to the tendency of toddlers and preschool children to be shy and with-drawn in unfamiliar situations. Assessment of behavioral inhibition is conducted in a laboratory situation, in which a child is evaluated on a series of age-appropriate cognitive tasks. The aim is to obtain an index of child's behaviour with an unfamiliar examiner under a mild cognitive stress. Each sessions are videotaped and scored, following which the chil-dren are dichotomized as being "inhibited" or "not inhibited". Some examples of inhibited behavioural responses include cessation of ongoing activity and vocalization, avoidance, clinging to parent, and extended latency to interact with novel persons.

The Revised Dimensions of Temperament Survey (DOTS-R; Windel & Lerner, 1986) assesses nine temperament dimensions: actvity level, rhythmicity, adaptability, threshold, intensity, mood, attention span, distractibility, and approach/withdrawal. The DOTS-R is available in two versions, the DOTS-R (SELF) and the DOTS-R (CHILD). The DOTS-R (CHILD) version is completed by the parents, in which they rate the extend to which each statement describe their child as he/she was in elementary school. In the DOTS-R (SELF), the respondents rate as to how true each statement describe their behaviour. The items are to be rated on a scale from 1 (usually false) to 4 (usually true). The administration time has been reported to be about 20–25 minutes.

SUMMARY

Debate has ensued regarding the most reliable and valid methods of assessing childhood anxiety. Each method of measuring anxiousness has advantages and disadvantages (Table 3.2). Self-report measures are useful for eliciting information about internal states that are not readily observable in a child but are prone to social desirability bias. Behaviour rating scales provide useful information from multiple informants across multiple settings, but cross-informant consistency is quite low calling into question the validity of these instruments for internalising problems. Clinical interviews provide a reliable means for obtaining detailed information about a child's presenting problems and are necessary for establishing diagnoses, but rely heavily on clinical judgment and informant reliability. Finally, behavioural observation is an objective means of evaluating the frequency and duration of specific behaviours, but as an assessment method is time-consuming and highly idiographic. The choice of which type of assessment to use typically depends on the goal of the assessment itself and the hypotheses made by the clinician (Table 3.3).

Critical Analyses of Research on Developmental Issues

The first developmental issue that arises in the assessment of child-hood anxiety is the lack of an age-appropriate diagnostic system

Table 3.2   Assessment methods for anxiety symptoms and disorders

Methods	Advantages	Disadvantages
Rating Scales	• Available normative data • Available psychometric properities • Inexpensive in terms of professional time and training requirement • Based on rater's experience	• No established cutoff scores for most scales • Problems involving bias of response • Difficult to report unobserved anxiety symptoms
Self-report Questionnaires	• Has sound psychometric properities • Easy and inexpensive to administer • Obtain information directly from the child	• Low level of agreement among informants • Information limited to the child's perspective
Direct Observation	• Assessment of actual behavior • Identification of environmental contingencies	• Can be expensive • Problem with observer drift • Needs proper coding systems
Diagnostic Interview	• Exploration of child's response • Direct observation of behavior • Reduces variability in obtaining information especially in structured diagnostic interview schedules	• May be time consuming to administer • Semi-structured interview needs to be conducted by clinicians • Can be expensive when a large sample size is required • Due to the "gated" nature of the screening items in some diagnostic interview, there may be loss of information

Table 3.3 Selection of assessment instruments and methods for anxiety

Areas of consideration	Areas of interest	Assessment methods/comments
Anxiety phenomena	• Frequency of anxiety disorders and comorbid disorders • Frequency and severity of anxiety symptoms • Effect of treatment of disorders and problems	• Diagnostic interview (structured or unstructured). • Rating scales; self-report of questionnaires. • Diagnostic interview; rating scale; self-report questionnaire; behavioural observation; measures of psychosocial impairment or quality of life.
Age of the sample	• Children • Adolescents	• Diagnostic interview (unstructured); parent interview; behavioural observation; rating scales by significant others (e.g., parents, teachers). • Diagnostic interview; self-report questionnaire.
Informants	• Child/Adolescent • Parent • Teacher	• Diagnostic interview; parent interview. • Rating scales; diagnostic interview; behavioural observation. • Rating scales; behavioural observation.
Personnel available	• Clinician • Non-clinician	• Diagnostic interview (structured or unstructured); rating scale; behavioural observation. • Highly structured interview; rating scale; behavioural observation.
Psychometric properties	• Reliability, validity, sensitivity, specificity	• Used instruments with established norms and psychometric properties.

(Essau *et al.*, 1997). The DSM-IV currently assumes that children, adolescents, and adults experience the same manifestations of anxiety. On the contrary, research has demonstrated that fears and worries change across the lifespan. At different ages, the symptoms experienced by children is relative to their cognitive, social, and bodily development (Costello and Angold, 1995). Hence, anxious symptomatology is best evaluated on the basis of developmental norms or age-appropriate functioning (Essau *et al.*, 1997). Separation anxiety in a 5-year-old, for example, would be considered normal based on the developmental level of young children and relatively high prevalence in young children and, but would be maladaptive in an adolescent. Given that DSM-IV provides one set of criteria for all individuals regardless of age, the decision of whether to assign a diagnosis to a particular child is left to the clinical judgement of the interviewer.

Secondly, the methods of assessing self-reported anxiety in children is currently limited to instruments administered to children across many age groups, ranging from early childhood to late adolescence. The lack of recognition for the differences in the manifestion of anxiety symptoms at different ages is surprising given the developmental context in which most fears occur. One means of overcoming this problem is through the provision of norms which compare children with their same-aged peers. The utility of these norms is dependent, however, on the number and cultural diversity of participants, as well as the recency of the norm development. There are also very few self-report measures for children under the age of 9 years, mostly due to the questionnable reliability and validity of the symptoms they report. This, however, leaves a large gap in the assessment of younger children with anxiety problems. Furthermore, no instruments have been developed specifically for adolescents.

Thirdly, it is widely accepted that the best method of assessing psychopathology in children is via multiple informants. The most common means of obtaining information from observers is through behaviour rating scales, such as the CBCL. While parents and teachers are accurate reporters of externalising problems in children where problem behaviour is overtly apparent, they are less satisfactory as informants of internalising problems (Klein, 1991; Loeber *et al.*, 1990). Parent-child consistency in diagnostic interviews for anxiety disorders is also quite low. This finding is perhaps not surprising given that anxiousness is an internally-derived experience, however, the lack of a "gold standard" for combining information from multiple informants makes the assignment of diagnoses difficult.

In summary, assessment is a critical first step in identifying problem areas and developing amerliorative strategies to reduce the distress and impairment associated with maladaptive thoughts, feelings, and behaviours. An important consideration when evaluating assessment information is the developmental context in which the problem occurs. Current assessment procedures are flawed from a developmental perspective in terms of: (i) the lack of an age-specific diagnostic system; (ii) the application of assessment instruments to a broad age range; and (iii) the unresolved issue of combining information from multiple sources. The first issue is a general concern of classification and diagnosis. Given that many assessment instruments are designed based on the symptoms defined in DSM-IV, the failure of the system to take developmental context into account presents with obvious validity concerns. The other two issues vary according to the stage of child development. The following section describes these concerns as they pertain to the assessment of anxiety problems across infancy, middle childhood, and adolescence.

ASSESSMENT OF INFANTS AND TODDLERS

The assessment of young children has lagged far behind that of school-aged children and adolescents. Merrell (1998) reported five main reasons for this: (i) appropriate instruments are unavailable; (ii) psychometric properties of existing instruments are inadequate; (iii) high variability in the behaviour of young children; (iv) behaviour in young children is highly influenced by context; and (v) instruments used with older children are extremely difficult to implement with young children. A further issue is the inappropriateness of many of the diagnostic categories of the DSM-IV with children younger than 5 years. A classification system for children aged 0 to 3 years has been developed but has yet to be widely accepted (Merrell, 1998).

Clinical interviews have been criticised for not being useful with young children. Indeed, one can intuitively assume that a structured diagnostic interview is likely to be an unreliable and invalid source of information from a 4-year-old, given the verbal competence and degree of insight required to respond to the questions. While unstructured interviews are commonly used with young children, the utility of this technique will depend on the clinician's ability to communicate on the same level as the child. Young children tend to want to give answers that please adults, thus leading questions can confound a child's response. A further consideration is that separation fears are very common at this age. Special efforts typically need to be made to make the child feel comfortable being alone with the interviewer. Overall, the clinical interview can provide valuable information about a child, but should only be used as one part of a comprehensive assessment (Merrell, 1998).

Self-report methods have been applied to preschool children, although the psychometric data are less than encouraging (Merrell, 1998). The main reasons for the difficulty in applying this assessment technique are due to young children lacking the "ability to read and understand test items, the cognitive maturity or sophistication to make specific incremental judgements in responding to test items, and the ability to correctly translate these judgements into the marking of the appropriate answer" (Merrell, 1998, p. 352). The second reason is the main sticking point in using self-report methodologies with pre-schoolers. As a general rule, it can be concluded that pen-and-paper assessments have limited, if any, utility with young children. Pictorial scales, such as the Pictorial Scale of Perceived Compence and Acceptance for Young Children (Harter and Pike, 1984), have the potential to be effective methods of obtaining self-report information. The basic requirements of this style of instrument are the elimination of reading demands and the inclusion of simple response types, such as pointing to a picture.

Behaviour rating scales are frequently used with younger populations and rely heavily on the observation skills and objectivity of parents and teachers. Target behaviours include externalising problems, social skills, sleep problems, destructive behaviour, as well as internalising problems. Only two instruments specifically include questions about degree of anxiousness: the Behavior Assessment System for Chlidren (BASC; Reynolds and Kamphaus, 1992) and the Child Behavior Checklist 2–3 (CBCL/2–3; Achenbach et al., 1992). Both instruments provide T-scores and percentile ranks for different problems and the psychometric properties are adequate.

Direct observation is also one of the most commonly used methods of assessment for young children. No standardised methods for assessing anxiety in this population have been developed, with the exception of the Preschool Observation Scale of Anxiety (POSA) (Glennon and Weisz, 1978). As described previously, this instrument demonstrates adequate interrater reliability but no relationship was found between scores on this scale and childrens' perceptions of their own anxiety. Cross-informant consistency in this age group is an issue that is relatively unexplored to date, most probably due to difficulty of reliably and validly obtaining self-reports of anxiousness from very young children.

Overall, assessment instruments for infants and toddlers are very limited in number and scope. One reason for the apparent lack of interest in developing appropriate measures is the question of the appropriateness of diagnosing anxiety problems in this cohort and the stability of such diagnoses as the child matures. Within the last two decades, temperament has received increasing attention from researchers. Studies of social behaviours in toddlers aged between 1 and 2 years, demonstrate two types of behaviour: inhibited and unhibited. Children classed as inhibited tend to show extreme fear or avoidance of unfamiliar situations and shyness with strangers; uninhibited children show a tendency to approach rather than avoid and are sociable with unfamiliar people (Kagan, 1996). In a review by Kagan (1996), it was concluded that not all inhibited children grow to be anxious adolescents and not all anxious adolescents were inhibited children. However, approximately one-third of toddlers who are characterised as inhibited, tend to display this tendency in late childhood and adolescence. This raises important issues for the prevention of anxiety problems in children. If children can be reliably identified at a young age as being at risk for developing an anxiety disorder, then certain ameliorative strategies may be designed and implemented to prevent the child experiencing such problems later in life. To achieve this goal, methods for assessing children under the age of 6 years need to be developed and longitudinal studies exploring the predictive validity of these instruments need to be designed.

ASSESSMENT OF SCHOOL-AGE CHILDREN

Research has indicated that school-aged children with an anxiety disorder experience significant personal and school problems compared to their nonanxious peers. Anxious children tend to be less like, even neglected, by their classmates (Laurent and Potter, 1998). They also report higher levels of depression and poorer self-concepts. It is becoming increasingly recognised that children do not always "grow out of" their fears (Beidel et al., 1996); indeed, the prevalence rates of anxiety disorders tend to increase with age, with the exception of separation anxiety disorder which has a 50% recovery rate (Cantwell and Baker, 1989). Anxiety disorders are also more common in girls than boys in nonclinical samples (Laurent and Potter, 1998). The most commonly used assessment tools for identifying targets for intervention with school-age children are self-report measures and behaviour rating scales.

Most self-report measures can be implemented with school-aged children. The RCMAS has the lowest age limit at 6 years although, interestingly, the same scale is used with individuals up to the age of 17 years. Self-report scales have the advantage over behaviour rating scales of measuring the individual perceptions and internal states of the child. Given that this approach relies heavily on the child's ability to understand and process the question being asked, as well as the honest reporting of the given answer, many self-report instruments may actually fail in this basic goal (Kendall and Flannery-Shroeder, 1998). Social desirability and a hypersensitivity towards the evaluation of others may influence the child's disclosure on a questionnaire about thoughts and feelings.

Dadds and colleagues (1998) investigated the tendency for anxious children to report in a socially desirable manner on the RCMAS. The RCMAS is unique in its inclusion of a Lie Scale consisting of 9 items, such as "I am always good", to assess the desire to present oneself in a favourable manner. The RCMAS was completed by a large sample of almost two thousand 7 to 14 year olds drawn from grades 3 to 7 of eight primary schools. Additionally, teachers were asked to nominate up to three children in their class who were perceived as anxious. The results indicated no relationship between self-reported anxiety and social desirability, thus anxious children were no more likely to be concerned with self-presentation than nonanxious children. Clinical experience suggests that social desirability is an important factor to consider when working with anxious children, although this is not borne out in these results. The results did, however, demonstrate important age and gender influences. Firstly, girls rated as anxious by their teachers had higher Lie scores. Secondly, boys who reported being anxious and were rated as anxious by their teachers showed lower Lie scores compared to boys who were identified by teachers but denied being anxious. Lastly, the convergence between teacher ratings and childrens' self-reported anxiety was generally low. Thus, there appear to be important differences between childrens' willingness to acknowledge anxiety and the salience of that anxiety to adult observers.

Cross-informant consistency, or rather inconsistency, is a critical issue in the assessment of anxiety in children. It is not uncommon to find parents, teachers, and children reporting vastly different perceptions of the child's behaviour. Research demonstrates that children tend to be more valid informants of internalising problems than parents or teachers (Klein, 1991; Loeber, 1990). This is not surprising given the subjective experience of anxiety and the central role of thoughts and feelings in perpetuating anxiety prescribed by many theories (Beck *et al.*, 1961). Behaviour ratings scales, such as the Child Behaviour Checklist with its parallel versions for children and teachers, typically show low correspondence between informants (Achenbach *et al.*, 1987).

Diagnostic interviews are the only form of assessment that provide guidelines for combining information from more than one informant, although there does not exist a "gold standard" for this practice. Most studies find that the agreement between children and parents on standardised interviews increases with age (Rapee *et al.*, 1994; Silverman and Eisen, 1992); others have found no age effect (Angold *et al.*, 1987). This suggests that as children mature they are either better able to verbalise their fears, less concerned with social desirability, or both. The influence of childrens' cognitive and social development on the validity of assessment is an issue deserving of further investigation.

Anxiety in children tends to wax and wane over time. The continuity of anxiety problems in children is an important issue in terms of the necessity, or lack thereof, for direct intervention. It is reasonable to assume that the determination of a diagnosis is potentially limited by the instruments available to assess the problem. Beidel and colleagues (1996) investigated the continuity of anxious symptomatology in children aged 7 to 12 years using diagnostic interview, and child and parent reports. All children and their mothers were interviewed using the ADIS. The children also completed the STAI-C and the CBCL was administered to each child's mother. Of the 150 children interviewed, 31 met DSM-III-R criteria for an anxiety disorder. At 6 month follow-up the diagnoses of social phobia and overanxious disorder were retained for 33% and 50% of the sample, respectively. In 16% and 25% of cases, the diagnoses for social phobia and overanxious disorder alternated. The stability of avoidant disorder was unexamined due to participant attrition and 5 participants presenting with unidentified anxiety disorders were not discussed by the authors. None of the nonclinic children reported clinically significant anxiety symptoms at follow-up. Across time, correlations of STAI-C in the anxious group was poor ($r = 0.34$ for State anxiety; $r = 0.13$ for Trait anxiety). Parent reports on the CBCL were more stable with correlations ranging from 0.50 for externalising problems to 0.74 for internalising problems. Overall, there appears some stability in anxiety problems in this age group but a moderate degree of instability in the specific content of the problems and level of distress was also evidenced. This finding raises an interesting developmental question: which children "outgrow" their fears? The risk and protective factors present in children with a tendency towards being anxious is deserving of future exploration.

Another interesting finding of the Beidel *et al.* (1996) study was the poor test-retest reliability coefficients of the STAI-C. The authors propose that this may be improved through the development of more specialised instruments focusing on specific psychopathology, such as social-evaluative concerns. Another means of improving the self-report assessment approach would be to design age-specific instruments, taking into consideration the developmental stages of children in terms of the content and manifestations of their fears and worries at different ages. Instruments for primary-school children, for example, might focus more on separation fears and less on social-evaluative concerns; while the opposite could be true for adolescents. The development of age-specific instruments also enables the questions to be written in an appropriate language for the age group, thereby decreasing the error due to misunderstanding the question.

The current view on parents' ability to report on their childrens' anxious symptomatology is that it is less accurate than for externalising problems. It seems reasonable to expect this outcome given the lack of overt signs associated with anxiety compared to disruptive or hyperactive behaviour. If this were completely true, however, diagnostic interviews with parents would be ineffective methods of assessment for internalising symptoms. The strength of interviews, it seems, lies in the asking of numerous, specific questions targeting each DSM-IV diagnosis. Yet to date, no self-report instruments for anxiety problems have been developed for parents either as a separate measure or in parallel with existing measures. The development of parallel versions for the self-report measures for children is also likely to assist future investigations of the importance of cross-informant consistency (Beidel *et al.*, 1996).

ASSESSMENT OF ADOLESCENTS

There are many self-report instruments available for the assessment of anxiety in adolescent populations. Unlike the younger cohorts, adolescents typically have the cognitive maturity and insight to answer questionnaires assessing their thoughts and feelings. However, concerns about self presentation and evaluation by others are amongst the most prevalent fears in adolescence, hence the issue of social desirability remains. To date, no anxiety measure has been designed specifically for adolescents despite the changes in both cognitive processing and social development for this age group.

Cross-informant studies have shown that adolescents are more accurate reporters than parents or teachers of their perceptions and internal states. Cantwell *et al.* (1997) interviewed 1,709 adolescent students aged 14 to 18 years using the K-SADS interview schedule. From these participants, 281 parent interviews were completed. Inter-rater reliability of the interviews for most disorders was good ($\kappa=0.80$), although the reliability coefficients for current anxiety disorders was significantly lower ($\kappa=0.60$). Overall, adolescents reported more disorders and core symptoms than their parents, particularly for anxiety and depression. Cronbach alpha coefficients were 0.51 for separation anxiety disorder, and 0.33 for all other anxiety disorders. Interestingly, of the 41 participants meeting diagnostic criteria for an anxiety disorder according to either adolescent or parent report, only 11 (27%) were reported by both respondents. Twenty-four diagnoses (58%) were based on adolescent report only and 6 (15%) on parent report. Thus, with the exception of separation anxiety, parent-adolescent agreement for anxiety disorders was poor, although it is important to note that this is possibly a function of prevalence rates for the other anxiety disorders in this study. Statistical analyses yielded no age or gender differences nor effect of parent education, age at onset, and severity of the disorder. Thus with this age group, the inclusion of parent report may not be necessary to reliably identify the majority of cases. The peer group is particularly important in adolescence. According to Erik Erikson's stages of psychosocial development, the goal of this period is to establish an identity; failure to do so is theorised to lead to role confusion. The prevalence of social anxiety in adolescents would intuitively appear to be directly or indirectly related to an individual's status amongst his or her peers. One study examined the relationship between peer nominations and self-reported social anxiety in a large group (n=973) of 11 to 14 year olds (Inderbitzen *et al.*, submitted). Based on behavioural descriptors (e.g. "liked", "starts fights the most"), children were classified as popular, average, rejected, neglected, or controversial. Those young people categorised as rejected or neglected, reported significantly higher social anxiety compared to the other groups. The status of an individual according to one's peers appears to be important in the experience of anxiety in adolescence.

We are currently investigating the influence of peers on the information processing of young adolescents. Adapting the ambiguous situations paradigm developed by Barrett and colleagues (1996), children aged between 7 and 14 years complete the Spence Children's Anxiety Scale. Based on their self-reported anxiety, participants are categorised as low, medium, or high anxiety. Each participant is presented with a series of ambiguous situations and asked to provide an interpretation and plan of action for each. Following this, participants are paired with another young person from the same category and asked to discuss the situations for 5 minutes each. Responses are taken again individually to assess the influence of peers on the processing of ambiguous information. We expect the high anxious group to give more threat-based and avoidant responses after the discussion, compared to before the interaction, while the low anxious group—similar to nonclinic families in the Barrett et al. (1996) study—is expected to demonstrate the opposite response style. We are also implementing group treatment for anxiety problems in this cohort of young people and intend to examine the ambiguous situations task at pre- and post-treatment. If the results of our investigation yield the expected results, this would demonstrate the potential importance of the peer group to inadvertently model and reinforce anxiety. Extrapolating from this, the best way to prevent the development of anxiety disorders may be in the context of the classroom. Suicide risk is a significant problem among adolescents. Investigations with depressed adults have revealed that anxiety is a significant predictor of completed suicide at 1 year follow-up (Fawcett et al., 1990).

Ohring and colleagues (1996) administered the State-Trait Anxiety Inventory for adults (Spielberger et al., 1976) and Beck Depression Inventory (BDI; Beck et al., 1961) to 46 Israeli adolescents aged between 12 and 19 years who were hospitalised following a suicide attempt. A control group of 72 adolescents admitted for other psychiatric problems but with no history of attempted suicide were also recruited. The results indicated that suicide attempters had significantly higher state and trait anxiety than nonattempters independent of age and gender. Scores on the BDI were also higher and correlated moderately highly with state and trait anxiety ($r = 0.59$ and $r = 0.51$, respectively). When depression scores were controlled, attempters had signficantly higher trait anxiety but not state anxiety, compared to nonattempters. Other authors have reported a similar finding with respect to trait anxiety and suicide attempts (De Wilde et al.,1993). Given this, the assessment of anxiety in adolescents, particularly those at risk, is of critical importance. To date, only the STAI assesses trait anxiety but the age of this instrument (nearly 30 years) and its correspondingly out-of-date norms suggests it is currently an inadequate instrument for this purpose.

Adolescents are widely considered to be the most accurate reporters of their internal state. Unlike younger children, adolescents are much more able to understand and process the questions being asked. For this reason, assessment of adolescents is a relatively straight forward process that typically relies heavily on self-report measures and diagnostic interviews. In adolescence, fears about self presentation and evaluation by others are more prominent (March and Albano, 1998) as the peer group becomes increasingly important to the young person. The effect of peers on the development of anxiety is a relatively new area of research. Suicide risk also increases with age and is particularly prevalent in young males. Anxiety is an important risk factor for suicidal behaviour in adults, thus reliable assessment of anxiousness in teenagers is potentially critical to prevention.

Summary and Future Directions

The goal of assessment is to classify, evaluate, and investigate (Kendall and Flannery-Shroeder, 1998) and multiple methods currently exist for assessing anxiety problems in children. Self-report measures and diagnostic interviews have demonstrated reliability, although the validity of most instruments remains to be proven. One possible reason for the lack of discriminant and construct validity is the lack of attention paid to developmental issues. Firstly, the main diagnostic system used by clinicians and researchers alike, DSM-IV, fails to recognise age as a factor in the assignment of diagnoses. Secondly, the assessment of childhood anxiety disorders has, for the most part, been broadly focused with little regard for age or stage of development. On a general level, the influence of childrens' cognitive and social development on the validity of assessment is an issue deserving of further investigation. This issue is particularly pertinent to very young children and adolescents, who each present with unique developmental issues that have been largely ignored in the assessment literature. Further investigations examining the temperament in young children as a predictor of anxiety problems in later life is warranted as research focuses on primary prevention. The relationship between anxiety in adolescence and peer relationships, as well as suicide risk is also deserving of future research. Our review has made us aware of numerous problems with regards to assessment of anxiety in children and adolescents, and which warrant consideration in future studies. The lack of clear or consistent cut-off criteria in studies based on self-report questionnaires limits our ability to describe "anxiety cases" and to compare findings across studies. Measurement of anxiety should include numerous methods of assessment (e.g., interview, observation) of psychosocial impairment since anxiety involves multiple dysfunction in various domains (e.g., cognitive, behaviour). One should go beyond symptom measures to develop adequate instruments that measure what anxious people do which may prolong, intensify, or maintain their anxiety. Finally, the development of internationally recognised and accepted criteria of comparing and combining information from multiple informants is essential.

References

Achenbach, T.M. & Edelbrock, C.S. (1983). *Manual for the Child Behaviour Checklist and Profile*. Burlington: University of Vermont.

Achenbach, T.M., McConaughy, S.H., & Howell, C.T. (1987). Child/adolescent behavioral and emotional problems: Implications of cross-informant correlations for situational-specificity. *Psychological Bulletin, 101*, 213–232.

Angold, A., Prendergast, M., Cox, A. *et al.* (1995). The child and adolescent psychiatric assessment (CAPA). *Psychological Medicine, 25*, 739–753.

Angold, A., Weissman, M.M., John, K., Marikangas, K.R., Prusoff, B.A., Wickramaratne, P., Gammon, G.D., & Warner, V. (1987). Parent and child reports of depressive symptoms in children at low and high risk of depression. *Journal of Child Psychology and Psychiatry and Allied Disciplines, 28*, 901–915.

Barrett, P.M., Rapee, R.M., Dadds, M.R., & Ryan, S.M. (1996). Family enhancement of cognitive style in anxious and aggressive children: Threat bias and the FEAR effect. *Journal of Abnormal Child Psychology, 24*, 187–203.

Beck, A.T., Ward, C.H., Mendelson, M., Mack, J.E., & Erbaugh, J. (1961). An inventory for measuring depression. *Archives of General Psychiatry, 4*, 561–571.

Beck, A.T. (1971). Cognitive, affect, and psychopathoogy. *Archives of General Psychiatry, 24*, 495–500.

Beidel, D.C., Fink, C.M., & Turner, S.M. (1996). Stability of anxious symptomatology in children. *Journal of Abnormal Child Psychology, 24*, 257–269.

Beidel, D.C., Neal, A.M., & Lederer, A.S. (1991). The feasibility and validity of a daily diary for the assessment of anxiety in children. *Behavior Therapy, 22*, 505–517.

Birmaher, B., Khetarpal, S., Brent, D., Cully, M., Balach, L., Kaufman, J., & McKenzie Neers, S. (1997). The Screen for Child Anxiety Related Emotional Disorders (SCARED): Scale construction and psychometric characteristics. *Journal of the American Academy of Child and Adolescent Psychiatry, 36*, 545–553.

Cantwell, D.P. & Baker, L. (1989). Stability and natural history of DSM-III childhood diagnoses. *Journal of the American Academy of Child and Adolescent Psychiatry, 28*, 691–700.

Cantwell, D.P., Lewinsohn, P.M., Rohde, P., & Seeley, J.R. (1997). Correspondence between adolescent report and parent report of psychiatric diagnostic data. *Journal of the American Academy of Child and Adolescent Psychiatry, 36*, 610–618.

Chorpita, B.F., Albano, A.M., & Barlow, D.H. (1996). Cognitive processing in children: Relation to anxiety and family influences. *Journal of Clinical Child Psychology, 25*, 170–176.

Costello, E.J. & Angold, A. (1995). *Developmental epidemiology*. New York: Wiley.

Costello, A.J., Edelbrock, C., Dulcan, M.K., Kalas, R., & Klaric, S. (1987). *The Diagnostic Interview Schedule for Children (DISC)*. Pittsburgh: University of Pittsburgh.

Dadds, M.R., Perrin, S., & Yule, W. (1998). Social desirability and self-reported anxiety in children: An analysis of the RCMAS Lie Scale. *Journal of Abnormal Child Psychology, 26*, 311–317.

De Wilde, E.J., Kienhorst, I.C.W.M., Diekstra, R.F.W., & Wolters, W.H.G. (1993). The specificity of psychologist characteristics of adolescent suicide attempters. *Journal of the American Academy of Child and Adolescent Psychiatry, 32*, 51–59.

Dong, Q., Yang, B., & Ollendick, T.H. (1994). Fears in Chinese children and adolescents and their relations to anxiety and depression. *Journal of Child Psychology and Psychiatry, 35*, 351–363.

Essau, C.A., Feehan, M., & Ustun, B. (1997). Classification and assessment strategies. In C.A. Essau & F. Petermann (Eds.), *Developmental psychopathology: Epidemiology, diagnostics, and treatment*. London: Harwood Academic Publishers.

Essau, C.A. & Wittchen, H-U. (1993). An overview of the Composite International Diagnostic Interview (CIDI). *International Journal of Methods in Psychiatric Research, 3*, 79–85.

Fawcett, J., Scheftner, W.A., Fogg, L., et al. (1990). Time-related predictors of suicide in major affective disorder. *American Journal of Psychiatry, 147*, 1189–1194.

Gullone, E. & King, N.J. (1997). Three-year follow-up normal fear in children and adolescents aged 7 to 18 years. *British Journal of Developmental Psychology, 15*, 97–111.

Gelfand, D.M. & Hartmann, D.P. (1984). *Child behavior analysis and therapy*. Boston, USA: Allyn & Bacon.

Glennon, B. & Weisz, J.R. (1978). An observational approach to the assessment of anxiety in young children. *Journal of Consulting and Clinical Psychology, 46,* 1246–1257.

Haynes, S.N. (1978). *Principles of behavioral assessment.* New York: Gardner.

Herjanic, B., & Reich, W. (1982). Development of a structured psychiatric interview for children: Agreement between child and parent on individual symptoms. *Journal of Abnormal Child Psychology, 10,* 307–324.

Inderbitzen, H.M., Walters, K.S., & Bukowski, A.L. (submitted). The role of social anxiety in adolescent peer relations: Differences among sociometric status groups and rejected subgroups.

Kagan, J. (1989). Temperamental contributions to social behavior. *American Psychologist, 44,* 668–674.

Kagan, J. (1996). Temperamental contributions to the development of social behavior. In D. Magnusson (Ed.), *The lifespan development of individuals: Behavioral, neurobiological and psychosocial perspectives.* London: Cambridge University Press.

Kearney, C.A. & Socha, K.E. (1997). Anxiety problems in childhood: Diagnostic and dimensional aspects. In J.A. den Boer (Ed.), *Clinical management of anxiety: Theory and practical applications.* New York: Marcel Dekker.

Kendall, P.C. & Flannery-Shroeder, E.C. (1998). Methodological issues in treatment research for anxiety disorders in youth. *Journal of Abnormal Child Psychology, 26,* 27–38.

Kendall, P.C. & Ronan, K.R. (1990). Assessment of children's anxieties, fears, and phobias: Cognitive-behavioral models and methods. In C.R. Reynolds & R.W. Kamphaus (Eds.), *Handbook of psychological and educational assessment of children: Personality, behavior, and context.* New York: Guilford Press.

Klein, R.G. (1991). Parent-child agreement in clinical assessment of anxiety and other psychopathology: A review. *Journal of Anxiety Disorders, 5,* 187–198.

La Greca, A.M. and Stone, W.L. (1993). Social anxiety scale for children-revised: Factor structure and concurrent validity. *Journal of Clinical Child Psychology, 22,* 17–27.

Last, C.G., Hersen, M., Kazdin, A., Orvaschel, H, & Perrin, S. (1991). Anxiety disorders in children and their families. *Archives of General Psychiatry, 48,* 928–934.

Last, C.G., Perrin, S., Hersen, M., & Kazdin, A.E. (1992). DSM-III-R anxiety disorders in children: Sociodemographic and clinical characteristics. *Journal of the American Academy of Child and Adolescent Psychiatry, 31,* 1070–1076.

Laurent, J. & Potter, K.I. (1998). Anxiety-related difficulties. In T.S. Watson & F.M. Gresham (Eds.), *Handbook of child behavior therapy.* New York: Plenum Press.

Loeber, R., Green, S.M., & Lahey, B.B. (1990). Mental health professionals' perceptions of the utility of children, mothers, and teachers as informants on childhood pathology. *Journal of Clinical Child Psychology, 19,* 136–143.

March, J.S. & Albano, A.M. (1998). New developments in assessing pediatric anxiety disorders. *Advances in Clinical Child Psychology, 20,* 213–241.

March, J.S., Parker, J.D.A., Sullivan, K., Stallings, P., & Conners, C.K. (1997). Multidimensional Anxiety Scale for Children (MASC): Factor structure, reliability, and validity. *Journal of the American Academy of Child and Adolescent Psychiatry, 36,* 554–565.

Merrell, K.W. (1998). *Behavioral, social, and emotional assessment of children and adolescents.* New Jersey: Lawrence Erlbaum Associates.

Moos, R.H. & Moos, B.S. (1986). *Family Environment Scale Manual* (2nd ed.). Palo Alto, C.A: Consulting Psychologists.

Nietzel, M.T., Bernstein, D.A., & Russell, R.L. (1988). Assessment of anxiety and fear. In A.S. Bellack & M. Hersen (Eds.), *Behavioral assessment: A practical handbook* (3rd ed.) (pp. 280–312). New York: Pergamon.

O'Brien, G.T. & Barlow, D.H. (1984). Agoraphobia. In S.M. Turner (Ed.), *Behavioral theories and treatment of anxiety.* New York: Plenum.

Ohring, R., Apter, A., Ratzoni, G., Weizman, R., Tyano, S., & Plutchik, R. (1996). State and trait anxiety in adolescent suicide attempters. *Journal of the American Academy of Child and Adolescent Psychiatry, 35,* 154–157.

Ollendick, T.H. (1983). Reliability and validity of the revised Fear Survey Schedule for Children (FSSC-R). *Behaviour research and Therapy, 21,* 395–399.

Ollendick, T.H., King, N.J., & Frary, R.B. (1989). Fears in children and adolescents: Reliability and generalizability across gender, age and nationality. *Behaviour Research and Therapy, 27,* 19–26.

Ollendick, T.H. & Yule, W. (1990). Depression in British and American children and its relations to anxiety and fear. *Journal of Consulting and Clinical Psychology, 58,* 126–129.

Olson, D.H., McCubbin, H.I., Barnes, H., Larsen, A., Muxen, M., & Wilson, M. (1985). *Family Inventories.* St. Paul, MN: Family Social Science.

Perrin, S. & Last, C.G. (1992). Do childhood anxiety measures measure anxiety? *Journal of Abnormal Child Psychology, 20,* 567–578.

Piacentini, J., Shaffer, D., & Fischer, P.W. (1993). The Diagnostic Interview Schedule for Children-Revised version (DISC-R): II. Concurrent criterion validity. *Journal of the American Academy of Child and Adolescent Psychiatry, 32,* 658–665.

Puig-Antich, J. & Chambers, W. (1978). *The Schedule for Affective Disorders and Schizophrenia for School-aged Children.* New York: State Psychiatric Institute.

Rapee, R.M., Barrett, P.M., Dadds, M.R., & Evans, L. (1994). Reliability of the DSM-III-R childhood anxiety disorders using structured interview: Inter-rater and parent-child agreement. *Journal of the American Academy of Child and Adolescent Psychiatry, 33*, 984–992.

Reich, W. & Welner, Z. (1988). *Revised version of the Diagnostic Interview for Children and Adolescents (DICA-R)*. St. Louis, MO: Department of Psychiatry, Washington University.

Reynolds, C.R. & Paget, K.D. (1983). National normative and reliability data for Revised Children's Manifest Anxiety Scale. *School Psychology Review, 12*, 324–336.

Reynolds, C.R. & Richmond, B.O. (1978). What I think and feel: A revised measure of children's manifest anxiety. *Journal of Abnormal Child Psychology, 6*, 271–280.

Reynolds, C.R. & Richmond, B.O. (1985). *Revised Children's Manifest Anxiety Scale*. Los Angeles: Western Psychological Services.

Richardson, S.A., Dohrenwend, B.S., & Klein, D. (1965). *Interviewing: Its forms and functions*. New York: Basic Books.

Robins, L.N., Cottler, L., Bucholz, K., & Compton, W. (1996). *The Diagnostic Interview Schedule, Version IV*. St. Louis: Washington University.

Robins, L.N., Helzer, J.E., Croughan, J., & Ratcliff, K.F. (1981). National Institute of Mental Health Diagnostic Interview Schedule: Its history, char-acteristics and validity. *Archives of General Psychiatry, 38*, 381–389.

Schwab-Stone, M., Fisher, P., Shaffer, D., Piacentini, J., Davies, M., & Gioia, P. (1993). The Diagnostic Interview Schedule for Children-revised version (DISC-R). II. Test-retest reliability. *Journal of the American Academy of Child and Adolescent Psychiatry, 32*, 643–650.

Silverman, W.K. & Albano, A.M. (1996). *The Anxiety Disorders Interview Schedule for DSM-IV: Child Version*. San Antonio, USA: Graywind.

Silverman, W.K. & Eisen, A.R. (1992). Age differences in the reliability of parent and child reports of child anxious symptomatology using a struc-tured interview. *Journal of the American Academy of Child and Adolescent Psychiatry, 31*, 117–124.

Silverman, W.K., Fleisig, W., Rabian, B., & Peterson, R.A. (1991). Childhood Anxiety Sensitivity Index. *Journal of Clinical Child Psychology, 20*, 162–168.

Silverman, W.K. & Serafini, L.T. (1998). Assessment of child behavior problems: Internalizing disorders. In A.S. Bellack & M. Hersen (Eds.), *Behavioral assessment: A practical handbook* (4th ed.) (pp. 342–360). Boston, USA: Allyn & Bacon.

Spence, S.H. (1997). Structure of anxiety symptoms among children: A confirmatory factor-analytic study. *Journal of Abnormal Psychology, 106*, 280–297.

Spielberger, C.D. (1973). *Manual for the state-trait anxiety inventory for children*. Palo Alto, CA: Consulting Psychologists Press.

Spielberger, C., Gorsuch, R., & Luchene, R. (1976). *Manual for the State-Trait Anxiety Inventory B Child Version.* Palo Alto, CA: Consulting Psychologists Press.

Spitzer, R.L., Williams, J.B.W., & Gibbon, M. (1988). *Structured Clinical Interview for DSM-III-R.* New York: New York State Psychiatric Institute.

Windle, M. & Lerner, R.M. (1986). Reassessing the dimensions of temperamental individuality across the life span: The Revised Dimensions of Temperament Survey (DOTS-R). *Journal of Adolescent Research, 1,* 213–230.

Wittchen, H-U, Robins, L.N., Cottler, L., Sartorious, N., Burke, J., Regier, D., & participants of the field trials (1991). Cross-cultural feasibility, reliability, and sources of variance of the Composite International Diagnostic Interview (CIDI)—Results of the multicenter WHO/ADAMHA Field Trials (Wave I). *British Journal of Psychiatry, 159,* 645–653.

PART II
ANXIETY DISORDERS

4 SEPARATION ANXIETY DISORDER

Andrew R. Eisen
Lisa K. Brien
James Bowers
Arielle Strudler

The central feature of separation anxiety disorder (SAD) is unrealistic and excessive anxiety upon separation or anticipation of separation from major attachment figures (American Psychiatric Association; APA, 1994). Primary symptoms include excessive worry about potential harm to oneself (e.g., getting kidnapped, becoming ill at school) and/or major attachment figures (e.g., car accident). The child may avoid situations that lead to separation from primary caregivers. Common situations include refusing to attend school, sleep alone at night, or visit with a friend. Children may resort to oppositional behaviours when avoidance becomes unlikely (e.g., temper tantrums, screaming, pleading, and threats). Physical complaints are also common and include stomachaches, headaches, nausea and vomiting. Recurrent physical symptoms necessitate a complete physical examination to rule out a general medical condition. Most somatic complaints are in response to the anticipated separation, and will lessen when the threat of separation is removed. In many cases, however, the physical symptoms are exaggerated to gain attention or postpone separation (Eisen and Kearney, 1995).

In the current version of the Diagnostic and Statistical Manual of Mental Disorders (DSM-IV; APA, 1994), SAD is the only anxiety disorder based on specific child criteria. The remaining anxiety disorder categories (e.g., panic disorder, social and specific phobias, obsessive-compulsive disorder) are based on adult criteria. DSM-IV SAD requires evidence of at least three (of eight) separation-related symptoms that cause (1) significant interference in social and academic functioning and (2) continuous disturbance for at least one month. These impairment criteria are important given that young children often experience developmentally appropriate separation anxiety (Rutter, 1981).

SAD can be differentiated from other anxiety disorders/problems by examining the context in which the symptoms occur. For example, school refusal behaviour is often observed in children with SAD (Last and Strauss, 1990). However, although school refusal behaviour may serve as a consequence of SAD, it is often also associated with other disorders and situations including specific phobias, social and generalized anxiety, and mood disorders (Kearney, 1995).

Children with specific phobias may fear situations related to school attendance (e.g., school building, teacher, and academic performance). In this case, the child's anxiety is related to specific school issues rather than the experience of separation from primary caregivers. Children with social anxiety may avoid school because of poor peer relations or fear of embarrassment in performance-based situations (e.g., giving an oral report, gym class). The anxiety, however, is directly related to the social situation rather than any discomfort associated with the absence of the caregiver. In addition, school refusal behaviour may be related to generalized anxiety disorder (GAD) or the presence of a mood disorder. Children with GAD tend to experience anxiety that is chronic in nature, lacks situational specificity and occurs even when the attachment figure is present. The presence of a mood disorder, particularly a major depressive episode, can be associated with problematic school attendance, poor peer relations, and academic problems. Careful assessment can help distinguish the function(s) of school refusal behaviour (Kearney, 1995). Panic attacks may also be observed in children with SAD whose intense anxiety over separation provokes the attack. This should be differentiated from panic disorder which involves recurrent panic attacks uncued in nature as well as a fear of having additional attacks (APA, 1994). Concern regarding the implications of panic attacks (e.g., losing control) is not characteristic of youngsters experiencing anxiety disorders in general, and SAD in particular.

Epidemiology

SAD is the most common anxiety disorder of childhood (Last et al., 1987). Prevalence estimates from community samples range from 3% to 5% for children (Anderson et al., 1987; Bird et al., 1988) and 0.01% to 2.4% for adolescents (Bowen et al., 1990; Fergussen et al., 1993; McGee et al., 1992). Prevalence estimates from childhood anxiety specialty clinics are appreciably greater. For example, Last and colleagues (1987) reported that SAD accounted for 33% of admissions compared to 15% of admissions for generalized anxiety, school phobia, and major depression, respectively.

SAD is more commonly observed in girls than boys (Last *et al.*, 1987, 1992). However, differences in symptomatology appear to be more a function of age rather than gender differences. For example, pre-school children often experience nightmares with separation-related themes. School-age and older children are more likely to experience intense discomfort upon separation and somatic complaints on school days, respectively (Francis *et al.*, 1987).

Risk Factors

A number of risk factors have been linked to the development and maintenance of childhood anxiety disorders in general and SAD in particular. In this section, we review familial/genetic, neurobiological, cognitive and psychosocial risk factors.

FAMILIAL/GENETIC INFLUENCES

Familial factors have been linked to the development of anxiety disorders in youth. Studies examining offspring of parents with anxiety disorders suggest that children are at risk for developing anxiety disorders themselves (Fyer *et al.*, 1990; Silverman *et al.*, 1988; Turner *et al.*, 1987; Weissman *et al.*, 1984). For example, Weissman and colleagues (1984) found that children of mothers with anxiety disorders (depression, panic, or GAD) had greater rates of SAD, panic, OCD and phobias compared to normal controls. Similarly, Silverman and colleagues demonstrated that children of parents with anxiety disorders not only displayed greater rates of anxiety symptoms but were more likely to receive a diagnosis if parental avoidance levels were strong. More strikingly, Turner and colleagues revealed that children of parents with anxiety disorders were seven times more likely to develop anxiety disorders than children of normal controls.

A number of studies have evaluated familial aggregation of anxiety disorders by examining the relatives of children who have been diagnosed with anxiety disorders. The majority of studies suggest that relatives of anxious youth have higher rates of anxiety disorders than relatives of children with other disorders or without any psychiatric history (Last *et al.*, 1987, 1991; Swedo *et al.*, 1989). For example, *Last et al.* (1991) examined the relatives of children with anxiety disorders, attention-deficit hyperactivity disorder (ADHD) or without any psychiatric history. The results revealed that relatives of anxious youth had the highest rates of anxiety disorders compared to the other groups. However, specific familial aggregation for anxiety disorders has not always emerged. For example, Livingston and colleagues (1985) demonstrated that affective disorders (probable depression, bipolar disorder) and alcoholism were more common than anxiety disorders in the relatives of children diagnosed with overanxious disorder (OAD) and SAD. In fact, only one relative (out of a sample of sixty-nine) was diagnosed with an anxiety disorder. Other studies support the finding that psychopathology in families of anxious youth is not limited to anxiety (Bell-Dolan *et al.*, 1990).

Collectively, these studies support the familial aggregation of anxiety disorders. However, both the mechanism of transmission (e.g., avoidance behaviour, parental psychopathology) and specificity of effects remains unclear. Furthermore, given the design of family studies, the contributions of genetics and family environment cannot be disentangled. Twin studies are needed to provide estimates of heritability.

Adult twin studies suggest a genetic transmission for anxiety disorders (Silove *et al.*, 1995; Torgersen, 1983). For example, Torgersen (1983) demonstrated that monozygotic (MZ) compared to dizygotic (DZ) twins had higher concordance rates (34% versus 17%) for any anxiety disorder. In a retrospective twin study, Silove *et al.* (1995) revealed that adults with panic disorder often experienced separation anxiety as children. Although these studies suggest genetic influence, the characteristics being transmitted remain unclear (e.g., temperamental variation, general biological vulnerability).

Twin studies during childhood and adolescence support environmental influences in the etiology of SAD and genetic variation for generalized anxiety. For example, Topolski *et al.* (1997) conducted a longitudinal study examining 543 MZ and 528 DZ twin pairs for SAD and 637 MZ and 630 DZ twin pairs for manifest anxiety. Manifest anxiety was measured by the Revised Children's Manifest Anxiety Scale (Reynolds and Richman, 1978). Symptom counts for SAD and OAD was measured by the Child and Adolescent Psychological Assessment (CAPS; Angold *et al.*, 1995) semi-structured interview. Model-fitting techniques were employed to examine additive genetic and shared environmental influences. The results revealed that additive genetic variation contributed little to the development of SAD. The heritability estimate was 0.04 when based on child reports. Alternatively, heritability estimates for manifest anxiety and OAD were 0.57 and 0.37, respectively. Regarding, shared environmental effects, the heritability estimate for SAD was 0.40. The authors suggested that attachment, sibling imitation, and negative life events were likely mechanisms. Surprisingly, shared environmental effects played a limited role for manifest anxiety and OAD. It is important to keep in mind that evaluation of anxiety in this study was limited to child reports.

Thapar and McGuffin (1995) reported a similar heritability estimate for manifest anxiety (0.59) when based on parent report. However, when the child was the respondent, shared environmental effects accounted for the data. Thus, genetic and environmental influences may vary depending upon who is the respondent. Overall, data from twin studies (child and adult) suggest a general biological vulnerability (Silove *et al.*, 1995) and moderate environmental influences in the development of SAD.

NEUROBIOLOGICAL INFLUENCES

Neurobiological dimensions of anxiety have been implicated in both animals and humans in the form of emotional reactivity (Suomi, 1981; Sapolsky, 1990) and neuroticism (Bouchard, 1994), respectively. However, the construct of behavioural inhibition is becoming increasingly recognized as an important neurobiological risk factor for anxiety disorders in general, and SAD in particular (Biederman *et al.*, 1990, 1993; Rosenbaum *et al.*, 1988).

Behavioural inhibition has been initially characterized by high motor activity (e.g., elevated heart rate) and high crying/fretting to novel stimuli. In early childhood, behavioural inhibition often translates to general fearfulness, cautiousness, irritability, and clinging/dependent behaviour. Behaviourally inhibited infants may be predisposed to possessing lower thresholds of excitability. Ten to fifteen percent of infants may be classified as behaviourally inhibited (Kagan, 1989). Evidence suggests that behaviourally inhibited infants may be more prone to developing anxiety disorders compared to their uninhibited counterparts. For example, children with parents who have anxiety disorders are more likely to display behavioural inhibition than children whose parents have other psychiatric disorders (Rosenbaum *et al.*, 1988). In another study, Biederman *et al.* (1990) examined the relationship between behavioural inhibition and the prevalence of childhood anxiety disorders. The study evaluated three groups of children, aged 5 to 8 years, and classified them as inhibited or uninhibited. One group had parents with a history of psychiatric disorders and another were considered healthy controls since there was an absence of medical or psychiatric problems. The prevalence of childhood anxiety disorders was based on a structured interview administered to parents. The results revealed that 27.8% of the behaviourally inhibited children met criteria for multiple anxiety disorders. Alternatively, none of the uninhibited children or healthy controls met these standards. Although behavioural inhibition appears to be an important neurobiological risk factor, the fact that most children failed to develop anxiety disorders underscores the importance of examining cognitive and psychosocial influences.

COGNITIVE INFLUENCES

In this section we discuss the role of cognitions in the development and maintenance of childhood anxiety and its disorders. Studies suggest that cognitive biases are associated with adult anxiety disorders (Butler and Mathews, 1983). Given that adults often report experiencing anxiety as children (Mattison, 1992), investigators are beginning to examine the nature of cognitive influences in anxious youth. Studies suggest that anxious children experience similar cognitive biases as adults with anxiety disorders. For example, compared to their non-anxious counterparts, children with anxiety disorders are more likely to attend to threatening cues (Dagleish and Watts, 1990), become distracted by worrisome thoughts (Prins et al., 1994), interpret ambiguous situations as threatening (Barrett et al., 1996; Chorpita et al., 1996) and focus on negative outcomes (Chorpita et al., 1996; Leitenberg et al., 1986).

Daleiden and Vasey (1997) described an information-processing model of childhood anxiety that targets these attentional, interpretive, and goal-oriented biases, and suggests cognitive mechanisms of change. Regarding attentional mechanisms, the model suggests attempting to clarify the nature of imminent threats. For example, distinguishing remote from genuine, possible from actual, and minor from severe threats, helps the anxious child attend less exclusively to threatening cues. In addition, modifying cognitive distortions appear to be fruitful targets of change. For example, a number of studies suggest that non-negative or healthy thinking (Kendall and Chansky, 1991) is more likely to be associated with behaviour change than positive thought processes (Eisen and Silverman, 1998; Prins et al., 1994). Finally, the model recommends problem-solving strategies to help anxious youth determine appropriate goals, and learn to regulate and cope with anxiety-provoking situations.

Along with identifying and modifying cognitive biases associated with childhood anxiety and its disorders, it is important to target family environments as well. For example, recent research suggests that both anxious youth and their parents process ambiguous information as threatening and are more likely to choose avoidant solutions than non-anxious youth and their families (Barrett *et al.*, 1996; Chorpita *et al.*, 1996). In addition, these studies also suggest that familial processing style may actually reinforce anxious children's cognitive biases. More recently, it has been shown that family environments that offer children minimal personal control are associated with childhood anxiety (Chorpita *et al.*, 1998).

Overall, cognitive biases play a role in the development and maintenance of childhood anxiety and its disorders. It remains unclear, however, whether these biases precede or accompany childhood anxiety. Additionally, these biases need to be examined in the context of a child's family environment.

PSYCHOSOCIAL INFLUENCES

In this section, we highlight the importance of parent-child attachment, family maintenance factors, and peers relations in the development and maintenance of separation anxiety.

Parent-Child Attachment: Bowlby (1973) suggested that separation anxiety was the result of adverse family influences or experiences (e.g., parental illness or repeated threats of abandonment). Through family interactions, children develop internal working models of the self. If the attachment figure satisfies a child's need for comfort, protection, as well as autonomy, the child's internal working model is likely to be competent. Alternatively, if the caregiver fails to meet these needs or is emotionally unavailable, the child's internal working model is likely to be unworthy. Such a model may result in distorted ways of processing (e.g., sources of threat) and predispose children to experiencing anxiety (Rubin and Mills, 1991).

Children who experience separation anxiety are likely to have an insecure-ambivalent attachment to the primary caregiver (Ollendick, 1998). This attachment style is characterized by a child's difficulty separating, exploring, and being comforted by the caregiver (Mattis and Ollendick, 1997), and is thought to result from an insensitive and inconsistent family environment (Isabella, 1993). A number of studies with anxious youth have characterized their families as higher in control and conflict and lower in warmth and support than the families of children without internalizing problems (Baumrind, 1989; Siqueland *et al.*, 1996).

Current developmental models suggest that attachment classification play an important role in the etiology of anxiety disorders. For example, Rubin and Mills (1991) outlined a pathway to anxiety disorders stemming from the interaction of temperament, family socialization experiences, and contextual conditions (e.g., stress, poverty). Their model suggests that temperamental wariness indirectly influence the security of attachment. For example, an infant's high intensity, fearful temperament may prompt the caregiver to become overprotective and overinvolved in attempt to soothe the infant. As a result, the infant's bids for exploration become restricted and an insecure attachment may develop. Keep in mind, however, that most children who develop anxiety disorders are not classified as having a behaviourally inhibited temperament (Rosenbaum et al., 1988).

Recently, Ollendick (1998) adapted Barlow's model (Barlow, 1988) to explain the development of childhood separation anxiety and its link with adult panic disorder. The model integrates biological and psychological sources of vulnerability. For example, biological vulnerability stems from a behaviourally inhibited temperament, characterized by heightened sympathetic activity under stress. Within this framework, the experience of separation may activate a strong neurobiological stress response (Rosenbaum et al., 1988).

Psychological sources of vulnerability stem from parent-child interaction patterns leading to internal working models of the world as unpredictable and uncontrollable. Ollendick suggests an insecure-ambivalent attachment captures the unpredictable-uncontrollable dimensions of the youngster's family environment and helps to explain the child's difficulties in separating, exploring and reuniting with the caregiver. As biological and psychological sources of vulnerability interact, the youngster becomes vulnerable to heightened reactions to separation-anxious events. Further sources of psychological vulnerability in the form of interoceptive conditioning and anxiety sensitivity (focus on internal somatic cues), maintain and intensify the cycle of anxious apprehension leading to the development of panic and possible agoraphobic avoidance.

Overall, both developmental models provide a useful framework for understanding the development of separation anxiety and adult panic disorder. Family maintenance factors, however, can help explain the durability and intensity of SAD.

Family Maintenance Factors: Eisen and colleagues (1998) outlined a parent-training program for SAD that addresses family maintenance factors. Parents of children with SAD often unknowingly reinforce their child's anxiety by falling prey to three traps. These include overprotection, excessive reassurance, and aversive parent-child interactions.

Parental overprotection occurs when a parent restricts a child from participating in potentially anxiety-provoking situations (e.g., playing contact sports, attending a relative's funeral). Overprotection is fueled by a parent's desire to keep their child safe and to minimize their own anxiety. Although parental overprotection is common and to some degree expected in these turbulent times, the nature of a child's SAD (i.e., preoccupation with harm) may stimulate a caregiver's protectiveness. Overall, if excessive restrictions occur, a child may be ill equipped to handle appropriate challenges and prone to experiencing anxiety. In addition, an overprotective family environment hampers an exposure-based treatment program for SAD.

In addition to protecting children from anxiety-provoking scenarios, parents of children with SAD often use excessive reassurance to comfort their child's fears/worries (e.g., "Don't worry", "Everything will be okay") of tragic outcomes. By doing so, a parent serves as the coping mechanism, and limits their child's opportunities to develop independent problem-solving skills.

Finally, the third trap is grounded in aversive parent-child interactions. In the event that a child experiences persistent separation anxiety, at times, frustrated parents may resort to more punitive methods (e.g., reprimands, punishment) to cease their child's fearful displays. The second and third traps encourage separation anxiety because the parent provides attention (positive or negative) during a child's fearful displays. A parent training program for SAD shifts these contingencies by encouraging parents to attend to their child's coping efforts and to ignore signals of anxious apprehension. This can be accomplished by utilizing differential reinforcement, shaping, and contingency management procedures (Eisen et al., 1998; Silverman, 1989).

Peer Relations: Like problematic family influences, poor peer relations may also place children at risk for experiencing psychopathology in general (Kupersmidt and Coie, 1990) and internalizing disorders (LaGreca and Stone, 1993) in particular. Poor peer relations in childhood are often associated with a rejected or neglected sociometric status. Rejected children tend to be actively excluded from the peer group whereas neglected children are largely ignored (LaGreca and Fetter, 1995). Both groups are at risk for experiencing internalizing disorders but rejected children are more likely to experience externalizing problems (Coie et al., 1990).

Children experiencing social anxiety are likely to have trouble initiating and maintaining peer activities (Vernberg *et al.*, 1992). Anxious
youth tend to have fewer friends than average, even when social
anxiety plays a minimal role (Eisen and Kearney, 1995). For example,
in the case of SAD, a child's refusal to leave the caregiver and/or their
preoccupation with harm may hamper both the frequency and quality
of peer interactions.

A number of studies have examined the relationship between peer
sociometric status and internalizing problems and/or disorders. For
example, Strauss and colleagues (1987) compared teacher ratings of
child anxiety with a peer nomination procedure. The results revealed
that children who were rated as highly anxious by their teachers were
more likely to be rated as shy and withdrawn by their peers.

Strauss and colleagues (1989) followed up their initial finding with two
studies examining sociometric status in carefully defined samples of
children with internalizing and externalizing disorders. Both studies
included a nonreferred peers control group. Overall, it was revealed that
anxious youth were more likely to be neglected and less socially competent than the other groups. Children with externalizing disorders did
experience social skill deficits, but the anxious sample was seen as more
shy and withdrawn. It is important to keep in mind, however, that 63%
of the children with anxiety disorders did not display problems in peer
status. Further research is necessary to determine the role of peers in the
development and maintenance of anxiety and its disorders.

PROTECTIVE FACTORS

A number of protective factors have been found to be associated with
positive long-term outcome irrespective of a child's diagnosis. These
include intelligence, quality of socialization, adequate coping skills and
emotional support both within and outside the home (Masten and
Coatsworth, 1995). Specific to SAD, protective factors in the form of
family, school, and peer interventions may help children negotiate the
experience of separation, and by doing so, may weaken or deactivate
strong neurobiological stress responses. For example, a secure attachment between parent and child facilitates the likelihood that an infant
will readily explore and separate from the primary caregiver. Similarly,
parent training interventions (Sheeber and McDevitt, 1998) can help
parents understand a child's temperament as well as to foster both
developmental competencies and problem-solving skills in their children (Fagot, 1996). In addition to helping children negotiate the expe-

rience of separation anxiety, interventions should also target other areas of vulnerability (e.g., cognitive biases, and poor peer relations) that may contribute to anxious apprehension. Early intervention efforts to promote child, family, and school-based competencies (Barrett *et al.*, 1996) are beginning to emerge and may help place the anxious child on more adaptive developmental pathways.

Comorbidity

Anxious youth rarely present for treatment with a single disorder. In children with SAD, 79% were found to have at least one other disorder, and 54% were found with two or more additional disorders. Overanxious disorder (OAD) was the most commonly occurring disorder, found in one third of the children with SAD. Other anxiety disorders likely to coexist with SAD were social phobia (8.3%) and simple phobia (12.5%) (Last *et al.*, 1987).

Recent research has supported the co-occurrence of SAD in children with OCD. Although prevalence estimates for SAD with OCD typically range between 4% and 7% (Brynska and Wolanczyk, 1998; Spence, 1997), rates have been found to be as high as 24% to 34% in OCD patients (Geller *et al.*, 1996; Valleni-Basile *et al.*, 1994).

Given the association between anxiety and depression in children (Brady and Kendall, 1992), it's not surprising that SAD is frequently comorbid with depression. As many as one third of children with SAD develop a depressive disorder (Last *et al.*, 1987, 1996). Bernstein and Garfinkel (1986) found comorbid anxiety and depression in 61.9% of a sample of children with school refusal behaviour. This finding is compelling given that as many as 75% of children with SAD also experience some form of school refusal behaviour (Last *et al.*, 1992). Finally, behaviour disorders are also likely to co-exist with SAD. Attention-deficit hyperactivity disorder (16.7%), oppositional-defiant disorder (16.7%), and enuresis (8.3%) were found to be the most frequent comorbid disorders with SAD (Last *et al.*, 1987).

Course and Outcome

Separation anxious symptoms often begin as innocuous complaints (e.g., stomachache, and nightmare) to parental separation. Such symptoms may serve an attention-getting function or are the result of genuine fearfulness associated with anticipated harm to the child and/or caregiver. The frequency and intensity of the child's symptoms often is determined by the degree of parental accommodation. For example, allowing a child to miss school or sleep in the parental bed may strengthen the child's initial symptoms. If the accommodation becomes consistent and excessive, parental efforts to foster indepen- dence are often resisted with fierce temper tantrums. SAD may adversely affect school performance (e.g., marginal attendance, preoccupation with separation), peer relations/extracurricular activities (e.g., refusal to participate without caregiver present), and family life (e.g., power struggles surrounding child's avoidance, restricted social activities of caregiver).

SAD can be chronic in nature but is more commonly triggered by life transitions. Typical events include becoming integrated to novel environments (school, neighborhood), or coping with major stressors (e.g., divorce, family illness). The course for SAD generally follows a developmental progression. For example, younger children (7 to 8 years) tend to experience fewer and less distressing symptoms (e.g., nightmares with themes of separation) whereas older children and adolescents experience greater avoidance levels and frequent somatic complaints (Francis et al., 1987; Last, 1991). Evidence suggests that separation anxious symptoms may linger into adulthood. Young adults experiencing separation anxiety have been found to have greater adjustment problems, tension, worry, and somatic complaints than individuals who reported SAD only as children (Ollendick et al., 1993).

Although SAD may be experienced throughout the lifespan, most children are able to negotiate the related difficulties. Some youngsters, however, remain vulnerable to developing anxiety disorders in adult- hood. A number of investigations (Ayuso et al., 1989; Laraia et al., 1994; Yeragani et al., 1989) have supported the link between SAD in childhood and panic disorder in adulthood. In general, these studies suggested that adult patients with panic disorder and agoraphobia (PD- Ag) had higher rates of separation anxiety as children compared to other disorders. However, these findings need to be interpreted with caution due to strong methodological constraints. For example, the majority of studies were retrospective in nature, employed differing definitions PD-Ag and SAD/school phobia, utilized problematic assessment measures, and failed to account for diagnostic comorbidity. In addition, several studies have either failed to demonstrate this association (Thyer *et al.*, 1986) or suggested that SAD served as general risk factor for adult anxiety disorders (Lipsitz *et al.*, 1994; van derMolen *et al.*, 1989).

In an attempt to improve retrospective assessment of SAD, Silove *et al.*, (1993) developed the Separation Anxiety Symptom Inventory (SASI), a self-report measure designed to assess childhood separation anxious experiences. Using the SASI, Silove and colleagues (Silove and Manicavasagar, 1993; Silove *et al.*, 1993, 1995) demonstrated that childhood separation anxiety was associated with a lifetime history of panic disorder. Overall, the bulk of the literature supports a link between early SAD and PD. It remains unclear, however, whether SAD is exclusively associated with PD or represents a general risk factor for anxiety disorders in adulthood (Lipsitz *et al.*, 1994; van der Molen *et al.*, 1989).

Assessment

A range of assessment methods is available to assess childhood anxiety disorders in general and SAD in particular. These include structured interviews, behavioural observations, and self-report and physiological measures.

Several structured interviews have been developed to assess child psychopathology in general and anxiety disorders in particular. These include the Diagnostic Interview Schedule for Children (DISC; Costello *et al.*, 1984), Schedule for Affective Disorders and Schizophrenia for School-Age Children (K-SADS; Puig-Antich and Chambers, 1978), Diagnostic Interview Schedule for Children and Adolescents (DICA; Herjanic and Reich, 1982) and the Anxiety Disorders Interview Schedule for Children (ADIS-C; Silverman and Nelles, 1988).

In general, each of these interview schedules have demonstrated adequate psychometric properties (Silverman, 1991). However, in our work with anxious youth, we employ the most recent version of the ADIS-C, which is based on DSM-IV (Silverman and Albano, 1996). The ADIS-C and the ADIS-P (parent version) provide the most comprehensive coverage of DSM-IV anxiety disorders. In addition, the section on SAD covers anxiety symptoms and etiology, provides a functional analysis of the disorder, and even covers early developmental precursors. The ADIS-C and ADIS-P also permits differential diagnosis of the majority of other child behaviour disorders and/or problems.

In addition to structured interviews, self-report measures are useful in identifying important characteristics of anxiety disorders (e.g., anxiety sensitivity, worry) and features of SAD. Measures that are especially relevant for SAD include the State-Trait Anxiety Inventory for Children (STAIC; Spielberger, 1973), Fear Survey Schedule for Children—Revised (FSSC-R; Ollendick, 1983), Revised Children's Manifest Anxiety Scale (RCMAS; Reynolds and Richman, 1978) and the Child Anxiety Sensitivity Index (CASI; Silverman *et al.,* 1991).

The STAIC contains two 20-item scales that measure state (variable) and trait (stable or chronic) anxiety. Both scales possesses strong psychometric properties (Spielberger, 1973), and contain relevant items for assessing SAD. For example, "I worry about school" and "I worry about my parents." The trait version has been found to be sensitive to treatment outcome (Eisen and Silverman, 1998).

The FSSC-R contains 80 items, possesses strong psychometric properties (Ollendick, 1983), and measures general fearfulness. Relevant items for assessing SAD include "Having to go to school," "Being alone" and "Being left at home with a sitter." The FSSC-R has been shown to discriminate overanxious children from those who fear going to school (Last *et al.,* 1989).

Because children with SAD often experience comorbid anxiety disorders, it is helpful to include the RCMAS and CASI in the assessment process. The RCMAS contains 37 items, possesses strong psychometric properties, and yields four subscales including worry/oversensitivity (e.g., "I worry when I go to bed at night), physiological (e.g., "Often I feel sick in my stomach), concentration (e.g., "I have trouble making up my mind) and lying (e.g., "I am always good). The four subscales are helpful in determining treatment targets (e.g., relaxation for somatic complaints, cognitive techniques for worry) and whether or not the child responded in a truthful manner. In addition, elevated scores on the worry/oversensitivity index are useful for discriminating anxiety disorders from other psychiatric populations (Mattison *et al.,* 1988).

Similarly, the CASI is a useful measure to include when assessing anxiety disorders in general and SAD in particular. The CASI contains 18 items, possesses strong psychometric properties (Silverman *et al.,* 1991) and measures how aversive children view the experience of physical sensations (e.g., "It scares me when I feel shaky"). Many youngsters with SAD are afraid to experience uncomfortable physical feelings such as stomachaches or headaches. In our work with anxious youth, elevated scores on the CASI are characteristic of children with GAD and suggest relaxation-based interventions. Overall, the RCMAS and CASI are helpful in determining the nature of anxious apprehension in youngsters.

Given that discrepancies between parent and child self-reports often emerge (Barrios and Hartmann, 1988), parent-completed measures should also be part of the assessment process. The most widely used parent measure is the Child Behavior Checklist (CBCL; Achenbach, 1991a). The CBCL contains separate age and gender profiles, possesses strong psychometric properties, relies on a national normative base, and covers the range of internalizing and externalizing behaviour problems. Relevant subscales for assessing SAD include withdrawn, somatic complaints, and anxious/depressed.

In addition to affording a more complete clinical picture to emerge, parent self-reports should also assess parental psychopathology, especially anxiety (e.g., Fear Questionnaire; Marks and Mathews, 1979) and depression (Beck Depression Inventory; Beck *et al.*, 1961). Such measures can help determine the impact of parental problems on child behaviour disorders as well as a parent's ability to participate in a family-based treatment program.

Additional measures that can contribute to a multimethod-multi-source assessment include measures of family dynamics. The Family Environment Scale (FES; Moos and Moos, 1986) and the Family Adaptability and Cohesion Evaluation Scales-III (FACES-III; Olsen *et al.*, 1985) both possess strong psychometric properties and can be used to assess the family environments of anxious youth. The FES contains 90 items and ten subscales. Relevant subscales for assessing SAD include independence, cohesion, expressiveness and control. The FACES-III addresses the degree to which families are enmeshed, disengaged, separated or neglected. Research has suggested that separation anxiety is associated with enmeshed families (Pilkington and Piersel, 1991; Kearney and Silverman, 1995).

In addition to child, parent, and family measures, teacher reports are useful in the event that a child's difficulty separating from caregivers generalizes to the school environment. Teacher measures can help clarify the relationship between a child's academic performance and anxious apprehension. The most widely used teacher measure is the Teacher Report Form (TRF; Achenbach, 1991b). Like the CBCL, the TRF contains separate age and gender profiles, possesses strong psychometric properties, contains a national normative base and covers both internalizing and externalizing behaviour problems. In addition, the TRF examines a child's work habits and academic performance. In our work with anxious youth, a teacher's willingness to complete the TRF creates a liaison between the clinician, school and family, and helps to ensure a child's continued progress. In order to circumvent potential biases associated with child, parent, family and teacher self-report measures, behavioural observations should be incorporated into the assessment process. During therapy sessions, clinicians can make use of key signals of a child's anxious apprehension such as nervous laughter, crying, poor eye contact (Kendall, 1994). More importantly, behavioural observations can be measured during exposure-based assignments. In the clinic setting, children with SAD can be instructed to spend increasingly greater amounts of time alone (e.g., sitting in the waiting area). As a child develops their coping skills, exposures should become more anxiety-provoking. For example, a parent can be encouraged to spontaneously run an errand and leave the child with the therapist. At home, parents can monitor behavioural observations as they arrange for their child (under guidance of therapist) to remain alone in a variety of situations while varying the timing (day vs. night), duration, and predictability of the exposures.

Finally, physiological measures can be an important part of the assessment process, given frequent desynchrony across assessment modalities. Heart rate and sweat gland activity have been found to be useful in assessing changes associated with anxious apprehension (Silverman and Kearney, 1993). Although practical constraints often preclude their use, it is helpful to measure physiological indexes during behavioural observations. Children may respond in socially desirable ways when completing self-report measures or deny fear during behavioural observations. However, altering ones heart rate may prove too difficult a task. With portable digital pulse monitors available, clinicians can measure a child's pulse during separation-related exposures. Several reports have demonstrated the utility of measuring behavioural observations and physiological indexes concurrently (Beidel, 1988; Eisen and Silverman, 1991).

Intervention

COGNITIVE-BEHAVIOURAL TREATMENT METHODS

There is a paucity of controlled empirical studies investigating cognitive-behavioural interventions for SAD. The majority of SAD treatment studies are limited to descriptive case reports. For example, Thyer and

Sowers-Hoag (1988) reviewed 11 published case reports that utilized cognitive-behavioural treatment of SAD. Although the studies tended to be methodologically flawed, positive therapeutic results were generally demonstrated using operant techniques and systematic desensitization.

Recently, two large-scale cognitive-behavioural treatment outcome studies (Kendall, 1994; Kendall et al., 1997) have been conducted with anxious youth. Kendall (1994) conducted the first randomized clinical trial investigating the efficacy of cognitive-behavioural therapy with 47 children (aged 9–13 years) diagnosed with an anxiety disorder (SAD, OAD, avoidant disorder). Participants were randomly assigned to a 16 session cognitive-behavioural treatment (Kendall et al., 1990). Cognitive techniques (e.g., coping self-talk) as well as behavioural training strategies (e.g. modeling, in vivo exposure, role-play, relaxation training, and contingent reinforcement) were employed. Cognitive assessments, behavioural observations, and self, parent, and teacher-reports were used to evaluate treatment outcome. The results revealed that sixty-six percent of treated cases no longer met criteria for an anxiety disorder at posttreatment. Treatment gains were generally maintained at one-year follow-up.

Kendall et al. (1997) conducted a second randomized clinical trial of their integrated cognitive-behavioural treatment protocol with 94 children, aged 9–13 years, with primary anxiety disorder diagnoses (SAD, OAD, or avoidant disorder). Similar measures were utilized to evaluate treatment outcomes. The results revealed that over 50% of the participants failed to meet criteria for an anxiety disorder at posttreatment. Treatment gains were generally maintained at one-year follow-up. In addition, Kendall and Southam-Gerow (1996) reported that treatment gains of their integrated treatment protocol were largely maintained two to five years (mean = 3.35 years) after completing treatment (Kendall, 1994).

Although the findings from the two randomized clinical trials are impressive, the inclusion of multiple treatment components does not permit an isolation of the active ingredients responsible for behaviour change. To address this issue, Silverman and colleagues (in press) separately examined the effects of contingency management (CM), self-control (SC), and education/support (ES) in 81 children (6 to 16 years) with phobic disorders. The CM and SC groups contained an exposure-based component. In general, all three treatments produced clinical improvements on child and parent completed measures as well as structured diagnostic interviews. Specifically, 88%, 55%, and 56% of participants failed to meet diagnostic criteria at posttreatment for SC, CM, and ES, respectively. Surprisingly, the non-exposure ES group produced similar clinical improvements as the exposure-based groups. This was particularly true at follow-up. The lack of group differences underscores the importance of prescriptive treatment strategies, i.e., linking specific symptoms (e.g., worries, somatic complaints, avoidance behaviour) or functions (e.g., positive and negative reinforcement) with consistent treatment interventions (Eisen and Silverman, 1998 for GAD; Kearney and Silverman, 1990 for school refusal behaviour).

FAMILY-BASED TREATMENT METHODS

Family-based treatment studies with anxious youth are beginning to emerge given the importance of family variables in the etiology and maintenance of child anxiety and its disorders (Kearney and Silverman, 1995). For example, Barrett and colleagues (1996) examined a family-based treatment for childhood anxiety and found that parent intervention improved overall outcomes. Participants included children meeting diagnostic criteria for SAD (n = 30), OAD (n = 30) or social phobia (n = 19). Participants were randomly assigned to either cognitive-behavioural therapy (CBT), CBT plus family management (CBT + FAM), or a wait-list control group. In general, the results revealed that 69.8% of the children in the treatment groups failed to meet diagnostic criteria for an anxiety disorder at posttreatment. This was true for 26% of the control participants. In addition, seventy-three percent of the children treated with CBT and 95.6% of the children in the CBT + FAM condition did not meet diagnostic criteria at the 12-month follow-up. Regarding children with SAD, 77.8% were free from a diagnosis at posttreatment and 94.1% were without an anxiety disorder diagnosis at 12-month follow-up. Overall, cognitive-behavioural parent and/or family training programs appear promising in the treatment of anxiety disorders in general, and SAD in particular. However, more research is needed to address both the individual and additive contributions of family-based treatments to standardized, emprically proven CBT methods (Eisen et al., 1998).

PHARMACOLOGICAL TREATMENT METHODS

Psychopharmacologists have made notable progress in establishing the safety and efficacy of pharmacological therapy for childhood behaviour disorders (Gadow, 1992). Traditionally, most of the literature has concentrated on children with disruptive behaviour disorders, autism, or mental retardation. More recently, however, internalizing disorders such as depression and anxiety are receiving attention. In general, psychopharmacotherapy tends to be a controversial issue, with uncertainties regarding the appropriateness of medication (e.g., efficacy, safety, toxicity) or adequacies of clinical services (e.g., drug evaluation procedures, professional training) (Gadow, 1992).

Although the pharmacotherapy of SAD and school refusal behaviour has been extensively studied, data have demonstrated equivocal results. A limited number of controlled studies have examined the treatment of SAD with antidepressant agents (Berney et al., 1981; Bernstein et al., 1990; Birmaher et al., 1994; Gittelman-Klein and Klein, 1980; Klein et al., 1992). Data suggest therapeutic effects for the tricyclic, imipramine (IMI) and the specific serotonin reuptake inhibitor (SSRI), fluoxetine. For example, in a double-blind placebo-controlled study with children exhibiting school refusal behaviour, Gittelman-Klein and Klein found evidence supporting the therapeutic efficacy of IMI. Ninety-three percent of the children experienced separation anxiety. IMI was administered to the treatment group (n = 16) at 100 to 200 mg/day (mean dosage = 150 mg/day). There were 19 participants in the placebo control group. Both groups of children (ages 7 to 15) also received behaviourally-oriented therapy for 6 weeks. Child, parent, and clinician ratings demonstrated improvements with respect to somatic complaints, fearfulness, and separation anxiety. Children treated with IMI had an impressive rate of returning to school compared with children on placebo (i.e., 81% vs. 47%, respectively).

More recently, Birmaher et al. (1994) demonstrated the efficacy of fluoxetine (Prozac) for children and adolescents with SAD. Their study included 21 participants with OAD, social phobia (SOP) or SAD who were previously unresponsive to psychotherapy and pharmacological treatments. Participants were treated openly with fluoxetine (mean dose = 25.7 mg/day) for up to 10 months. Results indicated that fluoxetine was effective, safe, and well tolerated in these children. Specifically, 81% (n = 17) of the participants showed moderate to marked improvement in their anxiety symptoms based on clinical global ratings.

The promise of antidepressant treatment has not been realized in other investigations. For example, Berney et al. (1981) conducted a double-blind investigation with a heterogeneous sample of 46 children (ages 9 to 14) with school refusal behaviour (87% experienced significant separation anxiety). Clomipramine (CMI, Anafranil) was administered for 12 weeks with dosages ranging from 40 to 75 mg/day.

Concurrent with medication treatment, participants received individual therapy and casework was done with the parents. The results showed that CMI (n = 27) was not superior to a placebo (n = 19), and that half of the children treated with CMI continued to have difficulty attending school and/or experienced significant separation anxiety.

Contrary to previous findings, Klein et al. (1992) found that IMI demonstrated only marginal effectiveness when compared with placebo controls. Participants were first treated with behavioural therapy for 6 weeks. Participants who continued to meet full DSM-III-R diagnostic criteria for SAD then entered pharmacological treatment. Twenty-one of these children were randomly assigned to either an IMI (mean dosage = 153 mg/day) or placebo group for 6 weeks under double-blind conditions. Child, parent, teacher, and clinical ratings revealed that IMI showed no significant superiority compared to placebo (50% of participants improved in both IMI and placebo conditions). Klein and colleagues suggested that the small sample size, absence of school refusal behaviour, and presence of oppositional behaviour may have minimized IMI's therapeutic effect.

Benzodiazepines have also been utilized in the treatment of SAD. For example, Klein and Last (1989) examined the preliminary effects of alprazolam (APZ, Xanax) on 18 children diagnosed with SAD. Children received daily doses of 0.5 to 6.0 mg/day of APZ (mean = 1.9 mg/day) over a 6-week period. Participants were rated as significantly improved based on child (65%), parent and clinical (80%) reports.

Bernstein et al. (1990) compared the efficacy of APZ and IMI in two studies with children exhibiting school refusal behaviour. In the first study, there was an 8-week open trial of APZ (n = 10, mean dosage = 1.43 mg/day) or IMI (n = 7, mean dosage = 135 mg/day). In addition to the pharmacological treatment, participants received psychotherapy and were involved in a school reentry program. Clinical global ratings showed that 67% of children in both groups demonstrated significant improvement in symptoms of anxiety and depression.

To address methodological constraints of the first study (e.g., open trial, continuous therapy, use of only global ratings), the investigators utilized a double-blind placebo controlled design in the second study. Twenty-four children were randomly assigned to either an APZ (mean dosage = 1.82 mg/day), IMI (mean dosage = 164 mg/day), or placebo condition for 8 weeks and participated in a school reentry program. The results suggested that the clinician ratings favored the medication over placebo. However, the treatment groups did not differ significantly on measures of child anxiety and depression. Future comparative studies are needed to determine optimal drug agents for SAD.

Overall, the pharmacotherapy of SAD is extremely limited. Most studies are hampered by methodological constraints, including small sample sizes, diagnostic heterogeneity, brief active drug periods, continuous therapy, lack of placebo controls, reliance on clinical rating scales, and limited long-term follow-up data. Currently, there are no established guidelines for antidepressant or anxiolytic treatment for anxiety disorders in general and SAD in particular in youngsters (Eisen and Kearney, 1995). Thus, psychosocial treatments should be utilized as a first course of action when treating youngsters with SAD. If anxiety symptoms remain severe and chronic, and drug treatment is recommended, dosage levels should be determined by clinical response and presence of side effects (see Simeon and Wiggins, 1995).

PREVENTION

In a series of studies, the Queensland Early Intervention and Prevention of Anxiety Project (QEIPAP) demonstrated that early intervention efforts might prevent or reduce the rates of anxiety disorders in children. In the first investigation (Dadds et al., 1997), 1,786 children, aged 7 to 14, were initially screened for the presence of anxiety problems using child self-reports and teacher nominations. After several more screenings and diagnostic interviews, 128 children were selected to participate. Inclusionary criteria consisted of meeting DSM-IV criteria for primary anxiety disorders (moderate severity) or possessing features of anxiety without meeting full diagnostic criteria. Participants were randomly assigned to a 10-week school-based and parent-focused psychosocial intervention (Barrett et al., 1994) or a monitoring group. The monitoring group received no treatment but was monitored at key points throughout the study (i.e., post-treatment and follow-up). 4.9% and 3.0% of the intervention and monitoring groups, respectively, met diagnostic criteria for SAD. The results revealed that 54% of the children in the monitoring group who experienced features of anxiety, developed full-fledged anxiety disorders at the six-month follow-up point. Alternatively, only 16% of the children who received the intervention developed anxiety disorders. Thus, the results suggest that early intervention can reduce the rates of anxiety disorders.

In the second study, the QEIPAP group (Dadds et al., 1999) reported two-year follow-up data from their original sample. Rates of anxiety disorders were 20% and 39% for the intervention and monitoring groups, respectively. Predictors of poor adjustment in the children included the severity of initial problems, participating in the monitoring group, and elevated parental anxiety. Overall, these studies suggest the need for comprehensive models of assessing and treating anxious youth emphasizing early intervention and school/family-based treatment targets.

Concluding Remarks

Despite SAD's unique status as the only anxiety disorder in DSM-IV based solely on child criteria, the empirical treatment literature is not as well developed as for other disorders. Most studies of psychosocial treatments, thus far, include only descriptive case reports which are methodologically flawed. In addition, investigations of pharmacological interventions have demonstrated inconsistent support for their effectiveness and utility, either alone or in combination with psychosocial treatments. While recent large-scale treatment outcome studies (Kendall, 1994; Kendall *et al.*, 1997) have supported the efficacy for cognitive-behavioural interventions for anxiety disorders in general and SAD in particular, further research is necessary for clinical researchers to develop prescriptive treatment strategies (Eisen and Silverman, 1998) for this population.

Family variables are becoming increasingly recognized as involved in the etiology and maintenance of SAD. Risk and protective factors need to be further studied and understood, to help children negotiate the experience of separation. The field is moving towards early intervention models emphasizing family, school, and developmental interventions. Such an approach is likely to help children and their families contain developmentally appropriate separation anxiety and place youngsters on more adaptive developmental pathways (Eisen and Kearny, 1995; Wachtel and Strauss, 1995).

References

Achenbach, T.M. (1991a). *Manual for the Child Behavior Checklist/4–18 and 1991 Profile*. Burlington, VT: University of Vermont, Department of Psychiatry.
Achenbach, T.M. (1991b) *Manual for the Teacher's Report Form and 1991 Profile*. Burlington, VT: University of Vermont, Department of Psychiatry.

American Psychiatric Association (1994). *Diagnostic and Statistical Manual of Mental Disorders* (4th ed.). Washington, DC: American Psychiatric Association.

Anderson, J.C., Williams, S., McGee, R., & Silva, P.A. (1987). DSM-III disorders in re-adolescent children: Prevalence in a large sample from the general population. *Archives of General Psychiatry, 44,* 69–76.

Angold, A., Pendergast, M., Cox, A., *et al.* (1995). The child and adolescent psychiatric assessment. *Psychological Medicine, 25,* 729–753.

Ayuso, J., Alfonso, S., & Rivera, A. (1989). Childhood separation anxiety and panic disorder: A comparative study. *Progress in Neuropsychopharmacology and Biological Psychiatry, 13,* 665–671.

Barlow, D.H. (1988). *Anxiety and its disorders: The nature and treatment of anxiety and panic.* New York: Guilford Press.

Barett, P.M., Dadds,M.R., & Holland, D.E. (1994). *The coping koala: Prevention Manual.* Unpublished manuscript. The University of Queensland, Queensland, Australia.

Barrett, P.M., Dadds, M.R., & Rapee, R.M. (1996). Family treatment of childhood anxiety: A controlled trial. *Journal of Consulting and Clinical Psychology, 64,* 333–342.

Barrett, P.M., Rapee, R.M., Dadds, M.R., & Ryan, S.M. (1996). Family enhancement of cognitive style in anxious and aggressive children. *Journal of Abnormal Child Psychology, 24,* 187–203.

Barrios, B.A. & Hartmann, D.P. (1988). Fears and anxieties in children. In E.J. Mash & L.G. Terdal (Eds.), *Behavioral assessment of childhood Disorders,* 2nd ed., (pp. 196–262). New York: Pergamon.

Baumrind, D. (1989). Rearing competent children. In W. Darmon (Ed.), *Child development today and tomorrow.* San Francisco: Jossey-Bass.

Beck, A.T., Ward, C.H., Mendelson, M., *et al.* (1961). An inventory for measuring depression. *Archives of General Psychiatry, 41,* 561–571.

Beidel, D.C. (1988). Psychophysiological assessment of anxious emotional states in children. *Journal of Abnormal Psychology, 97,* 60–82.

Bell-Dolan, D.J., Last, C.G., & Strauss, C.C. (1990). Symptoms of anxiety disorders in normal children. *Journal of the American Academy of Child and Adolescent Psychiatry, 29,* 759–765.

Berney, T., Klovin, I., Bhate, S.R. Gauside, R.F., Jeans, J., Kay, B., & Scarth, L. (1981). School phobia: A therapeutic trial with clomipramine and short-term outcome. *British Journal of Psychiatry, 138,* 110–118.

Bernstein, G.A., Garfinkel, B.D., & Borchardt, C.M. (1990). Comparative studies of pharmacotherapy for school refusal. *Journal of the American Academy of Child and Adolescent Psychiatry, 29,* 773–781.

Bernstein, G. & Garfinkel, B. (1986). School phobia: The overlap of affective and anxiety disorders. *Journal of the American Academy of Child and Adolescent Psychiatry, 25,* 235–241.

Biederman, J., Rosenbaum, J.F., Bolduc-Murphy, E.A., Faraone, S.V., Chaloff, J., Hirshfeld, D.R., & Kagan, J. (1993). Behavioral Inhibition as a temperamental risk factor for anxiety disorders. *Child and Adolescent Psychiatric Clinics of North America, 2,* 667–684.

Biederman, J., Rosenbaum, J.F., Hirshfeld, D.R., Faraone, S.V., Bolduc, E., Gersten, M., Meminger, S., & Reznick, S. (1990). Psychiatric correlates of behavioral inhibition in young children of parents with and without psychiatric disorders. *Archives of General Psychiatry, 47,* 21–26.

Bird, H.R., Canino, G., Rubio-Stipec, M., *et al.* (1988). Estimates of the prevalence ofchildhood maladjustment in a community survey in Puerto Rico: The use of combined measures. *Archives of General Psychiatry, 45,* 1120–1126.

Birmaher, B., Waterman, S., Ryan, N., Cully, M., Balach, L., Ingram, J., & Brodsky, M. (1994). Fluoxetine for childhood anxiety disorders. *Journal of the American Academy of Child and Adolescent Psychiatry, 33,* 993–999.

Bowen, R.C., Offord, D.R., & Boyle, M.H. (1990). The prevalence of overanxious disorder and separation anxiety disorder: Results from the Ontario child health study. *Journal of the American Academy of Child and Adolescent Psychiatry 29,* 753–758.

Bowlby, J. (1973). *Attachment and loss: Vol. 2. Separation.* New York: Basic Books.

Brady, E. & Kendall, P.C. (1992). Comorbidity of anxiety and depression in children and adolescents. *Psychological Bulletin, 111,* 244–255.

Brynska, A. & Wolanczyk, T. (1998). Obsessive-compulsive disorder and separation anxiety. *Journal of the American Academy of Child and Adolescent Psychiatry, 37,* 350–351.

Bouchard, T.J. (1994). Genes, environment, and personality. *Science, 264,* 1700–1701.

Butler, G. & Mathews, A. (1983). Cognitive processes in anxiety. *Advances in Behaviour Research and Therapy, 5,* 51–62.

Chorpita, B.F., Albano, A.M., & Barlow, D.H. (1996). Cognitive processing in children: Relationship to anxiety and family influences. *Journal of Clinical Child Psychology, 25,* 170–176.

Chorpita, B.F., Brown, T.A., & Barlow, D.H. (1998). Perceived control as a mediator of family environment in etiological models of childhood anxiety. *Behavior Therapy, 29,* 457–476.

Coie, J.D., Dodge, K.A., & Kupersmidt, J.B. (1990). Peer group behavior and social status. In S.R. Asher & J.D. Coie (Eds.), *Peer rejection in childhood.* Cambridge, MA: Cambridge University Press.

Costello, A.J., Edelbrock, C.S., Dulcan, M.K., Kalas, R., & Klaric, S.H. (1984). *Report to NIMH on the NIMH Diagnostic Interview Schedule for Children (DISC).* Washington, DC: National Institute of Mental Health.

Dadds, M.R., Holland, D.E., Spence, S.H., Laurens, K.R., Mullins, M., & Barrett, P.M. (1999). Early intervention and prevention of anxiety disorders in children: Results at 2-year follow-up. *Journal of Consulting and Clinical Psychology, 67,* 145–150.

Dadds, M.R., Spence, S.H., Holland, D.E., Barrett, P.M., & Laurens, K.R. (1997). Prevention and early intervention for anxiety disorders: A controlled trial. *Journal of Consulting and Clinical Psychology, 65,* 627–635.

Dagleish, T. & Watts, F.N. (1990). Biases of attention and memory in disorders of anxiety and depression. *Clinical Psychology Review, 10,* 589–604.

Daleiden, E.L. & Vasey, M.W. (1997). An information-processing perspective on childhood anxiety. *Clinical Psychology Review, 17,* 407–429.

Eisen, A.R., Engler, L.B., & Geyer, B. (1998). Parent training for separation anxiety disorder. In J.M. Briemeister & C.E. Schaefer (Eds.), *Handbook of Parent Training* (pp. 205–224). New York: John Wiley & Sons, Inc.

Eisen, A.R. & Kearney, C.A. (1995). *Practitioner's guide to treating fear and anxiety in children and adolescents: A cognitive behavioral approach.* Northvale, NJ: Jason Aronson Inc.

Eisen, A.R. & Silverman, W.K. (1998). Prescriptive treatment of generalized anxiety disorder in children. *Behavior Therapy, 29,* 105–121.

Eisen, A.R., & Silverman, W.K. (1991). Treatment of an adolescent with bowel movement phobia using self-control therapy. *Journal of Behavior Therapy and Experimental Psychiatry, 22,* 45–51.

Fagot, B. (1996). *Temperament and parent guidance.* Paper presented at the Occasional Temperament Conference, Eugene, Oregon.

Fergusson, D.M., Horwood, D.J., & Lynskey, M.T. (1993). Prevalence and comorbidity of DSM-III-R diagnoses in a birth cohort of 15 year olds. *Journal of the American Academy of Child and Adolescent Psychiatry, 32,* 1127–1134.

Francis, G., Last, C.G., & Strauss, C.C. (1987). Expression of separation anxiety disorder: The roles of gender and age. *Child Psychiatry and Human Development, 18,* 82–89.

Fyer, A.J., Mannuzza, S., Gallops, M.S., *et al.* (1990). Phobias and fears: A preliminary report. *Archives of General Psychiatry, 47,* 252–256.

Gadow, K.D. (1992). Clinical issues in child and adolescent psychopharmacology. Journal of Consulting and Clinical Psychology, 59, 842–852.

Geller, D., Biederman, J., Griffin, S., Jones, J., & Lefkowitz, T. (1996) Comorbidity of juvenile obsessive-compulsive disorder in children and adolescents: phenomenology and family history. *Journal of the American Academy of Child and Adolescent Psychiatry, 35,* 1637–1646.

Gittelman-Klein, R., & Klein, D.F. (1980). Separation anxiety in school refusal and its treatment with drugs. In R. Gittelman (Ed.), *Out of school* (pp. 188–203). New York: Guilford.

Herjanic, B., & Reich, W. (1982). Development of a structured psychiatric interview for children: Agreement between child and parent on individual symptoms. *Journal of Abnormal Child Psychology, 10,* 307–324.

Isabella, R.A. (1993). Origins of attachment: Maternal interactive behavior across the first year. *Child Development, 64,* 605–621.

Kagan, J. (1989). Temperamental contributions to social behavior. *American Psychologist, 44,* 668–674.

Kearney, C.A. (1995). School refusal behavior. In A.R., Eisen, C.A., Kearney, & C.E. Schaefer (Eds.), *Clinical handbook of anxiety disorders in children and adolescents.* Northvale, NJ: Jason Aronson.

Kearney, C.A., & Silverman, W.K. (1995). Family environment of youngsters with school refusal behavior: A synopsis with implications for assessment and treatment. *The American Journal of Family Therapy, 23,* 59–72.

Kearney, C.A. & Silverman, W.K. (1990). A preliminary analysis of a functional model of assessment and treatment for school refusal behavior. *Behavior Modification, 14,* 340–366.

Kendall, P.C. (1994). Treating anxiety disorders in children: Results of a randomized clinical trial. *Journal of Consulting and Clinical Psychology, 62,* 100–110.

Kendall, P.C. & Chansky, T.E. (1991). Considering cognition in anxiety-disordered Children. *Journal of Anxiety Disorders, 5,* 167–185.

Kendall, P.C., Flannery-Schroeder, E., Panichelli-Mindel, S.M., Southam-Gerow, M., Henin, A., & Warman, M. (1997). Therapy for youths with anxiety disorders: A second randomized clinical trial. *Journal of Consulting and Clinical Psychology, 65,* 366–380.

Kendall, P.C., Kane, M., Howard, B., & Siqueland, L. (1990). *Cognitive-behavioral treatment of anxious children: Therapist manual.*Philadelphia: Department of Psychology, Temple University.

Kendall, P.C. & Southam-Gerow, M.A. (1996). Long-term follow-up of a cognitive-behavioral therapy for anxiety-disordered youth. *Journal of Consulting and Clinical Psychology, 64,* 724–730.

Klein, R.G., Koplewicz, H.S., & Kanner, A. (1992). Imipramine treatment of children with separation anxiety disorder. *Journal of the American Academy of Child and Adolescent Psychiatry, 31,* 21–28.

Klein, R.G., & Last, C.G. (1989). Anxiety disorders in children. In A.E. Kazdin (Ed.), *Developmental Clinical Psychology and Psychiatry* (pp. 32–34). Newbury Park, CA: Sage.

Kupersmidt, J.B. & Coie, J.D. (1990). Preadolescent peer status, aggression, and school adjustment as predictors of externalizing problems in adolescense. *Child Development, 61,* 1350–1362.

LaGreca, A.M. & Fetter, M. (1995). Peer relations. In A.R.. Eisen, C.A., Kearney, & C.E. Schaefer (Eds.), *Clinical handbook of anxiety disorders in children and adolescents.* Northvale NJ: Jason Aronson.

LaGreca, A.M. & Stone, W.L., (1993). Social anxiety scale for children-revised: Factor structure and concurrent validity. *Journal of Clinical Child Psychology, 22,* 17–27.

Laraia, M.T., Stuart, G.W., Frye, L.H., Lydiard, R.B., & Ballenger, J.C. (1994). Childhood environment of women having panic disorder with agoraphobia. *Journal of Anxiety Disorders, 8,* 1–17.

Last, C.G. (1991). Somatic complaints in anxiety disordered children. *Journal of Anxiety Disorders, 5*, 125–138.

Last, C.G., Francis, G., & Strauss, C.C. (1989). Assessing fears in anxiety-disordered children with the Revised Fear Survey Schedule for Children (FSSC-R). *Journal of Clinical Child Psychology, 18*, 137–141.

Last, C.G., Hersen, M., Kazdin, A.E., Orvaschel, H., & Perrin, S. (1991). Anxiety disorders in children and their families. *Archives of General Psychiatry, 48*, 928–934.

Last, C.G., Hersen, M., Kazdin, A.E., Finkelstein, R., & Strauss, C.C. (1987). Comparison of DSM-III separation anxiety and overanxious disorders: Demographic characteristics and patterns of comorbidity. *Journal of the American Academy of Child Psychiatry, 26*, 527–531.

Last, C., Perrin, S., Hersen, M., & Kazdin, A. (1996). A prospective study of childhood anxiety disorders. *Journal of the American Academy of Child and Adolescent Psychiatry, 35*, 1502–1510.

Last, C.G., Perrin, S., Hersen, M., & Kazdin, A.E. (1992). DSM-III-R anxiety disorders in children: Socio-demographic and clinical characteristics. *Journal of the American Academy of Child and Adolescent Psychiatry, 31*, 1070–1076.

Last, C.G., Philips, J.E., & Statfield, A. (1987). Childhood anxiety disorders in mothers and their children. *Child Psychiatry and Human Development, 18*, 103–112.

Last, C. & Strauss, C. (1990). School refusal in anxiety-disordered children and adolescents. *Journal of the American Academy of Child and Adolescent Psychiatry, 29*, 31–35.

Last, C., Strauss, C., & Francis, G. (1987). Comorbidity among childhood anxiety disorders. *Journal of Nervous and Mental Disorders, 175*, 726–730.

Lease, C.A., & Strauss, C.C. (1993). Separation anxiety disorder. In R. T. Ammerman & M. Hersen (Eds.), *Handbook of behavior therapy with children and adults* (pp. 93–107). Boston: Allyn and Bacon.

Leitenberg, H., Yost, L.W., & Carroll-Wilson, M. (1986). Negative cognitive errors in children: Questionnaire development, normative data, and comparisons between children with and without self-reported symptoms of depression, low self-esteem, and evaluation anxiety. *Journal of Consulting and Clinical Psychology, 54*, 528–536.

Lipsitz, J.D., Martin, L.Y., Mannuzza, S., Chapman, T.F., Liebowitz, M.R., & Klein, D.F. (1994). Childhood separation anxiety disorder in patients with adult anxiety disorders. *American Journal of Psychiatry, 151*, 927–929.

Livingston, R., Nugent, H., Radar, L., & Smith, G.R. (1985). Family histories of depressed and severely anxious children. *American Journal of Psychiatry, 142*, 1497–1499.

Marks, I.M. & Mathews, A.M. (1979). Brief standard self-rating for phobic patients. *Behaviour Research and Therapy, 17*, 263–267.

Masten, A.S. & Coatsworth, J.D. (1995). Competence, resilience, and psychopathology. In D. Cicchetti and D.J. Cohen (Eds.), *Develolpmental psychopathology, vol 2: Risk, disorder, and adaptation* (pp. 715–752). New York: John Wiley & Sons.

Mattis, S.G. & Ollendick, T.H. (1997). Panic in children and adolescents: A developmental analysis. In T.H. Ollendick & R.J. Prinz (Eds.), *Advances in Clinical Child Psychology, 19,* (pp. 27–74). New York: Plenum.

Mattison, R.E. (1992). Anxiety disorders. In S.R. Hooper, G.W. Hynd, & R.E. Mattison (Eds.), *Child psychopathology: Diagnostic criteria and clinical assessment* (pp. 179–202). Hiilsdale, NJ: Erlbaum.

Mattison, R.E., Bagnatto, S.J., & Brubaker, B.H. (1988). Diagnostic utility of the revised children's manifest anxiety scale in children with DSM-III anxiety disorders. *Journal of Anxiety Disorders, 2,* 147–155.

McGee, R., Feehan, M., Williams, S., & Anderson, J. (1992). DSM-III disorders from age 11 to age 15 years. *Journal of the American Academy of Child and Adolescent Psychiatry, 31,* 50–59.

Moos, R.H., & Moos, B.S. (1986). *Family Environment Scale manual (2nd ed.).* Palo Alto, CA: Consulting Psychologists Press.

Ollendick, T.H. (1998). Panic disorder in children and adolescents: New developments, new directions. *Journal of Clinical Child Psychology, 27,* 234–245.

Ollendick, T.H. (1983). Reliability and validity of the revised fear survey schedule for hildren (FSSC-R). *Behaviour Research and Therapy, 21,* 685–692.

Ollendick, T.H., Lease, C.A., & Cooper, C. (1993). Separation anxiety in young adults: A preliminary examination. *Journal of Anxiety Disorders, 7,* 293–305.

Olsen, D.H., McCubbin, H.I., Barnes, H., *et al.* (1985). *Family Inventories.* St. Paul Minnesota: Family Social Science.

Pilkington, C.L. & Piersel, W.C. (1991). School phobia: A critical analysis of the separation anxiety theory and an alternative explanation. *Psychology in the schools, 28,* 290–303.

Prins, P.J., Groot, M.J., & Hanewald, G.J. (1994). Cognitions in test-anxious children: The role of on-task and coping cognitions reconsidered. *Journal of Consulting and Clinical Psychology, 62,* 404–409.

Puig-Antich, J. & Chambers, W.J. (1978). *Schedule for affective disorders and schizophrenia for school-age children (K-SADS).* Unpublished manuscript.

Reynolds, C.R., and Richman, B.O. (1978). What I think and feel? A revised measure of children's manifest anxiety. *Journal of Abnormal Child Psychology, 6,* 271–280.

Rosenbaum, J.F., Biederman, J., Gersten, M., Hirshfeld, D.R., Meminger, S.R., Herman, J.B., Kagan, J., Reznick, J.S., & Snidman, N. (1988). Behavioral inhibition in children of parents with panic disorder and agoraphobia: A controlled study. *Archives of General Psychiatry, 45,* 463–470.

Rubin, K.H. & Mills, R.S.L. (1991). Conceptualizing developmental pathways to internalizing disorders in childhood. *Canadian Journal Behavioual Science, 23*, 300–317.

Rutter, M. (1981). Emotional development. In M. Rutter (Ed.), *Scientific foundations of developmental psychiatry.* Baltimore: University Park Press.

Sapolsky, R.M. (1990). Stress in the wild: Studies of free-ranging baboons in an African reserve are helping to explain why human beings can differ in their vulnerability to stress-related diseases. *Scientific American,* 116–123.

Sheeber, L.B., & McDevitt, S.C. (1998). Temperament-focused parent training. In J.M. Briesmeister & C.E. Schaefer (Eds.), *Handbook of parent training: Parents as co-therapists for children's behavior problems* (2nd ed., pp. 479–507). New York: John Wiley & Sons.

Silove, D., Harris, M., Morgan, A., Boyce, P., Manicavasagar, V., Hadzi-Pavlovic, D., & Wilhelm, K. (1995). Is early separation anxiety a specific precursor of panic disorder-agoraphobia? A community study. *Psychological Medicine, 25*, 405–411.

Silove, D. & Manicavasagar, V. (1993). Adults who feared school: Is early separation Anxiety specific to the pathogenesis of panic disorder? *Acta Psychiatrica Scandinavica, 88*, 385–390.

Silove, D., Manicavasagar, V., O'Connell, D., Blaszczyski, A., Wagner, R., & Henry, J. (1993). The development of the separation anxiety symptom Inventory (SASI). *Australian New Zealand Journal of Psychiatry, 27*, 477–488.

Silove, D., Manicavasagar, V., O'Connell, D., & Yates, A. (1995). Genetic factors in early separation anxiety: Implications for the genesis of adult anxiety disorders. *Acta Psychiatrica Scandinavica, 92*, 17–24.

Silverman, W.K. (1991). Diagnostic reliability of anxiety disorders in children using structured interviews. *Journal of Anxiety Disorders, 5*, 105–124.

Silverman, W.K. (1989). *Self-control manual for phobic children.* Unpublished treatment protocol. Miami: Florida International University, Department of Psychology.

Silverman, W.K. & Albano, A.M. (1996). *The anxiety disorders interview schedule for DSM-IV: Child and parent versions.*San Antonio, Texas: The Psychological Corporation.

Silverman, W.K., Cerny, J.A., & Nelles, W.B. (1988). The familial influence in anxiety disorders: Studies on the offspring of patients with anxiety disorders. In B.B. Lahey & A.E. Kazdin (Eds.), *Advances in Clinical Child Psychology, 11*, 223–248. New York: Pergamon Press.

Silverman, W.K., Fleisig, W., Rabian, B., & Peterson, R.A. (1991). The child anxiety sensitivity index. *Journal of Clinical Child Psychology, 20*, 162–168.

Silverman, W.K., & Kearney, C.A. (1995). Behavioral treatment of childhood anxiety. In V.B. Van Hasselt and M. Hersen (Eds.), *Handbook of behavior therapy and pharmacotherapy for children: A comparative analysis.* New York: Pergamon Press.

Silverman, W.K., Kurtines, W.M., Ginsburg, G.S., Weems, C.F., Rabian, B., & Serafini, L.T. (1999). Contingency management, self-control, and education support in the treatment of childhood phobic disorders: A randomized clinical trial. *Journal of Consulting and Clinical Psychology, 67,* 675–687

Silverman, W.K. & Nelles, W.B. (1988). The anxiety disorders interview schedule for children. *Journal of the American Academy of Child and Adolescent Psychiatry, 27,* 772–778.

Simeon, J.G. & Wiggins, D.M. (1995). Pharmacotherapy. In A.R. Eisen, C.A., Kearney, & C.E. Schaefer (Eds.), *Clinical handbook of anxiety disorders in children and adolescents.* Northvale, NJ: Jason Aronson.

Siqueland, L., Kendall, P.C., & Steinberg, L. (1996). Anxiety in children: Perceived family environments and observed family interaction. *Journal of Clinical Child Psychology, 25,* 225–237.

Spence, S. (1997). Structure of anxiety symptoms among children: A confirmatory factor-analytic study. *Journal of Abnormal Psychology, 106,* 280–297.

Spielberger, C.D. (1973). *Manual for the state-trait anxiety inventory for children.* Palo Alto, CA: Consulting Psychologists Press.

Strauss, C.C., Frame, C.L., & Forehand, R.L., (1987). Psychosocial impairment associated with anxiety in children. *Journal of Clinical Child Psychology, 16,* 235–239.

Strauss, C.C., Lease, C.A., Kazdin, A.E., Dulcan, M.K., & Last, C.G. (1989). multimethod assessment of the social competence of children with anxiety disorders. *Journal of Clinical Child Psychology, 18,* 184–189.

Suomi, S.J. (1981). Inherited and experiential factors associated with individual differences in anxious behavior displayed in rhesus monkeys. In D.F. Klein & J.G. Rabkin (Eds.), *Anxiety: New research and changing concepts* (pp. 179–199). New York: Raven Press.

Swedo, S., Rapoport, J., Leonard, H., & Lenane, M. (1989). Childhood obsessive compulsive disorder: Clinical phenomenology of 70 cases. *Archives of General Psychiatry, 46,* 335–341.

Thapar, A. & McGuffin, P. (1995). Are anxiety symptoms in childhood heritable? *Journal of Child Psychology and Psychiatry, 36,* 439–447.

Thyer, B.A., Nesse, R., Curtis, G., & Cameron, O. (1986). Panic disorder: A Test of the separation anxiety hypothesis. *Behaviour Research and Therapy, 24,* 209–211.

Thyer, B.A. & Sowers-Hoag, K.M. (1988). Behavior therapy for separation anxiety disorder. *Behavior Modification, 12,* 205–233.

Topolski, T.D., Hewitt, J.K., Eaves, L.J., *et al.* (1997). Genetic and environmental influences on child reports of manifest anxiety and symptoms of separation anxiety and overanxious disorders: A community-based twin study. *Behavior Genetics, 27,* 15–28.

Torgerson, S. (1983). Genetic factors in anxiety disorders. *Archives of General Psychiatry, 40,* 1085–1089.

Turner, S.M., Beidel, D.C., & Costello, A. (1987). Psychopathology in the off-spring of anxiety disorders patients. *Journal of Consulting and Clinical Psychology, 55,* 229–235.

Valleni-Basile, L., Garrison, C., Jackson, K., Waller, J., McKeown, R., Addy, C., & Cuffe, S. (1994). Frequency of obsessive-compulsive disorder in a community sample of young adolescents. *Journal of the American Academy of Child and Adolescent Psychiatry, 33,* 782–791.

van derMolen, G., van der Hout, M., van Dieren, A., & Griez, E. (1989). Childhood separation anxiety and adult onset panic disorders. *Journal of Anxiety Disorders, 3,* 97–106.

Vernberg, E.M., Abwender, D.A., Ewell, K, & Beery, S.H. (1992). Social anxiety and peer relationships in early adolescence: A prospective analysis. *Journal of Clinical Child Psychology, 21,* 129–196.

Wachtel, J.R. & Strauss, C.C. (1995). Separation anxiety disorder. In A.R. Eisen, C. A. Kearney, & C.E. Schaefer (Eds.), *Clinical handbook of anxiety disorders in children and adolescents* (pp. 53–81). Northvale, NJ: Jason Aronson Inc.

Weissman, M.M., Prusoff, B.A., Gammon, G.D., *et al.* (1984). Psycho-pathology in the Children (ages 6–18) of depressed and normal parents. Journal of the American *Academy of Child Psychiatry, 23,* 78–84.

Yeragani, V., Meiri, P., Balon, R., Patel, H., & Pohl, R. (1989). History of separation anxiety in patients with panic disorder and depression and normal controls. *Acta Psychiatrica Scandinavica, 79,* 550–556.

5 PANIC ATTACKS AND PANIC DISORDER

Chris Hayward
Cecilia A. Essau

Until recently panic attacks and panic disorder were considered primarily problems of adults populations. During, the first decade of active research regarding panic disorder spanning the 1980s there was very little published about panic in children and adolescents. In the early 1990s there was debate about the existence of panic in children. In particular, Nelles and Barlow (1988) challenged the concept that children could experience the catastrophic cognitions necessary to experience panic attacks. Klein (1995) further argued that in adults with panic disorder, retrospective recall of childhood spontaneous panic attacks was extremely rare. These pivotal publications cast doubt on the validity of panic phenomenology in children. As recently as 1990 there were only a handful of case reports describing panic attacks and panic disorder in children and adolescents (Alessi and Magen, 1988; Alessi et al., 1987; Ballenger et al., 1989; Black and Robbins, 1990; Moreau et al., 1989; Van Winters and Strickler, 1984; Vitiello et al., 1987, 1990). There were 2 population-based studies estimating the prevalence of panic attacks in high school-aged adolescents (Hayward et al., 1989; Warren and Zgourides, 1988) and no studies assessing the prevalence of panic in children and younger adolescents. In the 1990s there was an increase interest in panic in children and adolescents. It is now evident that panic attacks and panic disorder do occur in children, although they probably are quite rare (Ollendick et al., 1994) During adolescence, perhaps at puberty, panic attacks become more common (Hayward et al., 1992), although panic disorder is still rare (Essau et al., 1999). This chapter will review the diagnosis, epidemiology, risk factors, assessment, impairment and service utilization, and treatment related to panic attacks and panic disorder in children and adolescents.

Definition and Classification

In DSM-IV, panic disorder is defined by the presence of recurrent, unexpected panic attacks followed by a minimum of one month of persistent concern of experiencing future attacks, worry about the possible implications or consequences of the panic attacks, or a significant change in behaviour related to the attacks (American Psychiatric Association; APA, 1994). For the diagnosis of panic disorder, panic attacks cannot be the result of a direct physiological effect of a substance, or a general medical condition. Finally, the panic attacks cannot be accounted for by another psychiatric disorder such as social and specific phobia, obsessive-compulsive disorder, posttraumatic stress disorder, or separation anxiety disorder.

A panic attack is defined as a discrete period of intense fear or discomfort. At least four of the following thirteen cognitive or somatic symptoms must be present during the attack: palpitations, pounding heart, or accelerated heart rate; sweating; trembling or shaking; sensations of shortness of breath or smothering; feeling of choking; chest pain or discomfort; nausea or abdominal distress; feeling dizzy, unsteady, lightheaded, or faintness; derealization or depersonalization; fear of losing control or going crazy; fear of dying; paresthesias; and chills or hot flushes. By definition, panic attacks must have a sudden onset and build to a peak within 10 minutes. Panic attacks in which there are fewer than four symptoms, are defined as "limited symptom attacks".

With respect to panic attacks two major changes have taken place in DSM-IV. First, since panic attacks are not unique to panic disorder but occur in other anxiety or other psychiatric disorders, the criteria for panic attacks were extracted from the panic disorder section and placed at the beginning of the anxiety disorders category. Second, DSM-IV differentiates between three types of panic attacks characterized by the relationship between the onset of the attack and the trigger or lack thereof: (i) unexpected (uncued) panic attacks occur out of the blue. That is, the onset of the panic attack is not associated with a situational trigger; (ii) situationally bound (cued) panic attacks in which the panic attack almost invariably occurs immediately following exposure to a situational cue or trigger; and (iii) situationally predisposed panic attacks, which tend to occur on exposure to the situational cue or trigger, but are not invariably associated with the cue and do not necessarily occur immediately after the exposure.

Epidemiology

The prevalence of panic disorder among adolescents in the general population has been estimated to be about 1% (see review by Essau,

2000). In a study by Hayward *et al.* (1997), the lifetime prevalence of panic disorder based on DSM-III-R criteria was 1.7%. In the Bremen Adolescent Study (Essau *et al.*, 1999, 2000), 0.5% of the adolescents met the DSM-IV criteria for this disorder sometime in their life. In a slightly higher age group (14–24 years), Wittchen and colleagues (1998) reported a lifetime prevalence of panic disorder being 1.6% and the 12-month prevalence being 1.2%.

The prevalence of panic attacks among adolescents in community studies varies dramatically, depending to a large extent on whether or not a questionnaire or a standardized diagnostic interview is used for the diagnosis. In a series of studies by Hayward and colleagues, the lifetime prevalence of panic attacks obtained using a structured diagnostic interview was 11.9% in ninth graders (Hayward *et al.*, 1989), 5.4% in sixth- and seventh-grade girls (Hayward *et al.*, 1992), and 5.4% in seventh and eighth-grade girls (Hayward *et al.*, 1997). In the Bremen Adolescent Study (Essau *et al.*, 1999), 18% of the adolescents reported having had at least one panic attack in their lifetime. Of those who reported having panic attacks, 48% reported the attacks as spontaneous. In a study by Reed and Wittchen (1998), 4.3% of the 14 to 24-year olds reported a lifetime prevalence of DSM-IV panic attacks. Those with panic disorder without agoraphobia described their panic attacks as more likely to be predominantly uncued, as compared to those with panic disorder with agoraphobia.

Studies that use questionnaires yield lifetime prevalence rates of panic attacks that are much higher, ranging from 43% to 60% (King *et al.*, 1993; Warren and Zgourides, 1988). In fact, one study reported the 1-year prevalence of panic attacks being 63% (Macaulay and Kleinknecht, 1989). Among university undergraduates, Norton *et al.* (1985) found that 34.4% of the students reported having had a minimum of three attacks in the past three weeks. In a second study (Norton *et al.*, 1986), 35.9% of the students reported experiencing at least one panic attack in the past year, and 3.1% at least three attacks in the past three weeks. Similar findings have been found by Margraf and Ehlers (1988), who reported between 46% to 59% of the students having had at least one panic attack in the previous year. Between 1% to 2% of these students reported having had at least three attacks in the previous three weeks.

Thus, questionnaire-determined panic assessments in adolescents yield frequencies that are up to three-fold greater than those obtained from diagnostic interviews. Some panic attacks captured by questionnaire may be false positive attacks that involve a fearful response to a situation involving real threat (Hayward et al., 1997). Also, interview versus questionnaire assessments may result in different cut-off points along a continuum of severity.

RATES BY GENDER

Studies of panic attack frequencies in adolescents and young adults demonstrate relative equal rates of panic attacks in males and females (Essau et al., 1999; King et al., 1993; Telch et al., 1989). However, when panic attacks are separated by severity or number of symptoms, adolescent females tend to be more represented in the severe groups or four-symptom groups (Hayward et al., 1989; King et al., 1996; Macaulay and Kleindknecht, 1989). In one study, subjects equally divided by sex with "nonclinical" panic attacks were selected on the basis of resembling panic attacks experienced by patients, the resulting subgroup of panickers was 72% female (Wilson et al., 1992). Thus, females and males may be at near equal risk of panic attacks, but females may experience more severe attacks and perhaps respond differently to panic attacks than males. Consistent with this possibility is the finding reported by Hayward et al. (2000) that males are over-represented among those with limited-symptom attacks and females are overrepresented among those with four-symptom attacks. Similarly, King et al. (1996) in a study of adolescents with nonclinical panic attacks, reported female to male ratios that increased when comparing any panic attacks to four-symptom panic attacks (female to male ratio for any panic was 1.3:1 versus 2:1 for four-symptom panic). In Reed and Wittchen's study (1998), panic disorder and panic attacks were significantly more common among females than males. However, their finding also indicated this gender difference to be affected by age.

AGE OF ONSET

The frequency of panic attacks increases during adolescence compared to childhood. This is evident from studies of adults where age of onset of a first panic attack is retrospectively recalled (Eaton et al., 1994; Kessler et al., 1998; Von Korff et al., 1985). In these studies there is an increase in the incidence of first panic attacks during adolescence, even though the peak age for onset of panic disorder is later in young adulthood. Similarly, in a study of young adolescents, prior to puberty panic attacks are rare (Hayward et al., 1992). However, after puberty at least for girls there is an increasing frequency of panic attacks. In older adolescents the frequency of reported panic attacks is similar to the frequency of panic attacks reported by adults (Essau *et al.*, 1999; Klein *et al.*, 1992; Warren and Zgourides, 1988). Thus, although prepubertal panic attacks and panic disorder occur, the frequency in the population appears to be low compared with rates in post-pubertal adolescents.

COURSE AND OUTCOME

The course and outcome of panic disorder has rarely been examined in children and adolescents. In the Bremen Adolescent Study (Essau, 1999), none of the four cases with panic disorder at the index investigation met the same diagnosis at a follow-up investigation conducted 15 months later. Among adults, the course of panic disorder has been described as chronic or recurrent (Wittchen and Essau, 1993). If untreated, half of the cases with panic disorder have a risk of developing other psychiatric disorders such as major depression and substance use disorders. In an early study by Noyes and colleagues (1990), only 10% of the patients with panic disorder who participated in a drug treatment study were free of symptoms at a 3-year follow-up investigation. Worse outcome were associated with more severe initial symptoms, female gender, and low socioeconomic status.

Comorbidity

Panic disorder in adolescents is highly comorbid with other psychiatric disorders. In the Bremen Adolescent Study (Essau, 1999; Essau *et al.*, 1999), 80% of those with panic disorder also had depressive disorders. Fifty percent of adolescents with panic disorder also had a somatoform disorder and an equal percent had a substance use disorder. Within the anxiety disorders, panic disorder is highly comorbid with posttraumatic stress disorder and generalized anxiety disorder. Also, panic attacks in adolescents appear to be non-specific markers for other psychiatric disorders. In a recent study by Reed and Wittchen (1998), the conditional probability of developing other psychiatric disorders among these with a panic attack was 63% in males and 40% in females. This association with other psychiatric disorders was particularly evident for those with a late onset of panic attack (after the age of 18 years). Among the disorders that most commonly co-occurred with panic attacks were depressive disorders, other anxiety disorders, and substance use disorders.

In a study utilizing a clinical sample, Last and Strauss (1989) reported that 35% of children and adolescents with panic disorder had another anxiety disorder, 12% had major depression, 6% had attention deficit hyperactivity, and 6% had oppositional defiant disorder. With respect to alcohol use, Hayward *et al.* (1997) reported the use of alcohol in 32% of adolescents with panic attack, 24% of adolescents with panic disorder, compared to 14% of those with neither.

Some adolescents who report panic attacks also report phobic avoidance related to the panic attack or fear of having another panic attack. Among the 10% to 35% of those who avoided being in certain places or situations for fear of panic attack, the severity of avoidance in most cases was generally moderate (Kearney *et al.*, 1997). The experience of having a panic attack was associated with a number of concern or problems in adolescents (Essau *et al.*, 1999). The most common problem expressed by both boys and girls was "avoidance of a certain situation". The next frequent among girls was "persistent concern about having another attacks", and among boys it was "worry about the implication of the attack". In the study by Reed and Wittchen (1998), the most common complications of panic attacks included worry about having another attack, their implications, changed behaviour and avoidance. In the King *et al.*'s study (1993), 25% of adolescents with panic attacks avoided specific situations for fear of having another attack. In Warren and Zgourides' study (1988), 10% of the adolescents with a panic attack avoided specific situations for fear of panic attacks, and in the Hayward *et al.*'s study (1997), it was 11.8%. In another study by Hayward *et al.* (1995), girls with panic attack compared to those girls without were more likely to report school refusal. The kind of settings most avoided by young people are those that involve groups of people unknown such as being in a restaurants, crowds, and auditoriums (Kearney *et al.*, 1997). Thus, it appears that for some children and adolescents panic may provoke the development of phobic avoidance, but panic attacks do not necessarily herald the onset of phobic avoidance for a significant population of youth who suffer "nonclinical panic attacks".

Risk Factors

Many studies examining risk factors for panic symptoms utilize clinical samples of adults in cross-sectional designs (for a review see Wittchen and Essau, 1993). However, clinical samples do not adequately represent all those with panic symptoms, as the majority of those with panic attacks and panic disorder never receive treatment (King *et al.*, 1993). Further, in cross-sectional designs risk factors are difficult to distinguish from correlates or consequences related to the presence of the disorder (Kraemer *et al.*, 1997). Thus, risk factor studies are best conducted in prospective cohort designs on representative samples of those free from the first symptom of the disorder. In the case of panic disorder, the first symptom is the initial panic attack. Risk factors for first panic symptoms are therefore best identified in adolescent samples.

PSYCHOLOGICAL RISK FACTORS

Some studies provide support for an association between childhood separation anxiety disorder and adult panic and phobic disorders (see Black, 1995 for a review). In these studies, adults with panic disorder and agoraphobia retrospectively report higher rates of childhood separation anxiety disorder compared to those without agoraphobia and panic. Individuals with panic disorder generally avoid separating from attachment figures; in children this includes a fear of separating from a parent, and in adults it is spouses, other relatives, and close friends. Although this finding has been inconsistent and nonspecific, there are two longitudinal studies that support an association between panic and agoraphobia, and childhood separation anxiety disorder (Biederman *et al.*, 1993; Klein, 1995). In Klein's study (1995), panic disorder was the only disorder that was more common in adults who were diagnosed as children with separation anxiety disorder. In the Biederman *et al.'s* study, (1993) childhood separation anxiety disorder predicted agoraphobia 3 years later in a group of children previously identified as behaviourally inhibited. Some researchers contend therefore, that childhood separation anxiety disorder may be specifically important for the development of panic disorder and agoraphobia (Black, 1995; Klein, 1995).

There are also studies of predisposing cognitive factors in adolescents that are extensions of a body of literature in adults. The increased propensity to respond fearfully to anxiety symptoms predisposes to the development of panic attacks have been well studied in adults. This predisposition has been labeled anxiety sensitivity. Higher levels of anxiety sensitivity have been shown prospectively, to increase the risk of panic attacks in young adults and more recently, in high school-age adolescent populations (Ehlers, 1995; Hayward *et al.*, 2000; Maller and Reiss,

1992; Schmidt *et al.*, 1997). Clark (1988) argued that panic attacks can result from catastrophic misinterpretation of bodily sensations. Feelings commonly associated with anxiety (e.g., palpitation) are interpreted as dangerous signals of impending harm (e.g., heart attack). Such catastrophic misinterpretation is cruical in the vicious cycle which culminants in a panic attack and panic disorder. However, it is yet to be examined in future studies whether or not Clark's model, which was developed for adults, can be used to explain the development of panic attack in children and adolescents. Some authors (e.g., Nelles and Barlow, 1988) have argued that panic attack should be rare or non-existent in children since they are not yet able to catastrophically misinterpret the somatic symptoms that are associated with a panic attack. Nelles and Barlow (1988) claimed that internal and catastrophic attribution that characterize panic attack does not exit until the children reach adolescence.

There is also a reason to believe that prior Axis I disorders, particularly depression, probably increase the risk for panic attacks, as is the case for adults (Hayward *et al.*, 2000).

Assessment

For many adolescents who are seeking treatment, anxiety is a common complaint. One task as clinicians is to determine whether the symptom of anxiety represents a transient reaction to a recent stressor or developmental phase, or whether the anxiety is a manifestation of a more serious psychiatric disorder. Anxiety can often be the first manifestation of severe depression, obsessive-compulsive disorder, panic disorder, separation anxiety disorder, and even occasionally, impending psychosis. Thus, it is important to do a complete diagnostic assessment of current and past symptoms, and the extent to which symptoms are interfering with current functioning. When assessing children about the presence of panic attack, the developmental level of the child needs to be taken into account (see Chapter 3 this volume). This includes the use of simple and understandable words.

In general, the process of assessing adolescent anxiety disorders does not differ from any thorough psychodiagnostic assessment for any other disorder or problem. However, it is helpful to highlight a few areas that are of particular relevance to the diagnosis and treatment of panic and other anxiety disorders.

MEDICAL HISTORY

It is very important to obtain a thorough medical history, including family medical history, and ascertain when the adolescent last had a physical examination. There are a number of medical conditions that can be associated with anxiety symptoms. Hyperthyroidism, for example, can present with anxiety as the primary symptom. In addition, medications prescribed for medical illnesses can cause or exacerbate anxiety. One adolescent evaluated in our clinic complained that she felt "nervous" and "jittery". A careful review of her symptoms and medical history revealed that her anxious feelings occurred most frequently when she was taking steroids for severe asthma. Not every adolescent who first presents with anxiety requires a medical evaluation. However, if there are any new medical complaints in addition to the symptom of anxiety, or a family history of medical problems that commonly have anxiety as a symptom, then a complete medical evaluation is warranted.

SUBSTANCE ABUSE

Careful assessment of substance use, and the potential for abuse and dependence, is also important. The use of alcohol, stimulants, marijuana, and other illicit drugs can induce anxiety states, both during episodes of intoxication as well as during withdrawal. The presence of active substance abuse makes accurate diagnosis of any other Axis I psychiatric disorder difficult until the adolescent has been drug free for an acceptable period of time.

Although substance abuse or dependence may not be an issue for a particular adolescent, evaluation of patterns of "recreational" substance use may help to clarify an anxiety disorder diagnosis. Some adolescents "self-medicate" prior to entering situations that trigger anxiety. Additional substances to inquire about include caffeine consumption and use of over-the-counter medications. Excessive caffeine intake has been associated with increased levels of anxiety and can trigger panic attacks. Likewise, over-the-counter medications such as cold medications or diet pills can have similar effects.

FAMILY HISTORY

A thorough family assessment is essential, and should cover family history of mood and anxiety disorders, and the typical responses of the parents to displays of anxiety or fear by the adolescent. Evidence from a number of studies suggests the strong possibility of genetic heritability of panic disorder (Clark *et al.*, 1990). However, it is difficult to distinguish the contribution of genetics from the contribution of growing up in a family with anxious relatives who model fearful behaviour. In addition, the response of the parents to the fearful behaviour of a child can further shape, reinforce, and maintain maladaptive behaviour.

Additional areas to be covered in the assessment that may be relevant to complaints of anxiety include increased family discord, such as marital conflict, separations, and divorce, and any recent losses or perceived threats of loss. Similarly, exposure to frightening situations in school or in one's neighborhood, such as violence or gang activity, can precipitate a new onset of anxiety symptoms. Of course, traumatic events, such as physical or sexual abuse, are frequent triggers of anxiety.

Adolescents may be reticent to discuss the traumatic or stressful events that underlie their symptoms, nor will they necessarily make psychological connections between external events and internal anxiety states. Thus, it is important for the mental health practitioner to not only understand the events in the adolescent's life that may be contributing to the symptoms, but to carefully document the timing of events with relation to the onset of symptoms.

Further complicating the assessment process is the fact that many adolescents view their symptoms as weird, bizarre, or crazy, and they may not readily volunteer certain aspects of their experience. Questions such as "Is there anything you are afraid of which others aren't?" or "do you ever get scared all of a sudden for no particular reason?" can be useful leads to uncovering symptoms. If an individual reports a severe fear or phobia, then the clinician should always assess for the presence of panic attacks. Similarly, if adolescents describe clear panic attacks, there may be associated phobic avoidance. The presence of panic attacks warrants follow-up questions regarding depression and suicidality, as there is an association between panic in adolescents and suicidality (Pilowsky *et al.*, 1999).

One of the difficulties in making the diagnosis of panic attacks and panic disorder in children and adolescents is that they do not understand the concept of sudden onset. Nor are they easily able to differentiate panic induced from either objects of phobic fear (bridges or dogs) or spontaneous panic attacks from objects of external fear that would be normally frightening. For example, when asked about whether a subject has ever had a panic attack, children and adolescents often confuse the fact that they might have been scared by the dark, a stranger, or an episode of violence in their neighborhood and think that this is a panic attack when in fact most children or adolescents their age might have been afraid in a similar situation. Thus, it is important to differentiate episodes of normal fear from episodes of panic in response to a phobia fear or panic that develops spontaneously. In population-based studies, the assessment of panic attacks can be performed either by questionnaire or interview. In clinical samples it is preferable to have the subject, as well as his/her parent assessed with a clinical interview. In addition to discussing the phenomenology of purported panic attacks, assessing related comorbid Axis I disorders such as depression and phobias, is important. Obtaining a history from parents is particularly important in younger aged children. As is true in all child and adolescent psychiatry, it is important to evaluate the family to determine whether there are familial factors contributing to the onset of panic. Panic attacks are particularly common in life transitions of adolescents, including periods of separation from parent, moves, loss of a parent, separation or divorce, and one should ask about these important life events to assess the circumstances under which panic attacks first appear.

PSYCHOSOCIAL IMPAIRMENT AND MENTAL HEALTH SERVICE UTILIZATION

Among adolescents with panic disorder, about 40% of them are severly impaired during the worst episode of their illness (Essau et al., 1999). Most reported (60%) being mildly impaired by their attacks. In the Reed and Wittchen study (1998), 72.8% of subjects with panic attack and 47% with panic disorder reported their panic symptoms to somewhat interfere with their daily life. In the study by King et al. (1993), only 7% of those with questionnaire-determined panic attacks indicated their panic attacks as causing significant interference in their life.

The issue of treatment-seeking in those with panic attacks is an important one given the fact that the vast majority of children and adolescents who suffer from panic attacks or panic disorder have no knowledge of panic attacks as a clinical phenomena, and they most often never seek treatment. In terms of mental health service utilization, only one out of five adolescents with panic disorder sought professional help for emotional and psychiatric problems (Essau et al., 1999).When considering only those who had a panic attack, about 30% sought help for emotional/psychiatric problems.

Although there are anxiety disorder clinics that treat children and adolescents, these types of specialty clinics are rare. Thus, efforts to educate care-givers, educators, and parents about the common place nature of panic phenomena in adolescents would probably benefit the primary and secondary prevention efforts to avoid the sequelae of panic attacks that can occur.

Treatment

Treatment of adolescent anxiety disorders often requires a combined approach utilizing individual and family therapy, and in some cases the use of group approaches and psychopharmacology.

INDIVIDUAL THERAPY

An approach to initial treatment using individual therapy should utilize a cognitive-behavioural model. However, the treatment should also be informed and enhanced by psychodynamic theory and technique. For many patients, treatment can be thought of in two phases:

Phase I: Psychoeducation, symptom relief, understanding the symptom precipitant, and training in anxiety management techniques.

Phase II: Exploration of "deeper" issues.

Much of the adult literature on treatment of panic symptoms is based on a cognitive-behavioural model. In practice, augmenting the problem-focused, cognitive-behavioural approach with more traditional exploratory techniques may help subjects gain insight about relations with others, family of origin and defenses used to manage emotions, and may ultimately lessen long term susceptibility for symptom return (Taylor and Arnow, 1988). Even when an adolescent is curious about the context and meaning of their anxiety symptoms, their primary concern upon initiation of therapy is usually symptom relief. Ignoring this urgency can lead to non-compliance with treatment or stopping treatment altogether.

Following completion of the assessment, the first step is education about panic attacks and the cognitive-behavioural conceptualization of anxiety. Patients are also oriented to the collaborative nature of the therapeutic relationship.

The introduction to the cognitive-behavioural conceptualization of panic can include the three ways in which panic and reactions to panic are manifested:

- Bodily reactions, such as rapid heart rate, difficulty breath, light-headedness, etc.;
- Cognitions or thoughts, such as "They'll make fun of me if I talk in class", "I might do something really embarrassing"; and
- Actions or behaviours, such as avoiding feared objects or events (Silverman *et al.*, 1995).

Treatment focuses on each of the three areas utilizing a combination of cognitive and behavioural techniques, such as relaxation training to help with the somatic manifestations of anxiety, cognitive techniques to alter anxious thought patterns, and exposure to feared bodily symptoms. Listed in Table 5.1 are a number of cognitive and behavioural techniques that are commonly used in the treatment of anxiety disorders.

FAMILY INVOLVEMENT

Family sessions are an important part of anxiety disorder treatment for most adolescents. However, the frequency and focus of the sessions varies considerably depending on the nature of the issues in a particular family and the way in which family dynamics are influencing the adolescent's

Table 5.1 Cognitive and behavioural techniques

Techniques	Component/Methods
Cognitive Techniques	● Daily record of dysfunctional thoughts ● Identification of cognitive distortions ● Examination of evidence for maladaptive thoughts/beliefs ● Look for alternative explanations ● Teach relationship between maladaptive thought and underlying beliefs
Behavioural Techniques	● Relaxation training ● Activity scheduling ● Modeling and role playing ● Exposure (imaginal and in vivo) ● Systematic desensitization

difficulties. In some cases, the focus of family sessions is on psycho-education regarding the nature of anxiety and the necessary components of treatment. Periodic family sessions are scheduled to provide parents with feedback about their child's progress, discuss changes in the adolescent's behaviour observed by the parents, and explore the impact of these changes on overall family functioning. Older adolescents, because of their developmentally appropriate greater degree of independent functioning, may require fewer family sessions than younger teens. A greater degree of family involvement may be indicated in cases where it is clear that the response of the parents to the anxious behaviour reinforces and maintains that behaviour.

GROUP THERAPY

Group therapy can be a useful format for many adolescent issues and disorders. There are several potential advantages a group format offers over individual treatment, including vicarious learning, seeing others with similar problems, the availablilty of multiple role-play partners, and a range of people who can provide evidence to counter distorted thinking (Hope and Heimberg, 1993). Because of the availability of multiple group members for role playing, the group format facilitates the exposure component of treatment for panic associated with social anxiety.

MEDICATIONS

In some cases anxiety symptoms persist or have severe consequences, for example the patient who is having frequent panic attacks is con-vinced that she has a brain tumor and refuses to go to school. This individual may need additional symptom relief which can be achieved with the use of medications. Both anti-anxiety agents and antidepres-sants are effective for anxiety symptoms in adults and are probably equally so in adolescents (Ballenger et al., 1989; Biederman, 1987; Fairbanks et al., 1997; Lepola et al., 1996; Renaud et al., 1999; Simeon and Ferguson, 1987; Simeon et al., 1992).

In general the antidepressant medications have one advantage over the anti-anxiety medications in that there is no physiologic dependence. On the other hand their onset of action is much longer, two to four weeks versus one to two days. The best choice for antidepressants is one of the newer types called SSRIs (selective serotonin reuptake inhibitors), such as Prozac. The tricyclic antidepressants have many more side effects and can be lethal in overdoses.

Overall, progress in treatment can be affected by a variety of issues. One of the most important factors in working with adolescents with panic symptoms is the nature of the therapeutic relationship. Unlike most adults who seek treatment, many adolescents, even those who are experiencing a significant degree of panic, are not necessarily motivated to enter therapy. They are commonly brought to therapy by their parents, and may be struggling with feeling pressured into a process about which they are quite ambivalent. Younger adolescents may feel they have less of a choice than older adolescents, but issues around autonomy and trust are common to work with all adolescents.

PREVENTION

As has been the case in panic disorder in adults, education can go a long way in identification and getting people into treatment for secondary prevention. Similar efforts might well be done in a school setting or avenues of contact with adolescent populations in particular. The opportunities for primary prevention require better identification of risk factors. Although it does appear that primary prevention might best be targeted to young adolescents or latency-age children prior to puberty when the frequency of panic attacks increases. Future research might well focus on the risk factors associated with onset of panic attacks in children and adolescents, the differences between children, adolescents and adults in addition to treatments that can be tested and controlled in a double-blind manner. The hope that panic will not lead to some of the identified consequences, namely, phobic avoidance, suicide, depression, alcohol use and increased disability really requires that intervention and education be done when the disorder first begins by increasing amounts of education and access to mental health care providers.

It is only in the last decade that the study of panic has been extended to children and adolescents. Panic attacks are not uncommon among adolescents even though panic disorder may be rare. A small number of those who experience panic as children and adolescents will eventually develop panic disorder. Identifying risk factors ultimately offers the possibility of early intervention—if not prevention. Educating parents, teachers, and adolescents about panic symptoms may help adolescents who experience panic attacks feel less confused about what the symptoms mean and facilitate seeking help.

References

Alessi, N.E. & Magen, J. (1988). Panic disorders in psychiatrically hospital-ized children. *American Journal of Psychiatry, 145,* 1450–1452.
Alessi, N.E., Robbins, D.R., & Dilsaver, S.C. (1987). Panic and depressive dis-orders among psychiatrically hospitalized adolescents. *Psychiatric Reserach, 20,* 275–283.
American Psychiatric Association (1994). *Diagnostic and statistical manual of mental disorders (4th ed.).* Washington, DC: American Psychiatric Association.
American Psychiatric Association (1987). *Diagnostic and statistical manual of mental disorders (rev. 3rd ed.).* Washington, DC: American Psychiatric Association.
Clark, D.M. (1988). A cognitive model of panic attacks. In S. Rachman & J. Maser (eds), *Panic: Psychological perspectives* (pp. 71–90). Hillsdale, NJ: Lawrence Erlbaum.
Clark, D.B., Smith, M.C., Neighbors, B.D., Skerlec, L.M., & Randall, J. (1994). Anxiety disorders in adolescence: Characteristics, prevalence, and comorbidities. *Clinical Psychology Review, 14,* 113–137.
Ballenger, J.C., Carek, D.J., Steele, J.J., Cornish-McTighe, D. (1989). Three cases of panic disorder with agoraphobia in children. *American Journal of Psychiatry, 146,* 922–924.
Biederman, J.C. (1987). Clonazepam in the treatment of prepubertal children with panic-like symptoms. *Journal of Clinical Psychiatry, 48,* 38–41.
Biederman, J., Rosenbaum, J.F., Bolduc-Murphy, E.A., Faraone, S.V., Chaloff, J., Hirshfeld, D.R., & Kagan, J. (1993). A 3-year follow-up of children with and without behavioral inhibition. *Journal of the American Academy of Child and Adolescent Psychiatry, 32,* 814–821.
Black, B. (1995). Separation anxiety disorder and panic disorder. In J.S. March (Ed.), *Anxiety disorders in children and adolescents* (pp. 212–234). New York: Guilford Press.
Black, B. & Robbins, D.R. (1990). Panic disorder in children and adolescents. *Journal of the American Academy of Child and Adolescent Psychiatry, 29,* 36–44.
Eaton, W.W., Kessler, R.C., Wittchen, H.-U., & Magee, W.J. (1994). Panic and panic disorder in the United States. *American Journal of Psychiatry, 151,* 413–420.
Ehlers, A. (1993). Somatic symptoms and panic attacks: A retrospective study of learning experiences. *Behaviour Research and Therapy, 31,* 269–278.
Ehlers, A. (1995). A 1-year prospective study of panic attacks: Clinical course and factors associated with maintenance. *Journal of Abnormal Psychology, 104,* 164–172.

Essau, C.A. (1999). *Angst und Depression bei Jugendlichen. Habilitationschrift.* Bremen: Universität Bremen.

Essau, C.A., Conradt, J. & Petermann, F. (2000). Frequency, comorbidity, and psychosocial impairment of anxiety disorders in adolescents. *Journal of Anxiety Disorders, 14,* 263–279.

Essau, C.A., Conradt, J., & Petermann, F. (1999). Frequency of panic attacks and panic disorder in adolescents. *Depression and Anxiety, 9,* 19–26.

Fairbanks, J.M., Pine, D.S., Tancer, N.K., Dummit, E.S., Kentgen, L.M., Asche, B.K., & Klein, R.G. (1997). Open fluoxetine treatment of mixed anxiety disorders in children and adolescents. *Journal of the American Academy of Child and Adolescent Psychiatry, 7,* 17–29.

Hayward, C., Killen, J.D., Hammer, L.D., Litte, I.F., Wison, D.M., Simmonds, B., & Taylor, C.B. (1992). Pubertal stage and panic attack history in sixth- and seventh-grade girls. *American Journal of Psychiatry, 149,* 1239–1243.

Hayward, C., Killen, J.D., Kraemer, H.C., Blair-Greiner, A., Strachowski, D., Cunning, D., & Taylor, C.B. (1997). Assessment and phenomenology of nonclinical panic attacks in adolescent girls. *Journal of Anxiety Disorders, 11,* 17–32.

Hayward, C., Killen, J.D., Kraemer, H.C., & Taylor, C.B. (2000). Predictors of panic attacks in adolescents. *Journal of the American Academy of Child and Adolescent Psychiatry, 39,* 207–214.

Hayward, C., Killen, J.D., & Taylor, C.B. (1989). Panic attacks in young adolescents. *American Journal of Psychiatry, 146,* 1061–1062.

Hayward, C., Taylor, C.B., Blair-Greiner, A., Strachowski, D., Killen, J.D., Wilson, D.M., & Hammer, L.D. (1995). School refusal in young adolescent girls with nonclinical panic attacks. *Journal of Anxiety Disorders, 9,* 329–338.

Hope, D.A. & Heimberg, R.G. (1993). Social phobia and social anxiety. In D.H. Barlow (Ed.), *Clinical Handbook of Psychological Disorders.* New York: The Guilford Press.

Kearney, C.A., Albano, A.M., Eisen, A.R., Allan, W.D., & Barlow, D.H. (1997). The phenomenology of panic disorder in youngsters: An empirical study of a clinical sample. *Journal of Anxiety Disorders, 11,* 49–62.

Kessler, R.C., Stang, P.E., Wittchen, H.U., Bedirhan, U.T., Roy-Burne, P.P., & Walters, E.E. (1998). Lifetime panic-depression comorbidity in the national comorbidity survey. *Archives of General Psychiatry, 55,* 801–808.

King, N.J., Gullone, E., Tonge, B.J., & Ollendick, T.H. (1993). Self-reports of panic attacks and manifest anxiety in adolescents. *Behaviour Research and Therapy, 31,* 111–116.

King, N.J., Ollendick, T.H., Mattis, S.G., Yang, B., & Tonge, B. (1996). Nonclinical panic attacks in adolescents: Prevalence, symptomatology, and associated features. *Behavioral Change, 13,* 171–183.

Klein, R.G. (1995). Is panic disorder associated with childhood separation anxiety disorder? *Clinical Neuropharmacology, 18,* S7–S14.

Klein, D.F., Mannuzza, S., Chapman, T., & Fyer, A.J. (1992). Child panic revisited. *Journal of the American Academy of Child and Adolescent Psychiatry, 31,* 112–116.

Kraemer, H.C., Kazdin, A.E., Offord, D.R., Kessler, R.C., Jensen, P.S., & Kupfer, D.J. (1997). Coming to terms with the terms of risk. *Archives of General Psychiatry 54,* 337–344.

Kutcher, S. & Mackenzie, S. (1988). Successful clonazepam treatment of adolescents with panic disorder. *Journal of Clinical Psychopharmacology, 8,* 299–301.

Last, C.G. & Strauss, C.C. (1989). Panic disorder in children and adolescents. *Journal of Anxiety Disorders, 3,* 87–95.

Lepola, U., Leinonen, E., & Kopenen, H. (1996). Citalopram in the treatment of early-onset panic disorder and school phobia. *Pharmacopsychiatry, 29,* 30–32.

Macaulay, J.L. & Kleinknecht, R.A. (1989). Panic and panic attacks in adolescents. *Journal of Anxiety Disorders, 3,* 221–241.

Maller, R.G. & Reiss, S. (1992). Anxiety sensitivity in 1984 and panic attacks in 1987. *Journal of Anxiety Disorders, 6,* 241–247.

Margraf, J. & Ehlers, A. (1988). Panic attacks in nonclinical subject. In H.-U. Wittchen & I. Hand (Eds.), *Treatment of panic and phobias.* Berlin: Springer.

Nelles, W.B. & Barlow, D.H. (1988). Do children panic? *Clinical Psychology Review, 8,* 359–372.

Norton, G.R., Dorward, J., & Cox, B.J. (1986). Factors associated with panic attacks in non-clinical subjects. *Behaviour Therapy, 17,* 239–252.

Norton, G.R., Harrison, B., Hauch, J., & Rhodes, L. (1985). Characteristics of people with infrequent panic attacks. *Journal of Abnormal Psychology, 94,* 216–221.

Noyes, R., Reich, J., Christiansen, J., Suelzer, M., Pfohl, B., & Coryell, W.A. (1990). Outcome of panic disorder: Relationship to diagnostic subtypes and comorbidity. *Archives of General Psychiatry, 47,* 809–818.

Ollendick, T.H., Mattis, S.G., & King, N.J. (1994). Panic in children and adolescents: A review. *Journal of Child Psychology and Psychiatry, 35,* 113–134.

Pilowsky, D.J., Wu, L.T., & Anthony, J.C. (1999). Panic attacks and suicide attempts in mid-adolescence. *American Journal of Psychiatry, 156,* 1545–1549.

Pollard, C.A., Henderson, J.G., Frank, M., & Margolis, R.B. (1989). Help-seeking patterns of anxiety-disordered individuals in the general population. *Journal of Anxiety Disorders, 3,* 131–138.

Reed, V. & Wittchen, H.-U. (1998). DSM-IV panic attacks and panic disorder in a community sample of adolescents and young adults. How specific are panic attacks? *Journal of Psychiatric Research, 32,* 335–345.

Renaud, J., Birmaher, B., Wassick, S.C., & Bridge, J. (1999). Use of selective serotonin reuptake inhibitors for the treatment of childhood panic disorder: A pilot study. *Journal of Child and Adolescent Psychopharmacology, 9,* 73–83.

Schmidt, N.B., Lerew, D.R., & Jackson, R.J. (1997). The role of anxiety sensitivity in the pathogenesis of panic: prospective evaluation of spontaneous panic attacks during acute stress. *Journal of Abnormal Psychology, 106,* 355–364.

Silverman, W.K., Ginsburg, G.S., & Kurtines, W.M. (1995). Clinical issues in treating children with anxiety and phobic disorders. *Cognitive and Behavioral Practice, 2,* 93–117.

Simeon, J. & Ferguson, B. (1987). Alprazolam effects in children with anxiety disorders. *Canadian Journal of Psychiatry, 32,* 570–574.

Simeon, J., Ferguson, B., Knott, V., Roberts, N., Gauthier, B., Dubois, C., & Wiggins, D. (1992). Clinical, cognitive and neurophysiological effects of alprazolam in children with overanxious and avoidant disorders. *Journal of the American Academy of Child and Adolescent Psychiatry, 31,* 29–33.

Taylor, C.B. & Arnow, B. (1988). Approaching the anxious patient: An overview of symptom-focused treatment. In C.B. Taylor & B. Arnow (Eds.), *The Nature and Treatment of Anxiety Disorders* (pp. 69–87). New York: The Free Press.

Telch, M.J., Lucas, J.A., & Nelson, P. (1989). Nonclinical panic in college students: An investigation of prevalence and symptomatology. *Journal of Abnormal Psychology, 98,* 300–306.

Von Korff, M.R., Eaton, W.W., & Keyl, P.M. (1985). The epidemiology of panic attacks and panic disorder. *American Journal of Epidemiology, 122,* 970–981.

Warren, R. & Zgourides, G. (1988). Panic attacks in high school students: Implications for prevention and intervention. *Phobia Practice and Research Journal, 1,* 97–113.

Wilson, K.G., Sandler, L.S., Asmundson, G.J.G., Ediger, J.M., Larsen, D.K., & Walker, J.R. (1992). Panic attacks in the nonclinical population: an empirical approach to case identification. *Journal of Abnormal Psychology, 101,* 460–468.

Wittchen, H.-U. & Essau, C.A. (1993). Epidemiology of panic disorder: Progress and unresolved issues. *Journal of Psychiatric Research, 27,* 47–68.

Wittchen, H.U., Reed, V., & Kessler, R.C. (1998). The relationship of agoraphobia and panic in a community sample of adolescents and young adults. *Archives of General Psychiatry 55,* 1017–1024.

6 SOCIAL PHOBIA

Lynne Sweeney
Ronald M. Rapee

Social phobia is one of the most common anxiety disorders in children and adolescents (Verhulst *et al.*, 1997). About one in every five children presenting to a specialty anxiety clinic has significant social fears (Beidel and Turner, 1998). Social phobia, specifically, is associated with a range of psychosocial impairments including social withdrawal and avoidant behaviour, social skill deficits, poor peer relationships, test anxiety and impairment in academic performance, and in more severe cases, depression, conduct problems, and alcohol and substance abuse (Vernberg *et al.*, 1992; Beidel and Turner, 1998; DSM-IV, APA, 1994). Retrospective studies of adult anxiety patients have demonstrated that social phobia in the childhood years is predictive of anxiety in adulthood, with early diagnosis (that is, prior to 11 years of age) predictive of non-recovery in adulthood (Davidson, 1993; cited in Beidel and Turner, 1998).

Thus far, research on social phobia has focused primarily on understanding the nature and maintenance of the disorder. Etiological explanations of social phobia are scant. Few publications have included detailed assessment protocols for diagnosis and treatment planning. Only a handful of studies have examined psychological treatments designed specifically for the child or adolescent with social phobia. Furthermore, research examining the efficacy of pharmacotherapy in this population is in its infancy. With large numbers of children experiencing social fears and the evidence pointing to detrimental outcomes, research efforts to increase our understanding in these areas is imperative. This chapter will attempt to integrate available knowledge of children and adolescents with social phobia to assist in the development of best practice with these fearful children. The first part of the chapter examines psychopathology and epidemiology of social phobia in childhood. Next we evaluate specific assessment tools for use with children and adolescents with social phobia. This includes a discussion of critical considerations in assessing children and adolescents with social phobia. The next section presents a model of the etiology of social phobia followed by a comprehensive review of psychological and pharmacological interventions for childhood social phobia.

In this chapter we will use the words "childhood" and "children" to refer to both children and adolescents unless specifically referring to an adolescent population.

Definition and Diagnosis

Social phobia is defined as a "marked and persistent fear of one or more social or performance situations in which the person is exposed to unfamiliar people or to possible scrutiny by others". Exposure to the feared situation will almost always provoke "an immediate anxiety response". This anxiety response in children may include "crying, tantrums, freezing, or shrinking from social situations" rather than the "panic" more characteristic of adults. Avoidance of the feared social or performance situation is very common. In some cases, children will endure the feared situation with dread (DSM-IV, 1994, p. 416).

To meet diagnostic criteria, in addition to the above symptoms, the fear and avoidance behaviour must significantly interfere with children's daily functioning, and the behaviour must have been present for a period of at least 6 months. Also, children must show evidence of being able to have "age-appropriate social relationships with familiar people" and the social or performance fears must be present in situations involving peers and not just in adult interaction settings (DSM-IV, 1994, p. 416). Children who demonstrate fears in *most* social situations are diagnosed with the additional specifier, *generalised*.

Clinical Correlates

As mentioned above, children with social phobia experience a range of psychosocial impairments that can lead to detrimental effects in both the short and long term. In a recent study, Beidel et al. (1999) examined the clinical features of preadolescent children with a DSM-IV diagnosis of social phobia. Results indicated that these children experienced "seriously impaired interpersonal functioning" including poorer social skills and higher loneliness scores compared to normal controls (p. 648). Children with social phobia reported few friends, if any, experienced somatic complaints such as headaches and tummy aches and a temperamental style suggestive of "emotional overresponsiveness" (high neuroticism, low extroversion, see Beidel et al., 1999 for more details). An earlier study of children with DSM-III-R social phobia (Beidel, 1991) reported higher trait anxiety, lower levels of perceived competency, higher rates of daily social distress, and more negative coping strategies in children with a diagnosis of social phobia compared with normal controls.

A number of studies have examined the frequency of children's fears in relation to a variety of social and performance situations. Beidel *et al.* (1991) report that children with social phobia experience, on average, about one feared interaction every other day. Beidel and Turner (1998) report that most of the distressing events occur in the school environment with an "unstructured encounter with a peer" the most likely distressing event (p. 41). Other commonly feared interactions include performing in front of others, talking in front of others (e.g., reading aloud to the class), taking tests, and attending social events. Not surprisingly, several studies have reported high rates of school phobia or "fear of school" among children diagnosed with social phobia (see Last *et al.*, 1991; Strauss and Last,1993).

Age of Onset, Course, and Outcome

Adult retrospective reports indicate that the average age of onset for social phobia is mid adolescence (APA, 1994; Liebowitz *et al.*, 1985; Turner *et al.*, 1986). However, one study using an adult sample reported that almost half of their sample had suffered with social phobia before 10 years of age (Schneier *et al.*, 1992). Studies using child samples have also reported earlier onsets. For example, Strauss and Last (1993) reported onset at a mean age of 12.3 years, whereas Beidel and Turner (1988) report that children as young as 8 can meet full criteria for a diagnosis of social phobia. Rapee (1995) suggests that data supporting an average age of onset of social phobia in mid-adolescence may be misleading in that it overlooks the existence of social phobia and social evaluative concerns in younger children who may be at risk. Indeed, one study examining the prevalence of feared outcomes in children aged between 6 and 16 years reported a relatively constant fear of evaluative outcomes across all age groupings (Campbell and Rapee, 1994). It may be that social concerns are usually present from an early age, yet only become identified as a clinical disorder when they begin to cause interference in functioning—e.g., dating in adolescence.

There is evidence to suggest that social phobia is relatively stable, is associated with a range of adverse outcomes, and is likely to persist into adulthood. Retrospective reports of adults with social phobia have indicated negative outcomes including impaired academic functioning, restricted social interactions and relatedness, alcohol abuse, and depression\(see Turner *et al.*, 1991; Schneier *et al.*, 1992).

Epidemiology

Prevalence data are based largely on DSM-III-R criteria with rates of social phobia according to DSM-IV criteria expected to be even higher. Overall, changes in DSM-IV appear to have the benefit of restricting diagnostic possibilities for children with social fears to social phobia (Beidel and Turner, 1998). Researchers have speculated that these changes may affect prevalence rates with new estimates likely to be a more accurate reflection of the true prevalence rates of social phobia in childhood.

Most studies cite prevalence of social phobia to be approximately 1–2% of the general child population (Anderson *et al.*, 1987; Kashani and Orvaschel, 1990; McGee *et al.*, 1990). Anderson and colleagues (1987) sampled 11 year old children and reported a 12 month prevalence rate of 0.9%, whereas Kashani and Orvaschel (1990) reported an overall prevalence rate of 1%. One study was found that used DSMIV criteria. Essau, Conradt and Peterman (1999a) reported a population prevalence rate of 1.6% using an adolescent sample (age range 12–17 years). Rates of social phobia in samples of children presenting to anxiety disorder clinics range from 15–18% based on DSM-III-R criteria (Albano *et al.*, 1995; Kendall and Warman, 1997; Last *et al.*, 1992). Kendall and Warman (1997) reported notably higher rates of social phobia according to DSM-IV criteria (40%) than when DSM-III-R criteria were used (18%). More studies are needed that examine the DSM-IV rates of social phobia in community and clinic samples of children.

Several studies of community samples have indicated a greater proportion of females to males who meet criteria for social phobia (e.g., Anderson *et al.*, 1987). On the other hand, clinical sample studies have shown equal numbers of male and female social phobics seeking treatment (Last *et al.*, 1987, 1992; Strauss and Last, 1993). Given that parents and teachers are often the agents of referral for children, this discrepancy in gender ratios between community and clinical samples may point to differences in parental and community values for girls and boys. For example, a boy of Western cultural origin who actively avoids social situations (due to a fear of negative evaluation and over concern with saying or doing the wrong thing in social settings), may be more likely to cause distress to parents and teachers than a girl with similar problems, and thus be more likely to be referred.

Comorbidity

Based on DSM-III-R comorbidity data, children rarely present with social phobia alone. Children are highly likely to meet criteria for at least one other anxiety diagnosis, with fewer children meeting diagnostic criteria for affective and externalising disorders. For example, Last *et al.* (1992) reported that 87% of children with social phobia met criteria for at least one other anxiety disorder, whereas Strauss and Last (1993) reported that 10% of children with social phobia met criteria for depression. A recent study based on DSM-IV criteria reported that 60% of children met criteria for an additional Axis 1 diagnosis, with 35% of these comorbid disorders in the anxiety field (Essau *et al.*, 1999a). The most common diagnoses were generalised anxiety disorder, specific phobia, and attention deficit hyperactivity disorder (all 10%), with selective mutism marginally lower (8%). Depression as a comorbid diagnosis was evident in only 6% of cases.

Assessment of Childhood Social Phobia

Comprehensive and accurate assessment of social phobia (and child anxiety disorders, generally) is paramount to making clinical diagnoses, treatment planning, treatment evaluation and research (see chapter 2 in this volume). It is generally accepted that comprehensive assessment of childhood anxiety disorders includes the use of reliable and valid assessment tools that accurately determine the presence of symptoms across different domains, identify symptom clusters and symptom severity, include multiple informant options, and demonstrate sensitivity to outcome evaluations. In recent years, researchers have begun to examine various aspects of the assessment of childhood social phobia in particular. This has included the development of specific measures for the assessment of social phobia and social anxiety, examination of the relevance of various available instruments and assessment techniques for the assessment of social phobia, as well as exploration of such factors as cross-informant consistency, social desirability, and health services utilisation.

ASSESSMENT PROTOCOL

Beidel and Turner (1998) propose an assessment strategy for assessing children with social phobia. This protocol includes a thorough clinical evaluation comprising a semi-structured interview, self-report clinical rating scales, and a clinical interview. In addition to this standardized assessment approach, Beidel and Turner (1998) highlight the potentially important assessment information that can be obtained via self-monitoring strategies. While this method of assessment is not always viable in child populations, its value in adults with social phobia supports that it be given consideration. Furthermore, several researchers have begun to explore behavioural assessment tasks (BAT'S) as a method for obtaining additional clinical information about the extent of the child's fear. While the unstandardized nature of BAT'S precludes their inclusion as part of a standardized assessment, experimental studies and clinical reports suggest that they may represent a useful adjunctive assessment technique for children with social phobia.

DIAGNOSTIC INTERVIEW

Of the diagnostic interviews currently available for determining clinical diagnostic status, the Anxiety Disorders Interview Schedule (ADIS-IV-C, Silverman and Albano, 1995) offers a comprehensive and relevant assessment for a child with social phobia. In addition to assessing for all the anxiety disorders (including a new screening section for selective mutism), affective disorders, Attention-Deficit/Hyperactivity Disorder (ADHD), and screening questions for a range of other disorders, the ADIS-IV-C includes questions about socialisation and peer relationships that are particularly relevant for the child with social phobia. Also, the ADIS-IV-C opens with a series of questions about school thus enabling the socially anxious child time to settle before asking specifics about the child's worries (Beidel and Turner, 1998). The parent version (ADIS-IV-P) includes the additional diagnostic categories of conduct disorder and oppositional defiant disorder as well as screening for a range of other disorders including enuresis, pervasive developmental disorders, and learning disorders.

SELF-REPORT INSTRUMENTS

There are many self report measures that have been developed to assess general anxiety symptoms in the child population and several of these include a clear social anxiety subscale. Overall, these measures of anxiety appear to be reasonably reliable in children, can discriminate between anxious and non-anxious children (with less support shown for discriminant validity within the anxiety disorders), show utility in measuring the impact of change following treatment, and show relatively low cross-informant agreement between parent and child reports (see Schniering *et al.*, 2000).

In recent years, two self-report measures have emerged that have been designed specifically to assess social anxiety in children. The Social Anxiety Scale for Children—Revised (SASC-R, LaGreca and Stone, 1993) was developed to assess social fears in children by adapting two commonly used adult measures of social anxiety (Social Avoidance and Distress Scale and Fear of Negative Evaluation, Watson and Friend, 1969). The scale consists of 22 items that comprise three subscales: Social Avoidance and Distress in General, Social Avoidance and Distress in New Situations, and Fear of Negative Evaluation. In terms of reliability and validity of the SASC-R, La Greca and Stone (1993) report acceptable internal consistency for each of the three subscales ($\propto$ >.65), and respectable concurrent validity in a sample of preadolescent children.

More recently, a second self-report measure of social phobia in children has been developed called the Social Phobia and Anxiety Inventory for Children (SPAI-C, Beidel *et al.*, 1995). The measure, designed for children between the ages of 8 and 14, consists of 26 items that comprise three factors: Assertiveness/General Conversation; Traditional Social Encounters, and Public Performance Factor. The authors report excellent internal consistency, high test-retest reliability across both short (2 weeks = 0.82) and longer (10 months = 0.63) periods, moderate correlations between the SPAI-C and other related constructs such as fear of criticism and general competence, and reasonable discriminant validity between children with social phobia from children with other anxiety disorders, externalising disorders, and non-clinical controls (Beidel *et al.*, 1996a). A parallel parent form is in the development stages.

SELF-MONITORING

Drawing largely on the demonstrated usefulness of self-monitoring in samples of adults with social phobia, Beidel and Turner (1998) describe this approach as a potentially valuable method of obtaining relevant information to assist in diagnosis, aid the identification of suitable exposure situations and avoidance patterns, and to assist with treatment outcome evaluations. While less often used in child populations, Beidel *et al.* (1991) have demonstrated that such procedures can be succesfully completed across a wide range of ages in children, and that picture cues can assist with compliance and completion of self-monitoring forms in younger children (8–10 years). In our own lab, the inclusion of self-monitoring forms are an important part of treatment planning and treatment efficacy evaluations for children with social phobia (and children with anxiety disorders, generally). To assist with compliance, we have introduced a reward system both at the lab and for parents to use in the home where rewards are contingent on completion of self-monitoring procedures and behavioural practice exercises. Anecdotely, this approach appears to improve compliance.

BEHAVIOURAL ASSESSMENT TASKS AND BEHAVIOURAL OBSERVATIONS

Beidel and Turner (1998) illustrate the potential value of including behavioural measures such as a behavioural assessment task in the assessment of socially anxious children. Based on anecdotal reports from their anxiety clinic, the authors describe a number of referred children who fail to admit any concerns with anxiety or peer relationships, yet when asked to take part in a behavioural avoidance task of social skills and performance, these same children were unable to demonstrate friendship skills, maintain social interaction, or perform adequately on a social performance task. Thus, in these cases, the behavioural assessment task identified important information regarding the child's presenting difficulties.

Recently, a number of experimental studies have emerged, that have used behavioural assessment and observation tasks, to assess such things as family interaction, cognitive features and parental over-protection in children with broad-based anxiety disorders. Only one experimental study was found that used behavioural assessment and observation tasks in a sample of children diagnosed with social phobia. In a recent study by Spence *et al.* (1999) a behavioural assessment task and two behavioural observations were included (in addition to diagnostic interview and self- and parent-questionnaire data) to assess social features of children with social phobia. Using the Revised Behavioural Assessment Test for Children (BAT-CR,

Ollendick, 1981—a modification of the Behavioural Assessment Test for Children—Bornstein *et al.*, 1977), children participated in 12 role plays in social situations involving positive assertiveness in 6 of the role plays and negative assertion in the remaining 6 role plays. Three variables were derived to assess social performance across the 12 role plays: eye contact, latency or response, and length of response. Two behavioural observations were included to assess social competence: a naturalistic school observation and an observation of assertiveness during the BAT-CR.

Results on these measures indicated that children with social phobia responded with fewer words during the role playing tasks and were less assertive in role play situations than control children (BAT-CR—behavioural observation). Across *all* interactions, children with social phobia received fewer positive responses from peers and experienced more instances of being ignored than their non-anxious peers (school observation). Across interactions initiated by the socially anxious child, clinical children were more likely to be ignored than control children (school observation). These findings were consistent with both child and parent reports of social skills and social competence. That is, children with social phobia were rated by themselves and their parents as less socially skilled and as less socially competent than their non-anxious peers. Interestingly, children with social phobia did not differ from their non-anxious peers on the amount of eye contact used or in the length of time to respond in the role plays (BAT-CR). Also, when initiating a social exchange, children with social phobia did not differ from their non-anxious peers in the number of positive or negative outcomes they received.

CRITICAL CONSIDERATIONS IN ASSESSING SOCIAL PHOBIA

There are a number of critical issues in assessment that bear direct relevance to the assessment of children with social phobia. These include social desirability, cross-informant consistency, and developmental sensitivity.

Social Desirability: Anxious children appear particularly primed for responding in socially desirable ways to assessment measures or tasks. Many researchers have noted anxious children's tremendous concerns with self-presentation and hypersensitivity to evaluation by others and have recognised that these behaviours are likely to result in socially desirable responses on assessment tasks (see Kendall and Flannery-Schroeder, 1998; Schniering *et al.*, in press). Several empirical investigations have examined relationships between social desirability and anxious symptoms in children with mixed results (e.g., Dadds *et al.*, 1998). Given the salience of fears of negative evaluation and poor social performance in children with social phobia, social desirability concerns may be even more relevant in this subgroup of anxious children. While measures have been developed that include lie scales (e.g., Revised Children's Manifest Anxiety Scale, Reynolds and Richmond, 1979), these items rarely work with children. Further research is needed to clarify the relationships between social phobia and social desirability in child populations.

Cross-Informant Consistency: There have been sufficient studies to conclude that agreement between parent and child reports of anxiety in children is poor (Rapee *et al.*, 1994; Kendall and Flannery-Schroeder, 1998) These findings hold for questionnaire data as well as diagnostic interviews. A recent study by Dibartolo *et al.*, (1998) assessed cross-informant consistency in a sample of children with social phobia. Results indicated reasonable agreement between parent and child ratings on social fears, whereas parents reported much higher levels of social avoidance compared with child reports. Further analyses revealed that social desirability accounted, in part, for the low avoidance reports by the children.

Several explanations have been proposed to account for low cross-informant consistency in children with social phobia, including parental anxiety, over-reporting by parents to ensure their child's acceptance into treatment, items on self-report measures beyond the developmental level of the child, and social desirability. Concerns with cross-informant inconsistency may be addressed, in part, by including multiple methods of assessment for both parents and children.

Developmental Sensitivity: Developmental factors pose complex problems for the assessment of childhood social phobia (and anxiety, generally). Given that the majority of available measures are downward extensions of adult measures, the degree to which these measures actually measure the construct of interest remains unclear (see Campbell *et al.*, 1996; McCathie and Spence, 1991). In this regard, the SPAI-C, an instrument designed specifically for children with social phobia, is recommended for use with children aged between 8 and 14 only. This reflects consideration of developmental relevance of the items of the SPAI-C to the population being assessed. Furthermore, the development of children's understanding of emotion, their ability to introspect and to become self-aware is a process taking place during the childhood years. While research is limited, findings suggest that young children (<12 years of age) have not developed these concepts sufficiently to be able to answer some of the more complex questions about the experience of anxiety—e.g., questions about cause and effect (Schniering *et al.*, in press).

Additional Assessment Issues: Diagnostic comorbidity in children complicates assessment and treatment planning, as well as expectations for outcome. Children with social phobia often have an additional anxiety disorder or other psychiatric diagnosis. March and Albano (1998) highlight the need for assessors to consider both cross-sectional and longitudinal comorbidity in case formulation as this will impact prognosis expectations and thus treatment planning and outcome evaluations.

Culture and gender are also important variables to consider in assessment practice. In brief, studies have shown that cultural factors can influence self-report measures of anxiety. For example, Chinese children have been found to report significantly more social fears than Western children (Dong *et al.*, 1994). In addition, assessment instruments may not include relevant items that capture certain fears found only in Asian cultures (Chang, 1984, cited in Beidel and Turner, 1998). In terms of gender, the finding that more female children have social phobia in the general population compared to equal numbers of male and female children with social phobia in clinical populations, suggests that further research is needed to improve our understanding of the factors responsible for the relatively lower numbers of female children with social phobia in clinical settings.

SUMMARY OF ASSESSMENT

In summary, comprehensive assessment of children with social phobia is critical to determine diagnostic status, treatment planning, outcome evaluations, and for research studies. Standardized assessment tools that demonstrate respectable reliability and validity are included as the core assessment materials. Comprehensive assessment protocols include multiple methods across multiple informants.

An assessment protocol includes a diagnostic interview to assist in determining diagnostic status as well as self-report clinical rating scales. Recent experimental studies have used behavioural assessment tasks and direct observation of behaviour to assess social skills with samples of children with social phobia, family interaction patterns, cognitive features, and parental overprotection of children with broad-based anxiety disorders. While results from these studies are provocative, the unstandardized nature of the assessment methodology precludes inclusion of these measures in a standardized assessment protocol. However, Beidel and others recommend their inclusion along with self-monitoring procedures as potentially important tools that provide valuable additional data on characteristics of children with social phobia. Future research aimed at increasing the reliability and validity of these assessment approaches is warranted.

Several critical issues have been raised that bear on interpretation of assessment findings. Poor agreement between parent and child reports, children's potential to respond in socially desirable ways, the sometimes inappropriate match between child's age and developmental level of a questionnaire or assessment task, the impact of comorbidity, and issues of culture and gender, highlight the complexity of factors that need to be considered in the assessment of children with social phobia.

Aetiology

A thorough examination of factors relevant to the aetiology of social phobia is beyond the scope of this chapter. Interested readers are referred to (Chorpita and Barlow, 1998; Hudson and Rapee, 2000; Krohne and Hock, 1991; Rapee, in press). In brief, Rapee (in press) has described a comprehensive model of the development of generalized anxiety disorder that is most likely applicable to all of the anxiety disorders, including social phobia. According to this model, genetic factors as well as both shared and nonshared environmental factors all play a role in the development of anxiety. In addition, the model pays particular attention to gene-environment interactions as a central component in the development of the individual.

While there are assumed to be several pathways to the development of anxiety, it is suggested that many individuals who later develop anxiety disorders, are characterized as temperamentally vulnerable. This temperamental style is characterized initially by high arousal and emotionality (Kagan and Snidman, 1991) and later by withdrawal behaviours (Rubin et al., 1989). It is likely that there is a strong genetic input to this temperamental style. Considerable evidence has supported the importance of genetic factors in anxiety disorders in both adults (Kendler et al., 1992) and children (Thapar and McGuffin, 1995). Few studies have specifically examined social phobia, however, the general view from many of these studies is that the genetic component is largely a nonspecific one that is common to all of the anxiety disorders and possibly also depression (Andrews, 1996). One study has indicated that a small component of the variance in social phobia may be attributable to a specific genetic component in addition to the nonspecific component (Kendler et al., 1992), however, further research will be required to support this suggestion.

Little research has addressed the manifestation of the nonspecific genetic component to anxiety, however, there is some evidence that factors such as psychophysiological arousal and emotionality may be prime candidates (Rapee, in press). In addition, it has been hypothesised that the inherited characteristics may produce a tendency for certain individuals to be more prone to learning threat associations than others (Rapee, in press). If further research also supports the finding of an additional specific genetic component to social phobia, it is possible that some individuals may be characterized by a specific tendency to learn associations with intraspecific threat. Alternately, it may be that dominance/submission patterns within humans may be partly directly genetically mediated.

Rapee (in press) has argued that an individual's temperamental style influences much of that person's environmental interactions that, in turn, have an influence on the individual's temperament. For example, one influential environmental factor in early childhood is believed to be the role of an overprotecting parent (Hudson and Rapee, 1998; Rapee, 1997). While a small component of this parenting may be a result of the parent's own anxiety and hence emerge as a shared environmental influence, a large component is likely to be a reaction to the child's temperament in the first place interacting with the parent's own anxiety, largely a gene-environment interaction. Specifically, we suggest that an emotional and withdrawn child will elicit protection from a caring parent in order to avoid distress on the part of the child. Over time, the parent will begin to anticipate the child's distress and will intervene earlier and earlier. In turn, this will have the effect of maintaining and possibly increasing withdrawal and avoidance behaviours on the part of the child (Hudson and Rapee, 2000). In turn, this effect is likely to be even stronger with a more anxious parent. Our own laboratory-based observations have supported the association of overinvolved parenting with anxiety disorders in children (Hudson and Rapee, 1998). To date, numbers have not allowed examination of these effects by diagnosis. However, some earlier, retrospective research has indicated that parental overinvolvement may possibly be more of an issue for social phobia than for other anxiety disorders (Rapee, 1997).

We hypothesize that similar interactive processes affect the influence on the development of anxiety of other environmental factors such as parent socialization practices, peer socialization, non-specific stressors, and specific learning experiences (Hudson and Rapee, 2000; Rapee in press). For example, retrospective research has indicated that parents of socially phobic individuals socialise less than parents of nonclinical subjects (Bruch *et al.*, 1989; Rapee and Melville, 1997). While this difference may simply reflect the effects of shared genetics, at least one study has shown that the degree of socialising by nonbiological mothers of adopted children correlates with the child's shyness (Plomin and Daniels, 1986). Hence it is possible, that these effects reflect an environmental influence such as parental modeling. According to our model (Rapee, in press), the effects of modelling of anxious behaviours will be more pronounced in children who are temperamentally vulnerable to the development of anxiety.

Psychological Treatment

HEALTH SERVICES UTILISATION

An important question related to treatment is, "Which children with social phobia receive treatment, and why?" Most clinicians in tertiary treatment centres will report that children with social phobia, especially those without additional externalising or learning difficulties, are rarely treated in these facilities. A recent study by Essau *et al.* (1999a) reported that only 24% of children with social phobia received treatment. This low rate of access to mental health services for these children is a problem and research is needed to understand more about reasons for these patterns.

A number of researchers has begun to explore factors that may influence children's access to mental health care. For example, Weisz and Weiss (1991) examined the referability[1] of child clinical problems in a sample of preadolescent children and reported that, on average, when emotional and behavioural problems do occur, externalising problems were more likely to stimulate clinic referral than internalising problems, and that while some problems have been shown to be more referable in boys, the overall mean "referability index" was found to be higher in girls than in boys. That is, girls who show problems are more likely to be referred to clinics than boys with the *same* problems. A number of factors have been proposed to account for low referability of certain child clinical problems. These may include adult judgements as to the seriousness of the problem (e.g., parents, teachers, school counsellors, general practitioners), parent psychopathology, comorbidity, availability of services, and costs of treatment (see Essau *et al.*, 1999b; Weisz and Weiss, 1991). In the case of social phobia, the withdrawn behaviours, general obediance, and lack of assertiveness that characterize these children would often be viewed as positive by referral agents such as teachers and even parents. The intense personal suffering that may drive adults to seek help would be less apparent to referral agents.

TREATMENT OUTCOME STUDIES

There are very few treatment outcome studies that have included only children with social phobia. Indeed, while there is growing interest in the area, only a handful of outcome studies for anxiety disordered children exist. The next section will briefly review relevant findings from treatment studies of broad-based anxiety disorders in children, then move on to a more detailed review of those treatment studies that have examined children with a specific diagnosis of social phobia. To conclude, we describe current research from our laboratory on anxiety prevention in preschool age children.

TREATMENT OF BROAD-BASED ANXIETY

Seven studies of children with broad-based anxiety disorders were found that utilised either an individual treatment approach (Barrett *et al.*, 1996; Kendall, 1994; Kendall *et al.*, 1997) or group treatment approach (Barrett, 1998; Flannery-Schroeder and Kendall, in press; Silverman *et al.*, in press; Rapee, 1996). All seven studies included some children with a primary diagnosis of social phobia (or avoidant disorder based on DSM-III-R). Although studies differed, in some cases, on format of treatment (i.e., group versus individual, uncontrolled versus controlled), number of sessions, age range of children, number of children with social phobia, and extent of parent involvement, all studies reported positive results supporting the use of cognitive-behavioural intervention strategies in children with broad-based anxiety disorders. Four of the seven studies examined differential outcome by diagnosis and found that success of treatments was applicable to children with a primary diagnosis of social phobia. Rapee (1996) reported that, although findings were not marked, there was a tendancy for children with primary diagnoses of social phobia and generalised anxiety to respond less at post-treatment than children with separation disorder. However, this trend was not seen at 12 month follow-up. These results suggest that social phobia and generalised anxiety disorder may respond somewhat more slowly to treatment.

TREATMENT OF SOCIAL PHOBIA

Group Treatment-Uncontrolled Studies: Two uncontrolled studies were found that evaluated group treatment of children with a diagnosis of social phobia (Albano *et al.*, 1995b; Beidel *et al.*, 1996b). In the first of these studies, Albano *et al.* (1995) presented findings from a pilot study of five adolescents with a principal diagnosis of social phobia. The study examined a 16 session multi-component cognitive behavioural group treatment package designed specifically for use with an adolescent population. The components of the treatment were largely drawn from successful treatment studies of adults with social phobia (Heimberg *et al.*, 1993). In addition, specific skill building strategies for adolescents were included drawing largely from the work of Christoff *et al.* (1985). These treatment components comprised psychoeducation, social skills training, problem solving and assertiveness training, cognitive restructuring, exposure techniques, and weekly homework assignments. Parental involvement was also an important part of the treatment package with the inclusion of parents at four "key" points in the 16 week treatment program. At 3 months post treatment, 4 of the 5 subjects no longer met diagnostic criteria for social phobia, whereas the remaining subject received only a provisional diagnosis of social phobia. At 12 month follow up, all five subjects were free of a clinical diagnosis of social phobia with one subject receiving a "subclinical diagnosis of social phobia in partial remission" (Albano *et al.*, 1995, p. 652).

The impact of treatment on behavioural and heart rate measures was evaluated at post-treatment and 12 months follow up with four of the five subjects available for testing across all three time points. Results indicated decreases in subjective anxiety during a reading and impromptu speech task for all four subjects at post test and further decreases at 12 month follow up. In fact, subjective anxiety ratings were very low at 12 month follow up with heart rate data remaining unchanged. Interestingly, negative cognitions during the reading and impromptu tasks significantly decreased from pre to post treatment and this was accompanied by a significant increase in the number of neutral cognitions across the follow up period.

Using a younger sample of children with social phobia, Beidel *et al.* (1996b) have reported preliminary findings using their own treatment program called "Social Effectiveness Therapy for Children". As with the Albano *et al.* (1995b) treatment package, Beidel and colleagues based their treatment program on intervention strategies that have been demonstrated to be effective in treating adults with social phobia. The pilot study, comprised 16 children between the ages of 8 and 12, and consisted of 24 sessions over a twelve week period. The main treatment components were exposure and social skills training. Each week the children received one treatment session focused on exposure and the second treatment session on social skills training. Unique to this treatment program was the inclusion of a "peer-generalisation component" (Beidel and Turner, 1998, p. 256). Following the weekly social skills training session, children with social phobia were paired with non-anxious peers for a 90 minute outing. This created natural opportunities for the child with social phobia to practice the newly learned social skill with a non-anxious peer.

The children reported significantly less social anxiety concerns at post-treatment on several measures. Similarly, parent reports indicated a significant reduction in internalising behaviours from pre- to post-treatment. On behavioural tasks of reading aloud and role playing, children were rated by independent and blind observers as significantly more skilled and with significantly less observable anxiety than pre-treatment ratings. These results are encouraging to the extent that they support continued evaluation of this particular treatment program for social phobia in adolescents. Multiple assessment modalities- that is, questionnaire data and behavioural observations, as well as multiple informants were used with all reports indicating reductions in social anxiety.

Group Treatment-Controlled Studies: Two controlled treatment outcome studies of children with social phobia, provide even stronger support for the utility of cognitive-behavioural approaches for treating this population (Beidel *et al.*, 1999; Spence *et al.*, 2000). One study by Spence *et al.* (2000) compared the effectiveness of two different treatments (a cognitive-behavioural group [CBG; N = 17] versus a cognitive-behavioural group plus parent component [CBGPC; N = 19]), with a waitlist control group (N = 14). Children, ranging in age from 7 to 14 years, were randomly assigned to one of the three groups. Treated children received 12 weekly therapy lasting 1 and 1/2 hours with 2 booster sessions at 3 months and 6 months post-treatment. Parents in the CBGPC received 12 weeks of weekly sessions of 30 minutes duration, as well as observation of child sessions. The treatment package consisted of social skills training, problem solving, relaxation training, cognitive restructuring and exposure therapy (Spence, 1995). The parent treatment component included instructions in parent management techniques particularly for socially anxious children as well as modelling and reinforcing of treatment objectives. Parents in the CBGPC also observed their child's sessions. Significantly fewer children met criteria for a clinical diagnosis of social phobia at post-treatment in both active treatments compared with the waitlist control group: 87% diagnosis free in CBGPC; 58% in CBG; 7% in the waitlist control group. These gains were maintained at follow-up. On measures of general and social anxiety, both treatments showed significant reductions at post treatment compared with the waitlist group. Also, parent reports of children's social skills increased for both treatment conditions compared with the control group. While there was a trend towards better results in the cognitive behavioural treatment that included the parent component, this difference did not reach significance.

In a sample of 50 preadolescent children (8–12 years of age) diagnosed with social phobia, Beidel *et al.* (1999) compared the effectiveness of their Social Effectiveness Therapy for Children (SET-C; N = 30) with an active, but non-specific intervention (N = 20), primarily a test-taking and study-skills training program. Treatments were matched in terms of therapist contact time, group versus individual treatment time, the giving of homework, and number of weekly sessions. Results were very encouraging. At post-treatment, 67% of the children in the SET-C group were free of their principal diagnosis of social phobia, compared with only 5% of children in the non-specific group. Furthermore, 52% of the SET-C group were judged to be treatment responders, while only 5% of the non-specific group achieved this classification. Similar to the Spence *et al.* (in press) study, improvements were also evident on other measures of social anxiety and social skills performance. All gains were maintained at 6 months post-treatment.

Overall, these preliminary studies support the utility of a multi-component group cognitive-behavioural treatment approach for treating children with social phobia. The two controlled studies (Beidel *et al.*, 1999; Spence *et al.*, 2000) provide the most direct evidence of the efficacy of cognitive-behavioural interventions for children with social phobia, with exposure and social skills training the central treatment components in both studies.

Future studies need to employ deconstructive methodology to allow determination of which treatment components are most effective in treating children with social phobia. Also, controlled treatment outcome studies that examine the efficacy of cognitive-behavioural treatments in *adolescents* with social phobia are warranted, as are studies that examine an individual treatment approach with samples of children meeting diagnostic criteria for social phobia. Other research areas include further examination of the contribution of parents to the treatment package for this population.

EARLY INTERVENTION AND PREVENTION

In line with the increasing trend towards *early intervention* and *prevention* in mental health, particularly in child populations, researchers have begun to evaluate the potential for cognitive-behavioural treatments to be used effectively as an early intervention or preventative approach with children who are anxious. For example, Dadds *et al.* (1997) conducted a combined child- and parent-focused treatment for the prevention and early intervention of anxiety problems in children between the ages of 7 and 14. Of an initial cohort of 1,786 children, 128 met criteria for inclusion and agreed to participate in the school based treatment. Children who met inclusion criteria were considered "at risk" based on a combination of child self-report of anxious symptoms, teacher ratings of shyness and anxiety, and parent report on a structured diagnostic instrument (see Dadd's *et al.* [1997] for complete screening and inclusion details). The treatment consisted of a 10 week school-based cognitive-behavioural and family-based intervention compared with a monitoring group. Unfortunately, 75% of the selected children met criteria for an anxiety disorder at pre-treatment. Thus results from these children are not relevant to the issue of early intervention and simply reflect treatment of mild anxiety disorders. Surprisingly, treatment outcome for these children was not especially strong mainly due to marked changes in the untreated group. Less than 40% of untreated children met criteria for an anxiety disorder after two years suggesting considerable remission in mildly anxious children (Dadds *et al.*, 1999).

In terms of early intervention, the main interest centres on the 25% of children who showed symptoms of anxiety but did not meet criteria for an anxiety disorder at pre-treatment. Consistent with the mild anxiety disordered children described above, very few of these children developed an anxiety disorder two years later, even if left untreated

(16% in the waitlist group). Thus, the effects of early intervention were minimal. The results did not differ by diagnosis. The results of this study seriously question the assumption that mild symptoms of social phobia are markers for the later development of more severe social phobia. In turn, these data question the value of early intervention for social phobia using low level anxious symptomatology as the selection. It is possible that identification of other risk factors may be a more useful method of selecting subjects for early intervention in social phobia.

An alternate model is to focus on even younger children and examine the risk factor of temperament. We are currently conducting a longitudinal prevention project with preschool age children who show early signs of a withdrawn temperament and their parents (Rapee and Sweeney, 1999). Our "at risk" group comprises 3½–4½ year-old children who are identified as behaviourally inhibited ("BI"—see Kagan et al., 1989). We first ask parents of preschool age children to complete a temperament measure, then, if the child scores in the clinical range on the approach/withdrawal factor, an observational assessment is conducted in our lab. Parents of children who meet BI criteria (and who agree to participate) are randomly assigned to either a 6-week cognitive-behavioural education group or a wait-list control group. The 6-week program (Rapee and Sweeney, 1998) educates parents in how to deliver cognitive restructuring and exposure to their children, teaches parent management strategies, as well as helping parents to become aware of their own anxieties and ways to manage them.

Pilot testing of this program has indicated very promising results (Rapee and Jacobs, 1998). Children whose parents underwent the education program showed a marked and significant decrease in both anxious symptomatology and, more impressively, temperament scores on withdrawal. Effects continued to increase to at least 6 months. Preliminary data in our larger, controlled trial are showing similar trends (Rapee and Sweeney, 1999). To the extent that behavioural inhibition predicts the later development of anxiety disorders, including social phobia (Biederman et al., 1990), these results should lead to a reduced incidence of anxiety disorders in this population.

PHARMACOLOGICAL TREATMENT

Studies examining the efficacy of pharmacological interventions for children with social phobia, and broad-based childhood anxiety disorders, are scarce (with the exception of obsessive-compulsive disorder where a number of published studies exist). The paucity of studies in this area can be explained, in part, by the relatively recent interest in the area of medication management of anxiety disorders in childhood, and by recent changes to DSM that have resulted in social phobia only being used as a diagnosis for children since 1994.

Given that no controlled outcome studies of pharmacological treatment were found that included only children with a specific diagnosis of social phobia, this review will include studies of broad-based anxiety disorders (which included some children with diagnoses of social phobia or avoidant disorder) and case studies of children with social phobia. While several studies have examined medication effects in samples of children diagnosed with selective mutism (sometimes described as a childhood variant of social phobia), the inclusion of these studies goes beyond the scope of the present review (for further reading see Black and Uhde, 1992; Dummit *et al.*, 1996).

One study was found that examined the efficacy of fluoxetine for children with broad-based anxiety disorders (Birmaher *et al.*, 1994). Twenty-one children, ranging in age from 11–17 years, who had not responded to previously administered psychological or pharmacological treatment, were treated in an open trial with fluoxetine over an average of 10 months. Anxiety disorders in the sample included social phobia, overanxious disorder, and separation anxiety disorder. Many of the children met criteria for more than one disorder. Results were encouraging with 81% of children rated by child psychiatrists as significantly improved on the severity and improvement scales of the Clinical Global Improvement Scale (CGIS). Of importance to this review was the report that fluoxetine was judged to be effective across the three diagnostic groups. Future research utilising placebo-controlled studies is needed to allow for firmer conclusions to be made regarding the efficacy of fluoxetine in reducing children's fears.

Two studies have examined the efficacy of alprazolam, a benzodi-azepine in children with diagnoses of avoidant disorder or overanxious disorder (Simeon and Ferguson, 1987; Simeon *et al.*, 1992). Simeon and Ferguson (1987) conducted an open trial of alprazolam with 12 children, ranging in age from 8–16 years. Overall, 58% of children showed moderate improvement across several measurement indicators (clinician, parent, and teacher ratings). Simeon *et al.* (1992) conducted a double-blind placebo-controlled study of alprazolam with a sample of 30 children (8–16 years). Findings from this study indicated that while there was a trend towards greater improvement in the alprazolam group compared with the placebo group based on clinical global ratings, overall there was no significant difference between groups at post-treatment. The authors suggest that these findings may be explained, in part, by the relatively low dose of alprazolam and the short duration of the treatment trial (4 weeks), and suggest that future studies address these limitations.

Several case studies have investigated the efficacy of buspirone in children with a variety of anxiety disorders, however, only one case study was found where the primary diagnosis was social phobia. Zwier and Rao (1994) reported improvement in an adolescent's social phobia following the introduction of buspirone. Improvements were noted as early as 12 days following initiation of buspirone and were maintained at 1 year follow-up. Conclusions about the efficacy of buspirone for children with social phobia cannot be made based on this single case study.

In summary, only a handful of studies have examined the efficacy of medication in treating children with social phobia. The majority of these studies have included samples of children with broad-based anxiety disorders. Despite the promising findings based on single case and open trial studies, the only double-blind placebo controlled outcome study failed to report superior outcome for children treated with alprazolam compared with a placebo control group. In fact, following withdrawal of medication, children from the alprazolam group continued to decline whereas children in the placebo group maintained gains or continued to make further gains (Simeon *et al.*, 1992). Clearly, before conclusions can be drawn about the efficacy of pharmacological interventions for children with social phobia, we need more placebo-controlled trials of the various indicated medications, as well as studies that include carefully diagnosed samples of children with social phobia. However, given the promising efficacy of non-pharmacological treatment programs for socially phobic children, one may question the value of such an approach for a young population.

Summary and Conclusions

Epidemiological data indicate that social phobia is one of the most common anxiety disorders in children and adolescents, that such problems are associated with a range of psychosocial impairments, and that it often follows a chronic course when left untreated. While there are a number of studies aimed at understanding the nature and maintenance of social phobia, little research has focused on etiological explanations, assessment, or interventions designed specifically for the child with social phobia. Indeed research on social phobia in children is still relatively new.

Comprehensive and accurate assessment of children with social phobia requires the inclusion of standardized assessment tools that demonstrate acceptable reliability and validity data. Also, assessments should include multiple informants and use multiple methods where possible. A sample assessment protocol that meets the above criteria may include parent- and child-self-report on a diagnostic interview, clinical rating scales, and several additional questionnaires that assess characteristics of children with social phobia. Clinical research teams have reported the potential usefulness of including self-monitoring procedures in the assessment process with this population, however, these assessment procedures lack standardization. Further research in this area is warranted. Several issues also need to be considered as part of the assessment of social phobia in children including social desirability, cross-informant consistency, developmental sensitivity, comorbidity, gender and cultural issues.

While few studies have examined etiological factors in social phobia in children, several related areas of research such as social anxiety, shyness, social isolation, and social withdrawal may contribute to our developing understanding of the origins of the disorder. Based on the available research, we speculate that an inhibited and withdrawn temperament should be a central component in any model of the development of social phobia. In turn, several other influential factors, such as parenting styles, parent and peer socialization, learning experiences, and life events are likely to produce their effects in interaction with this temperamental component.

To date, few treatment studies have been conducted that include a specific focus on the treatment of socially phobic children. Nevertheless, results from seven studies of children with broad-based anxiety disorders are encouraging and support the value of cognitive-behavioural treatments for children with social phobia. Two pilot studies and two very recent controlled treatment outcome studies have examined cognitive-behavioural treatment programs for children specifically diagnosed with social phobia. The two controlled studies provide the most direct evidence of the efficacy of cognitive-behavioural interventions for children with social phobia, with exposure and social skills training as the central treatment components in both studies. Additional replication studies are needed.

Future efforts with samples of children with social phobia should also focus on using deconstruction methodology to assist in evaluating the effectiveness of different treatment components, conducting studies with adolescents and assessing the usefulness of an individual treatment approach. More recently, early intervention and prevention approaches for children with social phobia, and anxiety in general, have emerged. Preliminary findings support the possible usefulness of prevention in young children at risk for the later development of social phobia. Longer term follow-up is needed before any firm conclusions can be drawn.

Studies examining pharmacological interventions for children with social phobia are scant. The few studies that do exist have used samples of children with broad-based anxiety disorders, or single case study reports. While several studies have shown a reduction in anxious symptoms following the administration of medication (fluoxetine, buspirone, or alprazolam), only one placebo-controlled treatment study was found and results did not support the efficacy of medication over placebo effects. This finding and the overall limited number of studies prohibits any conclusion being drawn and awaits further research in this area.

Research into the nature and treatment of children with social phobia has not received great attention to date. However, this is changing. The decision in the DSM-IV to eliminate the diagnostic category of avoidant disorder should help to direct an increased focus onto social phobia. In addition, the general increase in world attention to early intervention and prevention has already begun to increase research input into child and adolescent disorders. Future years should witness a burgeoning research effort to build our knowledge of the nature and treatment of social phobia in children and adolescents.

Note

[1] Referability is a term meaning the power of various child clinical problems to *evoke* clinic referral. Referability involves studying the likelihood that a problem or disorder will stimulate a referral if it, in fact, exists. For example, examining differences in the referability of boys and girls would involve studying the relative likelihood that girls and boys will be referred to a mental health clinic, given that they have the *same* problem. Referability is measured by calculating a "referability index" (RI—see Weisz and Weiss [1991] for a detailed explanantion of the RI).

References

Albano, A.M., DiBartolo, P.M., Heimberg, R.G., & Barlow, D.H. (1995a). Children and adolescents: Assessment and treatment. In R.G. Heimberg, M.R. Liedowitz, D.A. Hope, & F.R. Schneier (Eds.), *Social phobia: Diagnosis, assessment and treatment* (pp. 387–425). New York: Guilford Press.

Albano, A.M., Marten, P.A., Holt, C.S., Heimberg, R.G., & Barlow, D.H. (1995b). Cogntive-behavioural group treatment for social phobia in adolescents: A preliminary study. *The Journal of Nervous and Mental Disease, 183,* 649–656.

American Psychiatric Association (1994). *Diagnostic and Statistical Manual of Mental Disorders* (4th Ed.). Washington D.C.: American Psychiatric Association.

American Psychiatric Association (1987). *Diagnostic and Statistical Manual of Mental Disorders* (3rd ed. Rev.). Washington D.C.: American Psychiatric Association.

Anderson, J.C., Williams, S., McGee, R., & Silva, P.A. (1987). DSM-III disorders in preadolescent children. Prevalence in a large sample from a general population. *Archives of General Psychiatry, 44,* 69–76.

Andrews, G. (1996). Comorbidity in neurotic disorders: The similarities are more important than the differences. In R.M. Rapee (Ed.), *Current controversies in the anxiety disorders.* (pp. 3–20). New York: The Guilford Press.

Barrett, P.M. (1998). Evaluation of cognitive-behavioural group treatments for childhood anxiety disorders. *Journal of Clinical Child Psychology, 27,* 459–468.

Barrett, P.M., Dadds, M.R., & Rapee, R.M., (1996). Family treatment of childhood anxiety: A controlled trial. *Journal of Consulting and Clinical Psychology, 64,* 333–342.

Beidel, D.C. (1991). Social phobia and overanxious disorder in school-age children. *Journal of American Academy of Child and Adolescent psychiatry, 30,* 545–552.

Beidel, D.C., Neal, A.M., & Lederer, A.S. (1991). The feasibility and validity of a daily diary for the assessment of anxiety in children. *Behaviour Therapy, 22,* 505–517.

Beidel, D.C. & Turner, S.M. (1998). *Shy Children, Phobic Adults: Nature and Treatment of Social Phobia.* Washington D.C.: American Psychiatric Association.

Beidel, D.C., Turner, S.M., & Fink, C.M. (1996a). The assessment of childhood social phobia: Construct, convergent and discriminative validity of the Social Phobia and Anxiety Inventory for Children (SPAI-C). *Psychological Assessment, 8,* 235–240.

Beidel, D.C., Turner, S.M., & Morris, T.L. (1995). A new inventory to assess childhood social anxiety and phobia: The Social Phobia and Anxiety Inventory of Children. *Psychological Assessment, 7*, 73–79.

Beidel, D.C., Turner, S.M., & Morris, T.L. (1996b). Social Effectiveness Therapy for Children: A Treatment manual. Unpublished manuscript, Medical University of Charleston, South Carolina.

Beidel, D.C., Turner, M., & Morris, T.L. (1999). Psychopathology of Childhood Social Phobia. *Journal of American Academy of Child and Adolescent Psychiatry, 38*, 643–650.

Biederman, J., Rosenbaum, J.F., Hirshfeld, D.R., et. al. (1990). Psychiatric correlates of behavioural inhibition in young children and parents with and without psychiatric disorders. *Archives of General Psychiatry, 47*, 21–26.

Birmaher, B., Waterman, G.S., Ryan, N., Cully, M., Balach, L., Ingram, J., & Brodsky, M. (1994). Fluoxetine for childhood anxiety disorders. *Journal of American Academy of Child and Adolescent Psychiatry, 33*, 993–999.

Black, B. & Uhde, T.W. (1992). Elective mutism as a variant of social phobia. *Journal of American Academy of Child and Adolescent Psychiatry, 31*, 1090–1094.

Bornstein, M.R., Bellack, A.S., & Hersen, M. (1977). Social skills training for unassertive children: A multiple baseline analysis. *Journal of Applied Behaviour Analysis, 10*, 183–195..

Bruch, M.A., Heimberg, R.G., Berger, P., & Collins, T.M. (1989). Social phobia and perceptions of early parental and personal characteristics. *Anxiety Research, 2*, 57–65.

Campbell, M.A. & Rapee, R.M. (1994). The nature of feared outcome representations in children. *Journal of Abnormal Child Psychology, 22*, 99–111.

Campbell, M.A., Rapee, R.M., & Spence, S. (1996). *Developmental changes in the interpretation of instructions on a questionnaire measure of worry.* Unpublished manuscript.

Chorpita, B.F. & Barlow, D.H. (1998). The development of anxiety: The role of control in the early environment. *Psychological Bulletin, 124*, 3–21.

Christoff, K.A., Scott, W.O.N., Kelley, M.L., Baer, G., & Kelly, J.A. (1985) Social skills and social problem-solving training for shy young adolescents. *Behaviour Therapy, 16*, 468–477.

Dadds, M.R., Holland, D.E., Spence, S.H., Laurens, K.R., Mullins, M., & Barrett, P.M. (1999). Early intervention and prevention of anxiety disorders in children: Results at 2 year follow-up. *Journal of Consulting and Clinical Psychology, 67*, 145–150.

Dadds, M.R., Perrin, S., & Yule, W. (1998). Social desirability and self-reported anxiety in children: An analysis of the RCMAS Lie Scale. *Journal of Abnormal Child Psychology, 26*, 4, 311–317.

Dadds, M.R., Spence, S.H., Holland, D.E., Barrett, R.M., & Laurens, K.R. (1997). Prevention and early intervention for anxiety disorders: A controlled trial. *Journal of Consulting and Clinical Psychology, 65,* 627–635.

DiBartolo, P.M., Albano, A.M., Barlow, D.H., & Heimberg, R.G. (1998). Cross-informant agreement in the assessment of social phobia in youth. *Journal of Abnormal Child Psychology, 26,* 213–220.

Dong, Q., Yang, B., & Ollendick, T.H. (1994). Fears in Chinese children and adolescents and their relations to anxiety and depression. *Journal of Child Psychology and Psychiatry and Allied Disciplines, 35,* 351–363.

Dummit, E.S., Klein, R.G., Tancer, N.K., Asche, B., & Martin, J. (1996). Fluoxetine treatment of children with selective mutism: an open trial. *Journal of Amercian Academy of Child and Adolescent Psychiatry, 35,* 615–621.

Essau, C.A., Conradt, J., & Petermann, F. (1999a). Frequency and comorbidity of social phobia and social fears in adolescents. *Behaviour Research and Therapy, 37,* 831–843.

Essau, C.A., Conradt, J., & Petermann, F. (1999b). Course and outcome. In C.A. Essau & F. Petermann (Eds.)., *Depressive disorders in children and adolescents: Epidemiology, risk factors and treatment.* New Jersey: Jason Aronson Inc. Publishers.

Flannery-Schroeder, E.C. & Kendall, P.C. (in press). Group and individual treatments for youth with anxiety disorders: A randomised clinical trial. *Cognitive Therapy and Research.*

Heimberg, R.G., Salzman, D.G., Holt, C.S., & Blendall, K.A. (1993). Cognitive-behavioural group treatment of social phobia: Effectiveness at 5 year follow-up. *Cognitive Therapy and Research, 17,* 325–339.

Hudson, J.L & Rapee, R.M. (1998). Parent-child interactions and anxiety. Paper presented at the *World Congress of Behavioural and Cognitive Therapies,* Acapulco, Mexico, July.

Hudson, J.L. & Rapee, R.M. (2000). The origins of social phobia. *Behavior Modification, 24,* 102–129.

Kagan, J., Reznick, J.S., & Gibbons, J. (1989). Inhibited and uninhibited types of children. *Child Development, 60,* 838–845.

Kagan, J. & Snidman, N. (1991). Infant predictors of inhibited and uninhibited profiles. *Psychological Science, 2,* 40–44.

Kashani, J.H. & Orvaschel, H. (1990). A community study of anxiety in children and adolescents. *American Journal of Psychiatry, 147,* 313–318.

Kendall, P.C. (1994). Treating anxiety disorders in children. Results of a randomized clinical trial. *Journal of Consulting and Clinical psychology, 62,* 100–110.

Kendall, P.C. & Flannery-Schroeder, E.C. (1998). Methodological issues in treatment research for anxiety disorders in youth. *Journal of Abnormal Child Psychology, 26,* 27–38.

Kendall, P.C., Flannery-Schroeder, E.C., Panichelli-Mindel, S., Southam-Gerow, M., Henin, A., & Warman, M. (1997). Therapy for youths with anxiety disorders: A second randomised clinical trial. *Journal of Consulting and Clinical Psycholog, 65*, 366–380.

Kendall, P.C. & Warman, M.J. (1997). Anxiety disorders in youth: Diagnostic consistency across DSM-III-R and DSM-IV. *Journal of Anxiety Disorders, 10*, 453–463.

Kendler, K.S., Neale, M.C., Kessler, R.C., Heath, A.C., & Eaves, L.J. (1992). The genetic epidemiology of phobias in women: The interrelationship of agoraphobia, social phobia, situational phobia, and simple phobia. *Archives of General Psychiatry, 49*, 273–281.

Krohne, H.W. & Hock, M. (1991). Relationships between restrictive mother-child interactions and anxiety of the child. *Anxiety Research, 4*, 109–124.

LaGreca, A.M. & Stone, W.L. (1993). Social Anxiety for Children—Revised: Factor structure and concurrent validity. *Journal of Clinical Child Psychology, 22*, 17–27.

Last, C.G., Hersen, M., Kazdin, A., Finkelstein, R., & Strauss, C.C. (1991). Anxiety disorders in children and their families. *Archives of General Psychiatry, 48*, 928–937.

Last, C.G., Perrin, S., Hersen, M., & Kazdin, A.E. (1992). DSM-III-R anxiety disorders in children: Sociodemographic and clinical characteristics. *Journal of the American Academy of Child and Adolescent Psychiatry, 31*, 928–934.

Last, C.G., Strauss, C.C., & Francis, G. (1987). Comorbidity among child-hood anxiety disorders. *Journal of nervous and mental Disease, 175*, 726–730.

Liebowitz, M.R., Gorman, J.M., Fyer, A.J., & Klein, D.F. (1985). Social phobia: Review of a neglected anxiety disorder. *Archives of General Psychiatry, 42*, 669–677.

March, J. & Albano, A. (1998).New developments in assessing pediatric anxiety disorders. In T.H. Ollendick, & R.J. Prinz (Eds.), *Advances in Clinical Child Psychology, 20*, 213–241. New York: Plenum Press.

McCathie, H. & Spence, S.H. (1991). What is the Revised Fear Survey Schedule for Children measuring? *Behaviour Research and Therapy, 29*, 495–502.

McGee, R., Feehan, M., Williams, S., Partridge, F., Silva, P.A., & Kelly, J.(1990). DSM-III disorders in a large sample of adolescents. *Journal of American Academy of Child and Adolescent Psychiatry, 29*, 611–619.

Ollendick, T.H. (1981). Assessment of social interaction skills in school children. *Behavioral Counseling Quarterly, 1*, 227–243.

Plomin, R. & Daniels, D. (1986). Genetics and shyness. In W.H. Jones, J.M. Cheek, & S.R. Briggs (Eds.), *Shyness: Perspectives on research and treatment.* (pp. 63–80). New York: Plenum.

Rapee, R.M. (1995). Descriptive psychopathology of social phobia. In R.G. Heimberg, M.R. Liebowitz., D.A. Hope, & F.R. Schneier (Eds.), *Social*

Phobia: Diagnosis, Assessment and Treatment (pp. 41–66). New York: Guilford Press.

Rapee, R.M. (1996). *Improved efficiency in the treatment of childhood anxiety disorders.* Paper presented at the 30th annual AABT convention. New York.

Rapee, R.M. (1997). Potential role of childrearing practices in the development of anxiety and depression. *Clinical Psychology Review, 17,* 47–67.

Rapee, R.M. (in press). The development of generalised anxiety. In M.W. Vasey & M.R. Dadds (Eds.), *The developmental psychopathology of anxiety.* New York: Oxford University Press.

Rapee, R.M., Barrett, P.M., Dadds, M.R., & Evans, L. (1994). Reliability of the DSM-III-R childhood anxiety disorders using structured interview: Interrater and parent-child agreement. *Journal of the American Academy of Child and Adolescent Psychiatry, 33,* 984–992.

Rapee, R.M. & Jacobs, D. (1998). *Prevention of anxiety disorders: A model and pilot treatment program.* Paper presented at the World Congress of Behavioral and Cognitive Therapies, Acapulco, Mexico, July.

Rapee, R.M. & Sweeney, L. (1998). *PIP's Parent Education Program for Shy Preschoolers.* Unpublished manual. Macquarie University.

Rapee, R.M. & Sweeney, L. (1999). Prevention of anxiety disorders: A model and pilot treatment program. Paper presented at the *Anxiety Disorders Association of America Annual meeting.* San Diego.

Reynolds, C.R. & Richmond, B.O. (1979). What I Think and Feel: A revised measure of children's manifest anxiety. *Journal of Abnormal Child Psychology, 6,* 271–280.

Rubin, K.H., Hymel, S., & Mills, R.S.L. (1989). Sociability and social withdrawal in childhood: Stability and outcomes. *Journal of Personality, 57,* 237–255.

Schneier, F.R., Johnson, J., Hornig, C.D., Liebowitz, M.R., & Weissman, M.M. (1992). Social phobia: Comorbidity and morbidity in an epidemiologic sample. *Archives of General Psychiatry, 49,* 282–288.

Schniering, C.A., Hudson, J.L., & Rapee (2000). Issues in diagnosis and assessment of anxiety disorders in children and adolescents. *Clinical Psychology Review, 20,* 453–478.

Silverman, W.K. & Albano, A.M. (1995). *Anxiety Disorders Interview Schedule for Children.* San Antonio, TX: Psychological Corporation.

Silverman, W.K., Kurtines, W.M., Ginsburg, G.S., Weems, C.F., Lumpkin, P.W., & Carmichael, D.H. (in press). Treating anxiety disorders in children with cognitive-behaviour therapy: A randomised clinical trial. *Journal of Consulting and Clinical Psychology.*

Simeon, J.G. & Ferguson, H.B. (1987). Alprazolam effects in children with anxiety disorders. *Canadian Journal of Psychiatry, 32,* 570–574.

Simeon, J.G., Ferguson, H.B., Knott, V., Roberts, N., Garthier, B., Dubois, C., & Wiggens, D. (1992). Clinical, cognitive, and neurophysiological effects of alprazolam in children and adolescents with overanxious and avoidant disorder. *Journal of American Academy of Child and Adolescent Psychiatry, 31*, 29–33.

Spence, S.H. (1995). *Social Skills Training: Enhancing Social Competence with Children and Adolescents.* Great Britain: NFER-Nelson.

Spence, S.H., Donovan, C., & Brechman-Toussaint, M. (2000). The treatment of childhood social phobia: The effectiveness of a social skills training based cognitive-behavioural intervention, with and without parental involvement. *Journal of Child Psychology and Psychiatry, 41*, 713–726.

Spence, S.H., Donovan, C., & Brechman-Toussaint, M. (1999). Social skills, social outcomes and cognitive features of childhood social phobia. *Journal of Abnormal Psychology, 108*, 211–221.

Strauss, C.C. & Last, C.G. (1993). Social and simple phobias in children. *Journal of Anxiety Disorders, 1*, 141–152.

Thapar, A. & McGuffin, P. (1995). Are anxiety symptoms in childhood heritable? *Journal of Child Psychology and Psychiatry, 36*, 439–447.

Turner, S.M., Beidel, D.C., Dancu, C.V., & Keys, D.J. (1986). Psycho-pathology of social phobia and comparison to avoidant personality disorder. *Journal of Abnormal Psychology, 95*, 389–394.

Turner, S.M., Beidel, D.C., & Epstein, L.H. (1991). Vulnerability and risk for anxiety disorders. *Journal of Anxiety Disorders, 5*, 151–166.

Vernberg, E.M., Abwender, D.A., Ewell, K.K., & Beery, S.H. (1992). Social anxiety and peer relationships in early adolescence: A prospective analysis. *Journal of Clinical Child Psychology, 21*, 189–196.

Verhulst, F.C., van der Ende, J., Ferdinand, R.F., & Jasius, M.C. (1997). The prevalence of DSM-III-R diagnoses in a national sample of Dutch adolescents. *Archives of General Psychiatry, 54*, 329–336.

Watson, D. & Friend, R. (1969). Measurement of social-evaluative anxiety. *Journal of Consulting and Clinical Psychology, 33*, 448–457.

Weisz, J.R. & Weiss, B. (1991). Studying the referability of child clinical problems. *Journal of Consulting and Clinical Psychology, 59*, 2, 266–273.

Zwier, K.J. & Rao, U. (1994). Buspirone use in an adolescent with social phobia and mixed personality disorder (cluster A type). *Journal of Amercian Academy of Child and Adolescent Psychiatry, 33*, 1007–1011.

7 SPECIFIC PHOBIA

Cecilia A. Essau
Fumiyo Aihara
Franz Petermann
Susanne Al Wiswasi

Specific phobia is defined in DSM-IV (simple phobia in DSM-III and DSM-III-R) as the presence of marked and persistent fear of circumscribed objects or situations (American Psychiatric Association; APA, 1994). The major focus of fear maybe anticipated harm from some aspects of the object or situation. That is, the fear is usually not of the object itself but of some dire outcome that the individual believes may result from contact with that object. For example, individuals with blood phobia do not fear blood, but instead, they fear the consequences of confrontation with blood (e.g., fainting). Exposure to the phobic stimulus almost immediately provokes an anxiety response which may take the form of a panic attack. The phobic stimulus may be avoided or endured with distress. Individuals with this disorder recognize that their fear is excessive or unreasonable, however, this feature may be absent in children. The avoidance, anxious anticipation, or distress in the feared situation(s) markedly interferes with the person's daily activities, occupational (or academic) functioning, or social activities or relationships, or there is considerable distress about having the phobia. As argued by Silverman and Rabian (1994), specific phobia can be differentiated from normal developmental fears in that the phobic reaction is excessive and out of proportion to the demands of the situation, leads to avoidance, persists over time, and is maladaptive. For individuals under age 18 years, the fear must have persisted for at least 6 months.

The fear of a circumscribed stimulus must not be the fear of having a panic attack (as in panic disorder), or fear of humiliation or embarrassment in certain social situations (as in social phobia). It should be determined whether the observed condition includes fears that are more characteristic of agoraphobia. The phobic stimulus must not be related to the content of the obsessions of an obsessive-compulsive disorder (i.e., fear of dirt among individuals with an obsession about contamination). A distinction should also be made between specific phobia and posttraumatic stress disorder (i.e., avoiding stimuli related to severe stressor).

Unlike its earlier versions, DSM-IV differentiates between five types of specific phobias which have been delineated to indicate the focus of fear or avoidance: animal type (i.e., fear cued by animals or insects), natural-environment type (i.e., fear cued by objects in the natural environment such as storms, darkness, or water), blood-injection-injury type (i.e., fear cued by seeing blood or an injury, or receiving an injection), situational type (i.e., fear cued by a specific situation such as public transportation, tunnels, bridges), and a miscellaneous "other" type (i.e., fear cued by stimuli such as loud noise and avoidance of situations which may lead to choking). The idea of classifying specific phobia into different subtypes was based on findings that specific phobias differ with respect to their etiology, age of onset, physiological response, and focus of apprehension (Craske and Sipsas, 1992; Curtis et al., 1990). However, the validity of the separate categories of specific phobia as stated in DSM-IV needs to be examined in future studies. In a study among adults by Fredrikson et al. (1996), the factor analysis of specific fears and phobias confirmed that animal and blood-injection-injury phobias to represent separate categories. Situational and natural environment phobia tend to cluster together. Based on these findings, they concluded that situational and natural-environment phobias could possibly "share a common underlying theme" (Fredrikson et al., 1996; p. 37). Similar results have recently been reported by Muris and colleagues (1999). Overall, these findings have been interpreted as supporting the validity of the separate categories of specific phobia as proposed in DSM-IV.

While these adult criteria for specific phobia can be diagnosed in childhood and adolescence, minor changes have been made for these age groups. First, children may not recognize their fear as excessive or unreasonable. Second, the exposure to the phobic stimulus may provoke an immediate anxiety response in adult, whereas in children the fear may be expressed in "childhood" manner through crying, tantrums, freezing or clinging. Third, the phobic symptoms must have persisted for a minimum of six months before the disorder can be diagnosed. This criteria represents one of the major progresses in DSM-IV, because it enables the distinction between normal and short-lived fears from clinical fears or phobias. As discussed in detailed by Ollendick et al. (chapter 1, this volume) mild fears occur commonly as a normal part of development, which make it difficult to decide when to regard fears in childhood as clinically significant.

Assessment

Several self-report questionnaires have been developed to assess specific fears, the most common being that of the Fear Survey Schedule for Children—Revised (FSSC-R; Ollendick, 1983) and the Revised Children's Manifest Anxiety Scale (RCMAS; Reynolds and Richmond, 1978). The FSSC-R contains a broad range of potentially threatening stimuli which can be grouped into five factors: fear of failure and criticism, fear of the unknown, fear of injury and small animals, fear of danger and death, and medical fears (see chapter 3 in this volume). The RCMAS contains information related to the nature and level of the child's anxiety. Its scores yield three subscales: physiological anxiety, worry/oversensivity, and social concern/concerntration. Recently, the Spence Children's Anxiety Scale (SCAS; Spence, 1998) has been developed to measure various forms of anxiety disorders, including that of specific phobia (specifically, fears related to physical injury). In adults, numerous questionnaires have been developed for each specific types of phobia. Some examples include the Injection Phobia Scale (Öst et al., 1992) to assess blood-injury-injection phobia, as well as the Corah's Dental Anxiety Scale (Corah, 1968) and the Dental Cognitions Questionnaire (de Jongh et al., 1995) to measure dental phobia.

   Another common method to assess specific fears and phobia is by using structured interview schedules, including the Kiddie-Schedule for Affective Disorders and Schizophrenia (Puig-Antich and Chambers, 1978), the Diagnostic Interview for Children and Adolescents (Herjanic and Reich, 1982), the Diagnostic Interview Schedule for Children (Costello et al., 1987), and the Anxiety Disorders Interview Schedule for Children (Silverman and Albano, 1996). All these interview schedules cover DSM criteria for specific phobia and thereby allows the assessment of their diagnosis. As an illustration, we will present some portions of the "specific phobia" section of the Anxiety Disorders Interview Schedule for Children (Silverman and Albano, 1996, pp. 23–26). The specific phobia section begins by asking the child about certain things which they are very scared and uncomfortable about ("Many kids feel really scared and uncomfortable about certain, specific things, so scared and uncomfortable that they might want to stay away from these things. Some kids might also cry, or even have a temper tantrum, or get angry when they have to be around these things. Does this sound like you?"). This question is followed by showing the child a list of items that are related to certain types of specific phobia (animal phobia [e.g., snakes, spiders, dogs, bees/

insects]; natural environment type [e.g., high places, going up a ladder or a really tall building, thunderstorms or lightning, water, darkness]; blood-injection or injury type [e.g., gettings shots, having blood tests, seeing blood from a cut or scrape]; situational type [e.g., cars, planes, buses]; other type [e.g., loud noises, costumed characters, doctors or dentists]). A positive answer to this question is followed by a series of questions related to:

- feelings of fear ("Now, using the Feelings Thermometer, tell me how afraid you feel you are of these things that you said 'Yes' to");
- avoidance ("Okay, you just told me how afraid you are of some things. Now I want you to tell me if you ever try to stay away from or avoid these things");
- interference ("Now, when you say you're afraid of [phobic stimulus], are you so afraid that it bothers you and messes things up for you with friends or school or your family? Does it stop you from doing the things you would like to do? Tell me how much by using our thermemeter"); and
- duration ("Have you been afraid of [feared stimulus] for at least six months?")

To meet the diagnosis of a specific phobia the following criteria must be present: some fear rating (a rating of least 4) for one or more objects or situations; avoidance or endurance of specific phobic situation, and an interference with the child's normal routine, academic functioning, or social activities; and the duration of at least 6 months.

Epidemiology

According to recent epidemiological studies, specific phobia represents one of the most commonly diagnosed anxiety disorders in children and adolescents (Essau, 1999). The prevalence rates of specific phobia in the general population have been estimated to range from 1.9% to 12.7% (Table 7.1). For example, in the Kashani *et al.'s* (1989) study, 3.3% of the children and adolescents had simple phobia. In the Dunedin Study (McGee *et al.*, 1990), the rate of simple phobia when the children were 11 years of age was 2.4%, and when they were 15 years of age, it was 3.6%. In the Bremen Adolescent Study (Essau *et al.*, 2000), 3.5% of the adolescents met DSM-IV criteria for at least one specific phobia. Among the subtypes of specific phobia, animal and natural-environment phobia

Table 7.1 Frequency of specific phobia in recent epidemiological studies

Authors	Age (years)	Instrument/ Criteria	Frequency (%) LT	1-yr/6-mth/curr
Lewinsohn et al. (1993)	14–18	K-SADS/ DSM-III-R	1.9	2.1
Fergusson et al. (1993)	15	DISC/ DSM-III-R	–	5.1
Feehan et al. (1994)	18	DIS DSM-III-R	–	6.1
Verhulst et al. (1997)	13–18	DISC/ DSM-III-R	–	12.7
Canals et al. (1997)*	18	SCAN/DSM-III-R SCAN/ICD-10	– –	1.7 5.5
Steinhausen et al. (1998)	7–16	DISC/ DSM-III-R	–	5.8
Essau et al. (2000)	12–17	CAPI/ DSM-IV	3.5	–

Note: * = simple and social phobia; LT = Lifetime diagnosis; 1-yr = 1-year prevalence; 6-mth = 6-month prevalence; curr = current prevalence; SCAN = Schedule for Clinical Assessment in Neuropsychiatry; DIS = Diagnostic Interview Schedule; DISC = Diagnostic Interview Schedule for Children; K-SADS = Schedule for Affective Disorders and Schizophrenia for School-age Children; CAPI = Computerized Munich Version of the Composite International Diagnostic Interview.

were the most common, each with a frequency of 1.1%. Situational phobia (0.9%), blood-injury (0.8%), and other subtype of specific phobia (0.4%), occurred less frequently. The 1-year prevalence of simple phobia reported by Lewinsohn and colleagues (1993) was 2.1%, and by Feehan et al. (1994) 6.1%.

The number of children and adolescents exhibiting fears are much higher, with estimated rates ranging from 8% to 43% (Essau, 1999). In most studies (Ollendick and King, 1994; Ollendick et al., 1989), both the number and intensity of fears tend to decrease with age. The focus of fears also changed with age. For example, common fears among preschool children are that of strangers, the dark and animal; among elementary school age children these included fear of animals, darkness, their own safety, or thunder and lightning (King, 1993; Ollendick et al., 1989; Silverman and Rabian, 1994; Strauss and Last, 1993). The most common fear reported by the 12 to 17 year olds were "not being able to breath", "bombing attacks or being invaded", and "being hit by a car or a truck" (Ollendick and King, 1994). In the Bremen

Adolescent Study (Essau *et al.*, 2000), the most common fear among the 12–17 year olds was the fear of blood (39.6%), followed by the fear of animals (28%), natural-environments (26%), and specific situations (23.7%). Of those with a fear of the natural-environment, fear of height, and fear of storm and lightning were the most frequent. In a study by Poulton *et al.* (1998), about 10% of the 18-year olds reported having had a dental fear, and 5% had fear for blood.

GENDER

Differences between boys and girls have been found for specific fears and specific phobias (Essau *et al.*, 2000; King *et al.*, 1989; Ollendick and King, 1994; Ollendick *et al.*, 1989). The types of fears commonly reported by females were those related to animals, natural-environment (storms/lightning, water), and specific situations such as flight and closed room (Essau *et al.*, 2000). While explanation for this gender difference is unclear, sex-role stereotyping has been suggested (Sarason *et al.*, 1960). That is, boys are expected to fulfil masculine characteristcs (i.e., be brave and fearless) and girls "feminine characteristics" (i.e., fearful or anxious). Therefore, it is not clear whether the gender differences reported in most studies reflect real differences in fear or differences in attitude towards admitting fear. According to Fredrikson and colleagues (1996), gender differences may reflect social transmission of fears and phobias through role modeling.

The finding that more girls than boys in the community had more fears could not be confirmed in clinical settings. As reported by Strauss and Last (1993), an equal proportion of boys and girls with specific phobia were referred.

AGE OF ONSET

Specific phobia belongs to one of the disorders with a very early onset. Based on the Epidemiologic Catchment Area Program, Burke *et al.* (1991) found the hazard rate for developing phobias is the highest in the 10- to 14-year olds. Acording to a recent publication of the National Comorbidity Survey (Magee *et al.*, 1996), the average onset of phobia was 15 years. In two early studies by Öst (1987, 1991), the onset for animal phobia among phobic patients was 7 years, blood phobia 9 years, dental phobia 12 years, and blood-injection-injury phobia between 7 and 9 years. Similar findings have been reported by Liddel and Lyons (1978), who found age of onset for most types of

specific phobia being all below 12 years. That is, the age of onset for
blood phobia was 8.8 years, dental phobia 10.8 years, and thunderstorm phobia 11.9 years. In a recent study by Hofmann et al. (1997),
adult patients with blood-injury-injection phobia reported the earliest
age of onset (9.5 years) compared to those with natural-environment
(23.5 years) and with situational subtype (27.5 years). It is not clear
why the age of onset for these two subtypes of specific phobia was
much later than those reported in other studies.

   Among children and adolescents who were referred for treatment,
Strauss and Last (1993) reported the peak age for specific phobias at
10–11 and 12–13 years, with the mean age of onset being 7 to 8 years. In
the Bremen Adolescent Study (Essau et al., 2000), almost all subtypes of
specific phobia began relatively early in life. All adolescents with animal
and natural-environment phobias, and about 80% of those with blood-
injection-injury and situational phobias reported the onset of their phobia
before the age of 10 years.

Psychosocial Impairment

One of DSM-IV criteria (criterion E) for specific phobia, is that "The
avoidance, anxious anticipation, or distress in the feared situation(s)
interferes significantly with the person's normal routine, occupational (or
academic) functioning, or social activities or relationships, or there is a
marked distress about having the phobia" (APA, 1994, p. 410).
Numerous studies have confirmed that children and adolescents with
specific phobia are impaired in various areas of their life. Based on
detailed assessments of lifetime and cross-sectional impairment, all cases
with specific phobia were found to be highly impaired in their routine
activities during the worst episode of their phobia (Essau et al., 2000);
infact compared to those with other subtypes of anxiety disorders, specific
phobia was most frequently associated with impairment. Although a high
number of these specific phobic had their phobia in the past (not
currently), many of them were also currently impaired at school, work,
leisure activities, and social contact. They also reported being psycho-
logically distressed, as shown by the high score on all the subscales of the
SCL-90-R. All adolescents who met the diagnosis of a specific phobia
(Essau et al., 2000) avoided the feared object or situation. Exposure to the
feared situation or object is associated with numerous panic symptoms,
the most frequent being that of palpitation, trembling/shaking, and
sweating. When considering those with fears (i.e., those not meeting the

diagnosis of specific phobia), about 50% of them avoided the feared object or situation. Almost 40% of the adolescents with fears of specific objects or situations report being impaired in their normal activities during the worst time of their fear.

In Ollendick and King's study (1994), more than 60% reported their fears to significantly interfer with their daily activities; another 26% reported some distress. The amount of interference was the highest for fears related to failing a test, being hit by a car or truck, getting poor grades. McCathie and Spence (1991) similarly reported a strong association between the frequency of fearful thoughts and avoidance behaviour. In a study (Poulton *et al.*, 1998) that examined the relationship between dental, blood and injection fear and oral health, adolescents with dental fear alone or comorbid with blood or injection fear had significantly worse oral health (i.e.. greater caries experience) compared to adolescents with blood-injection fear only or those in the control group (i.e., no fear). Furthermore, adolescents with dental and blood or injection fear had a significantly higher level of tooth decay compared to those with dental fear only. Thus, contrary to the traditional belief that fear is a non pathological phenomena, existing studies indicate this does not hold true for all children and adolescents. That is, for a high number of children and adolescents fear or specific phobia can be very distressing or are associated with high level of impairment.

Despite this high level of impairment, only a small proportion of those with specific phobia did seek treatment for their phobia (Essau *et al.*, 2000). That is, only one adolescent with animal phobia, two with blood phobia, one with natural-environment, and one with situational phobia sought treatment. In the Strauss and Last's study (1993), youth with simple phobia were referred for treatment services at an average of 3.3 years following the onset of their phobias. Future studies need to examine factors that predict health services utilization among specific phobics. Among adults, those with specific phobia generally seek treatment because of problems caused or associated with specific phobia, and not generally for phobias which they can avoid (Noyes and Hoehn-Saric, 1998).

Comorbidity

DSM-IV acknowledges that: "In many cases, more than one subtype of specific phobia is present. Having one phobia of a specific subtype tends to increase the likelihood of having another phobia from within the same subtype" (APA, 1994, p. 407). Despite this fact and also the findings that anxiety disorders frequently co-occur both within the anxiety disorders as well as with other psychiatric disorders (Emmelkamp and Scholing, 1997; Essau, 2000), only a few studies have examined the comorbidity of the subtypes of specific phobia.

The few studies which have examined the comorbidity of specific phobia in children and adolescents have been inconsistent. In an early study by Anderson *et al.* (1987), specific phobia did not co-occur with other disorders. Finding from the Oregon Adolescent study (Lewinsohn *et al.*, 1997) indicated that simple (specific) phobia was found to be significantly comorbid with social phobia, and with separation anxiety disorder. That is, 21.7% of adolescents with simple phobia met the diagnosis of a separation anxiety disorder, and 10.2% of those with separation anxiety disorder also had simple phobia. The percentage of social phobics who met the diagnosis of simple phobia was 15.8%, and those with simple phobia who met the diagnosis of social phobia was 13%. In Poulton *et al.*'s study (1998), 10% of the adolescents with dental fear also had blood fear, and 53.1% had fear of injections. In a recent study by Essau *et al.* (2000), about one-third of the adolescents who met the DSM-IV criteria for a specific phobia also met the diagnosis for depressive (36.1%) and somatoform disorders (33.3%). 8.3% of those with specific phobia additionally had substance use disorders. Within the anxiety disorders, specific phobia co-occurred the most common with posttraumatic stress disorder (13.9%), obsessive-compulsive disorder (11.1%), and anxiety NOS (not otherwise specified) (11.1%). When concentrating on those who met the diagnosis of a specific phobia, our finding indicated that 25% of them had "pure" (i.e., no other subtypes of specific phobia) animal phobia, 22.2% had "pure" natural-environment phobia, 16.7% had blood phobia, 13.9% had situational phobia, and 5.6% had other types of specific phobia.

Studies in clinical settings showed a somewhat different picture. In a study by Last *et al.* (1992), 75% of the children with specific phobia had at least one anxiety disorders (mostly that of separation anxiety disorder); 32.5% had depressive disorders, and 22.5% had any disruptive behaviour disorder. In another study (Strauss and Last, 1993), 39% of the children and adolescents with simple phobia showed evidence of a phobic disorder only. Overanxious disorder (16%), separation anxiety disorder (29%), and avoidance disorder (3%) accounted for most of the comorbid diagnoses; only 5% of the simple phobics demonstrated a comorbid affective disorders.

Course and Outcome

Little is known about the course and outcome of specific phobia. This deficiency is mostly due to the traditional view that fear or phobia in children is transient (Emmelkamp and Scholing, 1997). Although many childhood fears are indeed mild and transitory, some fears may become intense and persist over time which may cause distress in some children (Spence and McCathie, 1993). Research findings on the course and outcome of specific phobia have been inconsistent. Among clinically referred children, specific (simple) phobia was found to have the poorest rate of recovery (Last *et al.*, 1996). In Hampe *et al.*'s (1973) study, about 80% of the children ages 6 to 15 years who were treated for phobias no longer had phobias at the 2-year follow-up assessment; however, 7% of the children continued to display phobias, despite treatment.

In a classic study by Agras *et al.* (1972), 10 children under 20 years old and 20 adults with phobia were followed over a five-year period. All the children were regarded as "improved" without active intervention, and that children tended to improve more quickly than adults. However, according to Ollendick's interpretation (1979) these "improved" children were not entirely symptom-free, suggesting the persistence of phobia for some children. In Lewinsohn *et al.*'s study (1993) the prevalence of simple phobia among the adolescents at the first interview was 1.4% (2.0% female; 0.7% males) and at the second interview, it was 0.5% (0.6% female; 0.4% males). Recent finding from the Bremen Adolescent Study (Essau, 1999) indicated specific phobia to have a very stable course. 87.5% of the adolescents who met the diagnosis of a specific phobia at T1 still meet the same diagnosis about 15 months later.

Etiological and Maintenance Factors

CLASSICAL CONDITIONING

The use of classical conditioning model to explain the etiology of specific phobia can be traced back to Watson and Rayner's "little Albert" study in 1920. According to this model, specific phobia is believed to be a conditioned response acquired through the association of a feared object (conditioned stimulus) with a noxious experience (unconditioned stimulus). Avoidance of the feared object prevents or reduces this phobia. This model has however been criticized. First, most cases with specific phobia fail to report that their phobia began in association with a traumatic event (Davey, 1992; Menzies & Clarke, 1993). This is especially the case for spider, height or water phobia. Second, a high number of specific phobics acquire their fear not through direct experience with the traumatic events, but through observational learning (Menzies & Clarke, 1993). Other criticism of the model have been discussed in numerous review papers (Davey, 1997) and therefore will not be presented here.

FAMILIAL/GENETIC FACTORS

The role of genetic factors in the etiology of anxiety disorders in general, and in specific phobia in specific is well recognized. In a family study by Fyer *et al.* (1990), 31% of the first-degree relatives of specific phobics compared to only 11% of relatives of control probands reported having had a specific phobia. Their result also showed that 15% of the children of specific phobics met the diagnosis of a specific phobia; among children of the control probands, it was only 8%. Frederikson and colleagues (1997) similarly found a positive familial history of spider and snake phobia in women with these phobias.

Twin studies have found significantly greater concordance rates among monozygotic (MZ) twins than among dizygotic (DZ) twins for specific phobias. In an early study by Torgersen (1979), MZ twins were found to be more concordant than DZ twins for phobic fears. In addition to genetic factors, certain developmental factors (e.g., dependent, reserved, and less self-confident in childhood) may contribute to the vulnerability of developing specific phobia. According to several authors (Kendler *et al.*, 1992), genes play their greatest role in contributing to a general risk factors and not disorder-specific. In their study of female twins (Kendler *et al.*, 1992), higher heritability but lower familial and environmental influences were found among animal phobics. The reserve was found for situational phobia.

One other family factor which has been reported as important for the development of anxiety disorders, including that of specific phobia, is parenting style. This line of research has stemmed mostly from Bowlby's attachment theory (1973), which views anxiety as an insecurity response that is induced or promoted by threat of, or actual, separation from an attachment figure. In several studies, family environment of adults with anxiety can be described as low on parental warmth and high on overprotection or control (Gerlsma *et al.*, 1990). In a study by

Messer and Beidel (1994), the family environment of children with any anxiety disorders has been described as promoting less independence compared to those with no psychiatric disorders or those with test anxiety only.

PATHWAYS OF ACQUISITION

According to Rachman (1977) there are three pathways in which phobias can be acquired: direct classical conditioning, vicarious condition, and information/instruction. This model has been investigated in numerous studies on various types of specific phobias, in adults and in children or adolescents. In the study by Öst (1991), most (52%) of the adult patients with blood-injury or injection phobias attributed the onset of their phobias to traumatic conditioning experiences, and 24% to vicarious learning. Only a few (7%) of them reported the onset of their phobia due to transmission of information, whereas 17% failed to recall the onset of their phobias. Similar finding has been reported by Kleinknecht (1994). Among students fearful of blood-injury situations, 53% attributed the onset of their fear to traumatic conditioning, 16% to vicarious learning and 3% to information. The rest (27%) were unable to recall the conditioning of onset.

In the study by Ollendick and King (1991), children first indicated their levels of fear after which they reported whether: (a) they remembered having a frightening experience with the feared object (direct conditioning experience); (b) their parents or friends ever showed fear or avoidance of the feared object (vicarious conditioning), and (c) they had been told, or heard stories about frightening things from their parents, teachers, friends (instruction or information). Most of the fearful children attributed the onset of their fears to vicarious and instructional factors; these indirect factors were sufficient to evoke high levels of fear. However, for some specific fear, these indirect sources of fear have to be present or in combination with direct conditioning experiences.

Menzies and Clarke (1993) used parental reports to examine the events which may be related to their child's onset of water phobia. Parents indicated the way in which they believed played a role in the onset of their child's water phobia by completing a list of origins of phobias, which included Rachman's pathway to fear acquisition. More than half of the parents (56%) considered their child's phobia as being unrelated to direct experience or information/observation. In other words, the child's phobia was present from their very first contact with water. About 26% of the parents reported vicarious learning experience (or indirect learning), suggesting that other family members had experienced fearful encounter with water. Only 2% of the parents attributed their child's phobia to direct conditioning. The rest (16%) were unable to recall any traumatic experience. The authors concluded that fear of water may develop in the absence of any previous negative experience with the feared object in a non-associated way.

DISEASE-AVOIDANCE MODEL

Disease-avoidance model (Matchett and Davey, 1991) has been used to explain for the development of some types of specific fears and phobia. According to the disease-avoidance model, common and non-clinical animal fears may be associated with disgust reaction, one of whose adaptive benefits is the prevention of the transmission of disease. These animals have been associated with the spreading of disease, dirt or contamination.

Related to the disease-avoidance model is the concept of disgust sensitivity, which is believed to be involved in the development of some specific phobias. For example, the study by Matchett and Davey (1991) examined the relationship between disgust/contamination sensitivity and animal fears in students, aged 18 to 30 years. Results showed a strong association between fear of animals that are not considered to attack and harm human beings (e.g., rat, spider) and those animals which are normally considered to evoke revulsion (e.g., snail, slug). No relationship was found between disgust sensitivity and the fear of animals that are likely to attack or harm human beings. In Merckelbach et al.'s study (1993), women with spider fears were found to have a higher disgust and contamination sensitivity than individuals without such fears. When concentrating on women with spider phobia, those with high disgust reported more conditioning incidents (i.e., experiencing a painful event in connection with spiders) than those with low disgust. However, no significant group differences were found with regard to the perceived dirtiness of spiders.

In the study by De Jong and colleagues (1997) fear of spiders, disgust sensitivity and spiders disgust-evoking status was examined in girls with spider phobia who were treated for their phobia, in non-phobic girls, and in the parents of both groups of children. Girls with spider phobia had higher levels of disgust sensitivity compared to girls in the control group, and that they tend to consider spiders as more disgusting. Their result also showed a reduction in spider fear following treatment to parallell a decline in spiders' disgust-evoking status.

Mothers reported not only more spider fearful than fathers, they also reported higher levels of disgust and contamination sensitivity. This finding was interpreted as suggesting spider fears being transmitted from mother to daughter via same-sex modelling. Indeed, Davey *et al.'s* study (1993) has found a significant association between parents' and children's disgust scores. Infact, parental disgust sensitivity was the main predictor of the child's fear of animal.

Although the association between disgust sensitivity and spider phobia is quite strong, the mechanism that link these two remains unclear. Merckelbach *et al.* (1993) argued that disgust sensitivity operates via latent inhibition. That is, before the onset of these problems, individuals with high disgust sensitivity may have avoided spiders or places where contact with spiders are likely to be encountered. Due to their lack of familarity with spiders, persons with high disgust sensitivity may have been more prone to subsequent conditioning processes. Another explanation is related to the role of disgust sensitivity in the maintenance of spider fear. High disgust sensitivity may intensify avoidance and reduce exposure to spiders.

Some authors (Rozin and Fallon, 1987) argued that fear of animals is associated with disgust or contamination sensitivity, as characterised by a food-rejection response, and avoiding the object. Others (Matchett and Davey, 1991) argued that at least three ways may explain for the association between animal fear and disgust: spreading of disease and being the sources of contamination; being contingently associated with dirt or contamination (e.g. cockroaches, spiders); and that they have features which elicit disgust reactions (e.g., slugs).

MAINTENANCE FACTORS

Many years ago, Mowrer (1960) suggested that avoidance behaviour is responsible for maintaining phobic fear. That is, avoidance tend to minimize direct and prolonged contact with the fear-provoking stimulus. By avoiding the phobic stimulus, the phobic individuals will not have the chance to learn that the stimulus is actually not harmful. According to Thorpe and Salkovskis (1997), once a stimulus is perceived as threatening, several factors such as hypervigilance, avoidance, autonomic arousal, and the presence of anxiety are responsible for maintaining the belief that the stimulus is threatening.

Attentional bias has also been proposed as responsible for the maintenance of specific phobias. In a series of studies using the emotional

Stroop task (Watts *et al.*, 1986), children with spider phobia were much slower in their colour naming of threatening words than that of neutral words. It was argued that these children direct their attention to the content of the threatening words, which in turn interferes with their colour naming task. Interestingly, upon successful treatment of their spider phobia, the attentional bias for threat cues disappears (Lavy *et al.*, 1993; Watts *et al.*, 1986)

Treatment

Numerous strategies have been used to treat specific phobia in children and adolescents, the most common being a behavioural approach or its major components (e.g., systematic desensitization, contingency management, self-control training, modeling, and behavioural family intervention) (Table 7.2). Although most studies have shown the efficacy of these strategies, their findings should be interpreted with caution due to methodological limitations, including the lack of controlled studies; lack of formal diagnostic procedures; and lack of systematic follow-up procedures. These constraints make it difficult to draw definitive conclusions about the "best" method to treat specific phobia in children and adolescents. In this section, we will review findings of some studies that have used eye movement desensitization and reprocessing as well as the behavioral approach in children and adolescents with specific fear or phobia.

EYE MOVEMENT DESENSITIZATION AND REPROCESSING (EMDR)

The EMDR is a new therapeutic technique originally developed for the treatment of posttraumatic stress disorder, but has recently been used for other anxiety disorders, including specific phobia. During EMDR, lateral eye movements are induced by the therapist, and the children are to imagine themselves being expose to an aversive memory. Following each set of eye movements the children then report their images, feelings, and thoughts. This procedure is repeated until the negative affect associated with the aversive memory habituates. Two controlled studies by Muris and colleagues have demonstrated the effectiveness of EMDR for children with specific phobia. In their first study (Muris *et al.*, 1997), 22 children with spider phobia were treated with one session of exposure in vivo and one session of EMDR with a

Table 7.2 Major components of a behavioral approach

Components	Description
Systematic desensitization	Is a graded imaginal exposure technique. It consists of three components: – relaxation training, – development of a fear-producing stimulus hiearchy, and – in vivo exposure (i.e., actual presentation of the hierarchy items).
Flooding	Prolonged exposure, either in vivo or imaginally, to the most fear-producing stimulus.
Contingency management	Manipulation of consequences of phobic behaviour through: – positive reinforcement (i.e., rewarding the child following a behaviour that increases the probability that it will recur), – shaping (i.e., reinforcement of closer approximation to the desired approached behaviour), and – extinction procedures (i.e., discontinuation of the reinforcement of behaviour).
Modeling	Involves showing the child non-fearful behaviour in the anxiety-producing situation and showing him/her an appropriate response for coping with the feared stimulus.
Cognitive-based approachal	Inclusion of procedures to change perception, thoughts, images, and beliefs by restructuring dysfunctional cognitions.
Behavioural family intervention	Training parents to use contingency management strategies to deal with their child's anxiety and to facilitate their exposure to the phobic situation.

crossover design. That is, half of the children with spider phobia received one session of EMDR prior to exposure in vivo, and another half received exposure in vivo prior to exposure. The treatment comprised of one 90 minute session which involved the desensitization of the most aversive, the most recent aversive confrontation with the phobic object, and a future confrontation with the phobic objects. For each experience, children described the aversive event and formulated a cognition (positive and negative) and physical anxiey response related to this experience. Upon completion of this task, the eye movements procedure was carried out and repeated until the lowest level of disturbance was obtained. Results showed positive effects of EMDR on self-report measures, but less pronounced on behavioural improvement. Exposure in vivo was more superior in reducing avoidance behaviour and that no significant difference could be found between EMDR and exposure in vivo on a physiological index.

In another study, Muris *et al.* (1998) compared the efficacy of EMDR, exposure in vivo, and computerized exposure in the treatment of spider phobia. Participants were 26 girls, who received individual treatment for their spider phobia. During the first phase of the treatment, the children were randomly assigned to one of the three groups: the EMDR, the exposure in vivo, or the computerized exposure. During the second phase, all groups received exposure in vivo. Children's level of spider fear were assessed before and after treatment. The exposure in vivo session produced significant improvement on the self-reported fear and behavioural avoidance. EMDR produced a significant improvement on self-reported spider fear only, whereas no significant improvement could be found for computerized exposure. Thus, exposure in vivo seems to be the most effective treatment for spider phobia in children.

BEHAVIOURAL APPROACH

Most work that has examined the efficacy of behavioural therapy for children and adolescents with specific phobia are based on single-case studies. Since most of these studies have been described in detailed elsewhere (Barrios and O'Dell, 1998; Ollendick *et al.*, 1997), only a few will be presented in this section.

Matthey (1988) described the treatment of a five year old girl with phobic reactions to thunderstroms (e.g., screaming and crying). Treatment took place over a three month period, and consisted of seven sessions; two of which were held in the Health Centre, three in the child's home and two at her school. The treatment approach comprised of self-statement, positive reinforcement, peer modelling, exposure to a videotape of a weather report and exposure to an audiotape of stroms. Independent ratings of the girl's mother and her teacher showed a decrease in fear behaviour at the end of treatment. By the seven month follow-up, the girl no longer exhibited any of her previous fear behaviours, including no longer becoming quiet and withdrawn when dark clouds were visible. This improvement was maintained at the twelve month follow-up.

Ollendick and colleagues (1991) described the treatment of two girls (10 and 8 year old) with nighttime fear. A multiple baseline design was used in this study. After a monitoring phase, self-control training (comprising of relaxation, self-monitoring and verbal self-instruction) was implemented. Contingency management procedures were also added to the program. Follow-up investigation was conducted 1 to 2 years after the final treatment session. Results showed that the self-control procedures combined with reinforcement conditions for engaging in appropriate nighttime behaviours was effective in reducing nighttime fears. Significant reduction was also obtained in the "clinging" behaviour toward the mother and complaints of physical symptoms upon separation from the mother. The use of self-control training (without reinforcement) was only moderately effective in reducing the girl's state anxiety.

Heard and colleagues (1992) used a behavioural treatment package, in three adolescent girls with a diagnosis of simple phobia (fears of medical procedure, darkness and school). A multiple baseline design across subjects was used, targeting each subjects' specific avoidant behaviour. The therapy began with the development of hierarchies of anxiety evoking stimuli for in vivo exposure, combined with cognitive restructuring and relaxation techniques to anxiety evoking stimuli. Cognitive restructuring involved targeting "distorted" cognitions and perceptions of environmental phobic cues and rehearsal of active control during graded exposure; the latter involved the application of competence-mediating statements. Parallel to the implementation of exposure procedures, home contingency management of phobic behaviour(s) was also used. The latter procedure involved having the family minimising the attention to fear reactions and positively reinforcing appropriate behaviour relative to phobic stimuli. Result showed significant improvements of anxiety at overt-behavioural and cognitive level in all the three adolescents. The treatment gains were maintained at a 3-month follow-up.

The efficacy of different behavioral techniques for a broad range of specific phobia has been explored in the adult literature (Öst, 1997). In a series of studies, the so-called "rapid behavioral treatment" (i.e., treatment with a total therapy time of a maximum of 3 hours) has been shown to be effective in treating spider, snake, blood-injury-injection, claustrophobia, dental, flying, and height phobia (Öst, 1997). Major components of the rapid treatment are exposure in vivo and modelling. During exposure in vivo, the patient has to be in the phobic situation until the anxiety fades away; the therapy session will only be terminated when the anxiety level is reduced by at least 50%. Modelling involves therapist demonstrating how to interact with the phobic objects. Findings to date have shown rapid behavioral treatment as effective as the longer treatments. Furthermore, adult patients with different types of specific phobia who participated in the rapid behavioral treatment were significantly better than in the no-treatment or waiting-list groups (Öst, 1997). It would be of interest to examine in future studies the extend to which rapid treatment can be applied to children and adolescents with specific phobia.

Conclusion

Specific phobia is one of the most common anxiety disorders in children and adolescents. Specific fears are even more common, with rates ranging from 8% to 43%. Specific phobia is frequently comorbid with other disorders, and is associated with avoidance behaviour and psychosocial impairment in various life domains. Despite the frequent occurrence of specific fears and phobia in this age group, our knowledge about specific phobia is still lacking, especially its course and outcome, and comorbidity with other disorders. Future studies are also needed that examined the validity of the subtypes of specific phobia as proposed in DSM-IV. Furthermore, since specific fears occur rather frequently in this age group, it would be useful to identify the kind of fears that predict the development of phobia.

Another area which needs further attention is the gender difference in the prevalence of specific fears and phobia. The interaction of sex hormones and conditioning processes has been proposed; another explanation has been related to culturally transmitted ideas and values (Merckelbach et al., 1996). As reviewed earlier, children may learn from their parent(s) that certain animals or insects (e.g., spiders) are associated with disease or contamination (Davey et al., 1993). In order to examine which of these explanations are more appropriate for gender differences, cross-cultural studies are needed. In the area of treatment, we need more controlled studies in a large sample of cases with specific phobia. A large sample size may enable the examination of factors which may moderate or mediate treatment success.

References

Agras, W.S., Chapin, H.N., & Oliveau, D.C. (1972). The natural history of phobias: Course and prognosis. *Archives of General Psychiatry, 26,* 315–317.

Anderson, J.C., Williams, S., McGee, R., & Silva, P.A. (1987). DSM-III disorders in preadolescent children. Prevalence in a large sample from the general population. *Archives of General Psychiatry, 44,* 69–76.

American Psychiatric Association (1994). *Diagnostic and statistical manual of mental disorders* (4th ed.). Washington, DC: American Psychiatric Association.

Barrios, B.A., & O'Dell, S.L. (1998). Fears and anxieties. In E.J. Mash & R.A. Barkley (Eds.), *Treatment of childhood disorders* (pp. 249–338). New York: The Guilford Press.

Bowlby, J. (1973). *Attachment of loss: Vol.II: Separation, anxiety and anger.* New York: Basic Books.

Burke, K.C., Burke, J.D., Rae, D.S., & Regier, D.A. (1991). Comparing age of onset of major depression and other psychiatric disorders by birth cohorts in five US community populations. *Archives of General Psychiatry, 48,* 789–795.

Canals, J., Domenech, E., Carbajo, G., & Blade, J. (1997). Prevalence of DSM-III-R and ICD-10 psychiatric disorders in a Spanish population of 18-year-olds. *Acta Psychiatrica Scandinavica, 96,* 287–294.

Craske, M.G. & Sipsas, A. (1992). Animal phobias versus claustrophobias: Exteroceptive versus interoceptive cues. *Behaviour Research and Therapy, 30,* 569–581.

Corah, N.L. (1968). Development of a dental anxiety scale. *Journal of Dental Research, 48,* 596.

Costello, A.J., Edelbrock, C., Dulcan, M.K., Kalas, R., & Klaric, S. (1987). *The Diagnostic Interview Schedule for Children (DISC).* Pittsburgh: University of Pittsburgh.

Curtis, G.C., Hill, E.M., & Lewis, J.A. (1990). *Heterogeneity of DSM-III-R simple phobia and the simple phobia/agoraphobia boundary: Evidence from the ECA study* (Report to the DSM-IV Anxiety Disorders Work-group). Ann Arbor, MI: University of Michigan.

Davey, G.C.L. (1992). Classical conditioning and the acquisition of human fears and phobias: A review and synthesis of the literature. *Advances in Behaviour Research & Therapy, 14,* 29–66.

Davey, G.C.L. (1997). A conditioning model of phobias. In G.C.L. Davey (Ed.), *Phobias: A handbook of theory, research and treatment* (pp. 301–322). Chichester: John Wiley & Sons.

Davey, G.C.L., DeJong, P.J., & Tallis, F. (1993). UCS inflation in the aetiology of a variety of anxiety disorders: Some case histories. *Behaviour Research and Therapy, 31,* 495–498.

De Jong, P.J., Andrea, H., & Muris, P. (1997). Spider phobia in children: Disgust and fear before and after treatment. *Behaviour Research and Therapy, 35,* 559–562.

De Jong, A., Muris, P., Schoenmakers, N., & ter Horst, G. (1995). Negative cogniotions of dental phobics: Reliability and validity of the dental cognitions questionnaire. *Behaviour Research and Therapy, 33,* 507–515.

Emmelkamp, P.M.G. & Scholing, A. (1997). Anxiety disorders. In C.A. Essau & F. Petermann (Eds.), Developmental psychopathology: Epidemiology, diagnostics and treatment. (pp. 219–263). London: Harwood Academic Publishers.

Essau, C.A. (1999). *Angst und Depression bei Jugendlichen. Habilitationschrift.* Bremen: Universität Bremen.

Essau, C.A., Conradt, J., & Petermann, F. (2000). Frequency, comorbidity, and psychosocial impairment of specific phobia in adolescents. *Journal of Clinical Child Psychology, 29,* 221–231.

Feehan, M., McGee, R., Nada-Raja, S., & Williams, S.M. (1994). DSM-III-R disorders in New Zealand 18-year-olds. *Australian and New Zealand Journal of Psychiatry, 28,* 87–99.

Fergusson, D.M., Horwood, L.J., & Lynskeyl, M.T. (1993). Prevalence and comorbidity of DSM-III-R diagnoses in a birth cohort of 15 year olds. *Journal of the American Academy of Child and Adolescent Psychiatry, 32,* 1127–1134.

Fredrikson, M., Annas, P., Fisher, H., & Wik, G. (1996). Gender and age differences in the prevalence of specific fears and phobias. *Behaviour Research and Therapy, 34,* 33–39.

Fyer, A.J., Mannuzza, S., Gallops, M.S., Martin, L.Y., Aaronson, C., Gorman, J.M., Liebowitz, M.R., & Klein, D.F. (1990). Familial transmission of simple phobias and fears. *Archives of General Psychiatry, 47,* 252–256.

Gerlsma, C., Emmelkamp, P.M.G., & Arrindell, W.A. (1990). Anxiety, depression, and perception of early parenting: A meta-analysis. *Clinical Psychology Review, 10,* 251–277.

Hampe, E., Noble, M., Miller, L.C., & Barrett, C.L. (1973). Phobic children at 2 years post-treatment. *Journal of Abnormal Psychology, 82,* 446–453.

Heard, P.M., Dadds, M.R., & Conrad, P. (1992). Assessment and treatment of simple phobias in children: Effects on family and marital relationships. *Behaviour Change, 9,* 73–82.

Herjanic, B. & Reich, W. (1982). Development of a structured psychiatric interview for children: Agreement between child and parent on individual symptoms. *Journal of Abnormal Child Psychology, 10,* 307–324.

Hofmann, S.G., Lehman, C.L., & Barlow, D.H. (1997). How specific are specific phobias? *Journal of Behavioural Therapy & Experimental Psychiatry, 28,* 233–240.

Kashani, J.H., Orvaschel, H., Rosenberg, T.K., & Reid, J.C. (1989). Psychopathology in a community sample of children and adolescents: A developmental perspective. *Journal of the American Academy of Child and Adolescent Psychology, 28*, 701–706.

Kendler, K.S., Neale, M.C., Kessler, R.C., Heath, A.C., & Eaves, L.J. (1992). The genetic epidemiology of phobias in women: The interrelationship of agoraphobia, social phobia, situational phobia and simple phobia. *Archives of General Psychiatry, 49*, 273–281.

King, N.J. (1993). Simple and social phobias. In T.H. Ollendick & R.J. Prinz (eds.), *Advances in clinical child psychology* (Vol. 15, pp. 305–341). New York: plenum Press.

King, N.J., Ollier, K., Iacuone, R., Schuster, S., Bays, K., Gullone, E., & Ollendick, T.H. (1989). Fears of children and adolescents: A cross-sectional Australian study using the Revised-Fear Survey Schedule for Children. *Journal of Child Psychology and Psychiatry, 30*, 775–784.

Kleinknecht, R.A. (1994). Acquisition of blood, injury, and needle fears and phobias. *Behaviour Research and Therapy, 32*, 817–823.

Last, C.G., Perrin, S., Hersen, M., & Kazdin, A.E. (1992). DSM-III-R anxiety disorders in children: Sociodemographic and clinical characteristics. *Journal of the American Academy of Child and Adolescent Psychology, 31*, 1070–1076.

Last, C.G., Perrin, S., Hersen, M., & Kazdin, A.E. (1996). A prospective study of childhood anxiety disorders. *Journal of the American Academy of Child and Adolescent Psychology, 35*, 1502–1510.

Lavy, E., Van den Hout, M.A., & Arntz, A. (1993). Attentional bias and spider phobia: Conceptual and clinical issues. *Behaviour Research and Therapy, 31*, 17–24.

Lewinsohn, P.M., Hops, H., Roberts, R.E., Seeley, J.R., & Andrews, J.A. (1993). Adolescent psychopathology: I. Prevalence and incidence of depression and other DSM-III-R disorders in high school students. *Journal of Abnormal Psychology, 102*, 133–144.

Lewinsohn, P.M., Zinbarg, R., Seeley, J.R., Lewinsohn, M. & Sack, W.H. (1997). Lifetime comorbidity among anxiety disorders and between anxiety disorders and other mental disorders in adolescents. *Journal of Anxiety Disorders, 11*, 377–394.

Liddell, A. & Lyons, M. (1978). Thunderstorm phobias. *Behaviour Research and Therapy, 16*, 306–308.

Matchett, G. & Davey, G.C.L. (1991). A test of a disease-avoidance model of animal phobias. *Behaviour Research and Therapy, 29*, 91–94.

Matthey, S. (1988). Cognitive-behavioural treatment of a thunder-phobic child. *Behaviour Change, 5*, 80–84.

McCathie, H. & Spence, S.H. (1991). What is the revised fear survey schedule for children measuring? *Behaviour Research and Therapy, 29*, 495–502.

McGee, R., Feehan, M., Williams, S., Partridge, F., Silva, P.A. & Kelly, J. (1990). DSM-III disorders in a large sample of adolescents. *Journal of the American Academy of Child and Adolescent Psychiatry, 29,* 611–619.

Merckelbach, H., de Jong, P.J., Arntz, A., & Schouten, E. (1993). The role of evaluative learning and disgust sensitivity in the etiology and treatment of spider phobia. *Advances in Behaviour Research and Therapy, 15,* 243–255.

Merckelbach, H., de Jong, P.J., Muris, P., & van den Hout, M.A. (1996). The etiology of specific phobia: A review. *Clinical Psychology Review, 16,* 337–361.

Menzies, R.G. & Clark, J.C. (1993). The etiology of childhood water phobia. *Behaviour Research and Therapy, 31,* 499–501.

Messer, S.C. & Beidel, D.C. (1994). Psychosocial Correlates of Childhood anxiety disorders. *Journal of the American Academy of Child Psychiatry, 33,* 975–983.

Magee, W.J., Eaton, W.W., Wittchen, H.-U. *et al.* (1996). Agoraphobia, simple phobia, and social phobia in the National Comorbidity Survey. *Archives of General Psychiatry, 53,* 159–168.

Muris, P., Merckelbach, H., & Collaris, R. (1997). Common childhood fears and their origins. *Behaviour Research and Therapy, 35,* 929–937.

Muris, P., Merckelbach, H., Mayer, B., & Meesters, C. (1998). Common fears and their relationship to anxiety disorders symptomatology in normal children. *Personality and Individual Differences, 24,* 575–578.

Muris, P., Schmidet, H., & Merckelbach, H. (1999). The structure of specific phobia symptoms among children and adolescents. *Behaviour Research and Therapy, 37,* 863–868.

Noyes, R. & Hoehn-Saric, R. (1998). *The anxiety disorders.* Cambridge: Cambridge University Press.

Ollendick, T.H. (1979). Fear reduction techniques with children. In M. Hersen, R.M. Eisler, & P.M. Miller (Eds.), *Progress in behavior modification* (Vol. 8, pp. 127–168). New York: Academic Press.

Ollendick, T.H. (1983). Reliability and validity of the revised Fear Survey Schedule for Children (FSSC-R). *Behaviour research and Therapy, 21,* 395–399.

Ollendick, T.H. & King, N.J. (1994). Diagnosis, assessment, and treatment of internalizing problems in children: The role of longitudinal data. *Journal of Consulting and Clinical Psychology, 62,* 918–927.

Ollendick, T.H. & King, N.J. (1991). Origins of childhood fears: An evaluation of Rachman's theory of fear acquisition. *Behaviour Research and Therapy, 29,* 117–123.

Ollendick, T.H., King, N.J., & Frary, R.B. (1989). Fears in children and adolescents. Reliability and generalizability across gender, age and nationality. *Behaviour Research and Therapy, 27,* 19–26.

Ollendick, T.H., Hagopian, L.P., & King, N.J. (1997). Specific phobias in children. In G.C.L. Davey (Ed.), *A handbook of theory, research and treatment* (pp. 201–226). Chichester: John Wiley & Sons.

Ollendick, T.H., Yule, W., & Ollier, K. (1991). Fears in British children and their relationship to manifest anxiety and depression. *Journal of Child Psychology and Psychiatry, 32,* 321–331.

Öst, L.-G. (1997). Rapid treatment of specific phobias. In G.C.L. Davey (Ed.), *A handbook of theory, research and treatment* (pp. 227–246). Chichester: John Wiley & Sons.

Öst, L.-G. (1991). Acquisition of blood and injection phobia and anxiety response patterns in clinical patients. *Behaviour Research and Therapy, 29,* 323–332.

Öst, L.-G. (1987). Age of onset in differen phobias. *Journal of Abnormal Psychology, 96,* 223–229.

Poulton, R., Thomson, W.M., Brown, R.H., & Silva, P.A. (1998). Dental fear with and without blood-injection fear: Implication for dental health and clinical practice. *Behaviour Research and Therapy, 36,* 591–597.

Puig-Antich, J. & Chambers, W. (1978). *The Schedule for Affective Disorders and Schizophrenia for School-aged Children.* New York: State Psychiatric Institute.

Sarason, S.B., Davidson, K.S., Lighthall, F.F., Waite, R.R., & Ruebush, B.K. (1960). *Anxiety in elementary school children.* New York: Wiley.

Silverman, W.K. & Albano, A.M. (1996). *The Anxiety Disorders Interview Schedule for DSM-IV: Child Version.* San Antonio, USA: Graywind.

Silverman, W.K. & Rabian, B. (1994). Specific phobia. In T.H. Ollendick, N.J. King, & W. Yule (Eds.), *International handbook of phobic and anxiety disorders in children and adolescents* (pp. 87–109). New York: Plenum Press.

Spence, S.H. & McCathie, H. (1993). The stability of fears in children: A two-year prospective study: A research note. *Journal of Child Psychology and Psychiatry, 34,* 579–585.

Steinhausen, H.-U., Winkler Metzke, C., Meier, M., & Kannenberg, R. (1998). Prevalence of child and adolescent psychiatric disorders: The Zürich epidemiological study. *Acta Psychiatrica Scandinavica, 98,* 262–271.

Strauss, C.C. & Last, C.G. (1993). Social and simple phobias in children. *Journal of Anxiety Disorders, 7,* 141–152.

Rachman, S. (1977). The conditioning theory of fear acquisition: A critical examination. *Behaviour Research and Therapy, 15,* 375–387.

Reynolds, C.R. & Richmond, B.O. (1978). What I think and feel: A revised measure of children's manifest anxiety. *Journal of Abnormal Child Psychology, 6,* 271–280.

Rozin, P. & Fallon, A.E. (1987). A perspective on disgust. *Psychological Review, 94,* 23–41.

Thorpe, S.J. & Salkovskis, P.M. (1997). The effect of one-session treatment for spider phobia on attentional bias and beliefs. *British Journal of Clinical Psychology, 36*, 225–241.

Torgersen, S. (1979). The nature and origin of common phobic fears. *British Journal of Psychiatry, 134*, 343–351.

Verhulst, F.C., van der Ende, J., Ferdinand, R.F., & Kasius, M.C. (1997). The prevalence of DSM-III-R diagnoses in a National sample of Dutch adolescents. *Archives of General Psychiatry, 54*, 329–336.

Watson, J.B. & Rayner, R. (1920). Conditioned emotional reactions. *Journal of Experimental Psychology, 3*, 1–14.

Watts, F.N., McKenna, F.P., Sharrock, R., & Trezise, L. (1986). Colour naming of phobia-related words. *British Journal of Psychology, 77*, 97–108.

8 GENERALIZED ANXIETY DISORDER

Michael A. Southam-Gerow

Children with generalized anxiety disorder (GAD) are plagued by worries that most children are able to shrug off. Often regarded as "little adults," these youth are overly concerned with issues usually viewed as the business of adults such as the family finances, the neighbors' marital conflict, and the impact of the weather on driving conditions. For a youth with GAD, these worries become a central focus of cognitive activity and disrupt adjustment and development. For example, one youth constantly worried about what was going to happen next in family life (e.g., errands out of the home) and whether things were going okay (e.g., worried constantly about the driving route of his mother), leading to his persistently asking his mother for updates and information. The questions were a tremendous distraction for her and led to her feeling angry at the young boy. This chapter reviews the current state of the empirical knowledge concerning GAD in youth.[1] First, the current status of the classification of the disorder is examined, including a brief review of relevant theoretical work on anxiety and worry. Second, epidemiological, course and outcome, and comorbidity data are reported and discussed. Third, risk and protective factors associated with GAD are considered. Fourth, research on the assessment, treatment, and prevention of the disorder are reviewed. Finally, future directions are highlighted.

Definition and Classification

Although GAD in adults has been relatively well-studied (Borkovec and Roemer, 1994; Brown, 1997; Rapee, 1991), little is known about GAD in youth. Much of the lag is due to changes in the Diagnostic and Statistical Manual of Mental Disorders (DSM). Until the release of the fourth edition of the DSM (American Psychiatric Association; APA, 1994), over-anxious disorder (OAD; DSM-III; APA, 1980; DSM-III-R; APA, 1987), was considered the diagnosis for youth who worried excessively. As a result, most of the research on worrying youth has almost exclusively focused on youth with OAD. Therefore, though this chapter's focus is nominally on GAD, relevant research on OAD is also reviewed. In this first section, the diagnostic criteria for both GAD and OAD are considered. Next, I review the empirical evidence in the debate over which diagnostic category—OAD or GAD—is most appropriate for youth who worry too much. Finally, I briefly summarize a current theory that has relevance to the classification of GAD.

The core symptoms of GAD in DSM-IV are (a) excessive worry about multiple topics; (b) difficulty controlling or regulating the worry; (c) somatic symptoms that accompany the worry; and (d) functional impairment resulting from the worries. The duration of these symptoms must be at least six months. Because there is a high rate of comorbidity among anxiety disorders (see below), an important diagnostic consideration relates to the focus of the youth's worries. If restricted to (a) separation from an attachment figure (separation anxiety disorder [SAD]); (b) social situations (social phobia); or (c) a specific event, stimulus, or situation (specific phobia), GAD is not the appropriate diagnosis.

Though GAD and OAD share conceptual overlap (i.e., both are designed to identify youth who worry too much), there are criterion-level differences that merit mention. One major difference between OAD and GAD concerns the requirement for GAD that youth experience at least one somatic symptom when worrying. Somatic symptoms are *not* required for a diagnosis of OAD, though some are included as criteria. Another difference is that OAD symptoms are described with a greater level of detail and some of these aspects of OAD are not captured in the broader, less specific criteria for GAD. For example, self-consciousness, overconcern with competence, and need for reassurance are all separate symptoms for OAD that do not correspond with a GAD symptom. A final criteria-related difference between GAD and OAD is that to meet criteria for GAD, the child must experience the worry as uncontrollable whereas this criterion or an analogue is not included among the criteria for OAD.

THE OAD-GAD DEBATE

The reasons for the elimination of OAD from the DSM were primarily related to (a) its high degree of overlap with GAD and (b) the contention by some that OAD may be a subsyndromal state. However,

OAD's inclusion in the DSM was in part an attempt to address possible developmental differences (i.e., child versus adult) in symptom presentation. Developmental psychopathologists balk at applying the same set of criteria for adults and children without sound empirical evidence to support such application. Although the framers of the recent version of the DSM have "ruled" in favor of having only one diagnostic category for excessive and interfering worry across the lifespan, current empirical evidence does not uniformly support the decision. In the following section, I review the evidence that has been amassed on the relative merits of OAD and GAD as diagnostic categories for youth who worry too much.

Investigators have examined the legitimacy of OAD as a diagnosis from at least three angles: (a) Can the diagnosis be reliably made? (b) Does the category possess discriminant validity? (i.e., Are OAD symptoms non-normative?) and (c) Is there impairment associated with OAD symptoms and diagnosis? The reliability (inter-rater and retest[2]) of OAD is one of the lowest of the anxiety disorders and has ranged widely (from poor to good) across a number of studies (see Werry, 1991 for review). For example, concerning inter-rater reliability, Silverman and Nelles (1988) found that the inter-rater kappa coefficient for OAD (0.54) was the lowest for all disorders examined and substantially lower than the mean for other diagnoses (0.78). Other researchers have reported even lower inter-rater reliability coefficients (e.g., Canino et al., 1986). Silverman and Rabian (1995) reported that the retest reliability of child-report of OAD symptoms was moderate to poor for more than half of the symptoms (i.e., 4 of 7). In addition, Werry's (1991) review revealed largely unsatisfactory data on the retest reliability of OAD at both the symptom and diagnosis level across several studies. More recently, though, Silverman and Eisen (1992) found better retest reliability for OAD for youth (0.85) and parent report (0.64) at the diagnostic level. Overall, reliability data for OAD are mixed, with more evidence suggesting moderate to low moderate reliability for the category.

Research has addressed the discriminant validity of OAD. For example, Bell-Dolan et al. (1990) examined anxiety symptomatology in a non-referred sample of 5 to 18 year olds, using the Schedule for Affective Disorders and Schizophrenia for School-Age Children (K-SADS). They found that many anxiety disorder symptoms—particularly symptoms of OAD and simple phobia—were relatively common in youth who did not meet criteria for any disorder. Additionally, many of these symptoms attenuated after one year:

many of the at-risk participants at the initial assessment were no longer at-risk at the follow-up assessment.

Additional evidence on the discriminant validity of OAD was reported by Beidel (1991). She compared a sample of anxiety-disordered youth (diagnosed with either OAD or social phobia by the Anxiety Disorders Interview Schedule for Children [ADIS-C]) to matched non-referred youth to determine if the pairs could be distinguished on a variety of measures. Although youth with social phobia could be discriminated from their matched peers, youth with OAD could not. Across most areas measured, OAD youth did not differ from their matched non-disordered counterparts. For example, youth with OAD did not differ from youth in the control group on measures of state anxiety, perceived competence, temperament, distress during a test, number of anxiety-provoking events reported, and distress during those reported events.

A more recent study examining the discriminant validity of OAD was conducted by Beidel et al. (1996b). They compared three samples of youth: (a) Clinic-Referred (CR) youth referred for treatment at a child anxiety clinic who received a diagnosis of OAD; (b) Community-Test-Anxious (C-TA) non-referred youth recruited through a school district to participate in a test anxiety study and found to be highly test anxious and diagnosed with OAD; and (c) Community-Non-Test-Anxious (C-NON) classmates of the community test-anxious sample who were not test anxious Beidel et al. (1996b) found no difference between the CR and the C-TA groups in terms of OAD symptom endorsement (both maternal and youth report), suggesting that a high number of OAD symptoms alone may not be a reason for clinical referral.

Beidel et al.'s (1996b) study also provides some suggestive evidence concerning whether OAD is related to clinical impairment. The CR and C-TA groups differed in terms of comorbidity and covariation: the CR group reported an average of 2.2 additional diagnoses compared to 0.3 for the C-TA group (and 0 for the C-NON group) and scored higher on CBCL scales. It is not possible to determine from this data if the impairment leading to clinical referral for the CR group was related to OAD or to the additional diagnoses and problem areas. However, given that youth in the C-TA group were not referred for treatment, it is tempting to conclude that the CR group's impairment was related more to the other diagnoses/problems and not to OAD per se.

Despite all of the negative evidence, some research has lent support to the possible legitimacy of OAD as a diagnostic category. For example, Last et al., (1992) found that 51% of youth diagnosed with OAD developed the diagnosis after the remission of another disorder, an unexpected result if OAD was a subsyndromal state. In addition, they found that youth with OAD experienced psychosocial impairment. However, because their sample was a clinical one with high rates of comorbidity, it cannot be determined for certain that the impairment was related to the OAD per se (Beidel *et al.*, 1996b). However, impairment scores were not different between youth with both OAD and social phobia compared to youth with OAD without social phobia.

Other evidence supporting the possible legitimacy of OAD (and GAD) was reported by Muris *et al.* (1998). In a community sample in Holland, they found that youth diagnosed with OAD (and GAD) differed on several different measures of clinical severity from those children not diagnosed with either disorder. For example, the two groups were discriminable by number of worries, scores on anxiety measures, and use of distraction coping, with the diagnosed youth exhibiting less adaptive functioning on each measure. However, the study did not address the relative validity of OAD versus GAD.

Other evidence supporting OAD was reported by Bowen *et al.* (1990). They found that youth self-diagnosed with OAD experienced OAD-related impairment, as measured by responses to questions assessing impairment in seven domains, including: (a) social problems; (b) impaired academic or behavioural competence; and (c) use of mental health services. The impairment assessment involved multiple informants, greatly strengthening the approach by reducing the problems with method variance. As Bowen *et al.* (1990) noted, impairment reported by youth with OAD and SAD was not significantly different from that reported by youth with externalizing disorders in all but two areas.

Overall, the evidence is mixed regarding OAD's validity, with most work that *explicitly* assessed OAD's legitimacy casting doubt on the category. However, OAD's nosological replacement GAD is not without its detractors and problems (Beidel *et al.*, 1996b; Silverman, 1998). As already mentioned, a prime criticism of GAD concerns applying the same criteria to adults and children despite obvious developmental differences. Developmental psychopathologists argue that psychological disorder will not be isomorphically identical across development and may even present a very different picture (Cicchetti, 1984). Specific to GAD, some have argued that the physiological symptoms associated with GAD in adults may not be present (or at least may be "undetected") in children (Bowen *et al.*, 1990; Last, 1991). The DSM-IV criteria for GAD make allowances for developmental differences in presentation of the disorder (i.e., fewer somatic symptoms required for diagnosis) but there are some who argue that this may not be sufficient (Silverman, 1998). An additional problem that some find with GAD is that the DSM-IV does not specify a set of functional impairment criteria (Beidel *et al.*, 1996). Instead, the DSM states "clinically significant impairment or distress" must be present, without detailing how this impairment might be manifest[3]. This problem could potentially lead to the same problems encountered with OAD, namely that the disorder will be over-diagnosed, with youth receiving the diagnosis without experiencing symptom-related impairment.

Because the nosological change was relatively recent, there is a paucity of studies on the validity and reliability of GAD. However, one recent investigation by Tracey *et al.* (1997) provides some evidence that supports the reliability and validity of GAD. They reported on a study of three samples of 7- to 17-year-old youth: those with GAD (GAD); youth without GAD but with other anxiety disorders (ANX); and non-clinic-referred youth without any anxiety disorder (NON). They compared the groups on several clinical indices, some of which were hypothesized to be specific to GAD (i.e., number of GAD and OAD symptoms from the ADIS, number of worries, scores on the RCMAS-Worry scale) and some of which were considered related to anxiety disorders more broadly (i.e., CDI, RCMAS-Anxiety scale) and on which they hypothesized no differences would be found between the anxiety disordered groups (GAD and ANX). Results supported the hypothesized specificity of symptomatology among GAD youth—worry number, RCMAS-Worry scale, and symptom counts of GAD and OAD discriminated between the GAD and ANX (and NON) groups as predicted.

Another issue addressed by Tracey *et al.* (1997) concerns the relative validity of GAD versus OAD for youth. To examine the question, they compared the number of reported GAD and OAD symptoms in the NON sample. Overall, the number of symptoms endorsed by the NON sample in both categories was low across both parent and child report. However, the NON youth and their parents endorsed a higher number of OAD symptoms (parent-report mean = 0.83; youth-report mean = 0.50) than GAD symptoms (parent-report mean = 0.22; youth-report mean = 0.06). Examined another way, only 1 NON youth and 2 NON parents endorsed any GAD symptom, 6 NON youth and 9 NON parents endorsed at least one OAD symptom. Thus, in the study, GAD appeared to possess somewhat better discriminant validity compared to OAD.

Tracey and colleagues (1997) also evaluated the appropriateness of DSM-IV's criterion C for GAD. Criterion C requires that a youth experience at least one of 6 somatic symptoms when worrying. As noted above, this particular criterion has been criticized because youth tend not to endorse high rates of somatic symptoms (Bowen *et al.*, 1990) and those symptoms that youth do tend to endorse are not included among the symptoms (e.g., headaches, stomachaches; see Last, 1991).[4] Two of Tracey *et al.*'s findings are relevant to the question. First, they found that youth *do* endorse somatic symptoms and the number of symptoms endorsed increased with age. In addition, they found that the positive predictive power of child-reported somatic symptoms exceeded that of parent-reported somatic symptoms. Both of these findings undermine arguments that criterion C lacks developmental sensitivity, at least for youth above age 7 years. Overall, Tracey *et al.*'s (1997) findings offered some support for the discriminant and convergent validity of the DSM-IV category of GAD for youth. In addition, they found preliminary evidence in favor of GAD as the better category compared to OAD. Finally, they did not find that criterion C posed the developmentally-linked problems that some have feared.

One final question arising from the change in the nosology concerns the applicability of past psychopathology and treatment research focused on youth with OAD to youth with GAD. In other words, would youth diagnosed with OAD in previous research meet criteria for GAD or would they represent a now undiagnosed group? Two recent studies have addressed this question. At a child and adolescent anxiety disorders clinic, Kendall and Warman (1996) applied both DSM-III-R OAD and DSM-IV GAD criteria (using the ADIS) to diagnose 40 youth at an anxiety disorders clinic. Overlap of youth with DSM-III-R OAD and DSM-IV GAD was high, 98% for parent-report and 93% for youth-report. In another investigation at a child anxiety disorders clinic, Tracey *et al.* (1997) found that all of the youth diagnosed with GAD also met criteria for OAD and vice versa. Both studies support the cautious application of research findings on youth OAD to youth with GAD. However, future work should test hypotheses based on the work with OAD samples to empirically test their validity with GAD youth. Overall, there is a critical need for considerably more research on this diagnostic question. Given extant work, though, the use of GAD appears better justified than OAD.

THEORETICAL NOTE ON NEGATIVE AFFECTIVITY: FEAR AND ANXIETY

A theoretical issue related to the distinction between *worry* and *fear* merits a few brief comments. Theory on negative emotions has played an important role in the categorization of emotional disorders. One current theory, the tripartite theory (Barlow *et al.*, 1996; Clark and Watson, 1991; Watson and Clark, 1984), has led to a swell of research in recent years (Chorpita *et al.*, 1998; Joiner *et al.*, 1996; Lerner *et al.*, 1999). In part, the theory addresses one categorization question that has been a focus of recent years: Are depression and anxiety distinct constructs or do they represent a unitary construct? Tripartite theory takes a middle road between the two extreme positions (i.e., unitary construct versus separate constructs), positing that anxiety and depression are each associated with a *unique* emotional component but that they share a common emotional component. The specifics of the theory have differed somewhat among various writers (Chorpita and Barlow 1998). Following the terminology of Barlow *et al.*[5] (1996), the common emotional component of negative emotions, *Fear*, represents general distress (i.e., autonomic arousal and panic) of the organism. The unique components are *Anxiety*—referring to tension, *worry*, and apprehension[6]—and *Depression*—referring to low positive affect, anhedonia, and hopelessness. The main symptoms of GAD overlap with the Anxiety component of the theory whereas the main symptoms of some other anxiety disorders (e.g., panic disorder, specific phobia) are more consonant with the Fear component. In theory, then, differential diagnosis could be enhanced by using assessment instruments based on the tripartite model. In preliminary support of this contention, the content of children's fears differs from the content of their worries (Muris *et al.*, 1997, 1998). However, additional work is needed to determine the value of the theory to classify anxiety- (and depression-) related problems in youth.

Epidemiology

As a result of the recent shift from the use of the diagnosis of OAD to GAD, there are very few studies that examine the epidemiology of GAD in youth. Because of the paucity of studies focused on GAD, I report studies that have examined the epidemiology of OAD and/or GAD. Future research will determine if the nosological change will impact the number of youth identified as having worry-related disorders. However, as reviewed in the previous section, research (Kendall and Warman, 1996; Tracey *et al.*, 1997) has suggested that youth diagnosed with OAD have tended to be diagnosed with GAD when DSM-IV criteria were applied. After reviewing the prevalence data for

OAD and GAD from both community and clinical samples, the literature on gender, ethnic, and developmental differences in OAD and GAD is examined. Then, the meager data on course and outcome of OAD and GAD are reviewed. Finally, data on comorbidity of OAD and GAD with other disorders are surveyed.

PREVALENCE OF DSM DISORDERS OF WORRY: OAD AND GAD COMMUNITY SAMPLES

There have been a number of epidemiological studies that have reported prevalence data for OAD and considerably fewer reporting data on GAD. Table 8.1 summarizes the prevalence data from these studies. As the Table indicates, prevalence for OAD has ranged from less than 2 to 19%. Though infrequently assessed and thus not as well estimated, rates of GAD appear lower, ranging from 0.4% to 4.2%. Prevalence rates have been more frequently assessed by youth report and when both parent- and youth-report data have been available, youth-report rates were always higher in community samples.

CLINICAL SAMPLES

Several childhood anxiety disorder treatment clinics have reported on the prevalence of disorders in their samples. In general, the prevalence of OAD and GAD in these clinics is quite high, from about 20% to over 70% depending on the clinic (e.g., Barrett et al., 1996b; Kendall, 1994; Kendall et al., 1997). In clinics serving a more general population, rates of OAD and GAD are considerably lower. For example, Weisz and Southam-Gerow (2000) found a past-year prevalence of OAD of 13.7% and 9.3% for GAD.

THE IMPACT OF ETHNICITY, GENDER, AND DEVELOPMENT

Despite calls for work with diverse samples, research with non-Caucasian ethnic groups has been rare in the childhood anxiety disorders literature. Little of the work that has been conducted was concerned with the diagnostic category of GAD specifically. However, some work on the relationship of ethnicity to anxiety disorders more broadly has been conducted[7]. For example, Canino et al. (1986) investigated symptom and diagnostic differences between African-American and Latino youth ages 5 to 16 in an outpatient clinic sample in New York City. Though they did not examine specific diagnostic differences, they did find that Latino youth were more likely than

Table 8.1 Prevalence of OAD and GAD in community sample

Study	Sample	Age	Interview and DSM version	% of OAD Parent/Youth	% of GAD Parent/Youth
Anderson et al. (1987)	New Zealand	11	DISC/DSM-III	2.9/-	-|-
Kashani et al. (1987)	USA	14 to 16	DICA/DSM-III	-|-	-|-
Costello et al. (1989)	USA	7 to 11	DISC/DSM-III	2.0/2.8	-|-
Velez et al. (1989)	USA-A	9 to 12	DISC/DSM-III	19.0/-	—
Velez et al. (1989)	USA-B	13 to 18	DISC/DSM-III	12.7-\-	
Velez et al. (1989)	USA-A	11 to 14	DISC/DSM-III	9.7/-	–
Velez et al. (1989)	USA-B	15 to 20	DISC/DSM-III	8.6/-	–
McGee et al. (1990)	New Zealand	13 to 15	DISC/DSM-III	5.9/-	–
Bowen et al. (1990)	Canada	12 to 16	Questionnaire/DSM-III-R	3.6/0	-|-
Fergusson et al. (1993)	New Zealand	15	DISC/DSM-III-R	2.1/6	4.2/1.7
Lewinsohn et al. (1993)	USA	14–17	K-SADS/DSM-III-R	.47/-(1.29/-)	-|-
Essau et al. (1999)	Germany	12–17	CAPI	-|-	0.4/-

NOTE: Rates are point prevalence rates; when lifetime prevalence rates were provided, they are listed in parentheses. Velez et al. (1989) was a longitudinal study; prevalence data reported are for two samples (marked A & B in the Table) at two timepoints; DISC = Diagnostic Interview Schedule for Children; DICA = Diagnostic Interview for Children and Adolescents; K-SADS = Schedule for Affective Disorders and Schizophrenia for School-age Children; CAPI = Computerized Munich version of the Composite International Diagnostic Interview.

African-American youth to report anxiety-related symptoms such as worrying or panic and school refusal due to fear. In a community sample, Silverman *et al.* (1995) found that African-Americans reported more worries compared to Latino and Caucasian youth. Additionally, Last and Perrin (1993) compared Caucasian and African-American youth ages 5 to 17 years presenting to an anxiety disorders clinic on many variables, including DSM-III-R diagnoses determined by K-SADS (combined parent-youth report). They found few differences between the two groups relevant to OAD/GAD (e.g., non-significant difference for prevalence of OAD between the groups). And Treadwell *et al.* (1995) found no ethnic differences in terms of OAD-related symptomatology and OAD diagnoses in a childhood anxiety disorders clinic. The different ethnic-related patterns found in these studies may be partly accounted for by the sample characteristics. The Canino *et al.* (1986) sample was a general clinical one, Silverman *et al.*'s (1995) was a community sample, and both the Treadwell *et al.* (1995) and Last and Perrin samples were drawn from anxiety disorders clinics. In particular, one would not expect large differences in anxious symptomatology in the two anxiety disorders clinic samples because the youth were selected on the basis of high levels of anxiety. The discrepant ethnic-related findings of the other two studies are harder to explain and require future work.

Gender differences in anxiety disorders among adults has been a consistent finding (Yonkers and Gurguis, 1995). In youth, this robust gender difference is also present, at least at the level of fears (e.g., Ollendick *et al.*, 1996) but differences regarding worry or GAD prevalence has been less frequently examined. At the symptom level, Silverman *et al.* (1995) found that females reported more worries than males. However, in two other studies examining worry frequency and severity in non-referred samples, mixed or no gender differences were found (Muris *et al.*, 1998; Vasey *et al.*, 1994). From a diagnostic perspective, most work has indicated that females were over-represented among youth with a current or past anxiety disorder, at least in adolescence (Bowen *et al.*, 1990; Lewinsohn *et al.*, 1993, 1998). Data for children suggests more equivalent rates of boys and girls with OAD or GAD (Last *et al.*, 1992; Werry, 1991).

Developmental theory (Vasey, 1993) predicts a developmentally-linked increase in risk for GAD and pathological worrying based on gains in cognitive abilities. Some work has addressed this idea. Strauss *et al.*, (1988) examined diagnostic differences among youth age 5 to 19 for OAD. Though they found no difference at the level of diagnosis, they did find that older children reported a greater number of symptoms and had higher levels of anxiety. In addition, as noted above, Vasey *et al.* (1994) found that a greater variety of worries, a greater ability to elaborate on outcomes of worry topics, and worries of increasing complexity is more common in children above 8-year-olds. Contrarily, Silverman *et al.* (1995) did not find developmentally-linked increases in worries, though the restricted age range of the sample may have reduced the chance of finding developmental differences.

Overall, the evidence on ethnic/cultural differences in worries, GAD, and OAD is insufficient to offer even tentative conclusions. The evidence on gender differences is somewhat better and suggests that beginning in adolescence, anxiety disorders in general and GAD/OAD in particular are more prevalent in females. Finally, although the evidence on developmental differences is sparse and not entirely conclusive, there does appear to be an increased developmental risk for worrying and for OAD symptomatology. However, that risk is theoretically countered by an increasing ability to cope with worry that also comes with development (Vasey, 1993).

Comorbidity

Overall, the comorbidity of anxiety disorders with other disorders is quite high (Brady and Kendall, 1992; Russo and Beidel, 1994). In fact, comorbidity rates in excess of 65% in epidemiological (Bird *et al.*, 1993; Fergusson *et al.*, 1993) and clinically-referred samples (Kendall *et al.*, 1997; Silverman and Ginsburg, 1998) have been reported. However, there is not a wealth of data on the comorbidity patterns specific to GAD. The data that does exist generally has examined the comorbidity patterns of OAD. This evidence is briefly reviewed here.

First, co-occurrence of OAD with other internalizing disorders is common. For example, rates of comorbidity with separation anxiety disorder and social phobia ranged from 20 to 30% in many studies (Kashani *et al.*,1990; Last *et al.*, 1987; Silverman, 1998). In addition, comorbidity of OAD with depressive disorders has also been a frequent finding, with reported rates as high as 50% though most studies have found the rate of co-occurrence to be in the 10% to 30% range (Bowen *et al.*, 1990; Brady and Kendall, 1992; McGee *et al.*, 1990; Silverman, 1998). Comorbidity is also extremely common in clinic-referred samples. For example, in a anxiety disorders clinic sample of 135 youth (Southam-Gerow *et al.*, in press), only 10% of the participants met criteria for a single diagnosis. Other anxiety disorders were frequently co-occurring, with 50% of youth meeting criteria for a secondary diagnosis of simple phobia, 29% for avoidant disorder or social phobia, 17% for separation anxiety disorder, and 2% for obsessive-compulsive disorder. Additionally, 5% of youth met criteria for dysthymia, and 4% for major depressive disorder. In a recent study on using DSM-IV criteria for GAD, Essau *et al.* (1999) found even higher rates—with 100% of youth with GAD also meeting criteria for at least one other anxiety disorder and at least one depressive disorder. However, the small size of the GAD sample limits the generalizability of these findings.

Co-occurrence of anxiety disorders (including OAD) with disruptive behaviour disorders has also been a common, though initially unexpected, finding (Russo and Beidel, 1994; Zoccolillo and Rogers, 1991). Most of the work has grouped all anxiety disorders together, making the specific comorbidity of OAD with externalizing disorders difficult. Using analyses from Russo and Beidel's (1994) review, greater than chance co-occurrence was found across most studies and for most disorder combinations, such as anxiety and conduct disorders, anxiety disorders and ADHD, and anxiety and oppositional defiant disorders. Comorbidity with externalizing disorders is also extremely common in clinic-referred samples with rates of co-occurrence reported by Russo and Beidel (1994) as highest for ADHD (as high as 40% in some samples), lower for ODD (ranging from 9 to 12%) and lowest for CD (ranging from 2 to 24%). These rates are consistent with those in the anxiety disorders clinic sample reported by Southam-Gerow *et al.* (in press): 15% ADHD, 9% oppositional defiant disorder, and 1% conduct disorder.

In addition, there is a small but suggestive set of studies that provide preliminary evidence of an overlap of anxiety disorders and substance abuse in adolescence (Deas-Nesmith *et al.*, 1998). None of the extant work has examined GAD (or OAD) specifically and thus future work must clarify whether the association between anxiety and substance abuse is specific to certain anxiety disorders (and certain substances) or if it is a more general association.

Course and Outcome

Data on the course and outcome of OAD and GAD is scanty. Some retrospective research with adults has suggested that the onset of GAD or at least symptoms of GAD begins at an early age (for review, see Brown, 1997). However, retrospective evidence is not as compelling as longitudinal work. Unfortunately, there is a paucity of prospective studies of childhood anxiety disorders. The work that does exist has little to say concerning GAD specifically. However, examining research on OAD provides a reasonable comparison. Overall, the disorder appears to be unstable over time (Cantwell and Baker, 1989; Last *et al.*, 1996; Beidel, *et al.*, 1996a). For example, Last *et al.* (1996) found that over 80% of anxiety disorders remitted during a 3- to 4-year longitudinal study. However, about 1/3 of the youth with anxiety disorders developed a new disorder, typically another anxiety disorder. This rate of new disorder acquisition was greater than that of non-disordered controls and not significantly different from the rate of acquisition of new disorders of a group of youth with ADHD. Specific to OAD, 80% of youth no longer met criteria after the follow-up period. However, among youth who had an anxiety disorder at the initial assessment, youth with OAD had the highest rate of new disorder acquisition at the follow-up point. Thus, although the diagnosis of OAD appears to be unstable over time, youth who have had OAD may be at increased risk for other future disorders. Whether these tentative findings are true for GAD remains to be determined.

Risk and Protective Factors

Recent effort has been made to elucidate factors (both risk and protective) associated with the development and presentation of anxiety disorders in youth. By specifying moderators and mediators of anxiety disorder development, the field will be in a better position to refine etiological models and design interventions. The direction the research has taken is manifold, congruous both with the notion that disorder involves multiple pathways (Kazdin and Kagan, 1994) and the concept of multifinality coming from the work of developmental psychopathologists (Cicchetti, 1984). Some researchers have focused on historically distal factors, like genetics, temperament, and early attachment. Others have focused on cognitive and family factors. In the next section, I review the research on possible etiological factors of anxiety disorders, indicating, when possible, which may have some specificity to GAD.

GENETICS AND TEMPERAMENT

Several recent studies have examined the effects of genetic (plus shared environmental and non-shared environmental) factors on the development of psychopathology (Eaves *et al.*, 1997; Kendler *et al.*, 1995; Topolski *et al.*, 1997). Contrary to the bulk of the other research on risk factors, this literature has a few studies focused on OAD and GAD specifically. The evidence suggests that there is an additive genetic basis for GAD in adults and OAD in youth (Eaves *et al.*, 1997; Topolski *et al.*, 1997). One potential specific mechanism, the dopamine transporter gene (DAT1), has been identified by Rowe *et al.* (1998), though its specificity to GAD is not certain. Additionally, evidence reported by Kendler and colleagues (Kendler, 1996; Kendler *et al.*, 1995) has suggested a common genetic factor for GAD and major depressive disorder in adult women. Although a genetic role in OAD and GAD has been demonstrated consistently, the evidence for an etiologic role of shared environmental factors has not been as favorable (Kendler *et al.*, 1995; Topolski *et al.*, 1997). However, extant data does support the important role of non-shared environmental factors in the development of OAD and GAD.

Temperament is a central topic of developmental and clinical research (Bates and Wachs, 1994; Chess and Thomas, 1990) and is viewed by many as a one possible behavioural manifestation of genetic factors predisposing individuals to various disorders. Arguably the most impressive body of evidence has come from the labs of Kagan, Biederman, and their colleagues. These researchers have provided strong evidence that (a) inhibited temperament is stable and (b) the style is associated with later internalizing disorders (anxiety disorders; Biederman, *et al.*, 1993; Kagan *et al.*, 1994; Rosenbaum *et al.*, 1992). Several other investigators have examined the importance of temperamental factors, including but not limited to inhibition, in the development of psychopathology. For example, Derryberry and Reed (1994) have posited two temperamental patterns that may serve as vulnerabilities for the development of psychopathology: (a) a reward/approach orientation that may create a vulnerability to impulsivity-related disorders and (b) a punishment/avoidance orientation that may place a child at risk for the development of an anxiety disorder. In addition, Eisenberg and colleagues have examined the relationship between the temperamental variable, emotional intensity (EI), and later outcomes. Although high negative EI (i.e., negative emotion like anger, sadness, or fear) has typically been the risk factor, high general and positive EI have also been linked to negative outcomes (Eisenberg *et al.*, 1996). Much of Eisenberg and colleagues research has examined behaviour problems as an outcome; however, some of the outcomes linked to EI are correlates of anxiety disorders. For example, poor social skills (Eisenberg, *et al.*, 1993) and increased shyness (and not low sociability; Eisenberg *et al.*, 1995) have been linked to elevated EI.

Overall, there is a growing literature on genetic and temperamental variables that place youth at risk for anxiety disorders. In addition, there is some evidence supporting a somewhat specific genetic mechanism for GAD (and depression).

COGNITIVE FACTORS

The literature on cognitive factors associated with anxiety disorders in youth is rapidly growing. Kendall (Kendall and MacDonald, 1993) has argued that cognitive *distortions*, defined as misinterpretations—typically with a negative bias—of social and interoceptive information, are characteristic of anxious youth[8]. Empirical evidence supports this contention. For example, two studies have demonstrated that anxious youth exhibit attentional biases toward threat in a few studies (Chorpita *et al.*, 1996; Vasey *et al.*, 1995). Furthermore. negative attributional style has also been associated with anxiety disorders in youth (Bell-Dolan, 1995; Bell-Dolan and Wessler, 1994). However, the association may not be specific to anxiety disorders because attributional style has been related to other forms of child psychopathology (Gladstone and Kaslow, 1995).

Additionally, anxiety sensitivity (Reiss and McNally, 1985) is another factor that has been studied as a risk factor for anxiety disorders, but a review of the literature by Silverman and Weems (1999) leaves the specificity of the findings in question. For example, Rabian and colleagues (1993) found that although anxiety sensitivity was useful in discriminating anxiety disordered youth from non-disordered youth, it did not discriminate behaviour-disordered youth from anxiety-disordered youth. Finally, Vasey (1993) has also suggested that youth with anxiety disorders also experience cognitive *deficiencies* such as deficits in self-control skills. Preliminary support of this notion has been offered by Southam-Gerow and Kendall (2000), who found that anxiety-disordered youth have deficits in their understanding of emotion regulation (i.e., how to hide and change feelings) compared to non-clinic-referred youth.

Anxiety-disordered youth also exhibit problem-solving deficits. For example, two studies have found that anxious youth tend to generate avoidant solutions to hypothetical situations (Barrett *et al.*, 1996a; Chorpita *et al.*, 1996). Buttressing these conclusions is some evidence that the bias in problem-solving is specific to anxiety disorders—aggressive and non-referred youth solve problems differently than anxious youth. This area of research will benefit from the inclusion of a depressed sample of youth to address further the specificity of the bias in problem-solving.

Though research on cognitive factors related to anxiety has been relatively abundant, no research to date has established the direction of the effect. In other words, it is not currently known if the cognitive factors discussed above are causes of or symptoms of anxiety disorders. Additionally, aside from the data on problem-solving biases, it is not certain to what extent some of the cognitive factors are specific to anxiety disorders and it is by far even less certain their specificity to GAD.

RELATIONAL FACTORS

Relational factors, in particular parental characteristics and practices, have been examined as risk factors for anxiety disorders. For example, there is preliminary evidence that insecure early attachment is related to the development of anxiety disorders (Manassis *et al.*, 1994; Warren *et al.*, 1997). In addition, the parents of youth with anxiety or depressive disorders exhibit high levels of anxiety (and depressive) symptoms and disorders themselves (Manassis and Hood, 1998; Velez *et al.*, 1989; for review, see Ginsburg *et al.*, 1995). In addition, the family functioning of anxiety-disordered youth's families is typically poor. For example, studies have found that anxious children's families are poor problem-solvers and that parents "enhance" anxious youths' tendency to select avoidant solutions (Barrett *et al.*, 1996a; Chorpita *et al.*, 1996). Additionally, research has shown that anxious children's families provide negative messages and expectations to the youth (Kortlander *et al.*, 1997; Stark *et al.*, 1993; see Ginsburg *et al.*, 1995 for review). Finally, there is evidence that the families have limited family participation in social/recreational activities (Ginsburg *et al.*, 1995).

Despite the growing evidence for a familial role in the development of anxiety disorders, there is a possibility, as suggested by preliminary evidence from genetic studies, that for GAD specifically, the role of the family (i.e., shared environmental factors) is not particularly important. Indeed, close examination of the genetic evidence suggests that for separation anxiety disorder, shared environmental factors play an important role but for GAD, shared environmental factors do not significantly contribute to hypothesized models. As research incorporates specificity models (Garber and Hollon, 1991) into risk factor paradigms, the specific role of the family in the development of GAD will be understood better. One possibility is that although relational factors may not be a direct cause of the onset of GAD, they may contribute to the maintenance of the disorder (e.g., Steinberg & Avenevoli, 2000). I considered this in the next section.

INTEGRATIVE MODELS AND PROTECTIVE FACTORS

Many researchers have focused on one type of risk factor without concurrent examination of other relevant factors. Typically this has been a result of scientific necessity and not as an argument of the primacy of a particular factor. Indeed, most researchers acknowledge that psychopathology is multi-determined. Some recent models have attempted to develop more integrative models, including multiple factors, to explain the development of psychopathology in general and anxiety disorders specifically. For example, the prolific work of Eisenberg and colleagues has examined the inter-relations of several factors including temperament, child emotion regulation, and caregiver behaviours and characteristics and their impact on social adjustment, broadly defined (Eisenberg et al., 1992, 1996, 1997a). Other multi-factor models have examined how temperament interacts with parenting practices or caregiver characteristics to produce various social adjustment outcomes (Nachmias et al., 1996; Park et al., 1997). For example, Rubin and colleagues (1991) reported that maternal depression interacted with child temperament and attachment to produce negative outcomes such as (but not limited to) anxiety disorders.

Specific to anxiety disorders, Chorpita and Barlow (1998) outlined a multi-factor model involving the mediation of perceived control (a cognitive factor) between stressful circumstances and anxiety. They reasoned, based on cognitive and neurobiological research, that early experience with uncontrollable and unpredictable stimuli would led to low perceived control and increased inhibition. As development proceeded, the negative control-related cognitions would reinforce the tendency toward inhibition and thus reciprocally "enhance" low perceived control. They also outlined how neuroendocrine (e.g., hyper-cortisol activity) and familial processes (parental control) are involved in the model (Chorpita et al., 1998b).

These broader models suggest protective factors at multiple levels. For example, Eisenberg's work indicates that moderate levels of EI relates to positive outcome (Eisenberg et al., 1997a, b), suggesting the protective role of certain temperamental styles. In addition, it is feasible that the negative outcomes associated with high EI may be moderated somewhat with higher levels of emotion regulation. (Eisenberg et al., 1992, 1994, 1997b). In addition, applying work from the emotional development literature, there is evidence for the moderating influence of the caregiver on temperamental style, for example. Some work has suggested that caregiver behaviours provide a "scaffolding" (Denham et al., 1995) or structure that enables and fosters a child's emotional development. Examples of this phenomenon include: (a) co-regulation of infant emotion that is sensitive to the infant's needs, (b) co-construction of emotion narratives by mother-child dyads that may serve as later emotion "scripts" for the child, and (c) maternal encouragement of autonomy as the child learns how to regulate independent of the mother (Calkins, 1994; Casey and Fuller, 1994; Kobak *et al.*, 1994; Oppenheim *et al.*, 1997). Absence of the scaffolding process could serve as a risk factor for psychopathology.

Overall, research on the etiological factors associated with anxiety disorders broadly and GAD specifically is only beginning. There is a need for more research, especially examining the inter-relations of multiple factors. In addition, work specifically examining protective factors is particularly lacking. Finally, the models discussed here are not specific to GAD. Future work should clarify whether a specific model is warranted and, if so, how development of GAD may differ from other anxiety disorders.

Assessment and Treatment of GAD

In this section I review different assessment procedures used to evaluate GAD in youth. In addition, research on treatment approaches that have been developed to address anxiety disorders in youth are also reviewed. Because only one treatment that I could find was specifically designed to treat OAD/GAD in youth (Eisen and Silverman, 1993; 1998), I focus on treatments developed to ameliorate anxiety disorders more generally. However, to be included in the review, the samples of the studies needed to include youth diagnosed with OAD or GAD. Psychosocial treatments have garnered the most support and thus the bulk of the section focuses on these approaches. In addition, the sparse evidence on pharmacological interventions is reviewed. Finally, studies examining the impact of preventive interventions are reviewed.

ASSESSMENT

Because children rarely refer themselves for clinical treatment, assessment of childhood psychopathology involves integrating the reports of multiple sources, typically the child and the parent(s), but sometimes also including a teacher as well as observational measures and physiological measurements. Assessment instruments specific to GAD are limited to structured diagnostic interviews, of which there are several (e.g., Anxiety Disorders Interview Schedule; Diagnostic Interview

Schedule for Children; Schedule for Affective Disorders and Schizophrenia for School-Age Children (K-SADS). Review of all of the instruments is beyond the scope of this chapter. Instead, I focus on one of the most widely used instruments, the Anxiety Disorders Interview Schedule for Children (ADIS-C; Silverman & Albano, 1996). The ADIS-C (and its parent-report version, the ADIS-P) is a structured diagnostic interview designed to assess the presence of all DSM diagnoses in children and adolescents. Supportive reliability data have been reported for the DSM-III-R (Silverman & Eisen, 1992; Silverman & Rabian, 1995) and the DSM-IV (Silverman, 2000) versions. Specific to GAD, reliability kappas were .63 for child-report, .72 for parent-report, and .80 for the composite diagnosis (i.e., clinician integration of parent and child report).

In addition to structured diagnostic interviews, there are several self-report and parent-report measures that assess chronic child anxiety. Again, because the review of all of these measures is beyond the scope of the chapter, only the most commonly used measures are listed. Preliminarily, it should be noted that none of these measures assesses GAD specifically; instead, they assess chronic anxiety more generally and as such provide useful though not specific information for GAD researchers. Child-report measures include Revised Clinical Manifest Anxiety Scale (RMCAS; Reynolds & Richmond, 1985), State-Trait Anxiety Inventory for Children (STAIC; Spielberger, 1973), the Child Anxiety Sensitivity Index (CASI), and the Negative Affectivity Self-Statement Questionnaire (NASSQ; Ronan, Kendall, & Rowe, 1994). Parent-report measures include a parent-report version of the STAIC (STAIC-P; Strauss, 1987; see also Southam-Gerow, Flannery-Schroeder, & Kendall, 2000), the Multidimensional Anxiety Scale for Children (MASC; March, Parker, Sullivan, Stallings, & Conners, 1997), the Screen for Child Anxiety Related Emotional Disorders (SCARED; Birmaher et al., 1997), and the Child Behavior Checklist (CBCL; Anxiety/Depression subscale; Achenbach, 1991a). In addition, a teacher report version of the CBCL (TRF; Achenbach, 1991b) also offers an assessment of child anxiety (and depression, using the Anxiety/Depression subscale).

Observational and psychophysiological assessments of childhood anxiety are less frequently employed. As with self- and parent-report measures, neither of the methods claims specificity to GAD; instead, they provide a more general assessment of anxiety. For example, Kendall and colleagues (e.g., Kendall, 1994; Kendall et al., 1997) have used a behavioral observation paradigm as a way to measure a child's anxiety response to a mildly stressful situation (i.e., giving a speech in front of a video camera). Various aspects of the child's behavior are coded (e.g., nervous hand movements; verbalizations of anxiety). The paradigm has shown sensitivity to treatment (i.e., children's behavior becomes less anxious after treatment). Additionally, some researchers have employed psychophysiological methods such as heart-rate measurement or sweat gland activity (see Eisen & Engler, 1995).

PSYCHOSOCIAL TREATMENTS

Until recently, there was not a literature on the treatment of childhood anxiety disorders. Most child clinical treatment research was focused on ADHD and antisocial behaviour in youth (Eyberg *et al.*, 1998; Pelham *et al.* 1998; Southam-Gerow and Kendall, 1997). The first randomized clinical trial examining a psychosocial treatment for childhood anxiety disorders did not appear until 1994 (Kendall, 1994), although case reports and multiple baseline studies had already begun to appear (Eisen and Silverman, 1993).

As noted, treatment approaches designed specifically for GAD in childhood are rare. More commonly, clinical researchers have developed and examined the efficacy of interventions for a broad range of anxiety disorders. Although historically a wide range of therapeutic modalities have been applied to treat anxiety in children, the lion's share of the recent empirical work has focused on behavioural and cognitive-behavioural approaches. The recent review of the child anxiety treatment research by Ollendick and King (1998), applying criteria for empirically-supported treatments (Chambless *et al.*, 1996), found that only behavioural and cognitive-behavioural approaches currently met some of the American Psychological Association's Division 12 (Clinical Psychology) Task Force on Promotion and Dissemination of Psychological Procedures (Div. 12 Task Force; 1995) criteria. In the following section, I review only those treatment approaches with empirical support for youth with GAD or OAD. Particularly, the review covers individual cognitive-behavioural therapies (ICBT), group cognitive-behavioural therapies (GCBT), and family cognitive-behavioural therapies (FCBT).

INDIVIDUAL COGNITIVE-BEHAVIOURAL THERAPIES (ICBT)

Kendall and colleagues have been one of the pioneers in developing and empirically testing treatment programs for childhood anxiety disorders at the Temple University child anxiety clinic. The ICBT developed by Kendall (Kendall *et al.*, 1990, 1992)—the Coping Cat program—has been the subject of rigorous study. The program is manual-based (Kendall, *et al.*, 1990) and is a primarily youth-focused, 16–20 session treatment. The program essentially involves (a) skills training and (b) exposure experiences. First, youth are taught a four-step coping plan called the FEAR steps (an acronym for steps to take when experiencing anxious distress: Feeling frightened, Expecting bad things to happen, Actions and attitudes to take, and Results and rewards) steps. The steps include: recognition of anxious feelings and somatic reactions; the role of cognition and self-talk in exacerbating anxious situations; the use of problem-solving and coping skills to manage anxiety; the employment of self-evaluation and self-reinforcement strategies to facilitate the maintenance of coping. After mastering the FEAR steps, the remaining eight to twelve sessions are dedicated to the implementation of the coping plan in increasingly anxiety-provoking situations that are tailored to each child's concerns. Throughout, behavioural strategies such as coping modeling, *in vivo* exposure, role play, relaxation training, and contingent reinforcement are used (see also Kendall *et al.*, 1990).

There is considerable empirical support for the program. Kane and Kendall (1991) reported a successful multiple baseline study (n = 4) of the program. Subsequently, two large-scale RCTs have been reported. In the first of these, Kendall (1994) compared the efficacy of ICBT to a waitlist (WL) control group. Results suggested that across youth-report, parent-report, teacher-report, diagnostic, and observational measures, the program was successful in alleviating anxiety in youth, both across time and in comparison to the WL control group. Kendall and Southam-Gerow (1996) reported that treated youth continued to experience significant gains from pretreatment functioning at a long-term follow-up assessment (mean follow-up 3.35 years, range 2 to 5 years).

The second RCT (Kendall *et al.*, 1997) included a larger sample, permitting, for example, an examination of the impact of comorbidity. Overall, the pattern of findings was similar to those reported by Kendall (1994): for example 71% of youth no longer met criteria—by parent report—for their pretreatment primary diagnosis at posttreatment. Youth self-report, parent-report, teacher-report and behavioural observation measures all supported the efficacy of the treatment program at posttreatment and at one-year follow-up. Additionally, no treatment differences were found based on primary diagnosis, age, or level of comorbidity.

In two multiple baseline studies, Eisen and Silverman (1993; 1998) have reported on a variant of ICBT that involves that prescriptive application of the treatment components of cognitive training (CT) and relaxation training (RT) for youth with OAD and GAD. A question addressed by these investigators was: Are youth helped best when the treatment approach is "aimed" at the central symptomatology? For example, would an anxious youth with a high number (and degree) of somatic complaints and a relatively lower level of ruminative worries respond better to a relaxation training (RT) compared to a cognitive therapy (CT)? And would a youth with a high number and severity of worries and a relatively lower level of somatic complaints respond best to CT? The first study (Eisen and Silverman, 1993) provided suggestive evidence for this hypothesis, and the second study (Eisen and Silverman, 1998) addressed the question directly. In the latter study, the primary symptoms of four participants (ages 8 to 12 years) with OAD and GAD were classified as falling into one of two response classes: somatic or cognitive. Two of the four participants were assigned to a treatment addressing the dominant symptom class (i.e., youth with more somatic symptoms matched to RT; youth with more "cognitive" symptoms such as worry assigned to CT). The other two participants were assigned to the treatment logically unrelated to the response class of their symptoms. Whereas all four youth improved regardless of matching, the prescriptive treatments led to better outcomes. In addition, the investigators found that RT led to improvements in the logically unrelated response class (e.g., worries) while CT was associated with no improvements and possible negative effects for the logically-unrelated response class (i.e., somatic symptoms).

Overall, ICBT is a promising approach for treating childhood GAD (and OAD). And as Ollendick and King (1998) conclude, Kendall's Coping Cat program has earned "probably efficacious" status according to the guidelines of the Div. 12 Task Force (Chambless *et al.*, 1996). In addition, the practice of prescribing particular treatment components based on the youth's particular set of problems merits continued empirical attention.

FAMILY COGNITIVE-BEHAVIOURAL THERAPIES (FCBT)

Considering the common finding that parental anxiety contributes to child anxiety and may have a deleterious effect on the outcomes of child-only treatments, increasing parental involvement in treatment is a logical step. Howard and Kendall (1996) tested the possibility that

FCBT may ameliorate childhood anxiety problems. They designed a family-involved treatment based on the ICBT tested by Kendall (1994). The treatment incorporated the parent(s) in each session—for example, learning the anxiety management skills and assisting in the exposure tasks. In a multiple baseline study, Howard and Kendall (1996) demonstrated preliminary evidence for the efficacy of this FCBT approach.

Barrett *et al.*, (1996b) developed a variant of the Kendall's (1994) ICBT, the "Coping Cat" program, that included a session-by-session parental involvement. The "Coping Koala" (FCBT) program involved fewer sessions than Coping Cat, twelve. Only four sessions were used for skills-acquisition (to 8 for "Coping Cat"), with the remaining 8 sessions involving in-vivo exposure. The "family" part of the treatment involved training of three sets of skills: (a) contingency management training, including how to reward courageous behaviour and extinguish fearful behaviour; (b) parental anxiety management skills; and (c) communication and problems-solving skills training for the parent.

Barrett *et al.* (1996b) tested the FCBT treatment against a waitlist condition and an adapted (i.e., briefer) version of Kendall's (1994) ICBT. Participants were youth ages 7 to 14 years who received a primary diagnosis of SAD, OAD, or social phobia using the ADIS and DSM-II-R criteria: 38% of the participants had a primary diagnosis of OAD. Results of the RCT were promising both for ICBT and FCBT. Both produced statistically and clinically significant change for participants. Head-to-head comparison of the two active treatments suggested an advantage for FCBT. For example, at posttreatment, 57% of the youth in the ICBT condition were disorder-free whereas 84% of the FCBT were. At one-year follow-up, this difference was still present: 70% for ICBT compared to 95.6% for FCBT. The superiority for FCBT was present for clinician ratings and some of the self- and parent-report measures. No differences were found regarding the effectiveness of the two treatments regarding primary diagnosis; however, FCBT was more effective for younger youth and females.

Cobham *et al.* (1998) adapted the FCBT examined by Barrett *et al.* (1996b) to test if (a) parental anxiety moderated treatment outcome for the ICBT approach, and (b) parental anxiety could be ameliorated by using only the parent-anxiety management component of FCBT. Youth ages 7 to 14 were randomly divided into two groups based on parental anxiety level (measured by the STAI-trait version): if one or both parents scored higher than 40 on the STAI, the youth was in the child anxiety plus parental anxiety group whereas youth with neither parent scoring above 40 were in the child anxiety only group. Within these groups, youth were randomly assigned to receive ICBT or FCBT. The family intervention in the study was limited to focusing only on one of the three components originally tested by Barrett *et al.* (1996b), namely parental anxiety management. Results supported the notion that for youth whose parents are also anxious, the FCBT was more effective: 39% of youth with anxious parents responded well to ICBT compared to 77% response to FCBT for youth with anxious parents. Finding in support of FCBT were not consistent across all measures. For example, independent clinician ratings and youth self-report findings did not support the superiority of the FCBT. It may be that the inclusion of only one of the three components from Barrett *et al.* (1996b) original intervention may have diluted the potency of FCBT. For youth without an anxious parent, results suggested that it did not matter which treatment they received: 82% responded to ICBT along and 80% responded to FCBT.

Overall, FCBT represents the most promising of the psychosocial treatments for youth, though its necessity for all youth with anxiety disorders is not certain (Cobham *et al.*, 1998). According to the Div. 12 Task Force criteria, the FCBT studied by Barrett *et al.* (1996b) is probably efficacious, awaiting only replication by another investigative team to rise to "well established" status (Ollendick and King, 1998).

GROUP COGNITIVE-BEHAVIOURAL THERAPIES (GCBT)

Recently, child anxiety treatment researchers have begun to examine the efficacy of group treatments for anxiety disorders in youth. The rationales for group treatments are several, including cost-effectiveness (for both therapist and family), natural opportunity for exposure to feared social situations, normalization of anxiety, and positive peer influence in group process. Three different investigators have reported on preliminary findings of the efficacy of a group approach. For example, Silverman *et al.* (1999) reported an RCT of a group approach based on their transfer of control model (Silverman and Kurtines, 1996). The model views the therapist as an expert consultant to the family who provides knowledge to the youth and the parent, typically in the form of skills development. The knowledge is tailored to effect change in the youth and the change is accomplished by transferring control from the therapist to the parent to the child. The key to treatment of anxiety in this model involves control of the occurrence and successful implementation of child exposure and approach behaviour. The goal is accomplished therapeutically through contingency management (for parent) and self-control training (for youth). The group treatment developed involved ten 80 minute sessions, 70 minutes of which were spent in two separate groups: children in one and parents of the children in the other. The final ten minutes of each session involved parents and children. The program addresses contingency contracting, group social skills training, self-control (cognitive) training, and exposure tasks. Parents are trained both on the anxiety processes of their children as well as the ways in which parental responses reinforce anxious behaviour. In the RCT comparing a group intervention to waitlist control, Silverman *et al.* (1999) reported that the intervention was efficacious at post-treatment, 3, 6, and 12 month follow-up points.

In another RCT, Barrett (1998) compared two different GCBT approaches, one modeled after the ICBT approach from Barrett *et al.* (1996b) and the other modeled after the FCBT approach from Barrett *et al.*, (1996b) to each other and to a waitlist control group. Results supported the efficacy of both group approaches compared to the waitlist control group. Head-to-head comparison of the two active treatments suggested a marginal advantage for the GCBT that involved parents. In a third RCT, Flannery-Schroeder and Kendall (in press) examined the relative efficacy of a group treatment adapted from the ICBT approach of Kendall (1994) compared to the original ICBT approach and to a waitlist control group. Results suggested that both GCBT and ICBT were superior to waitlist but no benefit for GCBT over ICBT was found. However, as Flannery-Schroeder and Kendall (in press) noted, the low power to detect differences between the two active treatments precludes firm conclusions about the relative efficacy of ICBT versus GCBT.

Overall, GCBT has good empirical support across all three RCTs. However, the specific treatments have differed notably across all three trials so none of them can at present be considered efficacious when applying the criteria for empirically supported treatments (e.g., Chambless *et al.*, 1996). To improve the empirical base for making treatment recommendations, investigators are encouraged to use and build on extant treatments rather than developing new ones. Additionally, future work with larger samples will be needed to clarify the relative efficacy of GCBT versus ICBT for childhood anxiety disorders.

PSYCHOPHARMACOLOGICAL TREATMENTS

Research on psychopharmacological treatments with anxiety-disordered youth has been infrequent and the number of controlled trials is quite small. As would be expected, there are no clinical trials examining the efficacy of pharmacotherapy for GAD in youth. Many studies that have been conducted have included behaviour therapy as an adjunct, thus muddying conclusions that can be drawn about the relative efficacy of the pharmacological treatments. In their review, Kearney and Silverman's (1998) concluded that pharmacotherapy alone was not as effective as pharmacotherapy plus behaviour therapy. Work that has examined pharmacotherapy alone has in general not supported the use of medications, particularly tricyclic antidepressants, as a treatment for OAD and other childhood anxiety disorders with the exception of obsessive-compulsive disorder, for which there is reasonably good evidence that medications are efficacious (March & Leonard, 1996)[9]. Evidence for the efficacy of the selective serotonin reuptake inhibitors is more promising (Allen *et al.*, 1995; Bernstein *et al.*, 1996, for reviews); however, no controlled trials for them have been reported to data for youth with GAD or OAD. Overall, there is inadequate evidence to date to assess the efficacy of medications for childhood GAD or OAD.

Prevention

Preventive interventions for anxiety disorders are only recently being developed. As evidence on risk factors for anxiety disorders has increased, the ability of prevention researchers to identify youth at-risk has expanded. In this section, two prevention programs are discussed. The first was designed for school-age children and the second was designed for preschool children. Different risk assessments were necessarily used in the different studies, based on developmental level. Other prevention work has focused on anxious attachment as a risk factor for later disorder (Crittenden, 1992; Lieberman *et al.*, 1991) but because of the unclear evidence on the specificity of the risk, these studies are not reviewed here.

Dadds and colleagues (Dadds *et al.*, 1997) have tested the efficacy of a prevention/early intervention model for anxiety disorders based on the Coping Koala program. The program involved 10 weekly group (5 to 12 youth) sessions with 3 parent sessions concurrent with child sessions. In the child sessions, the therapists taught youth an anxiety management plan, the FEAR steps (Kendall, 1994), and used group processes to reinforce positive strategies and individual efforts to overcome fears. The parent sessions focused on: child management skills; the FEAR plan and how parents could encourage/model coping with fears; and parental anxiety management skills.

Dadds *et al.* (1997) conducted a controlled trial of the intervention. Initially, they conducted 4 screening levels: (a) high RCMAS scores; (b) teacher nominations of anxiety problem; (c) rule-outs for developmental disabilities, non-English-speaking families, and invalid RCMAS completion; and (d) include youth with features of or with anxiety disorder and without primary externalizing disorder diagnosis on parent ADIS. Families of youth passing all four levels were invited to participate in the study and the final sample size was 128 from a screened sample of 1786 youth aged 7 to 14 years. Youth were randomly assigned to the intervention group or the monitoring group. Most youth participating had at least one diagnosis, with 14.8% of the intervention group meeting criteria for GAD (20.9% in the control group). There were no diagnostic or symptom differences between the groups at the initial assessment. Although at post-intervention, differences were not consistently in evidence between the two groups, at 6-months follow-up, a significant advantage for the intervention group emerged. Specifically, at the follow-up point, children in the intervention group had lower rates of anxiety disorder (16%) than their control group counterparts (54%). In addition, the intervention group demonstrated better outcomes on clinician rating measures. More recently, Dadds and colleagues (1999) reported on 1- and 2-year-follow-ups of the program. Regarding diagnostic rates, they found that the two groups converged at 1-year follow-up (37% for intervention group and 42% for monitoring group) but that at the 2-year follow-up, the intervention group showed a lower rate while the monitoring group's rate remained stable (20% to 39%). Clinician ratings showed parallel outcomes with two-year follow-up results favoring the intervention group. Overall, the program showed promise as a short-term early intervention program for youth at-risk for anxiety disorders.

Another group of investigators has attempted to intervene at an even earlier age. LaFreniere and Capuano (1997) tested an early intervention for preschoolers identified as anxious/withdrawn by teachers. The intervention involved 20 sessions designed to teach parenting and attachment promoting skills. For example, sessions focused on: child-directed play; behaviour modification of problematic behaviour; and education on developmental needs of children. The intervention was found to increase social competence of youth and parental use of appropriate control, compared to a no-treatment control group. However, differences were not found across all outcome areas. Though the intervention shows promise, further investigation is needed, especially focusing on subsequent rates of disorder and symptomatology across time in the two groups.

Overall, prevention of anxiety disorders is in its infancy. However, recent development of promising interventions has made rapid progress in the area possible. Synergy of the work from treatment, intervention, and general psychopathology researchers will enhance progress in this area.

Conclusions and Future Directions

A major weakness in the literature on GAD in youth is the lack of research specifically on GAD. Prior to the next DSM revision, it will be important to amass data on youth with GAD to evaluate any possible changes to diagnostic criteria. As Werry (1991) cautioned before DSM-IV revisions, premature changes to the criteria will impede scientific progress which requires relative stability of the criteria to proceed. Despite the paucity of specific data, the last decade has been one of increased attention to anxiety disorders in children. As a result, there are some general—though tentative—conclusions that can be offered as a coda to the chapter. With each conclusion, future research suggestions are offered.

First, anxiety disorders in general and clinical level of worry (i.e., GAD and OAD) in particular are relatively common problems in childhood. Future work should focus on establishing better prevalence estimates for GAD. In addition, examining developmental, ethnic/cultural, and gender differences in the prevalence and presentation of GAD will be important to sensitively address these problems in treatment programs (Szapocznik and Kurtines, 1993). Second, although clinical levels of anxiety and worry appear to be relatively unstable, a number of youth persistently experience clinical levels of anxiety without treatment. Future work should examine the moderators and mediators of anxiety disorder (and particularly GAD) stability. For example, what factors contribute to the maintenance of an anxiety disorder and what factors contribute to the "spontaneous remission" of disorder? Third, there appears to be a number of risk factors for anxiety disorders (in general), including genetic/temperamental, cognitive, and family factors. Increased effort to identify these factors and their specificity to GAD is recommended. Additionally, the development of multi-factor models (Chorpita and Barlow, 1998; Kazdin and Kagan, 1994) is strongly urged because often the multi-determined nature of disorder is over-shadowed by the dominance of single-factor research paradigms. Finally, several treatment programs for anxiety problems (including GAD) have been empirically tested and at least two appear efficacious according to the Div. 12 Task Force criteria. All of the tested models are cognitive-behavioural in orientation. Future work should take at least three directions. First, comparisons of ICBT, FCBT, and GCBT, incorporating prescriptive designs (Cobham et al., 1998; Eisen and Silverman, 1998) appears a logical next step for efficacy tests. In particular, the advantage of FCBT over ICBT found in some trials needs to be refined and the status of GCBT needs clarification. Second, the development and testing of other treatment approached based on non-cognitive-behavioural theory (e.g., play therapy, psychodynamic therapy, parent-focused approaches) is urged. Third, effort should be applied in the direction of public health trials (effectiveness trials) to test efficacious treatments in real-world settings (Kendall and Southam-Gerow, 1995; Weisz et al., 1992). Similar work has found success in the adult literature (Wade et al., 1998) and a current project at UCLA is focusing on the treatment of childhood anxiety disorders in community clinics.

Acknowledgement

The author thanks Aileen M. Echiverri, C. Ashley Borders, and Heather Santoro for research assistance.

Notes

[1] The terms youth and children will be used interchangeably to refer to both children and adolescents. Distinctions will be made explicit when required.

[2] Cross-informant agreement is another form of reliability that has been examined. I exclude it from consideration because low cross-informant agreement is a ubiquitous finding in the child literature (e.g., Frick et al.,

1994) and because the questionable relevance of this sort of agreement to the legitimacy of OAD (or any diagnostic entity).

3 Beidel *et al.* (1996) offer several suggestions for impairment criteria, including failure to attend school, presence of anxiety-related oppositional behaviour, and physical problems secondary to anxiety (e.g., hypertension).

4 Headaches and stomachaches were permitted as a valid symptom for OAD.

5 I follow this terminology largely because the theory is based (in part) on empirical research conducted with children (e.g., Chorpita *et al.*, 1998a).

6 The distinction between fear and anxiety is tied to different neurological systems, the behavioural inhibition system (BIS; anxiety) and the fight or flight system (FFS)—see Chorpita and Barlow (1998) for discussion.

7 Cross-cultural work on fears in children, though somewhat plentiful is not reviewed here because it is not directly applicable to GAD.

8 Cognitive distortions are not considered to be specific to anxiety disorders alone. Kendall (e.g., Kendall and McDonald, 1993) has noted that youth with depression and conduct disorder, for example, exhibit cognitive distortions as well.

9 Some have argued that selective mutism is a variant of social phobia; empirical support for medications has been reported for the treatment of selective mutism.

References

Achenbach, T.M. (1991a). *Manual for the child behavior checklists/4–18 and 1991 profile.* Burlington, VT: University of Vermont.

Achenbach, T.M. (1991b). *Manual for the Teacher Report Form and 1991 Profile.* Burlington, VT: Department of Psychiatry, University of Vermont.

Allen, A.J., Leonard, H.L., & Swedo, S.E. (1995). Current knowledge of medications for the treatment of childhood anxiety disorders. *Journal of the American Academy of Child and Adolescent Psychiatry, 34*, 976–986.

American Psychiatric Association (1987). *Diagnostic and statistical manual of mental disorders (rev. 3rd ed.).* Washington, DC: American Psychiatric Association.

American Psychiatric Association (1994). *Diagnostic and statistical manual of mental disorders (4th ed.).* Washington, DC: American Psychiatric Association.

Anderson, J.C., William, S., McGee, R., & Silva, P.A. (1987). DSM-III disorders in preadolescent children: Prevalence in a large sample from the general population. *Archives of General Psychiatry, 44*, 69–76.

Barlow, D.H., Chorpita, B.F., & Turovsky, J. (1996). Fear, panic, anxiety, and disorders of emotion. *Nebraska Symposium on Motivation: Perspectives on Anxiety, Panic*, (pp. 251–328). Lincoln, NE: University of Nebraska Press.

Barrett, P.M. (1998). Evaluation of cognitive-behavioural group treatments for childhood anxiety disorders. *Journal of Clinical Child Psychology, 27*, 459–468.

Barrett, P.M., Dadds, M.R., & Rapee, R.M. (1996b). Family treatment of childhood anxiety: A controlled trial. *Journal of Consulting and Clinical Psychology, 64*, 333–342.

Barrett, P.M., Rapee, R.M., Dadds, M.R., & Ryan, S.M. (1996a). Family enhancement of cognitive style in anxious and aggressive children. *Journal of Abnormal Child Psychology, 24*, 187–203.

Bates, J.E. & Wachs, T.D. (1994). *Temperament: Individual differences at the interface of biology and behavior.* Washington, D.C.: American Psychological Association.

Beidel, D.C. (1991). Social phobia and overanxious disorder in school-age children. *Journal of the American Academy of Child and Adolescent Psychiatry, 30*, 545–552.

Beidel, D.C., Fink, C.M., & Turner, S.M. (1996a). Stability of anxious symptomatology in children. *Journal of Abnormal Child Psychology, 24*, 257–269.

Beidel, D.C., Silverman, W.K., & Hammond-Laurence, K. (1996b). Overanxious disorder: Subsyndromal state or specific disorder? A comparison of clinic and community samples. *Journal of Clinical Child Psychology, 25*, 25–32.

Bell-Dolan, D.J. (1995). Social cue interpretation of anxious children. *Journal of Clinical Child Psychology, 24*, 2–10.

Bell-Dolan, D.J., Last, C.G., & Strauss, C.C. (1990). Symptoms of anxiety disorders in normal children. *Journal of the American Academy of Child and Adolescent Psychiatry, 29*, 759–765.

Bell-Dolan, D. & Wessler, A.E. (1994). Attributional style of anxious children: Extensions from cognitive theory and research on adult anxiety. *Journal of Anxiety Disorders, 8*, 79–96.

Bernstein, G.A., Borchardt, C.M., & Perwien, A.R. (1996). Anxiety disorder in children and adolescents: A review of the past 10 years. *Journal of the American Academy of Child and Adolescent Psychiatry, 35*, 1110–1119.

Biederman, J., Rosenbaum, J.F., Bolduc-Murphy, E.A, Faraone, S.V., Chaloff, J. Hirshfeld, D. R., & Kagan, J. (1993). A 3-year follow-up of children with and without behavioral inhibition. *Journal of the American Academy of Child and Adolescent Psychiatry, 32*, 814–821.

Bird, H.R., Gould, M.S., & Staghezza, B.M. (1993). Patterns of diagnostic comorbidity in a community sample of children aged 9 through 16 years. *Journal of the American Academy of Child and Adolescent Psychiatry, 32*, 361–368.

Birmaher B, Khetarpal S, Brent, D. A., Cully, M., Balach, L., Kaufman, J., Neer, S. M. (1997). The Screen for Child Anxiety Related Emotional Disorders (SCARED): scale construction and psychometric characteristics. *Journal of the American Academy of Child & Adolescent Psychiatry, 36*, 545–553

Borkovec, T.D. & Roemer, L. (1994). Generalized anxiety disorder. In M. Hersen & R.T. Ammerman (Eds.), *Handbook of prescriptive treatments for adults* (pp. 261–281). New York: Plenum Press.

Bowen, R.C., Offord, D.R., & Boyle, M.H. (1990). The prevalence of overanxious disorder and separation anxiety disorder: Results from the Ontario Child Health Study. *Journal of the American Academy of Child and Adolescent Psychiatry, 29*, 753–758.

Brady, E.U. & Kendall, P.C. (1992). Comorbidity of anxiety and depression in children and adolescents. *Psychological Bulletin, 111*, 244–255.

Brestan, E.V. & Eyberg, S.M. (1998). Effective psychosocial treatments of conduct-disordered children and adolescents: 29 years, 82 studies, and 5,272 kids. *Journal of Clinical Child Psychology, 27*, 180–189.

Brown, T.A. (1997). The nature of generalized anxiety disorder and pathological worry: Current evidence and conceptual models. *Canadian Journal of Psychiatry, 42*, 817–825.

Calkins, S.D. (1994). Origins and outcomes of individual differences in emotion regulation. *Monographs of the Society for Research in Child Development, 59* (2–3, Serial No. 240).

Canino, I.A., Gould, M.S., Prupis, S., & Shaffer, D. (1986). A comparison of symptoms and diagnosis in Hispanic and black children in an outpatient mental health clinic. *Journal of the American Academy of Child Psychiatry, 25*, 254–259.

Cantwell, D.P. & Baker, L. (1989). Stability and natural history of DSM-III childhood diagnoses. *Journal of the American Academy of Child and Adolescent Psychiatry, 28*, 691–700.

Casey, R.J. & Fuller, L.L. (1994). Maternal regulation of children's emotions. *Journal of Nonverbal Behavior, 18*, 57–89.

Chambless, D.L., Sanderson, W.C., Shoham, V., Johnson, S.B., Pope, K.S., Crits-Christoph, P., Baker, M., Johnson, B., Woods, S.R., Sue, S., Beutler, L., Williams, D.A., & McCurry, S. (1996). An update on empirically validated therapies. *The Clinical Psychologist, 49*, 5–18.

Chess, S. & Thomas, A. (1990). Continuities and discontinuities in temperament. In L. Robins & M. Rutter (Eds.), *Straight and devious pathways from childhood to adulthood* (pp. 205–220). Cambridge, UK: Cambridge University Press.

Chorpita, B.F., Albano, A.M., & Barlow, D.H. (1996). Cognitive processing in children: Relation to anxiety and family influences. *Journal of Child Clinical Psychology, 25*, 170–176.

Chorpita, B.F., Albano, A.M., & Barlow, D.H. (1998a). The structure of negative emotions in a clinical samples of children and adolescents. *Journal of Abnormal Psychology, 107*, 74–85.

Chorpita, B.F. & Barlow, D.H. (1998). The development of anxiety: The role of control in the early environment. *Psychological Bulletin, 124*, 3–21.

Chorpita, B.F., Brown, T.A., & Barlow, D.H. (1998b). Perceived control as a mediator of family environment in etiological models of childhood anxiety. *Behavior Therapy, 29*, 457–476.

Cicchetti, D. (1984). The emergence of developmental psychopathology. *Child Development, 55*, 1–7.

Clark, L.A. & Watson, D. (1991). Tripartite model of anxiety and depression: Psychometric evidence and taxonomic implications. *Journal of Abnormal Psychology, 100*, 316–336.

Cobham, V.E., Dadds, M.R., & Spence, S.H. (1998). The role of parental anxiety in the treatment of childhood anxiety. *Journal of Consulting and Clinical Psychology, 66*, 893–905.

Costello, E.J., Costello, A.J., Edelbrock, C., Burns, B.J., Dulcan, M.K., Brent, D., & Janiszewski, S. (1988). Psychiatric disorders in pediatric primary care: Prevalence and risk factors. *Archives of General Psychiatry, 45*, 1107–1116.

Crittenden, P.M. (1992). Treatment of anxious attachment in infancy and early childhood. *Development and Psychopathology, 4*, 575–602.

Dadds, M.R., Holland, D.E., Laurens, K.R., Mullins, M., Barrett, P.M., & Spence, S.H. (1999). Early intervention and prevention of anxiety disorders in children: Results at 2-year follow-up. *Journal of Consulting and Clinical Psychology, 67*, 145–150.

Dadds, M.R., Spence, S.H., Holland, D.E., & Barrett, P.M. (1997). Prevention and early intervention for anxiety disorders: A controlled trial. *Journal of Consulting and Clinical Psychology, 65*, 627–635.

Deas-Nesmith, D., Brady, K.T., & Campbell, S. (1998). Comorbid substance use and anxiety disorders in adolescents. *Journal of Psychopathology and Behavioral Assessment, 20*, 139–148.

Denham, S.A., Mason, T., & Couchoud, E.A. (1995). Scaffolding young children's prosocial responsiveness: Preschoolers' responses to adult sadness, anger, and pain. *International Journal of Behavior Development, 18*, 489–504.

Derryberry, D. & Reed, M.A. (1994). Temperament and the self-organization of personality. *Development and Psychopathology, 6*, 653–676.

Eaves, L.J., Silberg, J.L., Maes, H.H., Simonoff, E., Pickles, A., Rutter, M., Neale, M.C., Reynolds, C.A., Erikson, M.T., Heath, A.C., Loeber, R., Truett, K.R., & Hewitt, J.K. (1997). Genetics and developmental psychopathology: 2. The main effects of genes and environment on behavioral problems in the Virginia Twin Study of Adolescent Behavioral Development. *Journal of Child Psychology and Psychiatry and Allied Disciplines, 38*, 965–980.

Eisen, A.R. & Engler, L.B. (1995). Chronic anxiety. In A.R. Eisen, C.A. Kearney, & C.E. Schaefer (Eds.), *Clinical handbook of anxiety disorders in children and adolescents* (pp. 223–249). Northvale, NJ: Jason Aronson.

Eisen, A.R. & Silverman, W.K. (1993). Should I relax or change my thoughts? A preliminary examination of cognitive therapy, relaxation training, and their combination with overanxious children. *Journal of Cognitive Psychotherapy, 7,* 265–279.

Eisen, A.R. & Silverman, W.K. (1998). Prescriptive treatment for generalized anxiety disorder in children. *Behavior Therapy, 29,* 105–121.

Eisenberg, N., Fabes, R.A., Bernzweig, J., Karbon, M., Poulin, R., & Hanish, L. (1993). The relations of emotionality and regulation to preschoolers' social skills and sociometric status. *Child Development, 64,* 1418–1438.

Eisenberg, N., Fabes, R.A., Carlo, G., Troyer, D., Speer, A.L., Karbon, M., & Switzer, G. (1992). The relations of maternal practices and characteristics to children's vicarious emotional responsiveness. *Child Development, 63,* 583–602.

Eisenberg, N., Fabes, R.A., Guthrie, I.K., Murphy, B.C., Maszk, P., Holmgren, R., & Suh, K. (1996). The relations of regulation and emotionality to problem behavior in elementary school children. *Development and Psychopathology, 8,* 141–162.

Eisenberg, N., Fabes, R.A., & Murphy, B.C. (1995). Relations of shyness and low sociability to regulation and emotionality. *Journal of Personality and Social Psychology, 68,* 505–517.

Eisenberg, N., Fabes, R.A., Murphy, B., Karbon, M., Maszk, P., Smith, M., O'Boyle, C., & Suh, K. (1994). The relations of emotionality and regulation to dispositional and situational empathy-related responding. *Journal of Personality and Social Psychology, 66,* 776–797.

Eisenberg, N., Fabes, R.A., Shepard, S.A., Murphy, B.C., Guthrie, I.K., Jones, S., Friedman, J., Poulin, R., & Maszk, P. (1997a). Contemporaneous and longitudinal prediction of children's social functioning from regulation and emotionality. *Child Development, 68,* 647–664.

Eisenberg, N., Guthrie, I.K., Fabes, R.A., Reiser, M., Murphy, B.C., Holgren, R., Maszk, P., & Losoya, S. (1997b). The relations of regulation and emotionality to resiliency and competent social functioning in elementary school children. *Child Development, 68,* 295–311

Essau, C.A., Conradt, J., & Petermann, F. (1999). Haufigkeit und Komorbiditat der generalisierten Angststorung: Ergebnisse der Bremer Jugendstudie. *Nervenheilkunde, 18,* 46–51.

Fergusson, D.M., Horwood, L.J., & Lynskey, M.T. (1993). Prevalence and comorbidity of DSM-III-R diagnoses in a birth cohort of 15-year-olds. *Journal of the American Academy of child and Adolescent Psychiatry, 32,* 1127–1134.

Flannery-Schroeder, E.C., & Kendall, P.C. (in press). Group and individual cognitive behavioral treatments for youth with anxiety disorders: A randomized clinical trial. *Cognitive Therapy and Research.*

Frick, P.J., Silverthorn, P., & Evans, C. (1994). Assessment of childhood anxiety using structured interviews: Patterns of agreement among informants and association with maternal anxiety. *Psychological Assessment, 6*, 372–379.

Garber, J. & Hollon, S.D. (1991). What can specificity designs say about causality in psychopathology research. *Psychological Bulletin, 110*, 129–136.

Ginsburg, G.S., Silverman, W.K., & Kurtines, W.M. (1995). Family involvement in treating children with phobic and anxiety disorders: A look ahead. *Clinical Psychology Review, 15*, 457–473.

Gladstone, T.R.G. & Kaslow, N.J. (1995). Depression and attributions in children and adolescents: A meta-analytic review. *Journal of Abnormal Child Psychology, 23*, 597–606.

Howard, B.L. & Kendall, P.C. (1996). Cognitive-behavioral family therapy for anxiety-disordered children: A multiple-baseline evaluation. *Cognitive Therapy & Research, 20*, 423–443.

Joiner, T.E., Catanzaro, S.J., & Laurent, J. (1996). Tripartite structure of positive and negative affect, depression, an anxiety in child and adolescent psychiatric inpatients. *Journal of Abnormal Psychology, 105*, 401–409.

Kagan, J., Snidman, N., Arcus, D., & Reznick, J.S. (1994). *Galen's prophecy: Temperament in human nature.* New York: Basic Books.

Kane, M.T. & Kendall, P.C. (1989). Anxiety disorders in children: A multiple-baseline evaluation of a cognitive-behavioral treatment. *Behavior Therapy, 20*, 499–508.

Kashani, J.H., Beck. N.C., Hoeper, E.W., Fallahi, C., Corcoran, C.M., McAllister, J.A., Rosenberg, T.K., Reid, J.R. (1987). Psychiatric disorders in a community sample of adolescents. *American Journal of Psychiatry, 144*, 584–589.

Kashani, J.H. & Orvaschel, H. (1988). Anxiety disorders in mid-adolescence: A community sample. *American Journal of Psychiatry, 145*, 960–964

Kashani, J.H., Vaidya, A.F., Soltys, S.M., Dandoy, A.C., Katz, L.M., & Reid, J.C. (1990). Correlates of anxiety in psychiatrically hospitalized children and their parents. *American Journal of Psychiatry, 147*, 319–323.

Kazdin, A.E. & Kagan, J. (1994). Models of dysfunction in developmental psychopathology. *Clinical Psychology: Science and Practice, 1*, 35–52.

Kearney, C.A. & Silverman, W.K. (1998). A critical review of pharmacotherapy for youth with anxiety disorders: Things are not as they seem. *Journal of Anxiety Disorders, 12*, 83–102.

Kendall, P.C. (1994). Treating anxiety disorders in youth: Results of a randomized clinical trial. *Journal of Consulting and Clinical Psychology, 62*, 100–110.

Kendall, P.C., Chansky, T.E., Kane, M.T., Kim, R.S., Kortlander, E., Ronan, K.R., Sessa, F.M., & Siqueland, L. (1992). *Anxiety disorders in youth: Cognitive-behavioral interventions.* Needham Heights, MA: Allyn & Bacon.

Kendall, P.C., Flannery-Schroeder, E.C., Panichelli-Mindel, S.P., Southam-Gerow, M.A., Henin, A., & Warman, M.J. (1997). Treating anxiety disorders in youth: A second randomized clinical trial. *Journal of Consulting and Clinical Psychology, 65*, 366–380.

Kendall, P.C., Kane, M., Howard, B., & Siqueland, L. (1990). *Cognitive-behavioral treatment of anxious children: Treatment manual.* Available from the author, Department of Psychology, Temple University, Philadelphia, PA 19122.

Kendall, P.C. & MacDonald, J.P. (1993). Cognition in the psychopathology of youth and implications for treatment. In K.S. Dobson & P.C. Kendall (Eds.), *Psychopathology and cognition* (pp. 387–432). San Diego, CA: Academic Press.

Kendall, P.C. & Southam-Gerow, M.A. (1995). Issues in the transportability of treatment: The case of anxiety disorders in youth. *Journal of Consulting and Clinical Psychology, 63*, 702–708.

Kendall, P.C. & Southam-Gerow, M.A. (1996). Long-term follow-up of a cognitive-behavioral therapy for anxiety-disordered youth. *Journal of Consulting and Clinical Psychology, 64*, 724–730.

Kendall, P.C. & Warman, M.J. (1996). Anxiety disorders in youth: Diagnostic consistency across DSM-III-R and DSM-IV. *Journal of Anxiety Disorders, 10*, 453–463.

Kendler, K.S. (1996). Major depression and generalised anxiety disorder same genes, (Partly) different environments—Revisited. *British Journal of Psychiatry, 168 (Suppl. 30)*, 68–75.

Kendler, K.S., Walters, E.E., Neale, M.C., Kessler, R.C., Heath, A.C., & Eaves, L.J. (1995). The structure of the genetic and environmental risk factors for six major psychiatric disorders in women: Phobia, generalized anxiety disorder, panic disorder, bulimia, major depression, and alcoholism. *Archives of General Psychiatry, 52*, 374–383.

Kobak, R.R., Cole, H.E., Ferenz-Gillies, R., Fleming, W.S., & Gamble, W. (1994). Attachment and emotion regulation during mother-teen problem-solving: A control theory analysis. *Child Development, 64*, 231–245.

Kortlander, E., Kendall, P.C., & Panichelli-Mindel, S.M. (1997). Maternal expectations and attributions about coping in anxious children. *Journal of Anxiety Disorders, 11*, 297–315.

LaFreniere, P.J. & Capuano, F. (1997). Preventive intervention as means of clarifying direction of effects in socialization: Anxious-withdrawn pre-schoolers case. *Development and Psychopathology, 9*, 551–564.

Last, C.G. (1991). Somatic complaints in anxiety disordered children. *Journal of Anxiety Disorders, 5*, 125–138.

Last, C.G. & Perrin, S. (1993). Anxiety disorders in African-American and white children. *Journal of Abnormal Child Psychology, 21*, 153–164.

Last, C.G., Perrin, S., Hersen, M., & Kazdin, A.E. (1992). DSM-III-R anxiety disorders in children: Sociodemographic and clinical characteristics. *Journal* of the American Academy of Child and Adolescent Psychiatry, 31, 1070–1076

Last, C.G., Perrin, S., Hersen, M., & Kazdin, A.E. (1996). A prospective study of childhood anxiety disorders. Journal of the American Academy of Child and Adolescent Psychiatry, 35, 1502–1510.

Last, C.G., Strauss, C.C., & Francis, G. (1987). Comorbidity among childhood anxiety disorders. Journal of Nervous and Mental Disease, 175, 726–730

Lerner, J., Safren, S.A., Henin, A., Warman, M., Heimberg, R.G., & Kendall, P.C. (1999). Differentiating anxious and depressive self-statements in youth: Factor structure of the Negative Affect Self-Statement Questionnaire among youth referred to an anxiety disorders clinic. Journal of Clinical Child Psychology, 28, 82–93.

Lewinsohn, P.M., Gotlib, I.H., Lewinsohn, M., Seeley, J.R., & Allen, N.B. (1998). Gender differences in anxiety disorders and anxiety symptoms in adolescents. Journal of Abnormal Psychology, 107, 10–117.

Lewinsohn, P.M., Hops, H., Roberts, R.E., Seeley, J.R., & Andrews, J.A. (1993). Adolescent psychopathology: I. Prevalence and incidence of depression and other DSM-III-R disorders in high school students. Journal of Abnormal Psychology, 102, 133–144.

Lieberman, A.F., Weston, D.R., & Pawl, J.H. (1991). Preventive intervention and outcome with anxiously attached dyads. Child Development, 62, 199–209.

Manassis, K., Bradley, S., Goldberg, S., Hood, J., & Swinson, R.P. (1994). Attachment in mothers with anxiety disorders and their children. Journal of the American Academy of Child and Adolescent Psychiatry, 33, 1106–1113.

Manassis, K. & Hood, J. (1998). Individual and familial predictors of impairment in childhood anxiety disorders. Journal of the American Academy of Child and Adolescent Psychiatry, 37, 428–434.

March, J.S. & Leonard, H.L. (1996). Obsessive-compulsive disorder in children and adolescents: A review of the past 10 years. Journal of the American Academy of Child and Adolescent Psychiatry, 35, 1265–1273.

March, J.S., Parker, J.D.A., Sullivan, K., Stallings, P., & Conners, C.K. (1997). The Multidimensional Anxiety Scale for Children (MASC): Factor structure, reliability, and validity. Journal of the American Academy of Child & Adolescent Psychiatry, 36, 554–565.

McGee, R., Feehan, M. Williams, S., Partridge, F., Silva, P.A., & Kelly, J. (1990). DSM-III disorders in a large sample of adolescents. Journal of the American Academy of Child and Adolescent Psychiatry, 29, 611–619.

Muris, P., Meesters, C., Merckelbach, H., Sermon, A., & Zwakhalen, S. (1998). Worry in normal children. Journal of the American Academy of Child and Adolescent Psychiatry, 37, 703–710.

Muris, P., Merckelbach, H., & Collaris, R. (1997). Common childhood fears and their origins. *Behaviour Research and Therapy, 35*, 929–937.

Nachmias, M., Gunnar, M., Mangelsdorf, S., Parritz, R.H., & Buss, K. (1996). Behavioral inhibition and stress reactivity: The moderating role of attachment security. *Child Development, 67*, 508–522.

Ollendick, T.H. & King, N.J. (1998). Empirically supported treatments for children with phobic and anxiety disorders: Current status. *Journal of Clinical Child Psychology, 27*, 156–167.

Ollendick, T.H., Yang, B., King, N.J., Dong, Q., & Akande, A. (1996). Fears in American, Australian, Chinese, and Nigerian children and adolescents: A cross-cultural study. *Journal of Child Psychology and Psychiatry, 37*, 213–220.

Oppenheim, D., Nir, A., Warren, S., & Emde, R.N. (1997). Emotion regulation in mother-child narrative co-construction: Associations with children's narratives and adaptation. *Developmental Psychology, 33*, 284–294.

Park, S.Y., Belsky, J., Putnam, S., & Crnic, K. (1997). Infant emotionality, parenting, and 3-year inhibition: Exploring stability and lawful discontinuity in a male sample. *Developmental Psychology, 33*, 218–227.

Pelham, W.E., Wheeler, T., & Chronis, A. (1998). Empirically supported psychosocial treatments for attention deficit hyperactivity disorder. *Journal of Clinical Child Psychology, 27*, 190–205.

Rabian, B., Peterson, R.A., Richters, J., & Jensen, P.S. (1993). Anxiety sensitivity among anxious children. *Journal of Clinical Child Psychology, 22*, 441–446.

Rapee, R.M. (1991). Generalized anxiety disorder: A review of the clinical features and theoretical concepts. *Clinical Psychology Review, 11*, 419–440.

Reiss, S. & McNally, R.J. (1985). The expectancy model of fear. In S. Reiss & R.R. Bootzin (Eds.), *Theoretical issues in behavior therapy* (pp. 107–121). New York: Academic Press.

Reynolds, C.R. & Richmond, B.O. (1985). *Revised children's manifest anxiety scale (RCMAS): Manual.* Los Angeles: Western Psychological Services.

Ronan, K.R., Kendall, P.C., & Rowe, M. (1994). Negative affectivity in children: Development and validation of a self-statement questionnaire. *Cognitive Therapy and Research, 18*, 509–528.

Rosenbaum, J.F., Biederman, J., Bolduc, E.A., Hirshfeld, D.R., Faraone, S.V., & Kagan, J. (1992). Comorbidity of parental anxiety disorders as risk for childhood-onset anxiety in inhibited children. *American Journal of Psychiatry, 149*, 475–481.

Rowe, D.C., Stever, C., Gard, J.M.C., Cleveland, H.H., Sander, M.L., Abramowitz, A., Kozol, S.T., Mohr, J.H., Sherman, S.L., & Waldman, I.D. (1998). The relation of the dopamine transporter gene (DAT1) to symptoms of internalizing disorders in children. *Behavior Genetics. 28*, 215–225.

Rubin, K.H., Both, L., Zahn-Waxler, C., Cummings, E.M., & Wilkinson, M. (1991). Dyadic play behaviors of children of well and depressed mothers. *Development and Psychopathology, 3*, 243–251.

Russo, M.F. & Beidel, D.C. (1994). Comorbidity of childhood anxiety and externalizing disorders: Prevalence, associated characteristics, and validation issues. *Clinical Psychology Review, 14*, 199–211.

Silverman, W.K. (1998, October). *Diagnosis and classification of anxiety disorders.* Paper presented at the Conference on Treating Anxiety Disorders in Youth, Alexandria, VA.

Silverman, W.K. (2000). *Reliability data for the anxiety disorders interview schedule for children for DSM-IV.* Personal communication.

Silverman, W.K. & Albano, A.M. (1996). *Anxiety disorders interview schedule for DSM-IV: Child version.* San Antonio, TX: Psychological Corporation.

Silverman, W.K. & Eisen, A.R. (1992). Age difference in the reliability of parent and child reports of child anxious symptomatology using a structured interview. *Journal of the American Academy of Child and Adolescent Psychiatry, 31*, 117–124.

Silverman, W.K. & Ginsburg, G.S. (1998). Anxiety disorders. In T.H. Ollendick & M. Hersen (Eds.), *Handbook of child psychopathology (3rd Ed.)* (pp. 239–268). New York: Plenum Press.

Silverman, W.K. & Kurtines, W.M. (1996). *Anxiety and phobic disorders: A pragmatic approach.* New York: Plenum Press.

Silverman, W.K., Kurtines, W.M., Ginsburg, G.S., Weems, C.F., White-Lumpkin, P., & Hicks-Carmichael, D. (1999). Treating anxiety disorders in children with group cognitive-behavior therapy: A randomized clinical trial. *Journal of Consulting and Clinical Psychology, 67*, 995–1003.

Silverman, W.K. & Nelles, W.B. (1988). The anxiety disorders interview schedule for children. *Journal of the American Academy of Child and Adolescent Psychiatry, 27*, 772–778.

Silverman, W.K. & Rabian, B. (1995). Test-retest reliability of the DSM-III-R childhood anxiety disorders symptoms using the Anxiety Disorders Interview Schedule for Children. *Journal of Anxiety Disorders, 9*, 139–150.

Silverman, W.K. & Weems, C.F. (1999). Anxiety sensitivity in children. In S. Taylor (Ed.), *Anxiety sensitivity: Theory, research, and treatment of the fear of anxiety* (pp. 239–268). Hillsdale, NJ: Lawrence Erlbaum

Southam-Gerow, M.A., Flannery-Schroeder, E.C., & Kendall, P.C. (2000). *Psychometric evaluation of the parent-report STAIC.* Manuscript submitted for publication.

Southam-Gerow, M.A. & Kendall, P.C. (1997). Parent-focused and cognitive-behavioral treatments of antisocial youth. In D. Stoff, J. Breiling & J.D. Maser (Eds.), *Handbook of antisocial behavior* (pp. 384–394). New York: John Wiley & Sons.

Southam-Gerow, M.A. & Kendall, P.C. (2000). A preliminary study of the emotion understanding of youth referred for treatment of anxiety disorders. *Journal of Clinical Child Psychology, 29,* 319–327.

Southam-Gerow, M.A., Kendall, P.C., & Weersing, V.R. (in press). Examining outcome variability: Correlates of treatment response in a child and adolescent anxiety clinic. *Journal of Clinical Child Psychology.*

Spielberger, C. (1973). *Manual for the State-trait Anxiety Inventory for Children.* Palo Alto, CA: Consulting Psychologists Press.

Stark, K.D., Humphrey, L.L., Laurent, J., Livingston, R., & Christopher, J. (1993). Cognitive, behavioral, and family factors in the differentiation of depressive and anxiety disorders during childhood. *Journal of Consulting and Clinical Psychology, 61,* 878–886.

Steinberg, L. & Avenevoli, S. (2000). The role of context in the development of psychopathology: A conceptual framework and some speculative propositions. *Child Development, 71,* 66–74.

Strauss, C. (1987). *Modification of trait portion of State-Trait Anxiety Inventory for Children-parent form.* Available from author. University of Florida, Gainesville, FL.

Strauss, C.D., Lease, C.A., Last, C.G., & Francis, G. (1988). Overanxious disorder: An examination of developmental differences. *Journal of Abnormal Child Psychology, 16,* 433–443.

Szapocznik, J. & Kurtines, W. (1993). Family psychology and cultural diversity: Opportunities for theory, research and application. *American Psychologist, 48,* 400–407.

Task Force on Promotion and Dissemination of Psychological Procedures. (1995). Training in and dissemination of empirically-validated psychological treatments. *The Clinical Psychologist, 48,* 3–23.

Topolski, T.D., Hewitt, J.K., Eaves, L.J., Silberg, J.L, Meyer, J.M., Rutter, M., Pickles, A., & Simonoff, E. (1997). Genetic and environmental influences on child reports of manifest anxiety and symptoms of separation anxiety and overanxious disorders: A community-based twin study. *Behavior Genetics, 27,* 15–28

Tracey, S.A., Chorpita, B.F., Douban, J., & Barlow, D.H. (1997). Empirical evaluation of DSM-IV generalized anxiety disorder criteria in children and adolescents. *Journal of Clinical Child Psychology, 26,* 404–414.

Treadwell, K.R.H., Flannery-Schroeder, E.C., & Kendall, P.C. (1995). Ethnicity and gender in relation to adaptive functioning, diagnostic status, and treatment outcome in children from an anxiety clinic. *Journal of Anxiety Disorders, 9,* 373–384.

Vasey, M.W. (1993). Development and cognition in childhood anxiety: The example of worry. In T.H. Ollendick & R. Prinz (Eds.), *Advances in clinical child psychology* (Vol. 15, pp. 1–39). New York: Plenum Press.

Vasey, M.W., Crnic, K.A., & Carter, W.G. (1994). Worry in childhood: A developmental perspective. *Cognitive Therapy and Research, 18,* 529–549.

Vasey, M.W., Daleiden, E.L., Williams, L.L., & Brown, L.M. (1995). Biased attention in childhood anxiety disorders: A preliminary study. *Journal of Abnormal Child Psychology, 23,* 267–279.

Velez, C.N., Johnson, J., & Cohen, P. (1989). A longitudinal analysis of selected risk factors for childhood psychopathology. *Journal of the American Academy of Child and Adolescent Psychiatry, 28,* 861–864.

Wade, W.A., Treat, T.A., & Stuart, G.L. (1998). Transporting an empirically supported treatment for panic disorder to a service clinic setting: A benchmarking strategy. *Journal of Consulting and Clinical Psychology, 66,* 231–239

Warren, S.L., Huston, L., Egeland, B., & Sroufe, L.A. (1997). Child and adolescent anxiety disorders and early attachment. *Journal of the American Academy of Child and Adolescent Psychiatry, 36,* 637–644.

Watson, D. & Clark, L.A. (1984). Negative affectivity: The disposition to experience negative emotional states. *Psychological Bulletin, 96,* 465–490.

Weisz, J.R., Weiss, B., & Donenberg, G.R. (1992). The lab versus the clinic: Effects of child and adolescent psychotherapy. *American Psychologist, 47,* 1578–1585.

Weisz, J.R. & Southam-Gerow, M.A. (2000). Patterns of comorbidity in a community clinic sample. Manuscript in preparation.

Werry, J.S. (1991). Overanxious disorder: A review of its taxonomic properties. *Journal of the American Academy of Child and Adolescent Psychiatry, 30,* 533–544.

Yonkers, K.A. & Gurguis, G. (1995). Gender differences in the prevalence and expression of anxiety disorders. In M.V. Seeman (Ed.), *Gender and psychopathology* (pp. 113–130). Washington, DC: American Psychiatric Press.

Zoccolillo, M. & Rogers, K. (1991). Characteristics and outcome of hospitalized adolescent girls with conduct disorder. *Journal of the American Academy of Child and Adolescent Psychiatry, 30,* 973–981.

9 OBSESSIVE-COMPULSIVE DISORDER

Per Hove Thomsen

Obsessive-compulsive disorder (OCD) is defined by the presence of obsessions and/or compulsions, a definition which applies to children and adolescents, as well as adults. According to both ICD-10 (WHO, 1992) and DSM-IV (American Psychiatric Association; APA, 1994), OCD is defined by the presence of either obsessions and/or compulsions with the following clinical description of each: *Obsessions* are recurrent, persistent ideas, thoughts, images, or impulses, which are egodystonic and regarded as being senseless or repugnant. Attempts are made to ignore or suppress them. *Compulsions* are repetitive and seemingly purposeful for actions which are performed according to certain rules, or in a stereotyped fashion. The action is not an end in itself, but is designed to produce, or prevent some further event or situation. The activities are not realistically connected to the action, it is designed to produce or prevent, or it may be clearly excessive. The act is performed with a sense of subjective compulsion, coupled with a desire to resist the compulsion (at least, initially). A compulsion can be in the form of visible manifestation of stereotyped repetitive behaviour, although mental rituals are just as common. Mental rituals describe the phenomenon of performing compulsions within the child's mind, for example counting, saying specific phrases or words, calculating etc. These mental rituals are frequently just as disabling to the child as are overt compulsions. In diagnosing, one must include severity aspects. The obsessions or compulsions must be a significant source of distress to the individual, or interfere with social, or role functioning. DSM-IV include a new subcategory: *OCD with poor insight.* In DSM-IV field studies (Foa and Kozak, 1995) it was found that approximately 5% of adult OCD patients had, what they defined as constant poor insight. That is, the obsessions or compulsions were not clearly egodystonic. Furthermore, the patients were unable to rationalize and detach themselves from the symptoms, and therefore, were unable to recognise that their behaviour was both bizarre and illogical. Foa and Kozak (1995) also found that at some stage of their illness, approximately 25% of patients were not rational enough to describe their obsessions or compulsions as being egodystonic. The introduction of this sub-category leads to increased difficulty in distinguishing clearly between overvalued ideas, discrete psychotic symptoms and obsessions. In many children, this sub-category with poor insight might well apply. Frequently, children have poorer insight with regard to their symptoms (in particular, younger children) and are frequently resistant to their symptoms. Children and adolescents are, also, less secretive with regard to their symptoms than adult patients. ICD-10 does not include "obsessions with poor insight" as a diagnostic criterion. However, different subtypes are used: one subtype is used primarily with compulsions, one with obsessions, and one with both obsessions and compulsions. The majority of children and adoles-cents have both compulsions and obsessions, although there is a tendency that some patients show compulsions without obsessions (particularly in the case of children).

The clinical picture is most similar with regard to age. With the exceptions mentioned above, the content of obsessive-compulsive symptoms are remarkably similar. However, smaller children are more prone to include family-members in their obsessions and compulsions than adult patients.

Epidemiology

Obsessive-compulsive disorder in childhood and adolescence was pre-viously considered rare. It is still considered to be an underdiagnosed condition. Few studies have analysed the prevalence of OCD in a general child population. However, in these studies it is possible that not all cases have been recorded, since many patients with OCD tend to conceal their symptoms. Henderson and Pollard (1988) found that a majority of adult OCD patients were reluctant to seek professional treatment, only 28% of OCD individuals had sought help. They con-cluded, therefore, that estimates of OCD prevalence, based upon clini-cal populations, underestimate the prevalence of the disorder in the general population. Recent studies indicate that OCD is far more fre-quent in the general population, than previously believed. From five different American states Karno et al. (1988) found that in a general adult population, the lifetime prevalence was from 1.9% to 3.3%, approximately 25 to 60 times higher than expected, on the basis of epidemiological studies of psychiatric populations. In a Canadian pop-ulation Bland et al. (1988) found that 3% fulfilled OCD criteria (life-time prevalence). In an epidemiological study of 5.000 high-school students, Flament et al. (1988) found that 0.35% fulfilled OCD criteria, as defined by DSM-III (APA, 1980). They calculated a lifetime prevalence of 1%.

According to epidemiological studies performed in adolescent populations in New Zealand (Douglas *et al.*, 1995) and the United States (Valleni-Basile *et al.*, 1993) the current prevalence of OCD was 3–4%. Furthermore, the study performed by Douglas and colleagues (1995) was a longitudinal study, showing that having depression at the age of 14 increased the risk of fulfilling the OCD criteria at the age of 18. Esser *et al.* (1990) found the frequency of compulsions in 8 year old German children, to be 4.6% (moderate severity) and 2.8% (severe symptomatology). Later, the prevalence of compulsive checking within the same population (13 years old) was 3.4%, all of moderate severity. 2.3% reported a compulsion regarding cleanliness, and 4.0% experienced obsessive thoughts. However, Esser *et al.* (1990) did not use clear OCD criteria, neither did they use the DSM-III criteria, used by Flament *et al.* (1988). In a study by Esser *et al.* (1990), no distinction between OCD, obsessive-compulsive behaviour and other psychiatric disorders with obsessive-compulsive features was made. Their study merely shows that compulsions, to a "certain degree" are not uncommon in pupils. The study by Esser *et al.* (1990) is apparently one of the few recent European studies in which obsessive-compulsive symptoms have been rated amongst non-referred children. In a study using the Leyton Obsessional Inventory-Child Version (Berg *et al.*, 1986) in a population of non-referred Danish children and adolescents, it was found that obsessional habits/behaviour such as mental repetition of thoughts and words and difficulty in making decisions were the most common (Thomsen, 1993). These results are similar to that of the United States (Berg *et al.*, 1988). Approximately 4% of Danish children had a total interference-score in excess of 25, reflecting possible subclinical or clinical OCD. However, the screening was not followed by clinical interviews, thus, the prevalence of OCD was not estimated.

Phenomenology

The most common obsessive-compulsive symptoms seen in OCD children are anxiety regarding dirt and contamination and extreme washing rituals. These symptoms are seen in approximately 50% of OCD patients. Patients with such symptoms feel compelled to wash their hands or to shower incessantly, possibly up to 100 times a day. A fear of dirt and contamination may result in the patient becoming increasingly isolated due to avoidant behaviour in an attempt to avoid stimuli which may trigger the rituals. Another most frequent obsessive-compulsive symptom, seen in approximately 50% of the children is checking. Children with checking symptoms must ensure that the door is locked again and again, that the oven is turned-off, or they may even return to places they have visited to ensure that they have not driven in to anyone on their bicycle and, perhaps, hurt someone. These checking symptoms are frequently related to the obsessions that something terrible may happen. Many OCD children report that they are victims of repetitive behaviour, that is, they have to repeat daily routines again and again. Some children suffer from the obsession that they may harm themselves, or even others. One particular phenomenon, which has previously been classified as an obsession, although it is in fact a compulsion, is mental rituals of varying types. Children with these symptoms report that they feel impelled to undertake complicated calculations, count to a specific number, or to say certain words or sentences to themselves. Some compulsions are quite obvious whereas others are more discrete. Some OCD children may function poorly at school due to indecisiveness, or obsessive shyness. They experience difficulties in finishing their school work, and even minor tasks appear difficult for them. In these cases, the teachers may be the first to identify obsessions or compulsions in the child.

Rapoport *et al.* (1981) concluded, that the most striking feature of the symptoms seen in OCD children is the severity of the psychopathology in the absence of formal thought disorder. The child's mental state is relatively intact and he/she appears to be capable of relating to the illness. The child is able to discuss the symptoms sensibly, which is in contrast to the overall incapacitating nature of the symptoms.

Many OCD children suffer from an almost pathological doubting, varying from a mild form to an incapacitating form of extreme severity in which the child is uncertain as to his/her own perceptions. In these cases parents are frequently faced with the difficulty of answering repeated questions relating to almost all the child's activities (Rapoport *et al.*, 1981). Obsessional slowness, which is characterised by prolongation of routine activities, or pervasive and obvious difficulty initiating and completing them, appears to be more rare in children than in adult obsessive-compulsive patients. However, they have also been described in children (Rapoport *et al.*, 1981; Swedo *et al.*, 1989; Toro *et al.*, 1992; Thomsen, 1994a). Indecisiveness is frequently found in OCD children and adolescents (Swedo *et al.*, 1989; Thomsen, 1994a) and ranges from difficulty in making minor decisions, to the continual weighing-up of pros and cons regarding non-essentials. Thus, the child is unable to make any form of decision. As a result of their obsessions (usually obsessions relating to dirt and contamination, or the fear of harming others), many OCD children develop avoidant behaviour. Normally, this isolates them from other children and prevents them from participating in leisure activities.

There appears to be no significant inter-cultural differences in phenomenology, even between industrialised countries such as the USA, Denmark, Spain, and Japan, and developing countries such as India, China, and Turkey (Honjo *et al.*, 1989; Khanna and Srinath, 1988; Kerimoglu and Yalin, 1991; Swedo *et al.*, 1989; Thomsen, 1991). Symptoms such as excessive washing, obsessions of harming others or oneself, and checking behaviour, are the most common. Regardless of the location it is possible, however, that these similarities in various parts of the world are the result of referral-bias being based on clinical populations of referred children. It may be reasonable, particularly in countries where psychiatric aid is restricted, to imagine that only parents assimilated to a western life-style and to western psychiatric views, would refer their child for OCD treatment. The fact that phenomenology and prevalence are shown to be the same throughout the world, with extremely different social norms and cultural patterns, strongly supports the theory that OCD is a biological illness, independent of environ-mental influence.

The spectrum of symptoms is similar to those seen in adult OCD patients (Akthar *et al.*, 1978; Cooper and Kelleher, 1973; Karno *et al.*, 1988; Khanna and Srinath, 1988; Honjo *et al.*, 1989; Lo, 1967; Rasmussen and Tsuang, 1984; Zeitlin, 1986). There are, naturally, exceptions to this rule: that pervasive slowness is more common in adult patients, and that the number of patients with compulsions and no obsessions is found to be higher amongst children. More adult patients would appear to be "pure obsessionals" (i.e., having no compulsions) (Khanna and Srinath, 1988). Findings by Rettew *et al.* (1992) and Thomsen (1994b) show that the phenomenology of each individual is liable to change with time, i.e., even if symptoms persist, the form and content of obsessions and compulsions differ.

Risk and Protective Factors

Throughout the century the suggested causes of obsessive-compulsive disorder have varied. Already, Freud described OCD as a condition with

Table 9.1 Most common obsessive-compulsive symptoms in children and adolescents with OCD

Obsessions regarding	Seen in approximate
Dirt and infection	40%
Fear that something terrible will happen	20%
Disease	20%
Death	20%
Symmetry	15%
Sex	10%
Religious thoughts	10%
Anxiety of harming oneself or others	8%

Compulsions regarding	Seen in approximate
Washing rituals	50%
Checking	40%
Compulsive behaviour	40%
Fixing/arranging	30%
Other rituals	25%
Counting	20%

genetic impact. The biological causes and the view of OCD as a neuropsychiatric disorder have increased over the past few decades.

FAMILY GENETICS

Riddle and colleagues (1990) found that actually 19% of 21 OCD children had one OCD parent and as many as 52% had parents with obsessive-compulsive symptoms, without meeting OCD criteria, when parents were interviewed with standard clinical psychiatric assessments. This finding was supported by Thomsen (1994a). Swedo et al. (1989) found that 24% of referred OCD children had a first degree relative with OCD; Lenane et al. (1990) found that 9% of mothers and 25% of fathers of OCD children had suffered from OCD themselves. 2% of mothers and 20% of fathers suffered from OCPD (obsessive-compulsive personality disorder), and 13% of both mothers and fathers exhibited subclinical, obsessive-compulsive behaviour. Adams (1973) found that 71% of his patients had a positive family history of obsessions, or compulsions. He did not, however, distinguish clearly between OCD, obsessive-compulsive behaviour, and obsessive personality. Black et al. (1989) found that the morbidity risk for anxiety disorder was increased amongst relatives of obsessional subjects, compared with the relatives of psychiatrically normal controls, whilst the risk of OCD was not. However, when OCD was more "broadly defined" (including relatives with obsessions and compulsions not meeting criteria for OCD) the risk was increased amongst parents of obsessional subjects compared with the controls.

Pauls *et al.* (1986) have performed the largest family study of OCD to date. One hundred cases with OCD and their 633 relatives were identified and compared with 33 controls and their 110 control relatives. All the probands were interviewed and screened for obsessive-compulsive symptoms as well as tics and symptoms of Tourette's syndrome. Amongst the relatives of OCD patients it was found that as many as 10.1% fulfilled OCD criteria. A further 7–8% suffered from subclinical obsessive-compulsive symptoms, and as many as 4–5% had either Tourette's syndrome, or chronic multiple tics. In the group of relatives to control persons, only 1.9% had OCD (as would be expected from the above-mentioned population studies), a further 2% had obsessive-compulsive symptoms on a subclinical level and only 1% had either Tourette's syndrome or multiple tics. The authors concluded that the presence of Tourette's syndrome or tics was related to OCD onset at an early age.

A direct method of identifying a gnomic component to OCD is by undertaking a study of twins (Insel, 1992). There are no twin studies specifically designed for OCD. However, OCD has been described in studies of anxiety disorders in general (Torgersen, 1983). Twin-studies do not appear to support the genetic component for OCD. However, there is a tendency toward a higher concordance rate for obsessional-type features, and not for OCD per se (Carey and Gottesman, 1981; Insel, 1992). It is possible that what is inherited is a broader phenotype, which may even include a number of features similar to that of compulsive behaviour. Pauls *et al.* (1993) found that 52% of OCD children have a positive family history of OCD amongst first-degree relatives, and that the risk to relatives is related to the age of OCD onset amongst the probands: the earlier the onset of OCD in probands, the higher the risk of OCD or Tourette's syndrome in relatives.

FAMILY PATTERNS

It has been said that families with OCD children, frequently derive from the higher social-classes, as opposed to the general population, and particularly higher than other child psychiatric patients. In studies of children and adolescents (Adams, 1973; Apter *et al.*, 1984; Honjo *et al.*,

1989; Kerimoglu and Yalin, 1991; Rapoport, 1986; Rasmussen and Tsuang, 1984; Riddle *et al.*, 1990; Swedo *et al.*, 1989) the findings normally indicate that OCD patients are derived from white, middle- or upper-class, intact families. However, the findings of these studies may be subject to referral bias in that higher SES (i.e., high socio-economic status) parents are more effective in seeking evaluation and specialised treatment for their children, by way of specialist clinics, or research settings. Thomsen (1994c) analysed the social background of OCD children and psychiatric control patients, matched for age and sex. They were referred to a child psychiatric hospital, which provided virtually all psychiatric care for the local population. All families were from the local county, thus no referral-bias existed within the study. The author found that OCD children came from higher SES families than the majority of other child psychiatric patients, which called for an alternative explanation. For instance, mild OCD, or OCD features, which have been reported as being relatively common in parents of OCD children, may be socially and/or economically adaptive.

Certain myths have prevailed regarding families with OCD children. The families are frequently known to show a cultural behaviour emphasising cleanliness and perfection (Hoover and Insel, 1984). Adams (1973) has described them as being families with anal characters. It would appear that no systematic family based study has yet been conducted on larger groups of patients. Therefore, it has not been possible to establish whether these more or less causistic reports regarding the families are valid. It is unlikely that OCD is caused by the family structure itself. Family patterns may be regarded as a possible precipitating factor, for developing obsessive-compulsive symptoms in predisposed children. Family functioning was described in 20 Danish OCD children (Thomsen, 1994a), assessing adaptability and cohesion of the family (Olson, 1986). No specific type of OCD family pattern could be described, the only positive finding was that fathers of OCD children appeared to have more obsessional traits than fathers of other child psychiatric patients. However, it would appear that further information regarding OCD families is required in order to make strategies for therapies and consulting reports.

NEUROLOGICAL SOFT-SIGNS AND NEUROPSYCHOLOGICAL FINDINGS

Soft-signs are non-localized deviant performances in a motor, or sensory test, without other signs, or presence of focal neurological disorder. Soft-signs in child psychiatric patients have been well described, and the implications of soft-signs have been thoroughly analysed in general population of pre-school and school-children, and adolescent psychiatric patients.

The majority of studies conducted on OCD children have demonstrated an overweight of soft-signs, compared with normal control-groups (Adams, 1973; Hollander *et al.*, 1990; Insel *et al.*, 1983; Rapoport, 1986). Some of these studies have, however, been conducted without any psychiatric control groups. Thomsen and Jensen (1991) found neurological soft-signs in 18.6% of 61 OCD-children and adolescents compared with 14.4% in a control group, consisting of non-psychotic and non-retarded children and adolescents with psychiatric disorders other than OCD, referred to the same hospital. No significant differences were found between OCD-patients and the remaining child psychiatric population. Denckla (1989) found that 44 of 54 childhood OCD patients aged 6 to 22 years showed neurological abnormalities. Of these 44 patients, 18 had choreiform movements, 13 had non-specific neuro-developmental signs only, 8 had left hemisyndrome, and 5 had miscellaneous abnormalities.

The general conclusions drawn from conducted neuropsychological studies (mainly from adult OCD patients), are that a sub-group of OCD-patients exhibited impairment in several areas of cognitive functioning, whilst a further sub-group appeared to exhibit visuospatial/visuoperceptual deficits. It is possible that the first sub-group represented more globally deficient patients, with a general organic cause of OCD (Behar *et al.*, 1984; Boone *et al.*, 1991; Insel *et al.*, 1983; Reed, 1977).

In studies of children, a pattern of association between OCD and selected neurological disorders has been long recognized (Flament, 1993). A more specific pattern has emerged, implicating dysfunction of the basal ganglia an/or neuronal pathways, linking basal ganglia, the thalamus, and frontal cortex. Rapoport (1991) has proposed an ethological model for OCD and related disorders. The model suggests that the frontal cortex-basal ganglia-thalamic circuit may be the neural loci for phylogenetically old self-protective behaviour patterns, such as grooming and checking. The hypothesis of disturbances in the feedback loops, between nucleus caudatus, thalamus and the orbital frontal cortex is supported by recent studies made by Schwartz *et al.* (1996) and Baxter *et al.* (1992), who show a normalization of affected areas, following both behavioural therapy and medication. Compared with normal controls, on a battery of neuropsychological testing, OCD children do not differ on measures of memory and attention, reaction time, or decision time (Flament, 1993). However, there are specific deficits regarding tasks involving spatial perception and orientation, as well as the ability to learn by trial and error (an unknown pathway between two points). Similar patterns of spatial perceptual deficits have been reported in adult OCD patients (Flor-Henry *et al.*, 1979; Head *et al.*, 1989).

Most studies indicate neuropsychological deficits in childhood OCD, although the findings are still inconclusive and fail to demonstrate whether test results are primary or secondary to obsessive-compulsive symptoms. As yet, little is known as to what is specific for childhood OCD, compared with other child psychiatric disorders. The incidence of neurological and neuropsychological deficits in a child psychiatric population as a whole, is known to be higher than in a normal population. In studies regarding such deficits, control groups consisting of other child and adolescent psychiatric patients should be used.

As a support to the described etiological model for OCD, obsessive-compulsive symptoms have been described in a high proportion of children infected with betahaemolytic streptococ, resulting in Südenham's Chorea. In Südenham's Chorea antibodies to nucleus caudatus located in the basal ganglia have been demonstrated, further supporting the theory that the nucleus caudatus is involved in the pathogenesis of OCD.

NEUROTRANSMITTER STUDIES

In 1977, Yaryura-Tobias and Bhagavan introduced the hypothesis of the involvement of serotonin in OCD, showing that the OCD patients have lower levels of serotonin in the synapses than healthy persons. In 1980, Thorén *et al.* (1980) identified a group of OCD patients with high CSF 5-HIAA, who showed a positive response to chlomipramine treatment and a decrease in this metabolite, correlated with clinical improvement.

According to Insel (1992), at least two lines of evidence point to a neurochemical basis for, or a neurochemical abnormality in OCD. Pharmacological treatment studies, particularly those with serotonin reuptake inhibitors, and pathophysiological studies examining abnormalities of serotonin physiology in OCD patients, in the untreated state indicate that serotonin is involved. Only selective serotonin reuptake inhibitors are effective anti-obsessional compounds (Insel, 1992). Serotonin, therefore, appears to assist in the pharmacological relief of OCD, although whether it is involved in the pathophysiology of OCD is still unclear. Approaches to the latter have been made, indicating the extreme probability that serotonin is involved in this system (Zohar *et al.*, 1990).

Comorbidity

NORMAL DEVELOPMENT

Certain obsessions and compulsions are present in the normal development of most children. Most children go through phases in which they carry out certain rituals. For instance, most children are familiar with the expression: "step on a crack, break your mother's back" and at one time or another, have avoided stepping on a crack in the pavement. Children frequently, have certain bedtime rituals, they may also have lucky numbers. Normal rituals, however, normally vanish by the age of 8, whereas, childhood OCD normally sets in after the age of 7. It is only when rituals interfere with day-to-day life, or cause distress to the child, that an OCD diagnosis should be considered.

COMORBIDITY OF OCD WITH OTHER PSYCHIATRIC DISORDERS

OCD is frequently found in connection with depression, a finding which applies to children and adolescents, as well as adults. It is normally difficult to ascertain which symptoms (i.e., the depressive or obsessive-compulsive) occurred first. The majority of studies, find high comorbidity ranging from about 20% to more than 50% of OCD patients, who also suffer from depression at some stage of the illness (Rasmussen and Tsuang, 1984; Thomsen, 1994b). Follow-up studies indicate that depression occurs frequently in the course of OCD (Thomsen, 1994b).

Table 9.2 Rituals and superstitions in "normal" children

Rituals	Age-group
Bed rituals	Small children
Avoiding stepping on cracks	Younger children
Control/checking	Younger and older children (mild forms)
Counting/lucky numbers	Older children
Touching	Older children (when playing) – not common
Washing/showering	Pre-school children (mild), seldom in teenagers (unless OCD)
Fear of dirt and contamination	Younger children and older children (only in mild forms)

Eating disorders are frequently found in OCD females (Crisp *et al.*, 1987). Clear-cut anorexia nervosa can also co-occur with OCD. At least 3 points of evidence suggest the possible relationship between anorexia nervosa and OCD: Firstly, studies have illustrated that anorectic patients display high trait-scores in questionnaires assessing obsessive-compulsive features (these scores are comparable to that of OCD patients). Secondly, increased incidence of former anorexia nervosa in OCD patients is suggested, and during the course of the disorder some female OCD patients develop anorexia nervosa (Kaye *et al.*, 1992; Thomsen, 1994b). Thirdly, serotonin disturbance may, partially, contribute to the pathogenesis of both OCD and anorexia nervosa. Serotonin specific medications may also have some efficacy in anorexia nervosa (Crisp *et al.*, 1987). A prerequisite of applying an OCD diagnosis to an anorectic patient is that the patient must show "typical" compulsions (e.g., washing, checking, counting) and not only symptoms related to a food/eating disorder, or disturbed body image.

Anxiety disorders during adolescence are quite common, mainly in the form of generalized anxiety, panic disorder or specific phobia. In younger children, separation anxiety may be present, although generally, children in this age group are normally less distressed by other anxiety disorders than adolescent and adult patients. In the long term follow-up studies of OCD in children and adolescents, it was found that approximately 50% of the patients fulfilled the criteria for an anxiety disorder at some stage during the course of OCD (most commonly panic disorder (Kaye *et al.*, 1992; Thomsen, 1994b).

OCD is frequently found in children with Gilles de la Tourette's syndrome (TS). The opposite is less common, as TS itself is less common than OCD (Pauls *et al.*, 1986). Some studies have illustrated that the actual content of obsessive-compulsive symptoms in TS children vary somewhat from the most typical obsessive-compulsive symptoms seen in OCD patients not suffering from TS. Symptoms such as touching, counting, blinking and obsessions concerning lines and symmetry are more common in TS children. Clinically, it can be extremely difficult, to draw the line between a complex and elaborated motor tic (as seen in TS), and a compulsion (as seen in OCD).

Schizophrenia and OCD have been described as being comorbidly present in adult patients. In children, naturally, this comorbidity is seen to a much lesser degree; onset of schizophrenia normally occurs in the late teens, or early twenties. It is possible that obsessive-compulsive symptoms are overlooked in many adolescent cases, who receive a schizophrenia diagnosis. The essential difference between severe OCD and schizophrenia is that ego-functioning is only slightly impaired, or completely undamaged in OCD. Although bizarre obsessions and compulsions may be present, OCD patients have the rationality to detach themselves from the symptoms, and despite the severity of the psychopathology of OCD, formal thought disorders are non-existent.

The stereotyped and repetitive behaviour seen in autistic syndrome is not a part of an OCD. Autistic individuals normally suffer from a lack of conscience of mental state, and are thus unable to characterize whether certain acts are egodystonic, or to relate to the distress, resistance, or the futility of the symptoms. However, some cases of OCD have been reported in patients with Asperger's syndrome (Thomsen, 1994a). In diagnosing OCD in children with Asperger's syndrome, it is vitally important to focus upon the distress caused by the symptoms (as described by the child), as well as the resistance displayed by the child. The symptoms can then be characterized as undesirable, egodystonic, as opposed to the repetitive, specific circumscribed interests, typically associated with Asperger's syndrome.

Course and Outcome

Few follow-up studies have been conducted in child and adolescent populations. In a follow-up investigation of 15 adolescents suffering from OCD, approximately 7 years after first admission, Warren (1960) found that the majority had either a tendency toward mild obsessive-compulsive symptoms under stress (27%), or were more or less constantly handicapped to a moderate degree (27%). 33% suffered from constant, severe obsessional-pathology. Two to 7 years following the initial examination Flament et al. (1990) conducted a follow-up of 27 patients with severe primary OCD, with childhood/adolescent onset. A meagre 28% had no psychiatric diagnosis at follow-up, 68% still suffered from OCD, and 48% had an alternative psychiatric disorder, most commonly, anxiety or depression. Berg et al. (1989) conducted a two-year follow-up study of a community-based sample of adolescents, who had been identified in a previous epidemiological study (Flament et al., 1988) as having OCD, OCP, subclinical OCD, or any alternative psychiatric disorder with obsessive-compulsive features. The results showed that 50% of previous OCD patients received an identical diagnosis 2 years later. About 81% of the adolescents, who had previously been given a life-time diagnosis, were diagnosed as having either OCD or subclinical OCD at follow-up. The authors concluded that, contrary to earlier speculations, that adolescents who were initially diagnosed with subclinical OCD, did not develop into true cases of OCD. Zeitlin (1986) found a high individual continuity in obsessive-compulsive symptomatology from childhood to adulthood in patients with admission to a psychiatric hospital in both childhood and adulthood, and thereby, in a highly selected clinical sample.

A long-term follow-up study of European children with OCD (Thomsen, 1994b), with a follow-up period from 6 to 22 years, showed that the outcome could be roughly divided into four different categories: approximately 25% experienced no later OCD (even on a subclinical level), about 25% had OCD on a subclinical level (i.e., having obsessive-compulsive symptoms, but not fulfilling OCD criteria); 25% suffered from chronic OCD (from moderate severity to an incapacitating course of the illness), and the remaining 25% experienced episodic courses of OCD. That is, OCD would occur during periods of stress, interrupted by OCD-free intervals in which obsessive-compulsive symptoms had either totally disappeared or, more frequently, were at a subclinical level. Age at onset of OCD in childhood, and baseline OCD symptom severity did not appear to predict the prognosis. The course was, apparently, independent of social background, which is consistent with the findings of Leonard et al. (1993), in their treatment follow-up study. Many of the patients (still suffering from OCD) lived with parents, despite the fact that they had reached their mid-twenties, or were even older. Also, these patients exhibited avoidant behaviour (Thomsen, 1994b). Leonard et al. (1993) carried out a 2 to 7 year follow-up study of OCD children who had been treated with chlomipramine. They found that 43% still met diagnostic criteria for OCD, and that only 11% were totally asymptomatic. 70% of the subjects were on psychoactive medication at follow-up. Leonard et al. (1993) found that a parental axis-one diagnosis (any) was a negative predictor for prognosis.

Prevention and Intervention

PHARMACOLOGICAL THERAPY

Pharmacological treatment studies with serotonin reuptake inhibitors and pathophysiological studies, which examine abnormalities of serotonin physiology in OCD patients in the untreated state, indicate a neurochemical basis for OCD. Serotonin appears to be connected to the pharmacological relief of OCD, but whether it is involved in the patho-physiology of OCD is still unclear. Specific serotonin reuptake inhibitors (SSRI) are effective in the treatment of OCD, whereas other anti-depressants (such as imipramine and amitriptylin), which have no effect on the serotonin reuptake, do not show any efficacy in OCD. Most controlled double-blind studies, in children and adolescents with OCD, are still conducted with chlomipramine (De Veaugh-Geiss *et al.*, 1992; Flament *et al.*, 1985; Leonard *et al.*, 1989). All these studies show that chlomipramine is superior to both placebo and desipramine. SSRIs have, also, been included in the test, although mainly on adult patients. The SSRI-studies, however, show that these drugs are superior to placebo, whereas no apparent difference can be found in the efficacy of chlomi-pramine and SSRIs. Table 9.3 illustrates the psychopharmacological studies, with a controlled double-blind design.

Table 9.3 Studies on psychopharmacological treatment in childhood OCD with a controlled double-blind design

Study	Number	Treatment	Main results
Flament *et al.* (1985)	19	Clomipramine, 10 weeks (ds. 150 mg)	Clomipramine superior to placebo
Leonard *et al.* (1988)	48	Clomipramine, cross-over, 5 weeks (ds. 150 mg)	Clomipramine superior to desipramine
De Veaugh-Geiss *et al.* (1992)	60	Clomipramine 8 weeks (ds. 150–200 mg)	Clomipramine superior to placebo
Riddle *et al.* (1992)	14	Fluoxetine, 8 weeks (ds. 20 mg)	Fluoxetine superior to placebo
Riddle *et al.* (1996)	74	Fluvoxamine 10 weeks (ds. 200 mg)	Fluvoxamine superior to placebo
March *et al.* (1998)	184	Sertraline (ds. 200 mg)	Sertraline superior to placebo

The hypothesis of disturbance in the feed-back loops, between nucleus caudatus, thalamus and the orbitofrontal cortex is supported by recent studies made by Schwartz *et al.* (1996) and Baxter *et al.* (1992), who show a normalization of affected areas, following both behavioural therapy and medication.

When considering medication in the treatment of OCD children, it is important to note that medication alone is rarely as effective as medication combined with behavioural therapy. The main purpose of anti-OCD medication is to reduce the intensity of obsessive symptoms, as well as the distress and anxiety caused by them. In cases with primarily obsessions (with none or few compulsions present), behavioural therapy may seem more difficult to undertake.

Treatment with chlomipramine is frequently accompanied by side-effects, as a result of potential cardiotoxic effect. It is, also, a tricyclic antidepressant and therefore, SSRIs may be considered to be the preferred choice of drug. Not all SSRIs have been subject to controlled double-blind designs in children and adolescents. However, the clinical impression is that there are no major differences in the efficacy of the various SSRI-drugs. The main differences are found in their varying half-life periods, side-effect profile and interaction with other drugs.

As yet, the required dosage has not been determined for children and adolescents. In the case of adults, the required amounts appear to be higher than that of the treatment of depression. In children (i.e., up to the age of 12 to 13 years), a careful titration is suggested (i.e., commencing with a dosage of 10 mg (in cases of fluoxetine, citalopram or paroxetine), and gradually, increasing to 20, 30 or 40 mg depending upon the side-effects. In adolescents, titration to 60 mg, or in cases of sertraline 100, 150 or even 200 mg is suggested. When any improvement is seen, titration to a reduced dosage is recommended, in order to determine whether improvement continues on a reduced prescription.

SSRIs work somewhat slowly. It is, therefore, important not to discontinue medication at an early stage if no visible improvement is seen immediately. The response to treatment will normally take longer than in the case of depression. A period of two months is quite normal, before any significant improvement is visible. It is recommended that medication be continued for up till 12 weeks, giving slow responders a chance to show improvement. In cases, where no improvement has emerged following a period of 12 weeks, continuation with an alternative SSRI could be considered, or in cases of extreme OCD, augmenting factors should be considered. This should, however, be avoided with children, unless obsessive-compulsive symptoms are particularly disabling.

It is not easy to establish exactly how long treatment should be continued. Many patients show relapse of obsessive-compulsive symptoms after discontinuation of the treatment (Pato *et al.*, 1988). It would be reasonable to continue medication for a period of one year. Children and adolescents who respond well to combined medication and behavioural therapy, are able to function without medication after some time. Once again it is important, to consider the significance of behavioural therapy, perhaps arranging a few "booster-sessions", even after medication has been discontinued. This would support the child in his/her struggle against the obsessive-compulsive symptoms, should they appear again or deteriorate. In cases, where children or adolescents relapse, following discontinuation of medication, and where behavioural therapy does not satisfactorily improve the condition, continuation of medication should be considered.

The majority of studies, consistent with the clinical impressions illustrate that, even in cases of efficacy, medication alone is rarely, capable of total removal of the obsessions and compulsions. Where medication is effective the majority of patients experience a reduction of symptoms by approximately 50% to 75%.

PSYCHOLOGICAL INTERVENTIONS

Behavioural psychotherapy in the form of exposure and response prevention is regarded as an effective treatment of OCD in younger patients (March and Mulle, 1998). Exposure involves confronting the actual fear that cause stress to a person suffering from OCD. Response prevention, being to wilfully avoid the actions an OCD person would normally carry-out in order to relieve his/her anxiety such as washing hands, checking doors etc. Research involving adults has demonstrated just how effective this form of treatment can be. Results of behavioural therapy, however, vary from child to child. Children suffering from mild to moderate OCD respond most significantly from the treatment, particularly, those who have a desire to reduce their symptoms. Motivation is the key factor to the success of behavioural of therapy.

First of all, the exact problem must be defined. Following this, a neural framework is provided, reviewing the current scientific explanation of OCD. One must emphasize that OCD is not just a "bad habit", which must be corrected. The child is not responsible for his/her behaviour and there is nothing he/she could have done to prevent the situation.

At this point, it is important to describe the obsessions and compulsions in utmost detail. Which symptoms are present (i.e. checking, washing, rituals etc.)? At what time of the day (in which specific situations) do they occur? How much time is involved and to what degree do they interfere with the child's daily activities? It is, also, important to form a picture of the child's control over these symptoms, his/her resistance to them (smaller children in particular are inclined to yield completely to all compulsions without any attempt to resist them), and the distress caused by the symptoms. In order to plan the behavioural therapy sessions, a hierarchy of symptoms should be made, that is, which symptom is the most distressing. The hierarchy of rituals can be constructed, rated on the degree of anxiety experienced by the patients when they refrain from carrying them out. At each treatment session the patients are given a task to perform at home. These tasks are related to one, or more, of the items on the hierarchy, and could perhaps begin with the lowest rated item. Thus, the children gradually learn to suppress the urge to carry-out the rituals. Older children and adolescents are, frequently, provided with a diary, in which they are asked to record when, and how they perform their compulsions. Sometimes this task in itself may help to reduce the number of rituals performed. The purpose of this "homework" is that the OCD child must practise being master over the symptoms. The therapist must explain these "homework" assignments carefully to the child, emphasizing the importance of mastering OCD each and every day. The child must be aware that the homework is time-limited and specific, and therefore, will be under the child's control. Exposure and response prevention is the core of mastering OCD. Exposure requires the child to confront OCD triggers, for example, touching "contaminated" objects. Response prevention takes place when the child refuses to perform the compulsion (in this case, hand washing) which, normally, follows exposure to the trigger. When a child or adolescent is exposed to such a fearful situation, without having the opportunity of performing the compulsion, he/she will usually experience increased anxiety and must be encouraged to tolerate this anxiety. In cases where parents are involved in the child's rituals (particularly smaller children), it is important that the parents are, also, involved in the behavioural therapy. In such cases, as a child asking his/her parents a vast number of questions every day, one could perhaps, reduce this number as part of a "homework" assignment.

Behavioural therapy would appear to be successful in reducing OCD symptoms in approximately 50% of children (March and Mulle, 1998). Factors such as OCD severity, whether the child has other psychiatric disorders, the patient's age and the familial involvement in the obsessive-compulsive symptoms, aid in the explanation of varying responses to the same treatment. The interpretation of treatment results are invalidated by the lack of standardized rating criteria and deficiency in research design and random allocation in the studies performed (see Haan *et al.* [1998] and Thomsen [1996] for a review of behavioural therapy research). In a limited study by Haan *et al.* (1998), behavioural therapy produced stronger therapeutic changes than chlomipramine on the CY-BOCS and more extensive studies regarding its efficacy are recommended.

References

Adams, P. (1973) *Obsessive Children*. New York: Penguin Books.

Akhtar, S., Wig, N.N., Varma, V.K., Pershad, D., & Verma, S.K. (1978) Socio-cultural and clinical determinants of symptomatology in obsessional neurosis. *International Journal of Social Psychiatry, 24*, 157–162.

American Psychiatric Association. (1994). *Diagnostic and statistical manual of mental disorders* (4th ed.). Washington, DC: Author.

American Psychiatric Association. (1980). Diagnostic and statistical manual of mental disorders (3rd ed.). Washington, DC: Author.

Apter, A., Bernhout, E., & Tyrano, S. (1984). Severe obsessive compulsive in adolescence: A report of eight cases. *Journal of Adolescence, 7*, 349–358.

Baxter, L.R., Schwartz, J.M., Bergman, K.S., Szuba, M.P., Guze, B.H., Mazziotta, J.C., Alazraki A, Selin C.E., Ferng H.K., Munford P., Phelps M.E. (1992). Caudate glucose metabolic rate changes with both drug and behaviour therapy for obsessive-compulsive disorder. *Archives of General Psychiatry, 49*, 681–689.

Behar, D., Rapoport, J.L., Berg, C.J., Denckla, M.B,, Mann, L., Cox, C., Fedio, P., Zahn, T., & Wolfman, M.G. (1984). Computerized tomography and neuropsychological test measures in adolescents with obsessive-compulsive disorder. *American Journal of Psychiatry, 141*, 363–369.

Berg, C.J., Rapoport, J.L., Flament, M.F. (1986). The Leyton Obsessional Inventory-Child Version. *Journal of the American Academy of Child and Adolescent Psychiatry, 25*, 84–91.

Berg, C.J., Rapoport, J.L., Whitaker, A., Davies, M., Leonard, H.L., Swedo, S.E., Braiman, S., & Lenane, M. (1989). Childhood obsessive compulsive disorder. A two-year prospective follow-up study of a community sample.

Journal of the American Academy of Child and Adolescent Psychiatry, 28, 528–533.

Berg, C.J., Whitaker, A., Davies, M., Flament, M.F., & Rapoport, J.L. (1988). The Survey Form of the Leyton Obsessional Inventory-Child Version: Norms from an epidemiological study. *Journal of the American Academy of Child and Adolescent Psychiatry, 27,* 759–763.

Black, D.W., Yates, W.R., Noyes, R., Pfohl, B., & Kelley, M. (1989). DSM-III personality disorder in obsessive-compulsive study volunteers: a controlled study. *Journal of Personality Disorders, 3,* 58–62.

Bland, R.C., Orn, H., & Newman, S.C. (1988). Lifetime prevalence of psychiatric disorder in Edmonton. *Acta Psychiatrica Scandinavica. 77* (suppl. 338), 24–32.

Boone, K.B., Ananth, J., Philpott, L., Kaur, A., & Djenderedjian, A. (1991). Neuropsychological characteristics of nondepressed adults with obsessive-compulsive disorder. *Neuropsychiatry, Neuropsychology and Behavioural Neurology, 4,* 96–109.

Carey, G. & Gottesman, I.I. (1981). Twin and family studies of anxiety, phobic and obsessive disorders. In D.F. Klein & J. Rabkin (eds.). *Anxiety: New Research and Changing Concepts.* New York: Raven Press.

Cooper, J. & Kelleher, M.Y. (1973). The Leyton Obsessional Inventory: A principal components analysis on normal subjects. *Psychological Medicine, 3,* 204–208.

Crisp, A.H., Lacey, J.H., & Crutchfiels, M. (1987). Clomipramine and "drive" in people with anorexia nervosa. *British Journal of Psychiatry, 150,* 355–358.

Denckla, M.B. (1989). Neurological examination. In J.L. Rapoport (ed.) *Obsessive-Compulsive Disorder in Children and Adolescents* (pp.107–118). Washington, DC: American Psychiatric Press, Inc.

De Veaugh, G.J., Moroz, G., Biedermann, J. *et al.* (1992). Clomipramine hydrochloride in childhood and adolescent obsessive-compulsive disorder— a multi center trial. *Journal of the American Academy of Child and Adolescent Psychiatry, 31,* 45–49

Douglass, H.M., Morfitt, T.E., Dar, R., McGee, R., Silva, P. (1995). Obsessive-compulsive disorder in a birth cohort of 18-years-olds: Prevalence and predictors. *Journal of the American Academy of Child and Adolescent Psychiatry, 11,* 1424–1431.

Esser, G., Schmidt, M.H., & Woerner, W. (1990). Epidemiology and course of psychiatric disorder in school-age children. Results of a longitudinal study. *Journal of Child Psychology and Psychiatry, 31,* 243–263.

Flament, M.F. (1993). *The neurobiology of childhood OCD.* Presented at the First International OCD Conference, Italy.

Flament, M.F., Koby, E., Rapoport, J.L., Berg, C.J., Zahn, T., Cox, C., Denckla, M., & Lenane, M. (1990) Childhood obsessive-compulsive disorder: A prospective follow-up study. *Journal of Child Psychology and Psychiatry, 31,* 363–380.

Flament, M.F., Rapoport, J.L., Berg, C.J., Sceery, W., Kilts, C., Mellstrom, B., & Linnoila, M. (1985). Clomipramine treatment of childhood obsessive compulsive disorder: A double-blind controlled study. *Archives of General Psychiatry*, 42, 977–983.

Flament, M.F., Whitaker, A., Rapoport, J.L,. Davies, M., Bergt, C.Z., Kalikow, K., Sceery, W, & Shaffer, D. (1988). Obsessive compulsive disorder in adolescence. An epidemiological study. *Journal of the American Academy of Child and Adolescent Psychiatry*, 27, 764–771.

Flor-Henry, P., Yeydall, L.T., Koles, Z.J., & Howarth, B.G. (1979). Neuropsychological and power spectra EEG investigations of the obsessive-compulsive syndrome. *Biological Psychiatry*, 14, 119–130.

Foa, E.B. & Kozak, M.J. (1995). DSM-IV Field trial: Obsessive-compulsive disorder. *American Journal of Psychiatry*, 152, 90–96.

Haan, E.D., Kees, A.L., Hoogduin, M.D., Buitelaar, J.K., & Keijsers, G.P.J. (1998). Behavior therapy versus clomipramine for the treatment of obsessive-compulsive disorder in children and adolescents. *Journal of American Academic Child and Adolescent Psychiatry*, 37, 1022–1116.

Head, D., Bolton, D., & Hymans, N. (1989). Deficit in cognitive shifting ability in patients with obsessive-compulsive disorder. *Biological Psychiatry*, 25, 929–937.

Henderson, J.G. & Pollard, C.A. (1988). Three types of obsessive-compulsive disorder in a community sample. *Journal of Clinical Psychology*, 44, 747–752.

Hollander, E., Schiffman, E., Cohen, B., Rivera-Stein, M.A., Rosen, W., Gorman, J.M., Fyer, A.J., Papp. L., & Liebowitz, M.R. (1990). Signs of central nervous system dysfunction in obsessive-compulsive disorder. *Archives of General Psychiatry*, 47, 27–32.

Honjo, S., Hirano, C., Murase, S., Kaneko, T., Sugiyama, T., Ohtaka, K., Ayoma, T., Takei, T, Inoko, K, Wakabayashi, S. (1989). Obsessive-compulsive symptoms in childhood and adolescence. *Acta Psychiatrica Scandinavica*, 80, 83–91.

Hoover, C.F. & Insel, T.R. (1984). Families of origin in obsessive-compulsive disorder. *Journal of Nervous and Mental disease*, 172, 207–215.

Insel, T.R. (1992) Neurobiology of obsessive-compulsive disorder: A review. *International Clinical Psychopharmacology*, 7 (suppl. 1), 31–33.

Insel, T.R., Donnelly, E.F., Lalakea, M.L., Alterman, I.S., & Murphy, D.L. (1983). Neurological and neuropsychological studies of patients with obsessive-compulsive disorder. *Biological Psychiatry*, 18, 741–751.

Karno, M., Golding, J.M., Sorensen, S.B., & Burnam, M.A. (1988). The epidemiology of obsessive-compulsive disorder in five US communities. *Archives of General Psychiatry*, 45, 1094–1099.

Kaye, W.H., Weltzin, T.E., Hsu, L.K.G., Bulik, C.M., McCohona, C., & Sobkiewicz, T. (1992) Patients with anorexia nervosa have elevated scores on the Yale-Brown Obsessive-Compulsive scale. *International Journal of Eating Disorder*, 12, 57–62.

Kerimoglu, E. & Yalin, A. (1991) *Obsessive-compulsive disorder and histeria (conversion reaction) in children.* Poster presented at 9th Congress of European Society for Child & Adolescent Psychiatry, London.

Khanna, S. & Srinath, S. (1988). Childhood obsessive-compulsive disorder. 1. Psychopathology. *Psychopathology, 21,* 254–258.

Lenane, M.C., Swedo., S.E, Leonard, H.L., Pauls, D.L., Sceery, W., Rapoport, L . (1990) Psychiatric disorders in first degree relatives of children and adolescents with obsessive-compulsive disorder. *Journal of the American Academy of Child and Adolescent Psychiatry, 29,* 407–412.

Leonard, H.L., Swedo, S.E., Lenane, M.C., Rettew, D.C., Gershon, E.S., Rapoport, J.L. (1993). A two to seven year follow-up study of 54 obsessive compulsive children and adolescents. *Archives of General Psychiatry, 50,* 429–439.

Leonard, H.L., Swedo, S., Rapoport, J.L, Coby, E.V., Lenane, M.C, .Cheslow, D, & Hamburger, S.D. (1988). Treatment of obsessive compulsive disorder with clomipramine and desipramine in children and adolescents. *Archives of General Psychiatry, 46,* 1088–1092.

Lo, W. (1967). A follow-up study of obsessional neurotics in Hong Kong Chinese. *British Journal of Psychiatry, 113,* 823–832.

March, J.S. & Mulle, K. (1998). *OCD in Children and Adolescents. A Cognitive-Behavioral Treatment Manual.* New York, NY, USA: The Guilford Press.

Olson, D.H. (1986). Circumplex model VII: Validation studies and FACES III. *Family Process, 25,* 337–351.

Pato, M.T., Zohar-Kadouch, R., Zohar, J., & Murphy, D.L. (1988). Return of symptoms after discontinuation of clomipramine in patients with obsessive-compulsive disorder. *American Journal of Psychiatry, 145,* 1521–1525.

Pauls, D.L., Goodman, W.K., Rasmussen, S., & Alsobrook, J.P. (1993). *Familial risk of obsessive-compulsive disorder.* Presented at First International OCD Conference, Italy.

Pauls, D.L., Towbin, K.E., Leckman, J.F., & Zahner, G.E.P. (1986). Gilles de la Tourette's syndrome and obsessive-compulsive disorder. Presented at First International OCD Conference, Italy.

Rapoport, J.L. (1991). Recent advances in obsessive-compulsive dosorder. *Neuropsychopharmacology, 5,* 1–10

Rapoport, J.L. (1986). Childhood obsessive compulsive disorder. *Journal of Child Psychology and Psychiatry, 27,* 289–296.

Rapoport, J.L., Elkins, R., & Langer, D. (1981). Childhood obsessive-compulsive disorder. *American Journal of Psychiatry, 138,* 1545–1554.

Rasmussen, S.A. & Tsuang, M.T. (1984). The epidemiology of obsessive-compulsive disorder. *Journal of Clinical Psychiatry, 45,* 450–457.

Reed, G. (1977). Obsessional personality disorder and remembering. *British Journal of Psychiatry, 130,* 177–183.

Rettew, C.S., Swedo, S.E., Leonard, H.L., Lenane, M.C., & Rapoport, J.L. (1992). Obsessions and compulsions across time in 79 children and adolescents with obsessive-compulsive disorder. *Journal of the American Academy of Child and Adolescent Psychiatry, 31*, 1050–1056.

Riddle, M.A., Scahill, L., King, R.A., Hardin, M.T., Anderson, G.M., Ort, S.I., Smith, J.C. Leckman, J.F., & Cohen, D.J. (1992). Double-blind, crossover trial of fluoxetine and placebo in children and adolescents with obsessive-compulsive disorder. *Journal of the American Academy of Child and Adolescent Psychiatry, 31*, 1062–1069.

Riddle, M.A., Scahill, L., King, R., Hardin, M.T., Towbin, K.E., Ort, S.I., Leckman, J.F., & Cohen, D.J. (1990). Obsessive compulsive disorders in children and adolescents: Phenomenology and family history. *Journal of the American Academy of Child and Adolescent Psychiatry, 5*, 766–772.

Schwartz, J.M., Stoessel, P.W., Baxter, L.R. Kartin, K.M., & Phelps, M.E. (1996). Systematic changes in cerebral glucose metabolic rate after successful behaviour modification treatment of obsessive-compulsive disorder. *Archives of General Psychiatry, 53*, 109–113.

Swedo, S.E., Rapoport, J.L., Leonard, H., Lenane, M., & Cheslow, D. (1989). Obsessive-compulsive disorder in children and adolescents. Clinical phenomenology of 70 consecutive cases. *Archives of General Psychiatry, 46*, 335–341.

Thomsen, P.H. (1996). Treatment of obsessive-compulsive disorder in children and adolescents. A review of the literature. *European Child and Adolescent Psychiatry 5*, 55–66.

Thomsen, P.H. (1994a). Obsessive-compulsive disorder in children and adolescents. A study of phenomenology and family functioning in 20 Danish cases. *European Child and Adolescent Psychiatry, 3*, 29–36.

Thomsen, P.H. (1994b). Obsessive-compulsive disorder in children and adolescents. A 6–22 year follow-up study. Clinical descriptions of the course and continuity of obsessive-compulsive symptomatology. *European Child and Adolescent Psychiatry, 2*, 82–96.

Thomsen, P.H. (1994c). Children and Adolescents with obsessive-compulsive disorder. An analysis of sociodemographic background. *Psychopathology, 27*, 303–311.

Thomsen, P.H. (1993). Obsessive-compulsive disorder in children and adolescents. Self-reported obsessive-compulsive behaviour in pupils in Denmark. *Acta Psychiatrica Scandinavica, 88*, 212–217.

Thomsen, P.H. (1991). Obsessive-compulsive symptoms in children and adolescents. A phenomenological analysis of 61 Danish cases. *Psychopathology, 24*, 12–18.

Thomsen, P.H. & Jensen, J. (1991). Dimensional approach to obsessive-compulsive disorder in childhood and adolescence. *Acta Psychiatrica Scandinavica, 83*, 183–187.

Thorén, P., Åsberg, M., & Cronholm, B. (1980). Clomipramine treatment of obsessive compulsive disorder. I. A controlled clinical trial. *Archives of General Psychaitry, 37*, 1281–1285.

Toro, J., Cervara, M., Osefo, E., & Salermo, M. (1992). Obsessive-compulsive disorder in childhood and adolescence: A clinical study. *Journal of Child Psychology and Psychiatry, 33*, 1025–1937.

Torgersen, S. (1983). Genetic factors in anxiety disorders. *Archives of General Psychiatry, 40*, 1085–1989.

Valeni-Basile, L.A., Garrison, C.Z., Jackson, K.L., Waller, J.L., Mckeown, R.E., Addy, C.L., & Duffe, S.P. (1993). Frequency of obsessive-compulsive disorder in a community sample of young adolescents. *Journal of the American Academy of Child and Adolescent Psychiatry, 33*, 782–791.

Warren, W. (1960). Some relationships between the psychiatry of children and of adults. *Journal of Mental Science, 106*, 815–826.

World Health Organization. (1992). *The ICD-10 Classification of Mental and Behavioural Disorders*. Geneva, Switzerland: WHO Library Cataloguing in Publication Data.

Yaryura-Tobias, J.A. & Bhagavan, H.N. (1977). L-Tryptophan in obsessive-compulsive neurosis. *American Journal of Psychiatry, 134*, 1298–1299.

Zeitlin, H. (1986). *The natural History of Psychiatric Disorder in Children*. Institute of Psychiatry, Maudsley Monographs. Oxford: University Press.

Zohar, A.H., Murphy, D.L., & Zohar-Kadouch, R.C. (1990). Serotonin in obsessive-compulsive disorder. In E.F. Coccaro & D.I. Murphy (Eds.) *Serotonin in Major Psychiatric Disorder*. Wasthington DC: American Psychiatric Press.

0 POSTTRAUMATIC STRESS DISORDER

Daniel S. Schechter
M. Cevdet Tosyali

The study of posttraumatic stress over the past decade reflects an important paradigm shift in the field of psychiatry. Moving away from a simple nature-nurture dichotomy, the field can now attend to a far more complex mutual interaction of the environment and biology as these forces impact on the developing human brain. The study of post-traumatic stress has supported that autonomic nervous system responsivity and one's expectations of the world are fundamentally related. This chapter will review the literature on post-traumatic stress from infancy through adolescence, which by definition will cover some of the most exciting and influential research in the domain of developmental psychopathology.

Background

Posttraumatic stress reactions have long been recognized in adults following war-time combat as well as non-combat trauma. These reactions have been given a variety of names: soldiers heart, Da Costa's syndrome, irritable heart, effort syndrome, neurocirculatory asthenia, shell shock, battle fatigue, combat or war neurosis, gross stress reaction and transitional situational disturbances. Since Posttraumatic Stress Disorder (PTSD), a disorder which involves posttraumatic stress severe enough to cause significant distress and/or dysfunction to the individual, was introduced into the psychiatric nomenclature by the DSM-III in 1980 (American Psychiatric Association; APA,1980), it has been the object of enormous attention.

Children were once thought to experience only transient stress in the wake of traumatic events (Gurwitch *et al.*, 1998). Advances in the nosology of psychiatric disorders led to confirmation of clinical observations that PTSD also occurred in children with a similar duration of symptoms and course as found in adults. The range of severity was noted, as with adults, to be relative both to the nature, duration and frequency of traumatic exposure and to premorbid risk factors.

Diagnostic criteria for PTSD have evolved steadily since 1980, evidenced in the DSM-III-R (APA, 1987) and most recently in the DSM-IV (APA, 1994). The latter has incorporated the findings of researchers based on child interviews and clinical observations which take into account the child's chronological age as opposed to parent-reports alone (Gurwitch *et al.*, 1998). The DSM-IV criteria for PTSD for example include the following (p. 427–428): "The Person has been exposed to a traumatic event in which both of the following were present: (i) the person experienced, witnessed, or was confronted with an event or events that involved actual or threatened death or serious injury, or a threat to the physical integrity of self or others (ii) the person's response involved intense fear, helplessness, or horror. *Note*: In children, this may be expressed instead by disorganized or agitated behaviour". These initial criteria are followed by those of persistent *reexperiencing* of the traumatic event, persistent *avoidance* of stimuli associated with the trauma as well as numbing of general responsiveness, and finally persistence of symptoms of increased *arousal*. These symptoms must last more than one month and must cause clinically significant distress or impairment in social, occupational, or other important areas of functioning.

Throughout the DSM-IV criteria as seen in the example cited above, attempts are made to note not only that children have the disorder, but how "children" and particularly "young children" may differ in their presentation from that of adults. The DSM-IV implies that PTSD is a mental disorder whose childhood form is similar to that of adulthood yet with potential age-dependent differences in presentation.

PTSD AND HUMAN DEVELOPMENT

An alternative, and perhaps more complex view of the relationship of child PTSD to adult PTSD is offered by the model of developmental psychopathology (Cicchetti and Cohen, 1995; Cicchetti and Lynch, 1993). As Pynoos *et al.* (1995) describe in their developmental model of traumatic stress, traumatic experience during formative stages of human development contributes to the formation of expectations of the world by the child, as well as expectations of his or her place vis a vis others. Expressions of these expectations are found in thought, emotions, behaviour, and biology of the developing child and may "skew" the child's experience of the world. The young child's attempt to adapt to traumatic stress may lead to a heightened sympathetic nervous system response to traumatic reminders, and may result in vulnerability to psychopathology later in life.

What is adaptive in one risky situation at one point early in the life cycle, when generalized and/or persistent later, may become pathological. Indeed, several large studies (Breslau *et al.*, 1999; Yehuda *et al.*, 1998) have demonstrated that traumatic stress in childhood, and even moreso, PTSD in childhood are risk factors for later adult PTSD. More specifically, one recent study of 100 consecutive referrals to an inner-city child and adolescent psychiatry clinic concluded that out of the PTSD-afflicted 22% of the 59 children who had traumatic exposure as defined by the DSM-IV, the most significant associated risk factors by regression analysis for development of PTSD included physical abuse and domestic violence exposure; whereas, higher IQ was found to be a protective factor (Silva *et al.*, 2000). Wunderlich *et al.* (1998) in their study of 3021 young adults ages 14–24, found, after conducting multivariate comorbidity analyses, that the individuals at highest risk for suicide attempts were those suffering from anxiety disorders notably PTSD.

Recent research in developmental neurobiology (Perry *et al.*, 1995; Perry and Pollard, 1998; van der Kolk *et al.*, 1996) have attempted to explain the effects of traumatic stress in early childhood and its sequelae: Massive cortisol and catecholamine exposure to the developing nervous system essentially may lead to enduring effects on memory, attention, affect, pain and sympathetic nervous system regulation via alteration of synaptic connections and brain structure. Effects on cognitive functions can lead to academic and other vocational skills performance difficulties, creating further risk for the traumatized individual, who may additionally be at risk for affective, somatoform and substance use disorders. Individuals suffering from PTSD have also been found to be at increased risk to be re-traumatized. PTSD and dissociative symptoms in particular have been associated with risk for traumatized individuals to traumatize others (Coates and Moore, 1997; Lyons-Ruth and Block, 1996; Zeanah *et al.*, 1997). As many as one third of maltreated children are thought to perpetuate or "transmit" their violent trauma to their children intergenerationally (Oliver, 1993). PTSD among hospitalized, incarcerated or otherwise violent youths is noted as much higher than that of the general population (Cauffman *et al.*, 1998; Koltek *et al.*, 1998; Lipschitz *et al.*, 1999).

Recent research has gone as far as to offer a causal relation-ship between PTSD as a manifestation of altered sympathetic arousal affecting cognitive development and risk for violence, in that the capacity to reflect, verbalize, and inhibit aggresive impulses is often impaired when the individual is faced with a traumatic reminder (Moradi *et al.*, 1999).

THE DEFINITION OF TRAUMA AND WHAT IS "POST-TRAUMATIC STRESS"

Historically, Sigmund Freud (1959/1926) defined a traumatic event as one "in which external and internal, real and instinctual dangers con-verge." Thus, the experience of danger in the environment incorporates an estimation of the degree of threat, the degree of internal resources and external protection, such as that offered by others, and the degree of helplessness and irreversibility.

Terr (1987) reviewed the literature on childhood psychic trauma and her own studies such as that of the kidnapping of 26 schoolchildren who had been kidnapped and buried in a school bus in Chowchilla, California in 1976. She cited Sigmund Freud's definition above and Anna Freud's addition to this definition; namely, to be a trauma, an *external* event of sufficient magnitude so as to be perceived as life-threatening must take place. Terr developed the definition of trauma on which the DSM-IV description is based: "Psychic trauma occurs when a sudden unexpected intense external experience overwhelms the indi-vidual's coping and defensive operations, creating the feeling of utter helplessness" (Terr, 1987). What Terr terms as "the individual's coping and defensive operations" (i.e., "ego functioning") are determined in part by constitution, environmental input, and development as an interactive process involving both. In short, the perception of what is traumatic is relative to one's circumstances. The increasing capacity for agency, reflection, symbolic and language functioning, along with increasing physical growth, and the concomitant decreasing depen-dency on the caregiver with development, all contribute to a diminu-tion in the range of what may perceived as life-threatening over time. Increasing mobility and potential exposure to the new and unexpected paradoxically may increase the range. The DSM-IV definition of trau-matic event (APA, 1994) as "involving actual or threatened death or serious injury, or a threat to the physical integrity of self or other" already poses a problem if one considers the vantage point of a very young child. A preschooler who hears his traumatized mother's shrieks following receiving news of the death of her partner—or his psychotic mother's shrieks in response to an auditory hallucination, may hear his own death knell, even when there is no tangible threat to self or other. Analogous to "shared psychotic disorder" or *folie a deux*, shared or "relational" PTSD has been proposed as an alternative construct for this reason (Scheeringa *et al.*, 1995; Scheeringa and Zeanah, 1995). It is also for this reason some clinicians and researchers had advocated for abandoning the catastrophic event criterion in the DSM-III-R, feeling that a traumatic stress response alone regardless of the actual stimulus was sufficient (Drell *et al.*, 1993).

Indeed, from a developmental perspective, rolling off a sofa will not be traumatic for a healthy teenager; whereas for an infant or handicapped child, such an experience may seem life-threatening. For any age, however, being a passenger in a crashing car or being raped is likely to be traumatic. Being in a crashing car or being raped more than once, and surely, multiple times, is more likely to result in sustained PTSD than being traumatized once. This has been supported by research (Breslau *et al.*, 1999). Terr (1987) had put forth a simple distinction between isolated traumatic exposures or "Type I" traumas such as a traffic accident or natural disaster, and chronic repeated exposures or "Type II" traumas, the latter associated with child maltreatment or chronic illness.

Being traumatized once for someone predisposed to greater anxiety or from a more chaotic, emotionally unavailable family may produce the same degree of PTSD as for another individual with more protective factors, traumatized multiple times (Pynoos *et al.*, 1995). This question has been elegantly studied in the context of the Bosnian War and Palestinian Conflicts in which children exposed to violent combat suffered significantly more posttraumatic stress if their families were displaced or if they were otherwise deprived of basic needs than if not (Husain *et al.*, 1998). To complicate matters, the risk for being traumatized multiple times has been associated with familial disorganization, insecure and/or disorganized attachments, and emotional unavailability or neglect (Fergusson *et al.*, 1996; Lyons-Ruth and Block, 1996). Ruttenberg (1998) has schematized traumatic stressors for infants and very young children in terms of mild, moderate, severe and catastrophic. Most measures of PTSD will attempt to take severity of stressor, frequency and degree of exposure into account before assessing response (Carlson, 1997).

Phenomenology

Variation in symptom profiles across age groups from infancy through adulthood have been reported (Pfefferbaum, 1997). Reactions to traumatic events may differ depending on cognitive, social-emotional, and physical development (Pynoos *et al.*, 1995; Ruttenberg, 1998). Moreover, since other risk factors including psychopathology often accompany PTSD, age related variations in symptoms may also be related to factors such as security of primary attachment, availability of social supports, and child and adolescent comorbid disorders distinct from PTSD which, in turn, also vary with age (Cicchetti and Cohen, 1995; Cicchetti and Lynch, 1993).

Increased separation anxiety, exacerbated specific fears (e.g. of the dark, car noises, or other separation-associated and/or trauma-associated features), regressive behaviour (e.g. increased need for pacifier or bottle), somatoform complaints, and analogues of adult PTSD symptoms such as those clustering in the general categories of reexperiencing the event, avoidance, and arousal have all been noted for children one year-old and older (Gurwitch, 1998). In infants and toddlers, increased irritability and disruptive behaviour, exacerbation of startle response and other manifestations of dysregulation of affect, sleep, and feeding, along with, transient loss of milestones (such as bowel/bladder control or speech and language competence), and disorganization of attachment behaviour have been reported (Drell *et al.*, 1993; Thomas, 1995).

Reexperiencing the traumatic event(s) for preschoolers and school-age children may involve repetitive play in which themes of the traumatic event are expressed. Automatic-appearing activity that lacks the sense of fun, creative spontaneity and symbolic abstraction inherent in normative play are hallmarks of posttraumatic play (Terr, 1981). Such compulsive forms of play or reenactments of the trauma may, depending on the child and his/her developmental capacities, concretely resemble the traumatic event and/or may be displaced in content, yet contain the affective tone, rhythmicity, or other more abstract features of the event(s) or associated details.

General sexualized behaviour may be observed in children who have been sexually abused as functions of both reexperiencing the trauma and of increased arousal in relation to the trauma (Green, 1989). Similarly, increased hostile aggression directed towards self and/or others may be seen in children who have experienced physical abuse or who have itnessed violence (Kaplan and Pelcovitz, 1995). Importantly, posttraumatic play activity in the absence of a careful history may be missed or may seem bizarre or unrelated to the traumatic event. The following is an illustrative example:

> The first author evaluated and treated a 6 year-old boy with PTSD and Gender Identity Disorder, the former diagnosis, activated during a bout of tonsillitis when mother was considering surgery as a treatment option for him. This boy had had a series of life-threatening, ultimately successful operations and invasive procedures including multiple bone-marrow aspirations and chemotherapy to treat a rapidly advancing lymphoma at age 3. During his hospitalizations, his mother would leave the film *The Wizard of Oz* for him to watch with her and by himself when she could not be with him in his hospital room. During evaluation and subsequent treatment, this boy would rigidly repeat over and over the story from the film, taking the part of female characters Dorothy and the Wicked Witch. He carried a toy doctor-bag instead of a basket as he skipped along the imagined yellow brick road in his psychiatrist's office. He excitedly pretended to torture a small stuffed dog that he called Toto with toy syringes and surgical instruments, before waving a wand and magically healing him.

Pynoos *et al.* (1987) also have noted the insertion of fantasied rescue or undoing into posttraumatic play as a reparative effort. Incongruence of affect with content of the play, such as a 4 year-old child smiling while saying to his therapist that he has brought his murdered mother back to earth, may additionally relate to the developmentally-based inability to cognitively process the irreversibility of death and thereby to integrate affects of sadness and rage associated with loss. Children may also experience recurrent scary dreams, which similarly seem to be without recognizable content, yet which capture the affective tone, rhythmicity or other more abstract fragments of a traumatic experience (Terr, 1987).

Visual, auditory and somatosensory hallucinations as well as hypnogogic and hypnopompic illusions have been reported posttraumatically in children from early childhood through adulthood (Butler *et al.*, 1996; Haviland *et al.*, 1995). Transient deficits in reality testing of the individual with PTSD often coincide with internal and external efforts, such as by an abusive or frightened parent, to invalidate, disavow, or deny the traumatic experience. Further complicating the assessment of psychotic or pseudo-psychotic (i.e., vivid flashbacks) symptoms noted in the context of PTSD is the fact that PTSD is often comorbid with affective and/or substance abuse disorders, the latter being particularly relevant to adolescents (Butler *et al.*, 1996). Additionally, a child or adolescent may imitate the psychotic symptoms of a traumatizing caregiver in an effort to master the trauma (Haviland *et al.*, 1995). In a study of adolescent psychiatric outpatients without an identified psy-chotic disorder, hallucinations but not delusions were associated with PTSD (Haviland et al., 1995). There are conflicting reports of such hal-lucinations responding to anti-psychotic medications (Butler et al., 1996). Terr (1981) has also reported that children have described the sense of having been given a sign before trauma, called "omen forma-tion", and that some children suffered from a sense of foreshortened future. The latter has also been reported in adults (Schwarz and Kowalski, 1991). These symptoms can overlap with those related to depression frequently comorbid with PTSD.

It has been noted that avoidance behaviours will depend on the young child's motor capacity (Drell et al., 1993). For an infant up to the age of 12 months, subtle aversion of gaze, turning of the head, or closing the eyes may represent avoidance (Beebe and Lachmann, 1994). Marked anxiety reactions to strange situations in the 6–12 month period may be noted, with more active attempts to get away from trau-matic reminders as the child learns to walk and run. Avoidance behav-iours in young children may take on extremes of generalization perhaps due to developmentally based cognitive capacities. Preschool children who experienced windows being blown out in their day-care center while in the adjacent building to that which was destroyed in the Oklahoma City Bombing would go out of their way to avoid walking near windows in their subsequent schools for some time (Gurwitch, 1998). While social withdrawal, numbing and other dissociative or internalizing symptoms have been observed in very young children (Drell et al., 1993), it is thought that children below the age of 4 may be more likely to exhibit separation anxious clinging, overtly dysregu-lated and externalizing behaviours such as tantrums (Gurwitch, 1998; Perry et al., 1995; Scheeringa and Zeanah, 1995; Thomas, 1995). Terr found that young children tend, rather than to numb or deny the occurrence of an event as in older children and adults, often to day-dream and actively remember the event (Terr, 1987). Whereas denial of death or irreversible damage or change in adults may be defensive, apparent denial of death or permanence in a young child following trauma may relate to that child's developmentally-determined capacity (Pynoos et al., 1995).

In addition to difficulty falling or staying asleep, disruption of feeding schedules, inattention, and increased hypervigilance and startle responses, disturbances of arousal following trauma may take the form of increased irritability and affect dysregulation manifested by increased temper tantrums over minor events. The earlier version of the DSM (prior to DSM-III-R), in an effort to improve the nosology for infants, toddlers and preschool-age children, adds the presence of night terrors (*pavor nocturnis*) to the criteria for the PTSD analogue *Traumatic Stress Disorder*. As opposed to nightmares associated with reexperiencing the trauma, night terrors are considered to be a disturbance of arousal during sleep and involve abrupt awakening in distress often with screaming and crying. Efforts to devise other criteria specific to children and adolescents are ongoing (Scheeringa *et al.*, 1995) and await confirmation.

CULTURAL VARIANTS OF PRESENTATION OF PTSD

Research on cultural variants in the presentation of PTSD is needed. One recent study suggests that some culture-specific idioms of distress such as *ataque de nervios* ("attack of nerves"), a syndrome triggered by stressful events and found in the Caribbean Hispanic culture, may often represent paroxysmal affective and somatosensory dysregulation associated with post-traumatic stress (Schechter *et al.*, 2000).

Epidemiology

PREVALENCE OF PTSD IN THE COMMUNITY

In children and adolescents, PTSD community rates of 1.2% (Fisher *et al.*, 1993), 1.6% (Essau *et al.*, 1999) and 6.3% (Gianconia *et al.*, 1995) have been reported with structured interviews. A study conducted on an American Indian reservation yielded a rate of 3% (Jones *et al.*, 1997). Higher rates have been found with rating scales. For example, prevalence of 25% was reported in a study of 103 high school juniors (Berton and Stabb, 1996), and of 67% in a sample of adolescents attending an urban medical clinic (Horowitz *et al.*, 1995). Essau and colleagues (1999) reported that despite a prevalence of PTSD among 1035 adolescents from a large urban community in northern Germany of 1.6% (17 youths), as many as 22.5% (233) of the whole sample reported one or more traumatic life events.

PREVALENCE OF PTSD IN CHILDREN EXPOSED TO SPECIFIC TRAUMATIC EVENTS

Most studies of PTSD have examined groups exposed to specific traumatic events, and thus at risk for PTSD. Traditionally, these studies have been grouped based on the type of traumatic event, and we follow this categorization in our review. This approach seems sensible, as different events may have unique characteristics that may preclude generalizability to groups exposed to other types of traumatic events.

War: Refugees from conflict in Cambodia have been examined for effects of severe, long term traumatization, often including years spent in concentration camps. Studies of these adolescents and young adults who had been traumatized as children have yielded elevated lifetime rates of PTSD, ranging from 21.5% (Sack *et al.*, 1994) to 59% (Hubbard *et al.*, 1995), based on structured interviews. Other national groups have been studied. Among adolescent and young adult Afghan refugees a 13% rate of PTSD was obtained (Mghir *et al.*, 1995) and 27% in children exposed to the Lebanese Civil War (Saigh, 1989b). In the latter study, in addition to direct injury, threat of direct injury, seeing others injured, or learning of people injured (verbal mediation) all contributed to the development of PTSD. Less than four months after the Gulf War, a 31% PTSD rate was reported in a sample of Kuwaiti children (Nader *et al.*, 1993), but no effect was found for verbal mediation. Three weeks after the war, Israeli school children with high exposure to Scud missile attacks had a 24.9% PTSD rate, compared to 12.9% among those with low exposure (Schwarzwald *et al.*, 1993). Thirty months later, another study of Israeli children reported a rate of 7% (Laor *et al.*, 1997). Finally, applying DSM-IV criteria to a picture instrument, a 94% PTSD rate was reported in a cross sectional survey of 364 Bosnian children who had been displaced from their homes (Goldstein *et al.*, 1997). Disruption of provision for basic needs such as displacement from the home has been found to increase the rate of PTSD in war (Husain *et al.*, 1998). In a study of 239 children ages 6–11 exposed to war in Bosnia (Thabet and Vostanis, 1999), 72.8% were found to have at least mild PTSD symptoms. Forty-one percent were found to have moderate to severe symptoms with criteria met for PTSD among 26.8% of the total sample. This study concluded that the total number of experienced traumatic events was the best predictor of the presence and severity of PTSD symptoms. War, in any case, appears to be a powerful trigger for the development of PTSD in children.

Deliberate Attacks and Witness to Violence: Studies of attacks and violence concern children and adolescents who have witnessed or have been the target of violence, with the exclusion of war and physical and sexual abuse (*Abuse* is considered separate due to its distinguishing features, such as its repetitive nature and the child's frequent familiarity with the perpetrator). Based on clinical interviews, Malmquist reported that all of 16 children who had witnessed parental murder developed PTSD (Malmquist, 1986). Pynoos and Nader (1998) also reported prominent PTSD symptoms in all of 10 children who had witnessed sexual assault of their mothers. These studies, whose cases are perforce few, indicate a very high rate of PTSD in children who witness violence to parents. Two months after witnessing a suicide and accidental shooting on a school-bus, 14% of 32 children had PTSD while a random group from the community had none (0%), a non-significant difference (Brent et al., 1993a). A 36% PTSD rate was reported in 11 adolescents who had been attacked by gunmen while traveling in a van (Trappler and Friedman, 1996). In addition to subjects who witnessed violent events, some studies have included children who were in proximity to events or who were affected through association with victims. Nine months after a school bus accident which occurred during a school trip, 5.6% of 268 children were found to have scores reflective of PTSD on the PTSD-RI (Milgram et al., 1988). An 8% PTSD rate was reported in 64 children, 8–14 months after a school shooting (Schwarz and Kowalski, 1991), however, not all children had witnessed the shooting, and only 16% attended the classroom where the shooting occurred. One hundred and forty-six friends of adolescent suicide completers, some of whom had witnessed the suicide or discovered the body, were interviewed an average of 7 months after the events (Brent et al., 1993b). They had a 5.5% rate of new onset PTSD while a control group from the community had none.

Natural Disasters: Exposure to different natural disasters, including earthquakes, fires, and hurricanes, also has been implicated in PTSD. Pynoos et al. (1993) evaluated a random sample of 231 children 1.5 years after the large scale destruction caused by the 1988 Spitak earthquake in Armenia. A PTSD rate of 70.2% was obtained on the Children's PTSD-RI. In contrast, none of 22 children interviewed 6 months after the Loma Prieta earthquake had a PTSD-RI score associated with the diagnosis (Bradburn, 1991). Several studies have assessed children exposed to hurricanes after various intervals. Three months after hurricane Hugo, 5.42% of 5,687 school children were judged to have PTSD (Shannon et al., 1994). One year after the hurricane, a 4% PTSD rate was found in 1264 high school students (Garrison et al., 1993). Two months after hurricane Andrew, PTSD rates of 38.6% in a low impact, and 56.4% in a high impact area were reported based on self report questionnaires in 106 children. Between group PTSD-RI symptomatology scores were not significantly different (Shaw *et al.*, 1995). Four months later, six months after the hurricane, through telephone interviews with 400 adolescents, much lower PTSD rates were obtained, 9.2% in girls, 2.9% in boys, with an overall rate of 7% (Garrison *et al.*, 1995). In a controlled study, a 12% PTSD rate was reported in a group of 25 school boys who survived a dormitory fire, while among 13 adolescents who were not dormitory residents and thus had not experienced the fire, none had PTSD (Jones and Ribbe, 1991). PTSD was found in 9% of 33 children exposed to wild fires in southern California (Jones *et al.*, 1994), and 11.9% of 1,019 students, 9 months after a severe industrial fire in the community (March *et al.*, 1997).

Physical and Sexual Abuse: Most studies of PTSD in young victims of physical and sexual abuse have focused on referred samples. PTSD rates have ranged from 18.2% in 95 sexually abused children referred from community agencies (Merry and Andrews, 1994), to 90% in 10 preschoolers purportedly sexually abused in a day care setting (Kiser *et al.*, 1988). Few studies have focused on physical abuse alone. An 11% PTSD rate was reported in a study of 27 physically abused adolescents, however further investigation suggested that the PTSD may have been the result of previously undisclosed sexual abuse, rather than physical abuse (Pelcovitz *et al.*, 1995).

Studies have also compared rates between abused and non-abused children, and between various types of abuse. A chart review of 29 sexually abused, 29 physically abused, and 29 non-abused inpatients yielded respective PTSD rates of 20.7%, 6.9%, 10.3%, non-significant differences (Deblinger *et al.*, 1989). In another study, 26 sexually abused children had a 42.3% PTSD rate, compared to 8.7% in 23 non-abused clinical controls (McLeer *et al.*, 1994). In a study of 48 depressed inpatients, 24 of whom had a history of sexual abuse, PTSD was present in 45.5% of abused children vs. 0% in the non-abused (Brand *et al.*, 1996).

Most recently, a case-control study of victims of substantiated child abuse and neglect from 1967–1971 (N=676) were compared to an age- and socioeconomic status-matched control group of nonabused and non-neglected individuals (N=520) after being followed prospectively into adulthood (Widom, 1999). A total of 1,196 adult subjects were located and administered the Diagnostic Interview Schedule to assess PTSD. Childhood victimization was clearly associated with increased risk for lifetime and current PTSD: more than a third of the sexual abuse victims (37.5%) and 32.7% of the physical abuse victims not otherwise sexually abused, as well as 30.6% of the neglected individuals met DSM-III-R criteria for lifetime PTSD. The relationship between childhood maltreatment and number of PTSD symptoms persisted despite the introduction of covariates with risk for both (Widom, 1999).

Illness and Injury: In thirty 7–19 year old burn victims, with an average time since injury of 9 years, a present PTSD rate of 6.7%, and a lifetime rate of 30% were reported (Stoddard *et al.*, 1989). In fifty-seven 5–18 year old road traffic accident victims, PTSD was reported in 14%, 12–15 weeks after the accidents (Di Gallo *et al.*, 1997). In another study of 119 school-age child traffic accident victims as compared to a control group of 66 children who had sustained injuries during sports, 34.5% of the traffic accident victims were noted to have had PTSD; whereas, only 3% of the children with sports-related injuries met criteria for PTSD (Stallard *et al.*, 1998).

A 12% PTSD rate was reported in a follow up study of 64 pediatric leukemia survivors an average 6.7 years after treatment (Stuber *et al.*, 1996a). However, a study of 30 children who underwent bone marrow transplants found no instances of PTSD (Stuber *et al.*, 1996b). In a study of 23 adolescent cancer patients as compared to 27 physically abused adolescents, as many as 35% of the cancer patients met criteria for PTSD versus 11% of the physically abused children (Pelcovitz *et al.*, 1998). Increasing the risk for PTSD among the cancer patients in this study were poor family functioning and/or a parent with PTSD.

Assessment

Assessment of PTSD requires determining symptom severity and diagnostic thresholds, whether onset occurred following a traumatic event, and the presence of other disorders (Carlson, 1997). With children, assessment of PTSD should involve a face-to-face interview when possible, as well as observation of behavior during play for younger children and similar behavioral observation throughout the interview-process particularly for school-age children and adolescents. Parallel history from the caregivers, school, and when applicable, police, rescue and medical personnel or eye-witnesses is often important because even verbal children and adolescents may not report the full extent of traumatic exposure or range of posttraumatic stress symptoms (Nader *et al.*, 1991; Perrin *et al.*, 2000).

Structured and semi-structured diagnostic interviews aim to address many of these questions. However, they are time consuming and can be costly. Only two such interviews have demonstrated reliability and validity thus far (Perrin *et al.*, 2000): the Schedule for Affective Disorders and Schizophrenia for School-Age Children—Present and Lifetime Version, PTSD scale (K-SADS-PL: Kaufman *et al.*, 1997) and the Childhood PTSD Interview-Child Form (Fletcher, 1997). It is important to note that, therefore, most studies of child and adolescent PTSD have used self-rating scales such as the Impact of Events Scale (IES) (Horowitz *et al.*, 1979) and PTSD Reaction Index (PTSD-RI) (Frederick, 1985), which are easier and less expensive to administer than comprehensive diagnostic instruments. Cutoffs indicative of a diagnosis of PTSD have been put forth for the PTSD-RI. Goenjian and colleagues (1994, 1995) studied 60 earthquake survivors who were clinically interviewed in addition to being administered the PTSD-RI. Comparing the results of the two procedures, they found high sensitivity and specificity for detecting cases with a diagnosis of PTSD using the PTSD-RI (Goenjian *et al.*, 1994, 1995; Pynoos *et al.*, 1993).

Most recently, a cartoon-based measure of cardinal post-traumatic stress symptoms in school-age children has been published, the Darryl (Neugebauer *et al.*, 1999). The instrument measures exposure to community violence from child and parent reports and has shown good reliability overall and acceptable reliability for reexperiencing, avoidance, and arousal symptom clusters. A PTSD measure for very young children ages 12–48 months based on the Scheeringa criteria (1995) is being developed as part of the Infant Toddler Social Emotional Assessment (Briggs-Gowan and Carter, 1998).

Finally, while physiologic measures of arousal such as galvanic skin response, heart rate, and respiration may help validate self-reports and provide useful information for assessment especially of non-verbal children, these measures have not been validated for clinical purposes, are expensive, and not widely available (Perrin *et al.*, 2000).

Risk Factors

While many children exposed to traumatic events may develop PTSD, many do not. The question arises as to what factors place children at risk for PTSD. The identification of risk factors could ultimately facilitate identification of and prevention for children at risk. We address factors associated with a diagnosis of PTSD separately from symptoms of post-traumatic stress, since these may differ.

FEATURES OF THE TRAUMATIC EVENT

Degree of exposure: Trauma response has been shown to correlate with degree of trauma exposure, measured both in terms of physical and emotional proximity. Physical proximity may range from an event happening to the individual, versus witnessing an event from a spectrum of distances, to hearing of it or witnessing its after-effects. Emotional proximity refers to the degree of emotional involvement with the event. Physical proximity to the source of violent threat, severity of an earthquake, and number of traumatic incidents experienced are some of the ways by which severity of exposure has been defined. Comparisons have usually been made within exposed groups, with only a few exceptions that compare exposed to non-exposed individuals. The weight of the evidence supports a significant positive association between degree of exposure and PTSD (Burton *et al.*, 1994; Brent *et al.*, 1995; Hubbard *et al.*, 1995; Lonigan *et al.*, 1994; Mghir *et al.*, 1995; Sack *et al.*, 1993; Schwarzwald *et al.*, 1993). Many studies have also found an association between exposure and severity of post-traumatic stress symptoms (Bradburn, 1991; Jones and Ribbe, 1991; Longian *et al.*, 1991; Pynoos *et al.*, 1987; Nader *et al.*, 1993) with one exception (Shaw *et al.*, 1995). In a study of Kuwaiti children after the Gulf War, exposure to violence on TV was associated with post-traumatic stress symptom severity, as was having hurt someone during a confrontation (Nader *et al.*, 1993).

Emotional proximity to victims: Degree of friendship, or perceived closeness to victims of traumatic events, has been reported to be a potential contributor to PTSD. Closeness to victims was associated with PTSD in friends of adolescents who committed suicide (Brent *et al.*, 1995). Several studies have found an association between closeness to victims in a shared traumatic event and acute posttraumatic stress symptom severity (Goenjian *et al.*, 1995; Milgram *et al.*, 1988; Pynoos *et al.*, 1987, 1993), while one has not (Brent *et al.*, 1993a). Though found to have a significant effect on posttraumatic stress symptoms one month after a school shooting, at 14 month follow up, closeness to victims was associated with symptom levels only for children who had little exposure to the event themselves (Nader *et al.*, 1990). Therefore the significance of this effect may change over time, as may be the case with other risk factors.

Destruction of residence: Associations to degree of damage have been reported for PTSD after a hurricane (Lonigan *et al.*, 1994) and for posttraumatic stress symptom severity after wild fires in California (Jones *et al.*, 1994). Goenjian failed to find a similar association in Armenia, among survivors of an earthquake that led to large scale destruction (Goenjian *et al.*, 1995). Studies of children who lost their homes during the Bosnian War have shown a strong association to PTSD (Husain, 1998).

CHILDREN'S FEATURES

Age: Many studies have failed to find any relationship between age and PTSD (Burton *et al.*, 1994; Famularo *et al.*, 1993; Fisher *et al.*, 1993; Green *et al.*, 1994; Schwarzwald *et al.*, 1993). There have been reports of a positive association between age and PTSD (Brent *et al.*, 1995; Garrison *et al.*, 1993; Sack *et al.*, 1994), and one report of an opposite association, i.e. with younger age (Shannon *et al.*, 1994). With regard to symptom severity, findings are inconsistent. Several studies have found that older age is associated with severity (Longian *et al.*, 1991; Nader *et al.*, 1993) while others have not (Green *et al.*, 1994; Nader *et al.*, 1990; Pynoos *et al.*, 1987; Shaw *et al.*, 1995; Yule, 1992). This may have been related to the difficulty in applying standard criteria for PTSD to younger children (Drell *et al.*, 1993; Scheeringa and Zeanah, 1995).

Sex: Reports are equivocal about gender differences as they relate to risk for PTSD. Some studies have found girls to be over-represented among children who developed PTSD (Garrison *et al.*, 1993; Gianconia *et al.*, 1995; Shannon *et al.*, 1994). An association between female sex and PTSD symptoms has also been reported (Horowitz *et al.*, 1995; Hubbard *et al.*, 1995; Longian *et al.*, 1991; Pynoos *et al.*, 1993; Schwarzwald *et al.*, 1993; Yule, 1992), but not consistently (Nader *et al.*, 1990; Nader *et al.*, 1993; Garrison *et al.*, 1995; Pynoos *et al.*, 1987; Shaw *et al.*, 1995). Cauffman *et al.* (1998) reported that incarcerated girls had more and worse PTSD symptoms than incarcerated boys. One thought is that boys with disruptive behaviour and/or substance abuse may have PTSD that is missed.

Race/Ethnicity: In general, studies have not found any relationship between race/ethnicity and PTSD (Famularo *et al.*, 1993; Burton *et al.*, 1994; Garrison *et al.*, 1995; Shannon *et al.*, 1994). Similarly, several studies have been unable to find a race/ethnicity effect for posttraumatic stress symptoms (Nader *et al.*, 1990; Pynoos *et al.*, 1987;

Shaw *et al.*, 1995). In light of these studies, one report of an association of PTSD with being white (Garrison *et al.*, 1995), and another
with being African American (Lonigan *et al.*, 1991) are likely to represent chance findings. Some studies have suggested however that
refugees fleeing from violence and state terror such as in Southeast Asia
have an unusually high prevalence of PTSD (Mollica *et al.*, 1987). Such
prevalence could conceivably be misattributed to ethnicity by a socio-
culturally unaware researcher.

Income: A community study (Fisher *et al.*, 1993) found low income
to be associated with a heightened risk for developing PTSD, while
studies of Cambodian refugees (Sack *et al.*, 1993) and juvenile offenders (Burton *et al.*, 1994) did not. It is possible that lower income in the
population may aggravate consequences of traumatic events, whereas
this effect is not detectable in samples pre-selected for traumatic exposure from referred populations.

OTHER VARIABLES

Past psychiatric history: High trait anxiety ratings have been reported
to be associated with development of PTSD (Longian *et al.*, 1994).
Prospectively, while children post-natural disaster diagnosed with
PTSD tended to have depressive symptoms, premorbid depression was
not found to be a significant risk factor; premorbid anxiety symptoms
and/or disorder was associated with risk for PTSD (Asarnow *et al.*,
1999; La Greca *et al.*, 1998). In another study, while attention deficit
disorder was not associated with risk for trauma-exposure, bipolar disorder and/or depression independent of presence of attention deficit
disorder was suggested as a significant risk factor for subsequent exposure to traumatic stress (Wozniak *et al.*, 1999). Widom (1999) found a
significant association of three or more conduct disorder symptoms
prior to age 15 and any DSM-III-R diagnosis of alcohol or drug abuse
or dependence from childhood on, as associated with lifetime risk
factors for PTSD among adults with a verified history of childhood
abuse and/or neglect. In contrast, other studies have not found an association between PTSD and past psychiatric history (Burton *et al.*,
1994), or substance abuse history (Brent *et al.*, 1995). In adolescents
exposed to peer suicide, a previous history of suicide attempt was associated with post-traumatic stress symptoms (Brent *et al.*, 1995).
Inversely, child and adolescent psychiatric patients were found to experience more behaviour-dependent and -independent adverse life events
than either healthy controls or asthma patients (Sandberg *et al.*, 1998).

Attachment security: As suggested by the developmental model of traumatic stress (Pynoos *et al.*, 1995), traumatic stress can affect the developing young child's expectations of the world and of his/her place with other individuals. Conversely, the caregiving environment and the degree of security of attachment to the caregiver(s) in formative development can affect the child's vulnerability and response to traumatic stress (Cicchetti and Cohen, 1995; Cicchetti and Lynch, 1993; Scheeringa *et al.*, 1995). It has been hypothesized that the caregiver's protective function and ability to serve as a secure base can shield the child both from the occurrence of some traumatic events as well as the sequelae of traumatic events when they do occur (Bowlby, 1988). There is some evidence for this in the literature particularly in regard to sexual abuse related to which, the parent-child relationship, along with the parent's knowledge of the trauma's occurence and response to disclosure has been studied (Cohen and Mannarino, 1998; Fergusson *et al.*, 1996). When the caregiver on whom the child depends for survival, herself becomes a potential threat to survival as in the case of the maltreating parent, a complex adaptation involving hypervigilance, conflicting approach/avoidance behaviours, as well as an increased potential for dissociative phenomena develops. Such a complex response associated with "frightening/frightened behaviour" by the caregiver has been termed insecure attachment, disorganized-disoriented type (Lyons-Ruth and Jacobvitz, 1999). Disruptive and hostile-aggressive behaviour subsequently in the child has been associated with this type of attachment, linking it to intergenerational transmission of trauma (Lyons-Ruth *et al.*, 1993, 1997; Lyons-Ruth and Block, 1996; Zeanah *et al.*, 1997).

Other Family factors: Parental psychopathology, particularly anxiety, that might compromise parental capacity to cope with the child's traumatic stress and provide sufficient protective monitoring has been associated with increased occurrence of adverse life events and with diagnosis of PTSD in the child (Pelcovitz *et al.*, 1998; Tiet *et al.*, 1998). In a group of Cambodian refugees, children were more likely to have PTSD if their parents had PTSD (Sack *et al.*, 1995). Affective disorders, particularly bipolar disorder and substance abuse disorders diagnosed in the caregiver have been additionally associated with risk for inconsistent, impulsive, violent and poorly protective behaviour, placing the child at risk for traumatic stress, disruptive and/or violent behaviour, as well as disorganized attachment behaviour (Lyons-Ruth *et al.*, 1993; Lyons-Ruth and Block, 1996; Lyons-Ruth and Jacobvitz, 1999). A significant effect for family history was not found in social networks of suicide victims (Brent *et al.*, 1995). Continued maternal preoccupation with the event (McFarlane, 1987), irritable, depressed family atmosphere and separation from parents and change of family functioning after a disaster (McFarlane, 1987) have all been reported to be associated with post-traumatic stress symptoms in children. Widom (1999) found that family factors significantly associated with lifetime risk for PTSD among adult survivors of child maltreatment and neglect included: an arrested parent, a parent with substance abuse problems, and five or more children in the home.

Preoccupation with violence: While some children and adolescents with PTSD who have been victims of violent trauma, will attempt to avoid violence, preoccupation with violence may be a risk factor for PTSD. Viewing preferences of violent action television programs, associated with a caregiving environment in which viewing of such programs occurs, have not only been significantly associated with severity of PTSD symptoms and violent behaviour, but also with a higher level of traumatic life events in a community-based study of 2245 7–14 year-old children (Singer *et al.*, 1998).

Comorbidity

One study (Hubbard *et al.*, 1991) reported 59% of Cambodian refugees with PTSD had an accompanying diagnosis. Twenty-nine percent had somatoform pain disorder, 21% had generalized anxiety disorder, 19% had social phobia, 21% had current MDD, and 57% a lifetime history of MDD. Kinzie and colleagues (1989) reported that 50% of 30 Cambodian refugees with PTSD had a comorbid Major Depressive Disorder(MDD). Interestingly, 6 years later the MDD rate had dropped to 6%, while the PTSD rate remained relatively stable at 38% (Sack *et al.*, 1993). Other studies have also reported associations between PTSD and MDD (Brent *et al.*, 1995; Fisher *et al.*, 1993; Giaconia *et al.*, 1995; Sack *et al.*, 1994). Additionally, associations have been reported between PTSD and generalized anxiety disorder (Fisher *et al.*, 1993), conduct disorder (Cauffman *et al.*, 1998; Fisher *et al.*, 1993), attention-deficit hyperactivity disorder (ADHD) (Famularo *et al.*, 1996b), borderline personality disorder (Famularo *et al.*, 1991), and substance abuse (Deykin and Buka, 1997; Fisher *et al.*, 1993). One study reported that PTSD preceded or coincided with onset of substance abuse (Giaconia *et al.*, 1995), though onsets have not always been clearly separable (Deykin and Buka, 1997).

Course and Outcome

Two questions are relevant to the course of PTSD. One, when do symptoms first appear? Two, what is the time course of these symptoms? In a sample of children who had initially been studied one month after a sniper attack at school, symptoms had decreased significantly after fourteen months (Nader *et al.*, 1991). However, children who had been under the greatest threat were still symptomatic. Children who did not have an initial reaction to the event rarely (1%) developed symptoms. Similarly, a 9 month follow-up of children exposed to a bus accident found that there were few instances of delayed reactions (Milgram *et al.*, 1988). In a cohort of Cambodian refugees in which a 50% PTSD rate had initially been noted, the rate dropped to 38% over 6 years (Sack *et al.*, 1994). Other studies have similarly found that though rates decrease over time, many children continue to have symptoms of PTSD (Shaw *et al.*, 1996) and meet criteria for diagnosis (Green *et al.*, 1994). These findings suggest that identification of PTSD must take place soon after the traumatic experience, or it is likely that long term care will be required, but only in a subset of affected children.

Use of Health Care Services and Intervention

There are no published studies specifically of health care service utilization by child and/or adolescent patients with PTSD. One may infer that PTSD-associated disturbances in behaviour and somatosensory arousal regulation would lead to increased use of emergency care and crisis intervention services. Indeed, a high correlation between adolescent suicide attempts and PTSD has been noted (Wunderlich *et al.*, 1998). A non-specific association between functional socioemotional impairment including disruptive behaviour in preschool-age children and frequency of emergency department visits has also been described (Lavigne *et al.*, 1998).

Information on crisis intervention for children and adolescents with PTSD is limited. A two session debriefing procedure consisting of a problem solving approach based on cognitive behavioural methods was administered to adolescent survivors 10 days after a cruise-ship sinking (Yule, 1992). Five to nine months later, PTSD scores were significantly lower for students who had received the intervention compared to those who had not. There is some empirical evidence to support that early intervention with at-risk infants and mothers may improve the security of attachment and thereby lessen the risk for traumatic stress (van den Boom and Hoeksma, 1994). Additionally, studies of clinicians accompanying police officers to intervene at violent crime scenes, in which children have been exposed, are underway at Yale University and other U.S. sites.

PSYCHOTHERAPEUTIC TREATMENT

Post-traumatic conditions have been treated with psychotherapy for more than a century (Terr, 1987; Freud, 1959/1926). Many case-reports of children and adolescents describe abatement of distress, improved functioning and psychosocial development following a course of psychotherapy (Coates and Moore, 1997; Gaensbauer and Siegal, 1995; Pynoos and Nader, 1988; Terr, 1981; Zeanah et al., 1997). The principle by which most psychotherapy for PTSD in these case-reports is thought to be mutative lies essentially in the therapist's creating for the child a safe and tolerant atmosphere in which the child may communicate his or her traumatic experience through play, action and language. Painful affects (terror, rage, grief) associated with the experience, and which may have been dissociated from reenactment, such as in compulsive posttraumatic play, are labeled and reassociated with thoughts and actions gradually with the therapist's help. Assistance with the containment and regulation of negative affect along with reflection on the meaning of the trauma to the child, the latter involving the benefit of joint attention by the child and therapist, are essential components of the therapy. This occurs often through a reworking of the child's experience(s) through reparative play often with verbal clarification and interpretation by the therapist, who is both an empathic listener as well as the holder of an alternative perspective.

Whichever form of psychotherapy for childhood PTSD is employed, careful assessment of the child and environmental risk, along with establishment of a trusting treatment alliance with both child and caregivers, are prerequisite to any therapeutic work taking place (Perrin et al., 2000). One common barrier to success in psychotherapy with PTSD-afflicted children is the inability of the therapist to protect the child from further trauma such as in the instance of the child living with abusive caretakers or suffering from a life-threatening illness in an insufficiently supportive caregiving environment (Cohen and

Mannarino, 1998; Pynoos *et al.*, 1995). In such cases, no feasible frame nor adequate treatment alliance can be formed to support the therapy. Hence, the therapist may need to intervene as advocate for the child outside the therapist-patient relationship in order to protect the child and to allow the possibility for subsequent psychotherapy. Important to psychotherapy is a full and thoughtful evaluation that allows the child to tell the story of what he/she experienced freely through play and/or language whenever possible. What the child considers to be traumatic about an event may differ from what the clinician would assume to be traumatic (Pynoos *et al.*, 1995).

Despite the frequency with which psychotherapy is used to treat PTSD, outcome research is lacking, partly due to the inherent difficulty in carrying out controlled studies with a standard, manualized treatment. Studies that have been done to date often therefore involve discrete and operationalized therapies requiring highly trained clinicians. As such, Cognitive-Behavioral Therapy (CBT) is the most frequently studied form of treatment and has been subjected to the greatest number of rigorously controlled investigations for PTSD in adults (Foa and Meadows, 1997).

CBT for PTSD essentially combines classical and operant conditioning with cognitive restructuring to reduce anxiety. The treatment has four main components: (1) education/goal-setting, (2) coping skill development, (3) exposure, and (4) termination and relapse prevention (Perrin *et al.*, 2000).

While a careful study of 80 sexually abused children randomized to a traditional psychodynamically oriented treatment and CBT showed marked improvement for both groups with no significant differences (Berliner and Saunders, 1996), two similarly careful, longitudinal studies of 86 randomly assigned sexually abused preschoolers, and then 49 similar subjects of school-age, to either a trauma-focused CBT or nondirective supportive therapy, demonstrated in both age-groups that the CBT condition was associated with greater symptom reduction that was also maintained at 6- and 12-month follow-up assessments (Cohen and Mannarino, 1998). A 12-session cognitive behavioral treatment protocol was reported to decrease PTSD, as well as depressive and anxiety symptoms in 19, 3 to 16 year old sexually abused girls with PTSD (Deblinger *et al.*, 1990), and was subsequently found to be superior to traditional group therapy for this population (Deblinger *et al.*, 1999). Similarly, cognitive behavioral psychotherapy has been shown to diminish PTSD symptoms associated with single-incident stressors (March *et al.*, 1998).

Controlled studies in adults have also shown benefit of flooding, stress inoculation training, and prolonged exposure treatment (Foa *et al.*, 1991). In vitro flooding has been reported successful in case-reports of four children with PTSD (Saigh, 1989a). Eye movement desensitization and reprocessing (EMDR), involving therapist-induced saccadic eye movements to prompt physiologic regulation during imaging of the trauma as well as hypnotherapy are controversial treatments for PTSD that have not yet been systematically studied in children despite case-reports supporting their usefulness (Perrin *et al.*, 2000).

Psychodynamically-oriented parent-child treatment of preschool-age children who had been sexually abused showed sustained effects in 6- and 12-month follow-ups in one uncontrolled study, in which correlational and stepwise multiple regression analyses showed the best sustained outcome for children whose mothers had self-perceived adequate social supports and whom clinicians perceived were able to provide adequate support for their children during treatment (Cohen and Mannarino, 1998).

A 20 week group treatment program with therapeutic disclosure and processing of victimization memories led to decreased PTSD symptoms in 43 sexually abused adolescent girls at a group home (diagnoses are not reported) (Sinclair *et al.*, 1995). Last, a trauma and grief focused school-based treatment involving group and individual sessions was administered to 35 school children 18 months after a devastating earthquake (Goenjian *et al.*, 1997). Their outcome was compared to 29 children with similar PTSD rates who attended a school where the treatment was not implemented. The estimated PTSD rate was significantly lower in the treated compared to the untreated children, 28% vs. 69%.

PSYCHOPHARMACOLOGICAL TREATMENT

Medication can relieve PTSD symptoms leading to distress and dysfunction quickly. Psychopharmacologic treatment can also permit psychotherapy to begin or continue with a heightened sense of safety, as well as increased tolerance if not containment of anxiety. While more research is needed, a number of studies involving a variety of medications have been done.

In a 4 week open trial, 11 children with PTSD with a mean age of 8.5 years were treated with propranolol 0.8 mg/kg/d to 5 mg/kg/d (Famularo *et al.*, 1988). Mean PTSD scores were significantly lower with propranolol, compared to before treatment, and 3 weeks after discontinuation. In a study of 7 preschoolers with a clinical diagnosis of PTSD, treatment with clonidine, 0.1 to 0.2 mg/d led to general improvement in all children, and to decrease in PTSD specific symptoms in some (Harmon and Riggs, 1996). In another report, when a 7 year-old child with PTSD related nightmares ceased to benefit from clonidine treatment, guanfacine was substituted with success (Horrigan, 1996). Additionally, some medications FDA-approved for children for other indications, in open-trials with adults, such as cyproheptadine have been reported to reduce the frequency of nightmares (Neylan, 1999). Of note, there are no randomized placebo-controlled studies of any hypnotic medication for PTSD for children or adults. Carbemazepine was studied at doses of 300–1200 mg/d in 28, 8 to 17 year-old children with complex presentations, histories of repetitive trauma, and primary diagnoses of PTSD (Looff et al., 1995). Seventy-nine percent became asymptomatic and the remaining 21% improved moderately. Similarly promising randomized controlled studies of divalproex and gabapentin in victims of sexual abuse are ongoing (Donnelly et al., 1999; Goldberg et al., 1999).

As is the case with psychotherapy reports, the absence of controlled treatment contexts precludes inference about the clinical efficacy of the agents used in children with PTSD (Donnelly et al., 1999). While not yet well-studied in children, some randomized controlled pilot studies with adults have suggested for several years already that serotonin-reuptake inhibitors (SSRIs) such as fluoxetine, paroxetine and sertraline may be effective in reducing PTSD symptoms at least in the arousal cluster (Marshall et al., 1996). Sertraline is however the first medication with specific indication for PTSD to have been approved by the United States Food and Drug Administration (FDA) for adults (Gottlieb, 1999). Other SSRIs such as fluoxetine are under consideration for similar approval (Connor et al., 1999). In one of the largest randomized, controlled trials of sertraline involving study of 187 adult outpatients with PTSD, significant reduction of symptoms in the arousal and avoidance, but not reexperiencing clusters on the Clinician Administered PTSD Scale Part-2 (CAPS-2) was noted (Brady et al., 2000). While men showed a less significant effect between sertraline (flexibly dosed from 50 to 200 mg. per day) and placebo, gender differences in this study are difficult to assess given that 73% of the sample were women.

One recent controlled pilot study of treatment of 25 pediatric burn unit patients ages 2–19 years with imipramine versus chloral hydrate suggested a place for cautious initial use for such patients of imipramine to reduce symptoms of DSM-IV defined *Acute Stress Disorder* (i.e., a post-traumatic syndrome lasting 2 days to 4 weeks and occurring within 4 weeks of the traumatic event) (Robert *et al.*, 1999). Monitoring for cardiovasular risks associated with this medication is recommended.

Conclusion

Most of the research has been conducted on the epidemiology of children and adolescents exposed to specific traumatic events. Though there is considerable variation in rates, due in part to methodological differences such as sample selection, diagnostic criteria and instruments, it is clear that PTSD may develop from infancy through adolescence after exposure to various types of traumatic events. The scarcity of community studies precludes reasonable estimates of the prevalence of PTSD in the general child and adolescent population; however there is strong evidence indicating those exposed to war, natural disasters, violence, and sexual assault are at relatively high risk for PTSD. Among these, highest rates seem to result from war, possibly due to the pervasive effect of the trauma, not only on the child, but also the family and community.

Estimates have ranged from 13% to 94% depending on the specific population, degree of exposure to war, time elapsed since the traumatic events, and diagnostic method. PTSD rates of about 30% are the most common. Rates appear to increase when children have been brutalized, as was likely the case for those in concentration camps. In one study, rape was seven times more likely to lead to PTSD than other physical violence (Giaconia *et al.*, 1995). Direct threat or assault may not be necessary for PTSD symptoms to develop. Witnessing violence alone has been associated with PTSD.

Information about the immediate and subsequent psychological consequences of natural disasters has public health implications because it provides the basis for estimating the need for prompt implementation of potentially appropriate interventions in affected areas. From existing data, long term consequences of earthquakes appear highly inconsistent, with prevalence of PTSD varying from 0% in a small US sample (Bradburn, 1991) to 70% in Armenia (Pynoos *et al.*, 1993). It is likely that the immense destruction occurring in the latter played a significant role in the outcome. The limited scope of the US study precludes conjectures regarding potential cultural differences in children's responses to natural disasters. On the whole, rates of PTSD following natural disasters appear considerably lower than those associated with war.

While there is clear evidence of an association between sexual abuse and PTSD, a similarly strong relationship has not been established for physical abuse. The minimal data on physical abuse may be related to the frequent coexistence of various types of maltreatment, especially in referred samples. Children who are physically abused to a degree sufficient to warrant clinical attention may often also have histories of neglect or sexual abuse. Moreover, PTSD subsequent to illness, hospitalization, and medical procedures is understudied, especially in view of the large number of whom experience these stresses.

PTSD is often associated with other psychiatric diagnoses such as depressive disorders and anxiety disorders (Wunderlich et al., 1998; Wozniak et al., 1999). Depressive disorders and PTSD seem to co-occur frequently, although it is not clear if depression remains in chronic PTSD. The discrepancy between the co-occurence of major depressive disorder (MDD) at the initiation and maintenance points of PTSD precludes a straightforward interpretation of their relationship. It is possible that trauma may trigger both MDD and PTSD, but that the two disorders have independent origins and course. Associations between PTSD, anxiety disorders, and substance abuse have also been reported (Asarnow et al., 1999; Fisher et al., 1993; Wunderlich et al., 1998). What may link these disorders is dysregulation of affect and autonomic regulation as early as from infancy in at least some cases.

The study of treatment and prevention of child and adolescent PTSD have been seriously neglected. Though disasters have provided the opportunity to investigate early interventions aiming to prevent the development of PTSD, the evidence is limited. Systematic controlled studies will be necessary before preventive methods are assumed to be effective and are applied widely (Raphael and Meldrum, 1995). In clinical reports, psychotherapy as well as medication have been noted to provide benefit to children with PTSD. No controlled studies have been reported, and the field is still limited in its ability to infer merit for any one treatment of children with PTSD (Pfefferbaum, 1997).

As one can see from this review chapter, while a large and growing literature about PTSD in children has accumulated over the past decade, this literature remains predominantly phenomenological. The developmental considerations alluded to in this chapter await further study and elaboration. Similarly, neurohormonal and physiologic correlates of PTSD in children continue to become clearer (Perry *et al.*, psychotherapy 1995; Perry and Pollard, 1998). The neurodevelopmental role vis a vis etiology and the relationship to specific PTSD symptoms or symptom clusters, as well as their influence on long-term adaptation remain to be explored.

In sum, PTSD provides a fascinating opportunity for the study of the interplay of environment, biology, human psychology and development in the pathogenesis of a mental disorder. Prevention and effective intervention depend therefore on the interdisciplinary understanding of coping and resilience factors for children and their families from infancy through adulthood.

References

Allen, J.R., Heston, J., Durbin, C., & Pruitt, D.B. (1998). Stressors and development: A reciprocal relationship. *Child and Adolescent Psychiatric Clinics of North America, 7,* 1–17.

American Psychiatric Association. (1980). *Diagnostic and statistical manual of mental disorders* (3rd ed.). Washington, D.C.: Author.

American Psychiatric Association. (1987). *Diagnostic and statistical manual of mental disorders* (3rd ed. rev.). Washington, D.C.: Author.

American Psychiatric Association. (1994). *Diagnostic and statistical manual of mental disorders* (4th ed.). Washington, D.C.: Author.

Asarnow, J., Glynn, S., Pynoos, R.S., Nahum, J., Guthrie, D., Cantwell, D.P., & Franklin, B. (1999). When the earth stops shaking: Earthquake sequelae among children diagnosed for pre-earthquake psychopathology. *Journal of the American Academy of Child and Adolescent Psychiatry, 38,* 1016–23.

Beebe, B. & Lachmann, F. (1994). Representation and internalization in infancy: Three principles of salience. *Psychoanalytic Psychology, 11,* 127–165.

Berliner L, Saunders B.E. (1996). Treating fear and anxiety in sexually abused children: Results of controlled 2-year follow-up study. *Child Maltreatment, 1,* 294–309.

Berton, M.W. & Stabb, S.D. (1996). Exposure to violence and posttraumatic stress in urban adolescents. *Adolescence, 31,* 489–498.

Bowlby, J. (1988). *A secure base.* New York: Basic Books.

Bradburn, I.S., (1991). After the earth shook: Children's stress symptoms 6–8 months after a disaster. *Advanced Behavioral Research and Therapy, 3,* 173–179.

Brady K., Pearlstein T., Asnis G.M., Baker D., Rothbaum B., Sikes C.R., & Farfel G.M. (2000). Efficacy and safety of sertraline treatment of posttraumatic stress disorder: A randomized controlled trial. *Journal of the American Medical Association, 283*(14), 1837–1844.

Brand, E.F., King, C.A., Olson, E., Ghaziuddin, N., & Naylor, M. (1996). Depressed adolescents with a history of sexual abuse: diagnostic comorbidity and suicidality. *Journal of the American Academy of Child and Adolescent Psychiatry, 35*, 34–41.

Brent, D.A., Perper, J., Moritz, G., Friend, A., Schweers, J., Allman, C., McQuiston, L., Boylan, M.B., Roth, C., & Balach, L. (1993a). Adolescent witnesses to a peer suicide. *Journal of the American Academy of Child and Adolescent Psychiatry, 32*, 1184–1188.

Brent, D.A., Perper, J.A., Moritz, G., Allman, C., Schweers, J., Roth, C., Balach, L., Canobbio, R. & Liotus, L. (1993b). Psychiatric sequelae to the loss of an adolescent peer to suicide. *Journal of the American Academy of Child and Adolescent Psychiatry, 32*, 509–517.

Brent, D.A., Perper, J.A., Moritz, G., Liotus, L., Richardson, D., Canobbio, R., Schweers, J., & Roth, C. (1995). Post-traumatic stress disorder in peers of adolescent suicide victims: predisposing factors and phenomenology. *Journal of the American Academy of Child and Adolescent Psychiatry, 34*, 209–215.

Breslau, N., Chilcoat, H.D., Kessler, D., & Davis, G.C. (1999). Previous exposure to trauma and PTSD effects of subsequent trauma: Results from Detroit area survey of trauma. *American Journal of Psychiatry, 156*, 902–907.

Briggs-Gowan, M.J. & Carter, A.S. (1998). Preliminary acceptability and psychometrics of the Infant-Toddler Social and Emotional Assessment (ITSEA): A new adult-report questionnaire. *Infant Mental Health Journal, 19*, 422–445.

Burton, D., Foy, D., Bwanausi, C., Johnson, J., & Moore, L. (1994). The relationship between traumatic exposure, family dysfunction, and post-traumatic stress symptoms in male juvenile offenders. *Journal of Traumatic Stress, 7*, 83–93.

Butler, R.W., Mueser, K.T., Sprock, J., & Braff, D.L. (1996). Positive symptoms of psychosis in posttraumatic stress disorder. *Biological Psychiatry, 39*, 839–844.

Carlson, E.B. (1997). *Trauma assessments: A clinician's guide.* New York: The Guilford Press.

Cauffman, E., Feldman, S.S., Waterman, J., & Steiner, H. (1998). PTSD among female juvenile offenders. *Journal of the American Academy of Child and Adolescent Psychiatry, 37*, 1209–1216.

Chaffin, M., Kelleher, K., & Hollenberg, J. (1996). Onset of physical abuse and neglect: Psychiatric, substance abuse and social risk factors from prospective community data. *Child Abuse & Neglect, 20*, 191–203.

Cicchetti, D. & Cohen, D.J. (Eds). (1995). *Developmental psychopathology: Risk, disorder, and adaptation.* New York: John Wiley & Sons, Inc.

Cicchetti, D. & Lynch, M. (1993). Toward an ecological/transactional model of community violence and child maltreatment. *Psychiatry, 56*, 96–118.

Coates, S.W. & Moore, M.S. (1997). The complexity of early trauma: Representation and transformation. *Psychoanalytic Inquiry, 17*, 286–311.

Cohen, J.A. & Mannarino, A.P. (1998). Factors that mediate treatment outcome of sexually abused preschool children: Six and 12-month follow-up. *Journal of the American Academy of Child and Adolescent Psychiatry, 37*, 44–51.

Connor K.M., Sutherland S.M., Tapler L.A., Malik I., & Davidson J.R. (1999). Fluoxetine in PTSD: Randomised double-blind study. *British Journal of Psychiatry* 175(7), 17–22.

Deblinger, E., McLeer, S.V., Atkins, M.S., Ralphe, D., & Foa, E. (1989). Posttraumatic stress in sexually abused, physically abused, and non-abused children. *Child Abuse & Neglect, 13*, 403–408.

Deblinger, E., McLeer, S.V., & Henry, D. (1990). Cognitive behavioral treatment for sexually abused children suffering Posttraumatic stress: Preliminary findings. *Journal of the American Academy of Child and Adolescent Psychiatry, 29*, 747–752.

Deblinger E., Steer R.A., & Lippmann J. (1999). Two-year follow-up study of CBT for children suffering from posttraumatic stress symptoms. *Child Abuse and Neglect, 23*(12), 1371–1378.

Deykin, E.Y. & Buka, S.J. (1997). Prevalence and risk factors for posttraumatic stress disorder among chemically dependent adolescents. *American Journal of Psychiatry, 154*, 752–757.

Di Gallo, A., Barton, J., & Parry-Jones, W.L. (1997). Road traffic accidents: Early psychological consequences in children and adolescents. *British Journal of Psychiatry, 170*, 358–362.

Donnelly C.L., Amaya-Jackson L., March J.S. (1999). Psychopharmacology of pediatric PTSD. *Journal of Child and Adolescent Psychopharmacology, 9*(3), 203–220.

Draijer, N. & Langeland, W. (1999). Childhood trauma and perceived parental dysfunction in the etiology of dissociative symptoms in psychiatric inpatients. *American Journal of Psychiatry, 156*, 379–385.

Drell, M.J., Siegel, C.H., & Gaensbauer, T.J. (1993). Post-traumatic stress disorder in infants and toddlers. In C.H. Zeanah (Ed.), *Handbook of infant mental health* (pp. 291–304). New York: The Guilford Press.

Essau, C.A., Conradt, J., & Petermann, F. (1999). Haeufigkeit der Posttraumatischen Belastungsstoerung bei Jugendlichen: Ergebnisse der Bremer Jugendstudie. *Zeitschrift fuer Kinder-und Jugendpsychiatrie und Psychotherapie, 27*, 37–45.

Famularo, R., Fenton, T., Kinscherff, R., & Augustyn, M. (1996). Psychiatric comorbidity in childhood posttraumatic stress disorder. *Child Abuse Neglect, 20*, 953–61.

Famularo, R., Fenton, T., & Kinscherff, R. (1993). Child maltreatment and the development of posttraumatic stress disorder. *AJDC, 147*, 755–760.

Famularo, R., Kinscherff, R., & Fenton, T. (1988). Propranolol treatment of childhood PTSD, acute type. *AJDC, 142*, 1244–1247.

Famularo, R., Kinscherff, R., & Fenton, T. (1991). Post-traumatic stress disorder among children clinically diagnosed as borderline personality disorder. *Journal of Nervous and Mental Disease, 179*, 428–431.

Fergusson, D.M., Horwood, J., & Lynskey, M.T. (1996). Child sexual abuse and psychiatric disorder in young adulthood (Parts I and II). *Journal of the American Academy of Child and Adolescent Psychiatry, 14*.

Fisher, P., Hoven, C., Moore, R., Bird, H., Chiang, P.H., & Schwab-Stone, M. (1993). Evaluation of a method to assess PTSD in children and adolescents. *American Public Health Association Annual Meeting*.

Fletcher K. (1997). Childhood PTSD Interview-Child Form. In E Carlson (Ed.), *Trauma assessments: A clinician's guide* (pp. 248–250). New York: Guilford Press.

Foa E.B., Meadows E.A. (1997). Psychosocial treatments for post-traumatic stress disorder: A critical review. *Annual Review of Psychology, 48*, 449–480.

Foa, E.B., Olasov, R.B., Riggs, D.S., & Murdock, D.B. (1991). Treatment of PTSD in rape victim: A comparison between cognitive-behavioral procedures and counseling. *Journal of Consulting and Clinical Psychology, 59*, 715–723.

Frederick, C. (1985). Selected foci in the spectrum of PTSD. In J. Laube & S.A. Murphy (Ed.), *Perspectives on disaster recovery*. New York: Appleton.

Freud, S. (1959). Inhibitions, symptoms, and anxiety. In *The complete psychological works of Sigmund Freud*, Vol. 20, 94–129.

Gaensbauer, T.J. & Siegel, C.H. (1995). Therapeutic approaches to posttraumatic stress disorder in infants and toddlers. *Infant Mental Health Journal, 16*, 292–305.

Garrison, C.Z., Weinrich, M.W., Hardin, S.B., Weinrich, S., & Wang, L. (1993). Post-traumatic stress disorder in adolescents after a hurricane. *American Journal of Epidemiology, 138*, 522–530.

Garrison, C.Z., Bryant, E.S., Addy, C.L., Spurrier, P.G., Freedy, J.R., & Kilpatrick, D.G. (1995). PTSD in adolescents after Hurricane Andrew. *Journal of the American Academy of Child and Adolescent Psychiatry, 34*, 1193–1201.

Giaconia, R.M., Reinherz, H.Z., Silverman, A.B., Pakiz, B., Frost, A.K., & Cohen, E. (1995). Traumas and posttraumatic stress disorder in a community population of older adolescents. *Journal of the American Academy of Child and Adolescent Psychiatry, 34*, 1369–1380.

Goenjian, A.K., Karayan, I., Pynoos, R.S., Minassian, D., Najarian, L.M., Steinberg, A.M., & Fairbanks, L.A. (1997). Outcome of psychotherapy among early adolescents after trauma. *American Journal of Psychiatry, 154*, 536–542.

Goenjian, A.K., Najarian, L.M., Pynoos, R.S., Steinberg, A.M., Manoukian, G., Tavosian, A., & Fairbanks, L. (1994). PTSD in elderly and younger adults after the 1988 earthquake in Armenia. *American Journal of Psychiatry, 151*, 895–901.

Goenjian, A.K., Pynoos, R.S., Steinberg, A., Najarian, L.M., Asarnow, J.R., Karayan, I., Ghurabi, M., & Fairbanks, L.A. (1995). Psychiatric comorbidity in children after the 1988 earthquake in Armenia. *Journal of the American Academy of Child and Adolescent Psychiatry, 34*, 1174–1184.

Goldberg, F., Whiteside, J.E., Cloitre, M., Davis L.L., & Hyemee, H. (1999). Divalproex in PTSD resulting from sexual abuse. In new research: Program & abstracts. *152nd Annual Meeting of the American Psychiatric Association.*

Goldstein, R.D., Wampler, N.S., & Wise, P.H. (1997). War experiences and distress symptoms of Bosnian children. *Pediatrics, 100*, 873–878.

Gottlieb S (1999). Sertraline approved for PTSD. *British Medical Journal*, 319, 1089.

Green, B.L., Grace, M.C., Vary, M.G., Kramer, T.L., Gleser, G.C., & Leonard, A.C. (1994). Children of disaster in the second decade: A 17-year follow-up of Buffalo Creek survivors. *Journal of the American Academy of Child and Adolescent Psychiatry, 33*, 71–79.

Green, A.H. (1989). Overview of the literature on child sexual abuse. In D.H. Schetky, A.H. Green (Eds.), *Child sexual abuse* (pp. 30–54). New York: Brunner-Mazel.

Gurwitch, R.H., Sullivan, M.A., & Long, P.J. (1998). The impact of trauma and disaster on young children. *Child and Adolescent Psychiatric Clinics of North America, 7*, 19–31.

Harmon, R.J. & Riggs, P.D. (1996). Clonidine for posttraumatic stress disorder in preschool children.*Journal of the American Academy of Child and Adolescent Psychiatry, 35*, 1247–1249.

Haviland, M.G., Sonne, J.L., & Woods, L.R. (1995). Beyond posttraumatic stress disorder: object relations and reality testing disturbances in physically and sexually abused adolescents. *Journal of the American Academy of Child and Adolescent Psychiatry, 34*, 1054–1059.

Horowitz, K., Weine, S., & Jekel, J. (1995). PTSD symptoms in urban adolescent girls: Compounded community trauma. *Journal of the American Academy of Child and Adolescent Psychiatry, 34*, 1353–1361.

Horowitz, M., Wilner, W., & Alvarez, N. (1979). Impact of Events Scale: A measure of subjective stress. *Psychosomatic Medicine, 41*, 209–218.

Horrigan, J.P. (1996). Guanfacine for PTSD nightmares. *Journal of the American Academy of Child and Adolescent Psychiatry, 35*, 975–976.

Hubbard, J., Realmuto, G.M., Northwood, A.K., & Masten, A.S. (1995). Comorbidity of psychiatric diagnoses with PTSD in survivors of childhood trauma. *Journal of the American Academy of Child and Adolescent Psychiatry, 34*, 1167–1173.

Husain, S.A., Nair, J., Holcomb, W., Reid, J.C., Vargas, V., & Nair, J.S. (1998). Stress reactions of children and adolescents in war and siege conditions. *American Journal of Pediatrics, 155*, 1718–1719.

Jones, M.C., Dauphinias, P., Sack, W.H., & Somerville, P.D. (1997). Trauma-related symptomatology among American Indian adolescents. *Journal of Traumatic Stress, 10*, 163–173.

Jones, R.T. & Ribbe, D.P. (1991). Child, adolescent and adult victims of residential fire. *Behaviour Modification, 15*, 560–580.

Jones, R.T., Ribbe, D.P., & Cunningham, P. (1994). Psychosocial correlates of fire disaster among children and adolescents. *Journal of Traumatic Stress, 7*, 117–122.

Kaufman J., Birmaher B., Brent D., Rao U., Flynn C., Moreci P., Williamson D., Ryan N. (1997). Schedule for Affective Disorders and Schizophrenia for School-Age Children—Present and Lifetime version (K-SADS-PL): Initial reliability and validity data. *Journal of the American Academy of Child and Adolescent Psychiatry, 36*, 980–988.

Kinzie, J.D., Sack, W., Angell, R., & Clarke, B.R. (1989). A three-year follow-up of Cambodian young people traumatized as children. *Journal of the American Academy of Child and Adolescent Psychiatry, 28*, 501–504.

Kiser, L.J., Ackerman, B.J., Brown, E., Edwards, N.B., McColga, E., Pugh, R., & Pruitt, D.B. (1988). PTSD in young children: A reaction to purported sexual abuse. *Journal of the American Academy of Child and Adolescent Psychiatry, 27*, 645–649.

Koltek, M., Wilkes, T.C., & Atkinson, M. (1998). The prevalence of PTSD in an adolescent inpatient ward. *Canadian Journal of Psychiatry, 43*, 64–68.

La Greca, A.M., Silverman, W.K., & Wasserstein, S.B. (1998). Children's pre-disaster functioning as a predictor of posttraumatic stress following Hurricane Andrew. *Journal of Consulting and Clinical Psychology, 66*, 883–892.

Laor, N., Wolmer, L., Mayes, L.C., Gershon, A., Weizman, R., & Cohen, D.J. (1997). Israeli preschool children under Scuds: a 30 month follow-up. *Journal of the American Academy of Child and Adolescent Psychiatry, 36*, 349–356.

Lipschitz, D.S., Winegar, R.K., Hartnick, E., Foote, B., & Southwick, S.M. (1999). Posttraumatic stress disorder in hospitalized adolescents: Psychiatric comorbidity and clinical correlates. *Journal of the American Academy of Child and Adolescent Psychiatry, 38*, 385–392.

Lonigan, C.J., Shannon, M.P., Finch, A.J., Daugherty, T.K., & Taylor, C.M. (1991). Children's reaction to a natural disaster: Symptom severity and degree of exposure. *Advances in Behaviour Research and Therapy, 13*, 135–154.

Lonigan, C.J., Shannon, M.P., Taylor, C.M., Finch, A.J., & Sallee, F.R. (1994). Children exposed to disaster II: Risk factors for the development of post-traumatic symptomatology. *Journal of the American Academy of Child and Adolescent Psychiatry, 33*, 94–105.

Looff, D., Grimley, P., Kuller, F., Martin, A., & Shonfield, L. (1995). Carbamazepine for PTSD. *Journal of the American Academy of Child and Adolescent Psychiatry, 34,* 703–704.

Lyons-Ruth, K. & Block, D. (1996). The disturbed caregiving system: Relations among childhood trauma, maternal caregiving, and infant affect and attachment. *Infant Mental Health Journal, 17,* 257–275.

Malmquist, C.P. (1986). Children who witness parental murder: Posttraumatic aspects. *Journal of the American Academy of Child and Adolescent Psychiatry, 25,* 320–325.

March, J.S., Amaya-Jackson, L., Murray, M.C., & Schulte, A. (1998). Cognitive-behavioral psychotherapy for children and adolescents with PTSD after a single-incident stressor. *Journal of the American Academy of Child and Adolescent Psychiatry, 37,* 584–593.

March, J.S., Amaya-Jackson, L., Terry, R., & Costanzo, P. (1997). Posttraumatic symptomatology in children and adolescents after an industrial fire. *Journal of the American Academy of Child and Adolescent Psychiatry, 36,* 1080–1088.

Marshall, R.D., Stein, D.J., Liebowitz, M.R., & Yehuda, R. (1996). A pharmacotherapy algorithm in the treatment of posttraumatic stress disorder. *Psychiatric Annals, 26,* 217–226.

McFarlane, A.C. (1987). Post-traumatic phenomena in a longitudinal study of children following a natural disaster. *Journal of the American Academy of Child and Adolescent Psychiatry, 26,* 764–769.

McLeer, S.V., Callaghan, M., Henry, D., & Wallen, J. (1994). Psychiatric disorders in sexually abused children. *Journal of the American Academy of Child and Adolescent Psychiatry, 33,* 313–319.

Merry, S.N. & Andrews, L.K. (1994). Psychiatric status of sexually abused children 12 months after disclosure of abuse. *Journal of the American Academy of Child and Adolescent Psychiatry, 33,* 939–944.

Mghir, R., Freed, W., Raskin, A., & Katon, W. (1995). Depression and posttraumatic stress disorder among a community sample of adolescent and young adult Afghan refugees. *Journal of Nervous and Mental Disease, 183,* 24–30.

Milgram, N.A., Toubiana, Y.H., Klingman, A., Raviv, A., & Goldstein, I. (1988). Situational exposure and personal loss in children's acute and chronic stress reactions to a school bus disaster. *Journal of Traumatic Stress, 1,* 339–352.

Mollica, R.F., Whyshak, G., & Lavelle, J. (1987). The psychosocial impact of war trauma and torture on Southeast Asian refugees. *American Journal of Psychiatry, 144,* 1567–1572.

Moradi, A.U., Taghavi, M.R., Neshat Doost, H.J., Yule, W., & Dalgleish, T. (1999). Performance of children and adolescents with PTSD on the stroop colour-naming task. *Psychological Medicine, 2,* 415–419.

Nader, K., Pynoos, R., Fairbanks, L., & Frederick, C. (1991). Children's PTSD reactions one year after a sniper attack at their school. *American Journal of Psychiatry, 147*, 1526–1530.

Nader, K.O., Pynoos, R.S., Fairbanks, L.A., Al-Ajeel, M., & Al-Asfour, A. (1993). A preliminary study of PTSD and grief among the children of Kuwait following the Gulf crisis. *British Journal of Clinical Psychology, 32*, 407–416.

National Center for Clinical Infant Programs (1994). *Diagnostic Classification of mental health and developmental disorders of infancy and early childhood (DC:0–3)*. Arlington: Author.

Neugebauer, R., Wasserman, G.A., Fisher, P.W., Kline, J., Geller, P.A., & Miller, L.S. (1999). Darryl, a cartoon-based measure of cardinal posttraumatic stress symptoms in school-age children. *American Journal of Public Health, 89*, 758–761.

Neylan, T. (1999). Management of sleep disturbances in PTSD. From: Clinical frontiers in the sleep/psychiatry interface. *152nd Annual Meeting of the American Psychiatric Association*.

Oliver, J.E. (1993). Intergenerational transmission of child abuse: Rates, research, and clinical implications. *American Journal of Psychiatry, 150*, 1315–1324.

Pelcovitz, D. & Kaplan, D. (1996). Post-traumatic stress disorder in children and adolescents. *Child and Adolescent Psychiatric Clinics of North America, 5*, 449–469.

Pelcovitz, D., Kaplan, S., Goldenberg, B., Mandel, F., Lehane, J., & Guarrera, J. (1995). Post-traumatic stress disorder in physically abused adolescents. *Journal of the American Academy of Child and Adolescent Psychiatry, 33*, 305–312.

Pelcovitz, D., Libov, B.G., Mandel, F., Kaplan, S., Weinblatt, M., & Septimes, A. (1998). PTSD and family functioning in adolescents with cancer. *Journal of Traumatic Stress, 11*, 205–221.

Perrin S., Smith P., Yule W. (2000). Practitioner review: The assessment and treatment of post-traumatic stress disorder in children and adolescents. *Journal of Child Psychology and Psychiatry, 41*(3), 277–289.

Perry, B.D. & Pollard, R. (1998). Homeostasis, stress, trauma, and adaptation: A neurodevelopmental view of childhood trauma. *Child and Adolescent Psychiatric Clinics of North America, 7*, 33–51.

Perry, B.D., Pollard, R.A., Blakley, T.L., Baker, W.L., & Vigilante, D. (1995). Childhood trauma, the neurobiology of adaptation, and "use-dependent" development of the brain: How "states" become "traits." *Infant Mental Health Journal, 16*, 271–289.

Pfefferbaum, B. (1997). Posttraumatic stress disorder in children: A review of the past 10 years. *Journal of the American Academy of Child and Adolescent Psychiatry, 36*, 1503–1511.

Pynoos, R.S. & Nader, K. (1988). Children who witness the sexual assaults of their mothers. *Journal of the American Academy of Child and Adolescent Psychiatry, 27*, 567–572.

Pynoos, R.S., Frederick, C., Nader, K., Arroyo, W., Steinberg, A., Eth, S., Nunez, F., & Fairbanks, L. (1987). Life threat and posttraumatic stress in school age children. *Archives of General Psychiatry, 44,* 1057–1063.

Pynoos, R.S., Goenjian, A., Tashjian, M., Karakashian, M., Manjikian, R., Manoukian, G., Steinberg, A.M., & Fairbanks, L.A. (1993). Post-traumatic stress reactions in children after the 1988 Armenian earthquake. *British Journal of Psychiatry, 163,* 239–247.

Pynoos, R.S., Steinberg, A.M., & Wraith, R. (1995). A developmental model of childhood traumatic stress. In D. Cicchetti & D.J. Cohen (Eds). *Developmental Psychopathology: Volume 2: Risk, Disorder, and Adaptation* (pp. 72–96). New York: John Wiley & Sons, Inc..

Raphael, B. & Meldrum, L. (1995). Dose debriefing in psychological trauma work? *British Medical Journal, 310,* 1479–1480.

Robert, R., Blakeney, P.E., Villarreal, C., Rosenberg, L., & Meyer, W.J. (1999). Imipramine treatment in pediatric burn patients with symptoms of acute stress disorder: A pilot study. *Journal of the American Academy of Child and Adolescent Psychiatry, 38,* 873–882.

Ruttenberg, B.A. (1997). Traumatic stress disorder of infancy and childhood. In J.D. Noshpitz, S. Greenspan, S. Wieder, & J. Osofsky (Eds.). *Handbook of Child and Adolescent Psychiatry: Volume One* (pp. 520–536). NewYork: John Wiley & Sons, Inc..

Sack, W.H., Clarke, G., Him, C., Dickason, D., Goff, B., Lanham, K., & Kinzie, J.D. (1993). A 6-year follow-up study of Cambodian refugee adolescents traumatized as children. *Journal of the American Academy of Child and Adolescent Psychiatry, 32,* 431–437.

Sack, W.H., Clarke, G.N., & Seeley, J. (1995). PTSD across two generations of Cambodian refugees. *Journal of the American Academy of Child and Adolescent Psychiatry, 34,* 1160–1166.

Sack, W.H., McSharry, S., Clarke, G.N., Kinney, R., Seeley, J., & Lewinsohn, P. (1994). The Khmer Adolescent Project. I. Epidemiologic findings in two generations of Cambodian refugees. *Journal of Nervous and Mental Disease, 182,* 387–395.

Saigh, P.A. (1989a). The use of an in vitro flooding package in the treatment of traumatized Adolescents. *Dev Beh Pediatrics, 10,* 17–21.

Saigh, P.A. (1989b). The validity of the DSM-III post-traumatic stress disorder classification as applied to children. *Journal of Abnormal Psychology, 98,* 189–192.

Sandberg, S., McGuiness, D., Hillary, C., & Rutter, M. (1998). Indepence of childhood life events and chronic adversities: A comparison of two patient groups and controls. *Journal of the American Academy of Child and Adolescent Psychiatry, 37,* 728–733.

Schechter, D.S., Marshall, R., Salman, E., Goetz, D., Davies, S., & Liebowitz, M.R. (2000). Ataque de nervios and childhood trauma history. *Journal of Traumatic Stress, 13,* 529–534.

Scheeringa, M.S., Zeanah, C.H., Drell, M.J., & Larrieu, J.A. (1995). Two approaches to the diagnosis of PTSD in infancy and early childhood. *Journal of the American Academy of Child and Adolescent Psychiatry, 34,* 191–200.

Scheeringa, M.S. & Zeanah, C.H. (1995). Symptom expression and trauma variables in children under 48 months of age. *Infant Mental Health Journal, 16,* 259–270.

Schwarz, E.D. & Kowalski, J.M. (1991). Malignant memories: PTSD in children and adults after a school shooting. *Journal of the American Academy of Child and Adolescent Psychiatry, 30,* 936–944.

Schwarz, E.D. Kowalski, J.M. (1991). Post-traumatic stress disorder after a school shooting: effects of symptom threshold selection and diagnosis by DSM-III, DSM-III-R, or proposed DSM-IV. *American Journal of Psychiatry, 148,* 592–597.

Schwarzwald, J., Weisenberg, M., Waysman, M., Solomon, Z., & Klingman, A. (1993). Stress reaction of school-age children to the bombardment by Scud missiles. *Journal of Abnormal Psychology, 102,* 404–410.

Servan-Shreiber, D., Le Len, B., & Birmaher, B. (1998). Prevalence of PTSD and major depressive disorder in Tibetan refugee children. *Journal of the American Academy of Child and Adolescent Psychiatry, 37,* 874–879.

Shannon, M.P., Lonigan, C.J., Finch, A.J. Jr, & Taylor, C.M. (1994). Children exposed to disaster: I. Epidemiology of post-traumatic symptoms and symptom profiles. *Journal of the American Academy of Child and Adolescent Psychiatry, 33,* 80–93.

Shaw, J.A., Applegate, B., & Schorr, C. (1996). Twenty-one-month follow-up study of school-age children exposed to Hurricane Andrew. *Journal of the American Academy of Child and Adolescent Psychiatry, 35,* 359–364.

Shaw, J.A., Applegate, B., Tanner, S., Perez, D., Rothe, E., Campo-Bowen, A.E., & Lahey, B.L. (1995). Psychological effects of Hurricane Andrew on an elementary school population. *Journal of the American Academy of Child and Adolescent Psychiatry, 34,* 1185–1192.

Sinclair, J.J., Larzelere, R.E., Pain, M., Jones, P., Graham, K., & Jones, M. (1995). Outcome of group treatment for sexually abused adolescent females living in a group home setting, preliminary findings. *Journal of Interpersonal Violence, 10,* 533–542.

Singer, M., Slovak, K., Frierson, T., & York, P. (1998). Viewing preferences, symptoms of psychological trauma and violent behaviors among children who watch television. *Journal of the American Academy of Child and Adolescent Psychiatry, 37,* 1041–1048.

Silva, R.R., Alpert, M., Munoz, D.M., Singh, S., Matzner, F., & Dummit, S. (2000). Stress and vulnerability to posttraumatic stress disorder in children and adolescents. *American Journal of Psychiatry, 157,* 1229–1235.

Stallard, P., Velleman, R., & Baldwin, S. (1998). Prospective study of post-traumatic stress diesorder in children involved in road traffic accidents. *British Medical Journal, 317*, 1619–1623.

Stoddard, F.J., Norman, D.K., Murphy, J.M., & Beardslee, W.R. (1989). Psychiatric outcome of burned children and adolescents. *Journal of the American Academy of Child and Adolescent Psychiatry, 28*, 589–595.

Stuber, M.L., Christakis, D.A., & Kazak, A.E. (1996a). Posttraumatic symptoms in childhood leukemia survivors and their parents. *Psychosomatics, 37*, 254–261.

Stuber, M.L., Nader, K.O., Houskamp, B.M., & Pynoos, R.S. (1996b). Appraisal of life threat and acute trauma responses in pediatric bone marrow transplant recipients. *Journal of Traumatic Stress, 9*, 673–686.

Terr, L.C. (1987). Childhood psychic trauma. In J.D. Noshpitz (Ed), *Basic Handbook of Child Psychiatry, Volume 5: Advances and New Directions* (pp. 262–272). New York: Basic Books.

Terr, L.C. (1981). Forbidden games: Post-traumatic child's play. *Journal of the American Academy of Child and Adolescent Psychiatry, 20*, 741–760.

Thabet, A.A. & Vostanis P. (1999). Post-traumatic stress reactions in children of war. *Journal of Child Psychology and Psychiatry, 40*, 385–391.

Thomas, J.M. (1995). Traumatic stress disorder presents as hyperactivity and disruptive behavior: Case presentation, diagnosis and treatment. *Infant Mental Health Journal, 16*, 306–317.

Tiet, Q.Q., Bird, H.R., Davies, M., Hoven, C., Cohen, P., Jensen, P.S., & Goodman, S. (1998). Adverse life-events and resilience. *Journal of the American Academy of Child and Adolescent Psychiatry, 37*, 1191–1200.

Trappler, B. & Friedman, S. (1996). PTSD in survivors of the Brooklyn Bridge shooting. *American Journal of Psychiatry, 153*, 705–707.

van den Boom, D.C. & Hoeksma, J.B. (1994). The influence of temperament and mothering on attachment and exploration: An experimental manipulation of sensitive responsiveness among lower-class mothers with irritable infants. *Child Development, 65*, 1449–1469.

van der Kolk, B.A., Pelcovitz, D., Roth, S., Mandel, F.S., McFarlane, A., & Herman, J.L. (1996). Dissociation, somatization, and affect dysregulation: The complexity of adaptation to trauma. *American Journal of Psychiatry, 153*, 83–90.

Widom, C.S. (1999). Posttraumatic stress disorder in abused and neglected children grown up. *American Journal of Psychiatry, 156*, 1223–1229.

Winje, D. & Uluik, A. (1998). Long-term outcome of trauma in children: The psychological consequences of a bus accident. *Journal of Child Psychology and Psychiatry, 39*, 635–642.

Wozniak, J., Crawford, M.H., Biederman, J., Faraone, S.V., Spencer, T.J., Taylor, A., & Blies, K. (1999). Antecedents and complications of trauma in boys with ADHD: Findings from a longitudinal study. *Journal of the American Academy of Child and Adolescent Psychiatry, 38*, 48–55.

Wunderlich, U., Bronisch, T., & Wittchen, H.U. (1998). Comorbidity patterns in adolescent and young adults with suicide attempts. *European Archives of Psychiatry and Clinical Neurosciences, 248,* 87–95.

Yehuda, R., Schmiedler, J., Wainberg, M., Binder-Brynes, K., & Dudevani, T. (1998). Vulnerability to posttraumatic stress disorder in adult offspring of holocaust survivors. *American Journal of Psychiatry, 155,* 1163–1171.

Yule, W. (1992). Post-traumatic stress disorder in child survivors of shipping disasters: The sinking of the "Jupiter". *Psychotherapy & Psychosomatics, 57,* 200–205.

Zeanah, C.H., Finley-Belgrad, E., & Benoit, D. (1997). Intergenerational transmission of relationship psychopathology: A mother-infant case study. In L. Atkinson & K.J. Zucker (Eds.), *Attachment and Psychopathology* (pp. 292–319). New York: The Guilford Press.

PART III
EPILOGUE

1 PROGRESS AND UNRESOLVED ISSUES

Cecilia A. Essau
Franz Petermann
Berit Reiss
Melanie Steinmeyer

Major advances in anxiety research in children and adolescents have been made within the last decade. These have been made possible as a result of two related developments: the introduction of DSM-III (APA, 1980) and its subsequent versions which have provided an opportunity to examine anxiety disorders; and the development of diagnostic interview schedules which have allowed the systematic assessment of anxiety and other psychiatric disorders, as well as comparison of results across studies. However, there are a number of unresolved issues and challenges which need to be dealt with.

In this chapter, we will discuss the advances and unresolved issues in the area of anxiety disorders in children and adolescents. For the sake of discussion, these issues were grouped under: classification, assessment, epidemiology, comorbidity, risk factors, course and outcome, and treatment. Recommendations for further research will also be discussed.

Classification

Most studies of anxiety disorders in children and adolescents have used the adult criteria for anxiety based on the Diagnostic and Statistical Manual of Mental Disorders (DSM) or the International Statistical Classification of Diseases and Related Health Problems (ICD; World Health Organization, 1993). Since the introduction of DSM-III (APA, 1980), the criteria for making the diagnosis of anxiety disorders in terms of their symptoms, duration, and associated features have been explicitly and clearly described. Other characteristics of DSM-IV include multiaxiality, hierarchial organization, emphasis on phenomenological rather than etiological criteria, and attempts to establish reliability by large field trials (Werry, 1994). The advantage of using a multiaxial system is that it allows the assessment of certain types of disorders, aspects of environment, and different areas of functioning. The multiaxial system in DSM-IV includes five axes, on which each patient can be evaluated: Axis I (clinical disorders; other conditions that may be a focus of clinical attention), Axis II (personality disorders; mental retardation), Axis III (general medical conditions), Axis IV (psychosocial and environmental problems), and Axis V (global assessment of functioning). DSM-IV also employs the concept of diagnostic hierarchies in that individuals who meet the criteria for the diagnoses lower in the hierarchy are generally not given that lower diagnosis.

In the latest version of the DSM (DSM-IV; American Psychiatric Association, 1994), some changes have been made in the diagnostic criteria and categories of childhood anxiety disorders. Among the three anxiety disorders which were placed under childhood anxiety disorders, only separation anxiety disorder has remained the same category, although some of its criteria have been modified. Avoidant disorder has been changed to social phobia, and overanxious disorder to generalized anxiety disorder. In addition to the separation anxiety disorder, DSM-IV also lists nine other anxiety disorders (specific phobia, social phobia, panic disorder, obsessive compulsive disorder, generalized anxiety disorder, posttraumatic stress disorder, acute stress disorder, anxiety disorder due to a general medical condition, and substance-induced anxiety disorder) that can be used in children, adolescents, and adults. An unresolved issue is related to the application of adult criteria of anxiety disorders to children and adolescents. That is, little is known about the validity or the reliability of these criteria when applied to children. Furthermore, no studies have been made on the impact of putting the criteria of overanxious disorder and avoidant disorder under the "adult" section of the anxiety disorders (Eyberg *et al.*, 1998). Other major concerns include the poor definition, distinctiveness, treatment utility, and overall validity of many anxiety symptoms and syndroms (Kearney and Silverman, 1998).

Since DSM system is not sensitive enough to developmental issues, little attempt is made to specify the age at which specific diagnoses become valid (Eyberg *et al.*, 1998). This makes it difficult to decide whether symptoms occur frequently enough to be clinically significant because certain problematic behaviours may be developmentally-appropriate. Therefore, the diagnosis of anxiety in childhood and adolescence ought to be sensitive to the child's developmental stage as well as to constitutional and environmental factors that affect their developmental progress (Eyberg *et al.*, 1998).

Assessment

Some of the important functions of assessment include: evaluation of the presence and absence of specific behaviour and abilities; assignment of problems to a diagnostic category; specification of symptom severity; and monitoring the impact of treatment of anxiety and other disorders. However, in order to accomplish these functions, the instruments used to assess anxiety and other psychiatric disorders need to be reliable and valid.

Major sources of unreliability that result from variability in obtaining clinical information and diagnostic formulation can be substantially reduced by using highly structured diagnostic interview schedules (Essau et al., 1997). The main advantage of the structured diagnostic interview is its attempt to reduce observer, information, and criterion variance by specifying the items to be investigated and providing definitions for these items. On the other hand, a highly structured diagnostic interview generally takes longer to administer compared to an unstructured interview or the use of self-report questionnaire (see Chapter 3, in this volume). The average time of administrating the Diagnostic Interview Schedule for Children (DISC; Piacentini et al., 1993) is about 90 minutes. Given the children's restricted attention span, it is questionable whether the children can concentrate on the questions being asked, and consequently the reliability of the answer given. For example, Breton et al. (1995), in examining 9-11-year old's understandability of DISC, found questions related to time concepts being less understood compared to other questions. That is, less than 30% of the children understood questions related to time frame, length of symptoms, and "frequency of behaviour and emotion".

For young children who have not yet developed the cognitive ability to verbalize feelings, observational assessment provides perhaps the most objective method by which to quantify their distress (Eyberg et al., 1998). Structured diagnostic interviews with parents and rating scales obtained from parents or teachers may be useful. As children grow older, diagnostic interviews and self-report may be used to assess the children. Observational measures are difficult to standardize across ages, due to rapid changes of the children's problems. Since these different assessment methods and informants often produce inconsistent information, effort is needed to develop a criteria to make use of qualitative and quantitative information.

Children and adolescents at different ages may differ in their ability to report their emotions, feelings and behaviours. To evaluate similar characteristics across the age groups may require different measures, and include some changes of the same measures. However, any changes of assessment procedures may influence the results and consequently the conclusions, since the same items may be interpreted differently by youths at different developmental stages. Furthermore, in assessing age-appropriateness versus clinical relevance of children's behaviour, there is a need to know age-appropriateness of the behaviour. A challenge is to define "age appropriate" behaviours, and the way to operationalize them. In this respect, milestones of normal development may be useful. At the same time, the heterogeneity of child's development needs to be taken into account.

In order to have a comprehensive and an accurate picture of the youth's problem, especially among younger children, data needs to be gathered from multiple sources. Other reasons for using multiple informants include (Cantwell *et al.*, 1997): (i) children may not be able to provide a reliable and complete account of their problems; (ii) children may deny the presence of certain symptoms, or report only a mimimum number of symptoms due to social desirability; (iii) significant others may be unaware of the child's intrapsychic symptoms (e.g., obsession), or have little knowledge about the different situations in which the child display problematic behaviour; (iv) children and adults may differ in their threshold in defining behaviour as clinically significant and finally (v) the manifestation of the child's symptoms or behaviour may differ between settings.

Unfortunately, the agreement among informants on the frequency and severity of disorders, including anxiety among children, has been low (Achenbach *et al.*, 1987). For example, using data from the Oregon Adolescent Depression Project (Cantwell *et al.*, 1997), good parent-adolescent agreement was found for separation anxiety disorder, whereas poor agreement was found for other disorders and the core symptoms of obsessive-compulsive disorder. Given the low degree of agreement among different informants, an important question is to decide which information from which informants should be used. In clinical settings, it is usually the clinicians who weigh the information obtained from the different informants and make a decision about diagnosis and treatment. Unclear, however, is the way in which clinicians weigh discrepant information. In epidemiologic studies numerous methods have been used to analyze data from different informants, includung separate analysis of assessments provided by different informants (Offord *et al.*, 1996), the identification of "optimal" informants for specific categories of disorder (Hart *et al.*, 1994), the integration of data from all the informants (Bird *et al.*, 1993), and the use of latent variable methods to define disorders are pervasive phenomena (Fergusson and Horwood, 1987).

In addition to the continued problems of assessing anxiety in children, there are practical considerations and difficulties for clinicians, for example time contraints and the lack of norms for some measures. Therefore, there is a need to design assessment instruments of anxiety for use in clinical settings. However, some specific requirements need to be fulfilled (Wittchen and Essau, 1990). The instruments should: (1) be short so that they will not be time-consuming to administer, or interact significantly with the time constraints in clinical settings; (2) be easy to administer and should require only minimal training; (3) be comprehensive enough to detect the subtypes of anxiety disorder and their associated features such as onset, duration, and chronicity; (4) have high sensitivity and specificity to allow early detection and treatment; and (5) they should not be limited to the symptom level, but also some questions related to psychosocial functioning. From a clinical viewpoint, there is also a need for a short and reliable standardized assessment instruments for parents.

Epidemiology

The development of highly structured diagnostic instruments which can be administered by trained lay interviewers not only reduce costs, but also permit the investigations of large samples. These advances have attracted much interest in conducting epidemiological studies of anxiety and other psychiatric disorders. Epidemiological studies have the advantage of producing findings of greater generalizability than studies of clinical samples. Results from clinical settings may not be representative of individuals with anxiety or other disorders due to bias related to service attendance through restrictions in evaluating, access, and selection process in terms of help-seeking behaviour and chronicity (Essau *et al.*, 1997). Sample from the community and clinical samples may also differ in the risk factors, comorbidity, natural course, and response to treatment of their anxiety disorders.

While studies of general population samples may be more representative of the overall population than samples recruited from clinic setting, there are still some methodological problems. First, children need to be randomly selected from the whole child population. However, many children may be missed when research samples are selected by a dwelling-based or school-based process, or these who live in special settings (e.g. institutions). Second, bias may arise from groups of parents who refuse to give consent for their children to participate in research. According to some studies, characteristics of children missed in random child populations samples included the presence of parental psychopathology, poor social skills, and the presence of high number of symptoms reported from other sources (McGee *et al.*, 1990; Verhulst *et al.*, 1990). An unresolved problem in epidemiological studies is therefore related to the issue of representativeness of the samples.

Comorbidity

As discussed in different chapters in this volume, there are high comorbidity rates both within the anxiety disorders as well as between anxiety and other disorders (Emmelkamp and Scholing, 1997). Despite this high comorbidity rate, its meaning for etiological and classification issues remain unresolved (Angold and Costello, 1993; Nottelmann and Jensen, 1999), although several speculations have been put forward:

- *The high comorbidity of anxiety disorders may reflect the over-lapping diagnostic criteria or artificial subdivision of syndromes*: In a study among adults, Lepine *et al.* (1993) examined the extent to which high comorbidity rates between generalized anxiety disorder (GAD) and other psychiatric disorders are an artefact of shared symptoms. In DSM-III only four symptoms are unique to GAD, and the others are also used for classifying somatoform, panic, and major depressive disorders. To examine whether the high comorbidty rates between GAD and other disorders is an artefact of counting the same symptom towards the disorders, a separate analysis was done. For that analysis, symptoms were only counted towards the assessment of GAD if they were not counted at the same time as symptoms of panic, somatoform, and depressive disorders. Tetrachronic correlations between depressive disorders and GAD were no longer significant, as GAD's association with the anxiety cluster emerged more clearly. Certainly more studies of this nature need to be conducted especially among youth with anxiety disorders.

- *Comorbidity could have been the consequence of the same risk factors*: In attempting to explain the high comorbidity between anxiety and depressive disorders, a tripartite model has been proposed (Clark and Watson, 1991). According to this model, anxiety and depression share a nonspecific component of generalized affective distress or negative affect. In a recent analysis of the Bremen Adolescent Study (Essau, 1999), most factors that were found as risk factors for anxiety disorders are also risk factors for depressive disorders. These included parental psychopathology, cognitive dysfunction, low parent-child perceived attachment, and high number of life events. A more detailed analysis of the latter result showed that the events which differentiated anxious from depressed adolescents were those related to parents/family and health/illness.

- *It could also be that one disorder may represent an early manifestation of another disorder, or that one disorder causes or lowers the threshold for the expression of the other*: Issues related to the temporal sequences of disorders may be useful in testing this hypothesis. Among those with anxiety and depressive disorders, most studies have shown anxiety to generally begin before that of depression (Essau, 1999; Lewinsohn *et al.*, 1997). An important issue of relevance to the temporal sequence of disorders is related to the age of onset (see below), which may be affected by the problem of recall.

AGE OF ONSET

The ability to accurately date the onset of symptoms of anxiety disorders is important. There is, however, no general agreement on the definition of "age of onset". For some authors, it is defined as the age at which the person first experiences the full clinical picture of the disorder, or the time at which the syndromatic picture occurs.

The extent to which children could recall the date of onset of symptoms is unclear. Angold *et al.* (1996) examined the "precision" (i.e., margin of error in reporting onset date), "reliability" (i.e., similarity between onset dates for the same symptoms reported at multiple assessments), and "accuracy" (i.e., degree to which the age of onset is a true representation of the actual date on which the onset occurred) in dating the onset of symptoms of various disorders using the Child and Adolescent Psychiatric Assessment (CAPA; Angold and Costello, 1995) in the 8–16-year olds. The date of onset of a symptom for recall period longer than 3 months seemed to be unreliable. Given these findings, an effort ought to be devoted to developing strategies to help children and adolescents recall when their anxiety problems begin. Some strategies, commonly used in adults, such as the use of symptom lists and memory aids may improve lifetime recall and ease memory search.

Risk Factors

LIFE EVENTS

A high proportion of the anxious youths have been exposed to negative life events in the year before the onset of the anxiety, although it is not clear how these events exert their effects (see Chapters 4, 5, in this volume). Since not all individuals who were exposed to multiple life events remain well, future research ought to examine the mechanisms by which they act and the processes which result in their effects. Furthermore, life events do not appear to be a specific risk factor for anxiety disorder. As shown by Kendler et al. (1992), parental loss before the age of 17 years increase the risk for having five psychiatric disorders. In the same vein, in our Bremen Adolescent Study (Essau, 1999), life events were significantly associated with the presence of not only anxiety, but also with depressive and substance use disorders.

In addition to these conceptual problems, there are several methodological problems which need to be dealt with in future research: (i) Most of the studies that reported an association between anxiety and life events generally used cross-sectional design, and the use of life event checklists that cover only recent and negative events. Chronic difficulties, which generally fall outside the definition of life events, have rarely been included although they may also exert a significant effect on the risk of anxiety. Interview methods should be able to distinguish between negative and positive, chronic and recent events, and between the types of different recent events. (ii) Life event research should move away from the question of whether life events are causative or a consequence of anxiety disorder, to studying issues that maintain anxiety disorders. (iii) No reliable procedure is available for the retrospective assessment of life events. In our study, there tends to be a significant drop in the number of events reported by the adolescents as the period of time lengthens between assessment and the occurrence of these events (Essau, 1999). In this respect, it may be useful to test the impact of using memory aids on the retrieval process for past events.

FAMILY/GENETIC FACTORS

Anxiety disorders run in the family. In numerous family studies, children of parents with anxiety also have an increased risk of being anxious compared to children of non-anxiety parents (see Chapters 6, 7, 9, in this volume). Yet not all children of anxious parents have anxiety (Essau, 1999). These findings raise a question as to what constitute "shared risks" for siblings. That is, "to what extent do siblings share environments?" Given that they may share objective risks, the next question is related to the extent to which siblings make sense of their experiences similarly. Therefore, one needs to determine how shared risk factors such as parental anxiety impinge differentially on the children. In this respect, it may be useful to do a within-group and a within-individual analysis. A within-group analysis involves examining factors common among individuals in the group, whereas a within-individual analysis expands this focus to factors that are uncommon to those in the group members. As argued by Pike and Plomin (1996), experiences outside the family may even have a stronger effects on the child as siblings begin to make their own ways in life. Furthermore, the presence of anxiety disorders in adolescents was associated with maternal anxiety and depression, suggesting the unspecificity of the transmission of anxiety between parents and siblings (Essau, 1999).

Another strategy would be to examine the effect of multiple risk factors simultaneously, since anxious parents have several other risk factors such as life stressors, family dysfunction, and single parenthood. Future studies need to go beyond considering individual risk factors to addressing the question of whether any individual risk factors have unique variance in predicting anxiety disorders when assessed in the context of other powerful risk variables.

Numerous methodological issues also need to be considered in designing future family studies of anxious children. The most important deals with the choice of probands in the anxiety versus control groups. In order to have enough samples with anxiety disorders many family studies were conducted in clinical settings. However, data from clinical settings may be biased by methodological problems such as chronicity and severity of disorders, and selection process. Since some of the problems of clinical studies do not apply to epidemiological settings, more emphasis should be shifted to family studies in the general population. Furthermore, most family studies of anxious children are cross-sectional in nature. Longitudinal studies would be advantageous to examine the stability of the disorder and to tackle causal questions on the relationship between parental psychopathology and anxiety disorders in children. In addition to using family history studies to explore the specificity of transmission of anxiety disorders, more experimental conditions need to be developed. For example, the importance of early experience with uncontrollability in the development of anxiety disorders can be examined by studying a mother-child interaction using a longitudinal prospective design.

COGNITIVE FACTORS

Anxious children have more negative cognitive functioning than are their non-anxious counterparts (see Chapters 4, 5, 7, 8, in this volume). In interpreting this finding, it has often been argued that having cognitive dysfunction could lead to having anxiety. However, this interpretation is inconclusive because most studies are cross-sectional in nature. Furthermore, since anxiety is highly comorbid with depression, the dysfunctional cognition found in anxious children may not be specific to anxiety alone. As shown in our study (Essau, 1999), cognitive dysfunction was not only common to those with anxiety, but also to those with depressive disorders.

In addition to some methodological problems associated with each risk factor examined, one needs to be cautious in interpreting and generalizing the existing results. There is apparently a need to identify risk factors because factors tend to aggregate over time and contribute to anxiety. However, the same risk factors do not necessarily lead to anxiety in most people. It could be possible that a risk factor may interact with the person's characteristics such as age and gender. A great challenge would be to identify the contribution of each factors and as to how they may co-occur to produce anxiety.

Additionally, some factors may produce their effect differently. For example, marital discord may influence the child directly through exposure to an adverse situation at home, or indirectly through interference of the parent's ability to provide the child with a consistent discipline.

Course and Outcome

A prospective longitudinal study is an ideal approach to studying the course and outcome of anxiety disorders. Such an approach provides multiple measurement over time which may reduce biases due to reporting variations in situational data. Longitudinal data can be used to explore how chains of experiences could influence the course and outcome of anxiety disorders. However, despite these advantages, longitudinal studies are rare given their cost, logistical difficulty, and potential problems with attrition (Rutter, 1994). Attention must be paid to societal change over time, leading to the manifestation of cohort effects. A major challenge is to figure out a way in which to disentagle ageing effects (i.e., changes that occur with age) from period (i.e., influence of specific event to a particular time) and cohort effects (i.e., group of individuals who experience the same event during the same period). Other issues which present challenges for longitudinal research include the time intervals between the different assessments.

Finally, there is no general consensus as to what comprises the indices of course and outcome for anxiety. Given the integrative status of anxiety disorders, which comprise cognitive, behavioural, physiological and family factors, a wide range of indicators should be used to measure the course and outcome of anxiety disorders. These include: the presence of anxiety symptoms or disorder, psychosocial impairment, and health services utilization (Table 11.1).

Treatment

Two main categories of pharmacological agents often used to treat anxiety disorders in adolescents are antidepressants (e.g., imipramine and clomipramine) and anxiolytics (e.g., alprazolam and clon-

Table 11.1 Indicators of course and outcome of anxiety disorders

Domains	Examples
Symptoms and Diagnoses	• Presence of anxiety symptoms or anxiety disorders. • Presence of comorbid disorders.
Psychosocial Impairment	• Impairment in various areas of life (e.g., in school, at home, social life activities). • Quality of life.

Health Services Utilization	• Number and duration of health services used.
	• Type of health services used:
	  – Mental health speciality sector (e.g., psychiatrist, psychologist, social worker, counselor);
	  – Medical services from a nonpsychiatrist physician or a nurse;
	  – School-based and social services.
	• of health services: Inpatient, Outpatient, Telephone services.

azepam). However, most studies that examined the efficacy of these medications are problematic due to methodological limitations (Table 11.2). There are lack of double-blind, placebo-controlled studies which have evaluated the efficacy of pharmacological treatment of anxiety disorders in this age group (Kutcher *et al.*, 1992). Most studies are open trials with a small sample size, therefore, lack the statistical power to complete moderate medication effects. Standardized diagnostic procedure, well-defined outcome measures, and the used of a systematic side effect assessment have rarely been used. In addition to these methodological constraints, tricyclic antidepressant withdrawal may be associated with numerous symptoms such as severe nausea, vomitting, diarrhea, and restlessness (Kutcher *et al.*, 1992). The effects of benzodiazepines are dependent on the dose used, and may include drowsiness, slurred speech, and tremor (Kutcher *et al.*, 1992).

Psychological interventions commonly used to treat anxiety disorders include cognitive-behavioural therapy, or components of the behavioural approach. As shown in previous chapters, the cognitive-behavioural approach is generally effective in treating anxiety disorders. A major challenge is how to reach those who need

Table 11.2 Psychopharmacotherapy and psychological intervention for anxiety disorders

Pharmacologic treatment	Psychological intervention
Advantages	*Advantages*
• Short-term efficacy	• Established short- and long-term efficacy
• Can be integrated with medical treatment	• Time-limited, resulting in reduced cost in long-term
• Require little active participation of the anxious individual	• Little or no side effects
Disadvantages	*Disadvantages*
• Limited knowledge on long-term outcome	• Limited accessibility
• High relapse rate after withdrawal	• Takes more time and effort than pharmacologic treatment
• Risk of chemical dependency	• Require active participation of anxious youth and sometimes also their parents
• Negative side effects, leading to drop out	

the help the most. A large proportion of anxious children and adolescents in the community do not receive the professional help they need (Essau, 1999); most of those who sought treatment were treated in general medical or primary-care settings. Burns (1991) similarly reported that children with psychiatric disorders generally receive mental health services through non-mental health problems. However, for most children, the problem may not be detected by the primary-care physicians. Some explanations cited for underdetection, at least in adults, include characteristiscs of the health care systems (e.g., heavy work load of the general practioners) which allow only a brief consultation time, physician attitudes and experience, and a lack of training in diagnosing psychiatric disorders (Wittchen and Essau, 1990).

An important fact is that it is usually not the child him/herself who decides that behaviour needs attention and consequently makes the decision about referral, but an adult who is usually the parent or the teacher. Therefore, the factors which influence whether or not treatment is sought need to be identified. Parent's likelihood to seek help for their children may be influenced by the extent to which the child's behaviour is noticeable and bothersome, as well as by parent's mental health status and treatment history, and perceived benefits of treatment (Mash and Krahn, 1995). When summarizing this and other findings, factors which effect the child's referral can be divided to include the child, parents, and other's characteristics:

- Child Characteristics (e.g., severity and chronicity of depressive disorders; presence of comorbid disorders; psychosocial impairment; sociodemographic characteristic).
- Parent Characteristics (e.g., awareness of the problem; distress threshold level; family stress; psychopathology; sociodemographic characteristics).
- Other Characteristics (e.g., availability of services; cost and mechanism of financing)

Even if the children are in treatment, there is no guarantee that they join the treatment from the beginning to the end. According to Kazdin's review (1997), between 40 to 60% of families terminate the treatment prematurely.

Progress in developing an effective treatment is hindered by the studies' methodological problems, including the brief and time limited nature of treatment of nonclinical youths, which are usually done in university settings (Kazdin, 1997; Weisz et al., 1999). Also, group therapy has been the format of preference, probably due to their ease of administration, and also due to the fact that many studies are done in school. However, the use of manuals may make the treatment process rather inflexible, and encourage a tendency to ignore individual differences (Table 11.3). Differences in the approach used, and the severity and chronicity of anxiety seen in "research" and "clinical" therapy, make it is difficult to compare findings obtained in these two types of studies.

Furthermore, as presented in numerous chapters in this volume, most treatment studies have focused on general anxiety. Given the fact that adults are rarely treated for general anxiety, more research is needed into treatment for the different types of anxiety disorders in children and adolescents. Also, given the different features and risk factors associated with each subtypes of anxiety disorders, we cannot regard findings of existing studies as representative across all types of anxiety. This would mean a need to develop and empirically test treatment programs for the different types of anxiety disorders.

In order to achieve further progress towards developing an effective treatment including that of anxiety disorders (Kazdin, 1997), the following factors need to be considered: (i) the identification of factors related to the onset, maintenance, offset, and recurrence of anxiety; (ii) the development of a manual which contains clear and specific tasks for each session; (iii) the identification of the impact of treatment on anxiety symptoms and associated impairment; (iv) the identification of a treatment's component which produces or facilitates changes; and (v) which factors influence the effectiveness of treatment. A number of methodological issues relevant to the treatment of anxiety disorders in children and adolescents have also been proposed (Kendall and Flannery-Schroeder, 1998) (Table 11.3).

Summary

Although much progress has been achieved in anxiety research in children and adolescents, there are several issues which need to be resolved in the future. Some of the unresolved issues discussed in this chapter include: (i) The validity and reliability of using adult criteria for anxiety disorders among youths; (ii) The problem of the lack of agreement in the information from different informants; the way to deal with these disagreements also remains unresolved. Other problems associated with assessment issues are those related to designing age-related questionnaires or interview schedules, given the rapid and heterogenous nature of development; (iii) The meaning of comorbidity between anxiety and other psychiatric disorders for classification and etiology; (iv) The nonspecificity of risk factors for anxiety. That is, the risk factors usually found for anxiety have also been found for several other disorders; and (v) Low rates of mental health services utilization in children and adolescents with anxiety disorders.

Throughout this chapter, we have attempted to pose numerous questions related to each of these unresolved issues, with the hope of stimulating future research in anxiety among children and adolescents.

Table 11.3 Methodological issues in treatment research for anxiety disorders*

Methodological issues	Potential problems	Potential ameliorative strategies
Procedure		
• Use of manual	May limit therapist creativity; Lack of individualization	Quality assurance checks to examine treatment integrity
• Duration of treatment and control conditions	More attrition among youths in the waitlists than treatment groups	Frequent contacts with youths in the waiting group
• Psychoactive medications	Impact of medication on the dependent variables	Exclude youths on antianxiety and antidepression medication
Assessment		
• Child self-reports	May be affected by social desirability	Use multimethod assessment
• Parent and teacher reports	Not aware of the child's internal states	Use multimethod assessment
• Behavioural observations	Lack of standardized codes for behavioural observation	Use of peers/parents in the observational tasks
• Child and parents diagnostic interviews	Lack of among informants consistency	Use of various assessment procedures

Table 11.3 Methodological issues in treatment research for anxiety disorders* (*continued*)

Methodological issues	Potential problems	Potential ameliorative strategies
Treatment outcome		
Symptom focus and comorbidity	High comorbidity rates	Use a diagnostic interview schedule to identify the presence or anxiety and other disorders
Attrition and intent-to-treat analysis	Loss of participants before the end of treatment	Assess treatment gains based on pre- and posttreatment scores
Focus on the target client	Evaluating therapeutic effects on the child only may miss knowing its effects on the family members	Assess parental attitudes and family functioning
Clinical significance	Relying on statistical significance may lead to treatment gains as potent, although they may be clinically insignificant	Assess treatment outcomes in term of its clinical and statistical significance

*Source: Slightly modified from Kendall and Flannery-Schroeder (1998).

References

Achenbach, T.M., McConaughy, S.H., & Howell, C.T. (1987). Child/ adolescent behavioral and emotional problems: Implications of cross-informant correlations for situational specificity. *Psychological Bulletin, 101*, 213–232.

American Psychiatric Association (1980). *Diagnostic and Statistical Manual of Mental Disorders* (3rd ed.). Washington, DC: Author

American Psychiatric Association (1994). *Diagnostic and Statistical Manual of Mental Disorders* (4th ed.). Washington, DC: Author.

Angold, A., Erkanli, A., & Rutter, M. (1996). Precision, reliability and accuracy in the dating of symptom onsets in child and adolescent psychopathology. *Journal of Child Psychology and Psychiatry, 37*, 657–664.

Angold, A. & Costello, E.J. (1993). Depressive comorbidity in children and adolescents: Empirical, theoretical, and methodological issues. *American Journal Psychiatry, 150*, 1779–1791.

Angold, A. & Costello, E.J. (1995). A test-retest reliability study of child-reported psychiatric symptoms and diagnoses using the Child and Adolescent Psychiatric Assessment (CAPA-C). *Psychological Medicine, 25*, 755–762.

Bird, H.R., Gould, M.S. & Staghezza, B.M. (1993). Patterns of diagnostic comorbidity in a community sample of children aged 9 through 16 years. *Journal of the American Academy of Child and Adolescent Psychiatry, 32*, 361–368.

Burns, B.J., Costello, E.J. Angold, A. *et al.* (1995). The great smoky mountains study of youth: mental health service use across the child service system. *Health Affiliation, 14*, 147–157.

Breton, J.J., Bergeron, L., Valle, J.P., Lepine, S., Houde, L., & Gaudet, N. (1995). Do children aged 9 through 11 years understand the DISC version 2.25 questions? *Journal of the American Academy of Child and Adolescent Psychiatry, 34*, 946–956.

Cantwell, D.P., Lewinsohn, P.M., Rohde, P., & Seeley, J.R. (1997). Correspondence between adolescent report and parent report of psychiatric diagnostic data. *Journal of the American Academy of Child and Adolescent Psychiatry, 36*, 610–619.

Emmelkamp, P.M.G. & Scholing, A. (1997). Anxiety disorders. In C.A. Essau & F. Petermann (Eds.), *Developmental psychopathology: Epidemiology, diagnostics and treatment* (219–263). London: Harwood.

Essau, C.A. (1999). *Angst und Depression bei Jugendlichen :[Anxiety and depression in adolescents]*. Habilitationschrift. Bremen: Universität Bremen.

Essau, C.A., Feehan, M., & Üstun, B. (1997).Classification and assessment strategies. In C.A. Essau & F. Petermann (Eds.), *Developmental psychopathology: Epidemiology, diagnostics and treatment* (19–62). London: Harwood.

Fergusson, D.M. & Horwood, L.J. (1987). The trait and method components of ratings of conduct disorder. Part I: Maternal and teacher evaluations of conduct disorder in young children. *Journal of Child Psychology and Psychiatry, 28*, 249–260.

Hart, E.L., Lahey, B.B., Loeber, R., & Hanson, K.S. (1994). Criterion validity of informants in the diagnosis of disruptive behavior disorders in children: A preliminary study. *Journal of Consulting and Clinical Psychology, 62*, 410–414.

Kazdin, A.E. (1997). A model for developing effective treatments: Progression and interplay of theory, research, and practice. *Journal of Clinical Child Psychology, 26*, 114–129.

Kearney, C.A. & Silverman, W.K. (1998). A critical review of pharmacotherapy for youth with anxiety disorders: Things are not as they seem. *Journal of Anxiety Disorders, 12*, 83–102.

Kendall, P.C. (1994). Treating anxiety disorders in youth: Results of a randomized clinical trial. *Journal of Consulting and Clinical Psychology, 62*, 100–110.

Kendall, P.C. & Flannery-Schroeder, E.C. (1998). Methodological issues in treatment research for anxiety disorders in youth. *Journal of Abnormal Child Psychology, 26*, 27–38.

Kendler, K.S., Neale, M.C., Kessler, R.C., Heath, A.C. & Eaves, L.J. (1992). Childhood parental loss and adult psychopathology in women. *Archives of General Psychiatry, 49*, 109–116.

Kutcher, S.P., Reiter, S., Gardner, D.M., Klein, R.G. (1992). The pharmacotherapy of anxiety disorders in children and adolescents. *Psychiatric Clinics of North America, 15*, 41–67.

Lepine, J.P., Wittchen, H.-U., & Essau, C.A. (1993). Lifetime and current comorbidity of anxiety and affective disorders: Results from the International WHO/ADAMHA CIDI field trials. *International Journal of Methods in Psychiatric Research, 3*, 67–77.

Mash, E.J. & Krahn, G.L. (1995). Research strategies in child psychopathology. In M. Hersen & R.T. Hammerman (Eds.), *Advanced abnormal child psychology* (105–133). Hillsdale, NJ: Lawrence Erlbaum.

McGee, R., Williams, S., Anderson, J., McKenzie-Parnell, J.M., & Silva, P.A. (1990). Hyperactivity and serum and hair zinc levels in 11 year old children from the general population. *Biological Psychiatry, 28*, 165–168.

Nottelmann, E.D. & Jensen, P.S. (1999). Comorbidity of depressive disorders in children and adolescents: Rates, temporal sequencing, course and outcome. In C.A. Essau & F. Petermann (Eds.), *Depressive disorders in children and adolescents: Epidemiology, risk factors, and treatment*. Northvale, NJ: Jason Aronson.

Offord, D.R., Boyle, M.H., Racine, Y., Szatmari, P., Fleming, J.E., Sanford, M. *et al.* (1996). Integrating assessment data from multiple informants. *Journal of the American Academy of Child and Adolescent Psychiatry, 35,* 1078–1085.

Piacentini, J., Shaffer, D., & Fischer, P.W. (1993). The Diagnostic Interview Schedule for Children–Revised version (DISC-R): II. Concurrent criterion validity. *Journal of the American Academy of Child and Adolescent Psychiatry, 32,* 658–665.

Pike, A. & Plomin, R. (1996). Importance of nonshared environmental factors for childhood and adolescent psychopathology. *Journal of the American Academy of Child and Adolescent Psychiatry, 35,* 560–570.

Rutter, M. (1994). Beyond longitudinal data: Causes, consequences, changes and continuity. *Journal of Consulting and Clinical Psychology, 62,* 928–940.

Verhulst, F.C., Koot, H.M., & Berden, G.F.M.G. (1990). Four-year follow-up of an epidemiological sample. *Journal of the American Academy of Child and Adolescent Psychiatry, 29,* 440–448

Weisz, J.R., Valeri, S.M., McCarty, C.A. & Moore, P.S. (1999). Interventions for child and adolescent depression: Features, effects, and future directions. In C.A. Essau & F. Petermann (Eds.). *Depressive disorders in children and adolescents: Epidemiology, risk factors, and treatment.* New Jersey: Jason Aronson.

Werry, J.S. (1994). Diagnostic and classification issues. In T.H. Ollendick, N.J. King, & W. Yule (Eds.), *International handbooks of phobic and anxiety disorders in children and adolescents.* New York: Plenum Press.

Wittchen, H.-U. & Essau, C.A. (1990). Assessment of symptoms and psychological disabilities in primary care. In N. Sartorius *et al.* (eds.), *Psychological disorders in general medical settings* (111–136). Bern: Hogrefe & Huber Publishers.

World Health Organization (1993). *International Classification of Mental and Behavioral Disorders.* Geneva: World Health Organization.

Subject Index